N.A.M. Rodger

THE WOODEN WORLD

AN ANATOMY OF
THE GEORGIAN NAVY

W. W. NORTON & COMPANY

NEW YORK • LONDON

For Susan

First published by William Collins in Great Britain 1986
First published as a Norton paperback 1996

Copyright © N.A.M. Rodger 1986

ISBN 0-393-31469-3

Printed in the United States of America
Manufacturing by the Courier Companies, Inc.

W. W. Norton & Company, Inc.
500 Fifth Avenue, New York, N.Y. 10110
W. W. Norton & Company Ltd.
10 Coptic Street, London WC1A 1PU

1 2 3 4 5 6 7 8 9 0

CONTENTS

ILLUSTRATIONS

Nos. 1, 6, 7, 8, 10, 11, 12, 13 and 14 are reproduced by permission of the Director and Trustees of the National Maritime Museum; no. 2 is reproduced by permission of the Trustees and Director of the Science Museum, London; nos. 3, 4 and 5 are reproduced by permission of the Ministry of Defence; no. 9 is reproduced by courtesy of the Marquis of Normanby; no. 15 is reproduced by permission of the British Library.

The illustration overleaf, by James Dodds, is reproduced from *Building the Wooden Fighting Ship* by James Dodds and James Moore (Hutchinson, 1984), by permission of Century-Hutchinson Ltd.

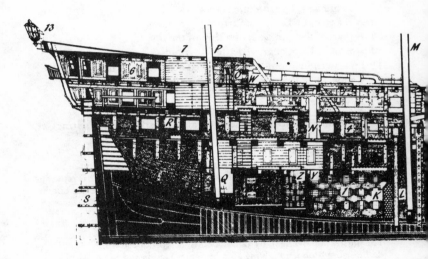

1 hold	8 forecastle deck	A bowsprit
2 palleting	9 waist	B fore mast
3 orlop deck	10 beak	C fore jeer bitts
4 gun deck	11 gripe	D filling room
5 upper deck	12 figurehead	E light room
6 quarter deck	13 stern lanterns	F bitts
7 poop deck		G galley stove
		H belfry
		I jeer capstan

THE LONGITUDINAL SECTION OF A
SEVENTY-FOUR-GUN SHIP

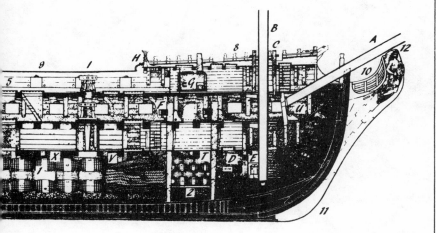

J	rollers and main jeer bits	S	rudder
K	shot lockers	T	powder
L	pump shafts	U	manger
M	main mast	V	cable tiers
N	main jeer capstan	W	box binnacle (two compasses)
O	wheel	X	water casks (packed in shingle ballast)
P	mizzen mast	Y	salted meat
Q	light (aft)	Z	'spirituous liquor'
R	tiller		

PREFACE

Anyone who writes a book such as this incurs many obligations of gratitude to those without whom it could never have reached the press. First among them are the owners and keepers of the manuscripts upon which it is based. My colleagues in the Public Record Office have shown me that practised forbearance which comes from years of dealing with tiresome individuals and unreasonable demands. Dr R.J.B. Knight and Dr Roger Morriss of the National Maritime Museum were equally generous with their scarcest resource, time. His Lordship the Marquis of Normanby kindly permitted me to consult the Mulgrave Castle Archives. Mr F.B. Stitt, the County Archivist of Staffordshire, and Dr Mary L. Robertson of the Huntington Library were particularly helpful when I worked in their archives, and Mr Clinton V. Black, the Archivist of Jamaica, went well beyond the line of duty in answering enquiries by post. In preparing illustrations I have been helped by Dr A.P. McGowan, Miss R. Prentice and Mr Roger Quarm of the National Maritime Museum, Dr Thomas Wright and Mr J. Roome of the Science Museum, Lieutenant-Commander Lawrence Phillips R.N.R. and Petty Officer M.P. McBarron R.N. In the notes and bibliography I have acknowledged the particular help on various points which I received from Mr A.W.H. Pearsall, Major H.G.R. Boscawen, Mr Thomas Pakenham and Professor T.J.A. Le Goff.

Some passages in Chapter VE and the Appendices originally appeared in the *Bulletin of the Institute of Historical Research*, and I am grateful to the Institute for permission to reproduce them. Documents in Crown Copyright are printed by permission of the Controller of H.M. Stationery Office.

This book would never have been finished but for the encouragement I have received throughout from my editor Mr Richard Ollard, who originally proposed that I should write it. It has benefited greatly from the wise advice of the late Professor John Bromley, the most rigorous of scholars of the eighteenth century, and of the Navy. He lived just long enough to read it in draft, and it was typical of his unselfishness that in his last illness he should spare strength to criticize and encourage. I owe him a great debt, but there is one greater still, indicated by the dedication to my wife, who married me and found she had acquired a book as well.

N.A.M.R.
Acton, Trinity Sunday, 1985

PREFACE TO THE FONTANA PRESS EDITION

In this edition I have not attempted any substantial revision, but I have taken the chance to make various small corrections, and to refer to some work published in the last two years. I am grateful to the friends and correspondents who have pointed out my mistakes.

N.A.M.R.
Acton, Trinity Sunday, 1987

INTRODUCTION

It has long ceased to be true that naval history is written solely as a disconnected series of battles or campaigns, related to the history of the nation, if at all, only at the level of grand strategy. In the past thirty years a great deal of important work has been done, notably by John Ehrman and Daniel Baugh,[1] to lay bare the eighteenth-century British Navy as an organization: the largest industrial unit of its day in the western world, and by far the most expensive and demanding of all the administrative responsibilities of the State. Nevertheless the Navy has in recent years been an unfashionable subject among professional historians in Britain, with the natural result that its historiography in many respects is old-fashioned and the received views of it do not well agree with modern understanding of the currents of British history as a whole.

This is particularly true of the social history of the Navy, which in spite of some pioneering efforts, remains largely unwritten in any detail for any period, and especially for the eighteenth century.[2] There is a common opinion, derived in considerable measure from Masefield's *Sea Life in Nelson's Time*,[3] that naval discipline was harsh and oppressive, officers frequently cruel and tyrannical, ratings drawn from the dregs of society, ill-treated and starved. The fact that this picture agrees very little with what is generally understood of eighteenth-century British society as a whole has reinforced professional historians' distaste for naval history, and contributed to the absence of detailed scholarly studies of the Navy in recent years. My object in undertaking this work was to test the traditional view of the internal life of the Navy by studying the evidence in detail for a limited period. This has the inevitable disadvantage of all such studies, that they do not by themselves offer a revealing perspective on changes over time, but I considered that it would not otherwise be possible to present the evidence in sufficient detail. I have tried to draw an anatomy of the inner life of the Navy. I am conscious that it is not a complete anatomy, that there are areas – religion and superstition, for example – which are hardly touched on because the evidence I have used says very little about them. Possibly the people I have here described appear more as social beings than as private individuals. I hope that other historians will be moved to remedy these and other deficiencies.

They will certainly find that even the evidence I have used, which comes largely from the Public Record Office, has not been exploited to the limit. In particular the ships' musters and pay books are a vast archive (there are about a quarter of a million of them, extending over two centuries) upon which any social history of the Navy ought to be founded, and the use of computers in analysis of such material makes it for the first time feasible to draw out their real value. I have not had that opportunity; the material presented in my appendices was derived without the benefit of a computer, and any historian possessed of one who cares to master these admittedly very technical documents should find a rich field of social analysis.

My study concentrates on the period of the Seven Years' War; that is to say, on the nearly nine years from the spring of 1755, when serious fighting between Britain and France broke out, at first in America and later at sea (war was not declared until May 1756), to the early months of 1763 when the preliminaries of peace were signed. With somewhat more caution, I have drawn evidence from, and would apply my conclusions to, the whole period from about 1740 to 1775. I do not claim that what was true of the middle years of the century applied either before or after. One of the banes of naval social history is the assumption, still widespread in the teeth of all probability, that nothing ever changed, so that something which can be shown to have happened once in, say, 1690, may be assumed to have been common at any period from the Restoration to the Regency.[*] This is emphatically not true; the Navy, like society in general, was continually developing. I believe that the traditional view of the social life of the Navy cannot be reconciled with the evidence for the middle years of the century, but it remains perfectly possible (though hardly probable) that it exactly describes the Navy at the end of the century – the period, in fact, to which it is most commonly referred. Another study is required to test how far sea life in Nelson's time really appeared in the bloody colours that Masefield painted.

In writing about the period of the Seven Years' War I have devoted almost no time to the events of the war itself. Those who are not familiar with the course of that war at sea and wish to become so should read Sir Julian Corbett's great work,[5] still unreplaced though much in need of revision, but it is not necessary to do so to understand this book. The reader need know no more than that a naval war against France (and from 1762, Spain) was in progress. After an unpromising start, that war was in the end a British triumph, and part of the object of this social anatomy is to examine what it was about the Royal Navy which made it an effective instrument of war. Many components of victory, notably money, are outside my focus, and I have not had the opportunity to make any comparative study of the French navy, but I believe that at least this book presents a plausible background to the victories which undoubtedly occurred, and are frankly difficult to account for if the Navy was run as a sort of floating concentration camp.

I have not attempted in this study to give more than a brief sketch of the administration of the Navy. It would be pointless, indeed impertinent to do again what has been so well and completely done by Daniel Baugh. I have made frequent reference to his works, but my debt to him goes much further than the detailed points referred to in my notes. Like all historians of the eighteenth-century Navy, I ground my study on the foundations which he has laid, and without which this book could not have been begun. I have also taken advantage of the recent work of John Harland[6] to avoid more than passing reference to the complex business of how a ship at sea was actually handled. This was the focus of the working lives of seamen, but it is also a subject so large and so technical that nothing less than a complete book can do it justice, and as that book has been written, far better than I could do it, I have not devoted much space to the subject in spite of its importance.

My title will remind those familiar with the eighteenth-century Navy of a satirical pamphlet of 1707, re-issued at intervals until at least as late as 1751, *The Wooden World dissected in the Character of a Ship of War*.[7] Its author, Ned Ward, was a London publican with some gifts for satire, but almost no knowledge of the

Navy, and his work does not deserve to be used as evidence. His title, however, is good, for the phrase 'the wooden world' was in colloquial use at sea in just the sense I require, to refer to the Navy not as a fleet of ships or an instrument of national policy, but as a society in miniature, a floating world with its own customs and way of life. In describing it I have avoided using not only Ned Ward, but also another writer whose works have perhaps been drawn on rather more than they deserve, Tobias Smollett. As he had served one voyage as a surgeon's mate he was not wholly unacquainted with the Navy, but he remains a poor, or rather an over-rich, substitute for documentary evidence. In picaresque novels a man is not upon oath, and I regard the attempt to guess which sea officer was the original of Commodore Trunnion or Lieutenant Bowling, and which of Smollett's incidents may be taken as faithfully reflecting sea life, as more amusing than useful for the historian.

The evidence I have used is briefly described in the Note on Sources, which also explains the conventions used in citing it. In quoting manuscripts, and also printed works which follow eighteenth-century conventions, I have used modern spelling, punctuation and capitalization. There are few real differences between the English of that time and our own, and I consider that the use of the original form is apt to distract the reader from the sense to a spurious quaintness of style. I have not hesitated to break this rule, however, when the form of the original conveys something material, for example about the literacy of the writer. In quotation, editorial omissions are indicated thus . . ., additions [thus], and all words in italic are emphasized in the original. Unambiguous abbreviations have been expanded without comment. I have as far as possible spelled surnames in the way their owners did, which is not always the form most common in secondary sources. It would be a tiresome affectation to write of the eighteenth-century Navy without using terminology some of which is technical, and some of which has fallen out of use. For the benefit of readers who may be unfamiliar with nautical terms in particular, I have supplied a short glossary. Printed works which appear in the bibliography are given in the notes by short title only. My main text is chaste, and most statistical passages I have confined to the decent obscurity of a learned appendix.

CHAPTER I

The Sea Service

A AFLOAT

Seamen have always dwelt on the fringes of settled society. The Greeks hesitated whether to count them among the living or the dead,[1] and eighteenth-century Englishmen were not much better informed. They were familiar with seafarers only as the inhabitants of modern European cities are familiar with tourists. They recognized their curious clothes and eccentric behaviour, they laughed at their oddities, they profited from their ignorance – but they did not understand seamen, and they knew nothing whatever of the world from which they came. Superficially familiar, the seaman remained to his contemporaries profoundly strange. They knew him only on land, out of his element. The sailor on a run ashore, probably drunk and riotous, was a popular image, but the sailor afloat and at work was quite unfamiliar to his countrymen. It is striking that almost all the prints of sailors show them in their flamboyant shore-going rig, never in their working clothes, nor at work. The shipboard world in which officers and men spent their active lives was probably less well-known to men of education than the remote countries described in the travel books then so popular, or the remote ages on whose history they had been brought up.

The lapse of two centuries has done nothing to make the eighteenth-century seafarer better known. In his own day the popular impression was a stereotype quite removed from reality. It was easy even for those quite close to the Navy – clerks in the Navy Office, for example – to fall into loose and convenient phrases like 'officers and seamen', when they meant the whole body of naval personnel. They knew if they stopped to think that there were many sorts of 'officers' and many ratings who were not seamen. Modern writers tend to assume that a ship's company really consisted of two separate groups, homogeneous within themselves and distinct from each other. Moreover they are apt to suppose that this great divide between officers and men corresponded to a class barrier which separated officers and gentlemen from those who were neither. It has been so in the services for a century and more, and to an extent it is so still, but the eighteenth-century Navy was different. In reality the company of every ship was divided in many overlapping, ambiguous and untidy ways, some ill defined by the regulations, and some not mentioned at all. Shipboard society was a complex world in which each person's place was defined by many invisible and subtle distinctions. Before any other aspect of naval life can be described, it is essential to disentangle this complexity.

The formal system of ranks and ratings distinguished commissioned officers (who were also sea officers), warrant officers who were sea officers and those who were reckoned only as inferior officers, petty officers with the status of inferior officers, and others who were simply ratings, slightly superior to the rest of 'the people', the common term for the ratings of the ship as a body. Both officers and ratings were divided another way by their professions; seamen were the largest group, but there were many other trades, and in each there were the qualified, the learners and the unskilled. Age divided and united, for a ship's company, though largely a body of young men, also included elderly officers and ratings, and a large number of children. Across all these boundaries, affecting them all but corresponding with none, lay the invisible distinctions of social class, distributing gentlemen and tradesmen, noblemen and artisans with careless impartiality among the ranks and ratings.

At the head of the seagoing Navy were the admirals. After the promotion of June 1756 there were thirty of them in all, one admiral of the fleet, six admirals, eight vice-admirals and fifteen rear-admirals. Many of them were too old for active service, some were otherwise occupied, some were not to be trusted with an active command, and many of the new rear-admirals had little experience, so the choice of commanders-in-chief was not large. Even the rank and status of a flag officer, with the fine uniform and substantial half-pay that went with it, was enviable enough, and actual command at sea was the object of every officer's ambition – especially command overseas, with the independence and opportunity that implied. But ambition was tempered by the heavy responsibility of an independent command. There was no chance to consult one's superiors, to weigh the advice of wiser and more experienced heads. Issues of war and diplomacy, of life and death turned on an admiral's unaided decisions, and if there were any who took them lightly, they did so no more after the death of Admiral Byng, shot in 1757 for failure in action. One captain actually refused promotion to rear-admiral.[2]

Though some admirals were commanders-in-chief, not all commanders-in-chief were admirals, for the limited number of flag officers was freely supplemented by commodores. A commodore appointed to command a squadron or station had most of the status of a rear-admiral while his broad pendant was flying, but reverted to captain's rank and seniority as soon as he hauled it down. It was possible to reach as far down the captains' list as one wished to make commodores, unlike admirals, and the possibility was often exploited to choose young and energetic commanders. When Commodore Keppel was made rear-admiral in 1762 he had recently commanded a fleet of sixty-three sail, with two other commodores under him – and he had the experience to do so, for he had been a commander-in-chief, off and on, for thirteen years.[3] There were also commodores without flag-captains, who had simply been ordered by their commander-in-chief to take charge of a detachment or division of ships, and who were distinguished only by a broad pendant and a title from the captains they had been and were to be.

An eighteenth-century admiral was accompanied to sea by a considerable 'retinue', but it did not include much of a staff, in the modern sense. A squadron of over twenty sail might, but did not usually, have a captain of the fleet, a senior captain or rear-admiral to assist the admiral, and sometimes the captain of a private ship (meaning a man-of-war not carrying an admiral) might act as an unofficial staff officer,[4] but most flag officers relied largely on their secretaries. An admiral's secretary was less a private amanuensis than the business manager of the squadron. He controlled, drafted, and sometimes even signed the admiral's correspondence;[5] he was heavily involved in victualling (on distant stations like the East Indies he was often himself the agent-victualler); he was usually the admiral's prize agent and often the squadron's as well. This was big business, and it demanded ability and experience. A secretary needed extensive connections and good credit in the world of business and finance, and he needed to move easily among senior officers afloat and great men ashore. Not surprisingly, secretaries were often members of families already prominent in the Navy or naval administration.

Apart from the secretary, an admiral's retinue usually included some domestics. Flag officers were expected to entertain in a style befitting their rank, especially abroad, so a cook was important, and men to wait at table. In the spartan conditions of sea life, however, there was a limit to the usefulness of domestics, and no flag officer filled up his retinue with them. Twenty for a vice-admiral or fifteen for a rear-admiral left some room for 'young gentlemen', the would-be officers under the admiral's patronage.

The number of admirals at sea was small, and a man might pass his whole career at sea without serving in a flagship. For most officers and men it was the captain who ruled their little world, and it was the captain who answered to the Admiralty for his ship and all who served in her. Properly the only captains were post-captains, commanding the rated or 'post' ships (that is, the largest ones), but 'masters and commanders' were always called 'captain', as indeed were most officers commanding vessels of any size, even in the merchant service, so that, as a satirical pamphleteer put it, a title 'bestowed on the elevated rank of the commander of a post ship, descends by prostitution, or courtesy, which you will, to the *commander of an oyster boat*'.[6] It was quite correct for the masters and commanders who commanded the smaller men-of-war to be addressed as 'captain' as though they had reached post rank, and though they had not, they shared the lonely responsibilities of command. Indeed, the decisions of a young commander of a sloop cruising alone might be more difficult than those of a senior post-captain commanding a private ship in a large squadron, seldom out of signalling range of the flagship. In return for responsibility, captains had power, independence, status, and some chance of wealth.

Admirals and commodores commanding usually flew their flags in one of the larger line-of-battle ships, fit to lie in the centre of the line in action, and to accommodate the flag officer in decent state at other times. The flag-captain who actually commanded the flagship was generally newly promoted and less experienced than the captains of smaller ships, so custom permitted and even required the admiral to interfere a good deal in the internal management of his flagship.[7] Flag-captains were therefore the least independent of all commanders.

The most junior commissioned officers were the lieutenants. Every combatant ship and vessel in the Navy had at least one. The larger line-of-battle ships had as many as six, each commissioned specifically as first lieutenant, second lieutenant and so on down. Sloops had only a single lieutenant to assist the commander, and the smallest men-of-war of all, the hired cutters and tenders, had as their only sea officer a lieutenant in command. Though their actual social backgrounds varied widely, lieutenants were always regarded as gentlemen, and expected to behave as such. To this extent it is permissible to speak of the break between commissioned and warrant rank as though it corresponded to the social distinction between gentlemen and the rest, but there were many commissioned officers who would never have been called gentlemen had they not risen in their profession, while on the other hand they were not the only gentlemen on board.

Next after the commissioned officers came the warrant officers, and first those who were included as 'sea officers', officers in the loose modern sense, exercising a general authority aboard ship. The fact that they received warrants rather than commissions was in itself an administrative accident, but it symbolized an important division which was both social and professional. Whatever their personal origins, commissioned officers as a class historically represented the military and governing classes come to sea to take their natural place in command of those who merely earned their living afloat. In Macaulay's phrase (quite untrue of the period to which he applied it), 'There were gentlemen and there were seamen in the navy of Charles the Second. But the seamen were not gentlemen; and the gentlemen were not seamen.'⁸ Professionally, the warrant officers were specialists, craftsmen responsible to the captain for their own departments, but also in a measure confined to them. In the time-honoured English fashion, the experts were kept in their place; it was the commissioned officers, educated only as seamen, who took command.

The master was the most senior of the warrant officers, and in some respects, including pay, his status was equal to that of the lieutenants. In merchant ships it was, as it is still, the master who holds command, but in the Navy the master was simply the navigator. He plotted the ship's position day by day, with his own instruments and on his own charts. In confined waters he conned (piloted) the ship. It was literally a vital task, on which many lives depended, but it was a task for which commissioned officers also were trained, and increasingly trained as well as masters or even better. There were fine navigators of high scientific attainments in both groups, and the masters, for all their long tradition and status, no longer had anything like a monopoly of their professional skill.

This at least was certainly not true of the surgeons. Though in their own profession their standing was far inferior to that of physicians, there were only a few physicians in the seagoing Navy, one to each of the larger squadrons overseas, and in every ship the surgeon was the medical man on whom officers and men relied in the face of illness and wounds. Depending on the size of the ship, the surgeon might be assisted by one or more surgeon's mates, warranted and qualified like him, but reckoned in the Navy only as inferior officers with the standing of petty officers. The social status and professional ability of surgeons varied very widely; there were at least two naval surgeons, or former naval surgeons, who had been knighted,⁹ but in general their pretensions to gentility were insecure. Many were certainly devoted men, and no more ignorant than the run of doctors of the day. Thomas Blakeaway, surgeon's first mate of the *Cambridge*, was 'an excellent assistant, who had been a very eminent operator in London for nails and corns' (which must have been a comfort to the ship's company), 'but from misfortune had taken refuge on board.'¹⁰ On the other hand the surgeon of the *York* was reported 'afraid to attend the sick from an apprehension of being liable to take the sickness himself', and a surgeon's mate appointed to the *Elizabeth* in 1758 was described by her captain as 'not fitly qualified, very idle, and ... they would not trust a sick favourite dog under his care'.[11]

Of all the officers of the ship, the purser occupied the strangest position. He was a warrant officer responsible for victualling the ship and providing other consumable articles. He did this in part as an officer charged with government stores for which he rendered accounts like the other warrant officers, but for many of his responsibilities he operated as a private contractor selling at his own risk articles the number, quality and price of which were fixed by the Navy. It was a most invidious position. Under-capitalized entrepreneurs in a highly risky business, pursers could only prosper with ability, credit and a good measure of luck. If they did prosper, they were liable to find themselves even more unpopular among the people than usual. When two or three Englishmen are gathered together, they grumble about the food, and eighteenth-century seamen grumbled about the purser who could, in certain circumstances, profit by cheating them, and was naturally suspected of doing so. To some extent pursers represent the seagoing version of that characteristic figure of the age, the 'man of business', and successful pursers were usually men with connections both to the mercantile world and to other sea officers. Even the best connections, however, did not ensure success. Sir James Barclay, baronet, died poor in 1756 after twenty years as a purser,[12] and so did many others of humbler birth.

The purser, together with the boatswain, gunner, carpenter and cook, was a standing officer, which meant that he was warranted to a ship when she was built (in practice when she was ordered to be built), and – in theory at least – stood by her or served in her throughout her life until he or she perished. When ships paid off into the Ordinary (the dockyard reserve) and lay at their moorings stripped to a gantline, the standing officers stayed, officially living on board, with a force of shipkeepers under their orders to maintain them. This meant that these officers, for whom there was no half-pay and limited chances of superannuation, had a fairly secure job for life. The standing officers of ships in Ordin-

ary did not have a very onerous task, though it was more demanding than that which faced the officer whose ship had not yet been
launched, or which had been left on the list long after she had been
broken up.[13] These sinecures were used to provide pensions for old
and disabled officers, and decent salaries for admirals' secretaries.
It was an approach characteristic of the age; the spirit of the naval
regulations was abused and the taxpayer suffered, but in a rough
and ready way the efficiency and humanity of the Service were
thereby served, and without the need to subvert an ancient and
settled constitution.

If standing officers had never changed ships it would have produced an impossibly inflexible system. In fact standing officers
were regularly promoted from small ships to larger, and there was
a good deal of 'exchanging for duty', whereby those who wanted
to go to sea swapped ships with those who did not, or could not. In
wartime all the standing officers in Ordinary who retained strength
or zeal would soon be at sea, and those remaining tended to be the
dregs. It was with much surprise that Commodore Boys, the commander-in-chief, found a good gunner in the Chatham Ordinary in
1760, and in recommending him to the Admiralty he was careful to
explain the circumstance (a serious illness) which had obliged a
deserving officer to retire thither in the midst of war.[14]

The gunner was another of the warrant sea officers. Unlike the
purser he usually had no pretensions to gentility, though there
were exceptions. One gunner was said to be the son of a captain,[15]
and young gentlemen hoping for a lieutenant's commission sometimes took a gunner's warrant as a stepping stone. Gunners were
of course responsible for guns and powder, and were unusual in
that they owed a dual allegiance. Their accounts were rendered to,
and their warrants received from, the Ordnance Board, an independent department not part of the naval administration nor
subordinate to the Admiralty. For purposes of discipline and shipboard organization gunners were as much officers of the Navy as
any, but administratively their loyalties were divided. Gunners had
usually begun their careers as seamen, and in some ships, particularly sloops with few officers, the gunner stood watches.[16]

Very similar in status to the gunner was the boatswain, another
warrant sea officer who had usually begun as a seaman. The boats-

wain indeed had a general responsibility for all the 'seamanlike' activities in the ship other than handling her, for rigging, sails, ground tackle and all the gear which went with them. He accounted to the Navy Board for these stores, and like all other sea officers he had to be a man of sufficient education to keep accounts and make reports in writing. It was virtually impossible to be an illiterate boatswain – one must say 'virtually', because there were in fact at least two boatswains in the Navy during the Seven Years' War who could not sign their names, Henry Cowley of the *Port Royal* sloop, and George Harwood of the *Wager*.[17] How they managed, even in such small ships, is difficult to see.

The last of the warrant sea officers was the carpenter, responsible for the maintenance of the hull, masts and spars of the ship. Carpenters were unusual in that they could and often did pass part of their careers in the dockyards and part in the Navy. All standing officers were paid on the books of the dockyard when their ships were out of commission, but carpenters had commonly begun their careers as apprentices in the yards, and not obtained their carpenters' warrants until they were qualified shipwrights of some years' standing. The carpenter was a highly skilled man in an essential craft, and though like the boatswain and gunner no gentleman, a good carpenter would enjoy the respect and favour of all sensible captains. In terms of long experience in a complex and demanding job, the carpenter had no rival among the non-seamen aboard.

The only other person on board who was sometimes, but not usually, reckoned as a sea officer was the chaplain. His position was an awkward one. Socially he was an inactive landman among busy seamen; his doubtful pretensions to gentility left him no comfortable home among either commissioned or warrant officers, and his actual duties were far from clear. Some chaplains, followers of admirals or well-connected captains, stood much in the position of domestic chaplains to a noble household: a proper ornament to a flag officer's retinue, who could say grace at table and help the secretary. A rather different picture is offered by a satirist:

> A sea chaplain is, generally speaking, a clerical beau; wears white stockings, ruffles to his shirt, and some-

times a long tail of borrowed hair tied to his own; frequents the coffee-house and makes advances publicly to the barmaid.[18]

But like so many contemporary views of the officers and men of the Navy, this shows the chaplain ashore. To what extent he could discharge a genuinely spiritual rôle afloat depended entirely on the quality of the man and the attitude of his captain.

Between the sea officers, both commissioned and warrant, and the body of the people was an amorphous and ill-defined body known as inferior officers. These were men with some claim to officer's rank, sufficient to distinguish them from ordinary ratings without raising them so high as the sea officers. Several of them were warrant officers, in the literal sense of being appointed by warrant, and like the warrant sea officers, their superiors, .they were usually among the specialists of the ship's company. Such were the armourer, and in large ships the gunsmith, subordinates of the gunner who maintained the great guns and small arms respectively; the sailmaker who was responsible to the boatswain; the schoolmaster who taught the youths of the ship navigation; the cook; the surgeon's mates; and the master-at-arms, often a former sergeant in the army, whose duty was to instruct the men in small arms drill, but who was tending to acquire some disciplinary responsibility. All these were warrant officers, holding a rank in the Navy which the captain could not alter, but ranking no higher than the petty officers whom he could rate or disrate as he pleased.

Two of these petty officers' rates, midshipman and master's mate, were counted among the inferior officers. The position of these two ratings well illustrates the curious amalgam of an official system of ranks and ratings with the social reality of class and education. In principle both midshipmen and master's mates (often just 'mates' for short) were a sort of superior petty officer with a more general authority, but they remained no more than ratings. Yet it was quite possible for an armourer, a warrant officer, to be court-martialled for striking a midshipman as his superior officer.[19] The reason for this was that midshipmen and mates were regarded as future sea officers, with the all-important social distinction of the right to walk the quarter deck. They were expected

24

to dress respectably and behave like officers; one pressed (i.e. conscripted) man intended as a midshipman was not permitted to assume the rating until he had clothes 'to appear properly as a quarter deck officer'.[20] In order to qualify as a lieutenant a young man had to have served at least two years as a midshipman or master's mate, so there were large numbers of young gentlemen in these rates learning their trade as officers, but it was not true in the 1750s that all midshipmen and mates were future lieutenants. Many mates were would-be masters, learning navigation in assisting the master, and many persons in both rates were simply steady and experienced seamen, well able to discharge their duties without having any real pretensions to commissioned or warrant rank. The age structure of midshipmen and mates shows a predominance of young men in their early twenties, together with a considerable number of much older men.[21] The number of midshipmen and mates was fixed for each rate of ship by the regulations,[22] but young men graduating from the Royal Naval Academy at Portsmouth to do their qualifying time could be accommodated as midshipmen ordinary, taking the place, and pay, of an able seaman, but otherwise rated as a supernumerary midshipman.

Beneath the inferior officers stood the body of the people, who in turn were divided in many ways. They were all ratings, that is to say that their position was both 'rank' and job, and depended only on the captain, who could rate or disrate without reference to higher authority. He chose some men to rate as petty officers, who were not officers at all in the ordinary acceptance of the word, but working men chosen to take charge of particular duties. There were petty officers, or men of petty officer's standing, among the craftsmen and specialists, but in common parlance the phrase tended to be used only of seamen petty officers. One spoke of 'petty officers and able' to distinguish the experienced seamen from ordinary seamen and landmen on the one hand, and from the idlers or daymen on the other. The distinction between seamen, who stood watches, and idlers, who worked by day and slept at night, was one of the most fundamental afloat. It divided the ship's company, officers and ratings, into two unequal parts. Among officers, the lieutenants and the master stood watches, in sloops sometimes the boatswain and gunner as well. So did the midshipmen and mates, the seamen petty officers, seamen, landmen and servants. The idlers, that is the specialist non-seamen, were the carpenter, purser, surgeon, chaplain, and their subordinates. Idlers of petty officer's standing were the sailmaker and his mates, the yeoman of the powder room, the armourer and his mates, the carpenter's mates, the purser's steward, the captain's clerk, the cook and his mate, and the schoolmaster. The gunner's mates, the master-at-arms and the corporal (his assistant) were also idlers, but in practice often exercised authority outside the gunner's department to which they strictly belonged. All these were petty officers, but colloquially the term was applied more to the seamen petty officers, the quartermasters and quartermaster's mates, yeomen of the sheets, boatswain's mates and the coxswain of the barge. These supervised, but also shared, the seamen's work. Among them, or more often from suitable able seamen, the captain would select men to act as captains of tops and parts of ship,[23] positions not officially established, but well understood as necessary to take charge of the topmen aloft, and of the forecastlemen, waisters and afterguard. There were also among the seamen one quarter gunner to every four guns, who assisted the gunner's mates in looking after them, and one captain of each gun, who was in charge of the gun's crew in action. Quarter gunners were officially established, and paid two shillings a month more than able seamen, but captains of guns, like captains of tops, received no official recognition.

The people below petty officer, 'private men' as they were sometimes called, were likewise divided into seamen and idlers. Among the latter were the carpenter's crew and sailmaker's crew ('crew' in this context meaning both the group in general and its least skilled members in particular), the steward's mate, cook's mate, yeomen of the boatswain's storeroom, captain's cook, cooper and barber. Seamen were, or could be, divided into able seamen, ordinary seamen and landmen. As a rule of thumb it was reckoned that one year at sea would make an ordinary, and two years an able seaman, but in peacetime the Navy hardly needed to bother, for there was no difficulty in filling up with able men.[24] When wartime shortages obliged captains to recruit where they could, a ratio of one-third able, one-third ordinary and one-third landmen was reckoned the minimum consistent with safety.

At sea the petty officers and seamen were divided into two watches,[25] and each watch into a number of 'parts of ship'. The least experienced, and most troublesome, joined the afterguard on the quarter deck, and the waisters in the waist. Here, under the immediate eye of the officers, they hauled on sheets, halliards and braces, work which called for collective strength and co-ordination, but little individual skill. The smart young seamen worked aloft as topmen, handing and loosing sail. Upper yardmen, the youngest of the topmen, often no more than older boys, worked on the topgallant and royal yards, the highest of all, whose sails and gear were lightest. Older seamen, no longer agile enough to work aloft, joined the forecastlemen under the boatswain, where they handled the headsails, and dealt with the vital and tricky work of clearing away the anchors to let go, and catting and fishing them when unmooring.

Among the people and, as far as their strength and abilities allowed, working with them, was one particular and very distinctive group, the servants. Every sea officer (plus the cook) was allowed one servant, except the boatswain, gunner and carpenter with two each, and the captain with four for every hundred of the ship's authorized complement. These servants were not actually servants, either in the eighteenth-century sense of employees, or in the modern sense of domestics. They were boys, being bred up to the sea life, almost as apprentices to their masters. Some indeed were really apprentices. The regulations prescribed that standing officers' servants were to be apprenticed to them, and other sea officers sometimes took apprentices as well – even admirals. Boscawen had an apprentice, a boy from Greenwich Hospital School, and Rear-Admiral Durrell took as an apprentice 'one of the mathematical boys in Christ's Hospital'.[26] Whether apprenticed or not, servants went to sea young. The regulations said that officers' sons might not be younger than eleven, nor others younger than thirteen, but it was a regulation often ignored. There were boys at sea of six or eight,[27] some of them young gentlemen aiming for the quarter deck, others just future seamen. Officers' servants could come from almost any background. There were noblemen's sons among them, but Captain Lord Harry Powlett took poor waifs from the streets of London, while Michael Pascal, first lieutenant of the *Roebuck* in 1757, had a black slave boy as his servant.[28] In the absence of any rating of 'boy' for future officers or future seamen, the great majority of officers, and some ratings, began their careers as officers' servants. The established numbers of servants amounted to between 6 and 10 per cent of the ship's company,[29] and the actual number of boys aboard could easily be higher, since it was common for some of the older boys to be rated able seamen. There were 'able seamen' as young as eleven or twelve,[30] and most young gentlemen on their way to the quarter deck served at least some time in these ratings. The actual work a young gentleman might be doing bore hardly any relation to his nominal rating. At various times he would work with the seamen, including working aloft which was regarded as an important part of a future officer's training, and learn navigation from the schoolmaster, if there was one, or from the master. At a suitable age the young man would be allowed to walk the quarter deck as a young gentleman, and even, if he were particularly favoured, to mess with the lieutenants in the wardroom.[31]

The final group of a ship's company which has not yet been mentioned was the marines. In previous wars marine regiments of the army had been raised, or ordinary marching regiments sent to sea, but the permanent corps of marines under Admiralty control was first established in 1755, so that during the Seven Years' War it was a new force. Every ship except the smallest carried a detachment of marines with their own officer or officers. They were taught to handle a musket, and expected to fight ashore if landing parties were needed, but they were certainly at least as ill-trained as the average British foot-soldier of the day.[32] Although not put in watches, and naturally not seamen, marines were expected to help with the work of the ship when required, usually in pulling and hauling, or walking round the capstan to raise the anchor. No marine could be ordered to work aloft, but they were encouraged to learn seamanship and some left the corps to become able seamen, earning not only higher pay[33] but a much higher social standing aboard ship.

Apart from their authorized complement of officers, ratings and marines, ships might be ordered to bear supernumeraries.

Sometimes these were pilots, sometimes newly raised men awaiting distribution to other ships, sometimes boat's crews, survivors
or others who had somehow become separated from their ships,
and sometimes soldiers or passengers embarked for some reason.
Flagships bore the admiral and his retinue as supernumeraries, and
occasionally ships were allowed by Admiralty order to bear permanent supernumeraries as an addition to their company for some
particular purpose.

A ship's company, large or small, was a microcosm of society
with a manifold division of ranks and ratings, of social class and
status, of skills and professions, and of age. The life of the ship can
only be understood in relation to these overlapping patterns. In
their dealings with one another, in tension and accommodation, in
fear and affection, in persuasion and command, men acted within
the constraints imposed by the complex internal structure of shipboard society.

B   ASHORE

The administration of the British Navy in the eighteenth century
was, like the government as a whole, a haphazard collection of
institutions whose responsibilities often overlapped and whose
relations were not well defined. On paper the arrangements were
chaotic, but they had evolved over a long time, they were familiar
to those who operated them, and in intelligent hands they functioned much more efficiently than might have been expected. This
was in spite of the fact that the Navy was by far the largest and
most complex of all government services, and indeed by a large
margin the largest industrial organization in the western world. It
faced problems of management and control then quite unknown in
even the greatest private firms. This was a powerful reason why it
strongly favoured continuity of service among its administrative

staff, for there was no pool of talent or relevant experience outside the naval service from which managers or administrators could be drawn, and they had to be bred up within the service.

At the head of the naval administration stood the Board of Admiralty, or to give it its proper title, the Commissioners for executing the Office of Lord High Admiral. There had been a Lord Admiral in office as recently as 1708, well within the service of some senior officers, and the Board was not yet regarded as the only possible form which the higher direction of the Navy might take, but it was well settled in its rôle by the start of the Seven Years' War. Its political head, the First Lord, generally sat in Cabinet and was unquestionably the dominant member of his Board, even though the signatures of three members were required to validate important orders. A weak or incompetent First Lord, like Lord Temple whom Pitt installed after his brief triumph in 1756, tended to paralyse the Board's work, for there was no alternative source of leadership.[1] The First Lord profited by, and if a civilian depended on, the presence of at least one other sea officer of ability on the Board, but many members were political placemen who played only a minor part in naval direction.

With the exception of Temple's short period in office, the First Lord from 1751 to his death in 1762 was Admiral Lord Anson, and for seven years before that he had been the leading naval member in the Boards of the Duke of Bedford and Lord Sandwich.[2] Anson was a remarkable character, whose achievements at the head of his service have more often been praised than understood. They are indeed difficult to describe, because Anson was a man who preferred to work unobtrusively. The changes he wrought were for the most part gradual, many concerned with crucial but unexciting administrative processes, and the presence of his own guiding hand is easier to sense than to prove. He effectively covered his tracks from the historian not only by not keeping papers, but by not creating them. He hated correspondence, and conducted the inescapable minimum by the hand of his secretary, Philip Stephens, who was installed as Second Secretary of the Admiralty in 1759, and succeeded John Clevland as Secretary in 1763. Even his wife was surprised to receive a letter in his own hand.[3] Reserved, austere and quite unclubbable, he was never very popular in the political world and cared nothing for society,[4] but in his own service he was widely admired, even loved, and his numerous followers spread his methods throughout the Service. His guiding principle was a rigorous devotion to high standards of training and conduct, and the transformation in a dozen years from the humiliating failures of the early 1740s to the triumphs of the Seven Years' War is his lasting monument. Anson is certainly one of the key figures in the creation of a distinctive naval ethos, not just the product of patriotism or self-interest, but the ingrained assumption that a man's first duty was to the good of the Service. No adequate biography of Anson has ever been written, and it would certainly be hard to do justice to a man who so effectively covered his tracks, but the Navy of the Seven Years' War was what Anson had made it, and the list of its virtues is to a great extent the list of his achievements.

The political position of the Board of Admiralty was peculiar, and unlike that of any other government department. The First Lord, as political head of the Board, sat in Cabinet and was of necessity a politician of standing, but for much of the century the First Lords were, so to speak, artificial politicians, officers whose professional success had raised them to political greatness. This was Anson's position; his wealth, his peerage, his political consequence and his marriage to the Lord Chancellor's daughter were all the effect, not the cause, of his naval triumphs. The qualities required of a First Lord, civilian or naval, were greater than those looked for in any other Cabinet post. 'Capacity is so little necessary for most employments,' Fox reproved that indefatigable schemer Bubb Doddington in March 1757 as Pitt's ministry approached collapse, 'that you seem to forget that there is one where it is absolutely so – viz. the Admiralty'. 'The First Lord of the Admiralty must needs be a man of real ability and great application.'[5] This was to some extent a conclusion born of unhappy experience of the lack of such a man under Carteret's administration in 1742–44, and it did not extend as far as the other members of the Board. Anson was unusual in having two other naval commissioners of real weight, Boscawen and Forbes. Forbes was shrewd and experienced, and moreover, because of his health, permanently ashore, unlike Boscawen. The other members of the

Board during the Seven Years' War were civilian politicians of no remarkable calibre, much like those who populated other boards and commissions, but their qualities were of only secondary importance, for Anson dominated his Board completely, and in his absence all but routine business was suspended.[6]

The routine business of the Admiralty consisted largely in co-ordinating the work of other departments. Its own primary responsibilities for the discipline and general direction of the Navy called for only a small staff – thirty in 1759.[7] The clerks were promoted strictly by seniority, and paid very well; 'ils sont trop bien payés', a French spy reported in disappointment, 'et risquent trop pour succomber aux appâts du gain.'[8] Precision was essential in their work, and a high sense of professionalism was expected.[9] At their head stood the Secretary of the Admiralty, the confidential servant of the Board in principle, but in practice an official of greater consequence in both the naval and political worlds than several of the Lords Commissioners. He managed not only the Admiralty's administrative business but also its political affairs, and he was the channel by which many promotions and appointments were arranged. He was the only official eyes and ears of the Board, to whom all correspondence was addressed, and from whom all correspondence (except formal orders requiring the signatures of three Lords Commissioners) came, signed 'by command of their Lordships'.[10] Politicians and officers who hoped to cultivate any influence at the Admiralty Board approached Clevland in preference to any member of the Board except Anson. Vice-Admiral Holburne, whose failure to take Louisbourg in the previous year had damaged his reputation as a sea commander, was in the spring of 1758 appointed commander-in-chief at Portsmouth. At once he wrote to Clevland in terms ingratiating to the point of servility, begging him to get the appointment changed, for 'I shall be very unhappy at that villainous Portsmouth'.[11] William Pitt, the Secretary of State and war minister, concerted strategic schemes with Clevland, and Lord Halifax declined any suggestion of becoming First Lord after Anson's death until he was sure that the Secretary would be staying in office.[12]

The Admiralty received the King's commands, that is to say the Cabinet's decisions, through the channel of one of the two Secretaries of State, during the Seven Years' War usually Pitt. By this mechanism the Cabinet's control of strategy was expressed, but in Anson's time the strategy had invariably been drawn up at meetings at which he was present and usually the dominant voice.[13] Major overseas expeditions involving both Services were directed by the Secretary of State himself, who sent orders straight to the naval and military commanders-in-chief. This could easily have led to dangerous confusion with the Admiralty, and in minor matters it sometimes did,[14] but so long as the Admiralty was kept fully informed, no real harm resulted, and co-operation between the Services was greatly assisted. In earlier periods the mechanism had been used to keep the Admiralty in the dark, but in Anson's time no politician, least of all Pitt, would have attempted such a move. The Secretary of State's orders were always communicated to the Admiralty, and admirals reported to it both what they had received from, and what they had sent to Pitt. At the beginning and end of expeditions, there was a formal transfer of control.[15]

The largest part of the routine administration of the Navy, including the management of the dockyards, the design, construction and repair of ships, and the supply of all sorts of naval stores, was the responsibility of the Navy Board, a body much larger (and much older) than the Admiralty.[16] This Board was formally entitled the Principal Officers and Commissioners of the Navy, and there was a distinction between the two. The Principal Officers were the Controller, the Surveyor, the Clerk of Acts, and the Controllers of Treasurer's, Victualling and Storekeeper's Accounts. The Controller, who was always a former sea officer, usually acted in practice as chairman of the Board, though in principle all its members were equal. The Surveyor, always a former shipwright, was responsible for ship design and construction. The Clerk of Acts, generally a former Navy Office clerk, supervised the large secretariat, and the civilian Controllers of Accounts managed the financial business of the Board.[17] Each of these had individual responsibility for a large department, but they also acted collectively as members of the Board in matters requiring the Board's sanction, and in this they were joined by the other commissioners, who had no departments of their own. These commissioners were always post-captains on half-pay, and a commissionership was regarded as the equivalent of a rear-admiral's flag in status. To accept it implied retirement from the sea service.[18] The boundary between the Board's collective responsibilities and the Principal Officers' individual tasks was drawn more by custom than constitution.

This was a potentially dangerous feature of the Board's organization, but still more curious was the position of the commissioners of the dockyards. They were members of the Navy Board on permanent detached service, but they were not actually in charge of the yards of which they were the heads. The senior officers of the yards received their orders either from the Board as a whole, or from one of the Principal Officers in particular. Three signatures was the minimum necessary to validate a Board order, and the commissioner of the yard could not sign one by himself. He could supervise, report, advise and warn, but he could not give orders. No dockyard had a single executive head, and only the Board in London could control its management. In practice this apparently unworkable arrangement functioned surprisingly well, but much depended on the personal relations of a commissioner with the Board and with the senior officers of his yard. It was often possible, for example, for an admiral arriving in port to arrange with the commissioner and the master shipwright of the yard to have his ships docked or repaired without waiting for the Navy Board's order to justify them, but in 1761 the Portsmouth yard officers refused to do this for Rodney.[19] The system left plentiful opportunities for confusion and delay. Its only advantage was that it was possible in emergency for two commissioners to come down from London to a dockyard and constitute a local Navy Board to deal with immediate problems,[20] but this meant that there were two Boards functioning simultaneously in different places, a situation too obviously pregnant with confusion to be of use except in a crisis.

The senior officers of each yard were the master shipwright (who in practice carried some sort of pre-eminence), the master or masters attendant, the storekeeper, the clerk of the cheque, and the master ropemaker, who ran the semi-independent ropeyard. The master shipwright was in charge of all building and repair, and of the major part of the workforce; the master attendant supervised the ships afloat and in reserve, moorings, yard craft and pilotage; the storekeeper kept all naval stores and supplies, and the clerk of the cheque was responsible for accounts. Each of these had numerous subordinates. Long experience and ability were the requirements for these offices, usually long experience in the yards, though the masters attendant were chosen from retired masters in the Navy. John Tovey, for example, began his career in 1739 as an apprentice and retired as master shipwright of Plymouth in 1801. Thomas Moulden was appointed master sailmaker of Sheerness in 1759, promoted to Chatham in 1768, and retired in 1802. Joseph Collins was a clerk in Portsmouth yard from 1715 to his death in 1763. Samuel Hemmans entered the *Minerva* as a captain's servant in 1760, and retired as master attendant of Chatham in 1810.[21] Services of over fifty years were not uncommon, which gave the yards an immense fund of experience at the cost, perhaps, of a certain institutional rigidity. Sea officers complained on occasion about the condition or design of their ships,[22] but they were not themselves experts in design or construction, and their remarks are not always to be taken at face value. There was praise, too, for yard officers' skill and zeal.[23]

The finance of the Navy as a whole, and the paying of officers and men in particular, was the responsibility of the Treasurer of the Navy, who was in theory a member of the Navy Board, but in practice entirely independent. His office superintended the system of bizarre complexity by which the ships of the Navy were paid,[24] and received monies voted by Parliament; the system of Navy bills, which effectively allowed the Navy to issue its own debt instruments and raise its own deficit finance without reference to Treasury or Parliament, was administered by the Navy Board.

The Navy Board was responsible for naval stores, that is, for ships, but victuals for men were dealt with by another body, the Victualling Board, autonomous within its own sphere of operations. It was second only to the Navy Board in its size and complexity, and maintained victualling yards and stores at the dockyard ports.[25] Yet another board, the Commissioners for Sick and Wounded Seamen, commonly known as the Sick and Hurt Board, maintained the naval hospitals and medical organization and also took charge of prisoners of war (of both services).[26] These two were under Admiralty orders, but the Navy drew its supplies of guns, ammunition and warlike stores from the Ordnance Board, an independent authority even older than the Navy Board, which was also responsible for fortifications, and ran the artillery and engineer corps and the wagon train which were attached to, but not part of, the regular army.[27] Warrant sea officers, though like all officers answerable in point of discipline to their captains and ultimately to the Admiralty, accounted for stores under their charge to the appropriate Board; Victualling Board for the purser, Sick and Hurt for the surgeon, Ordnance for the gunner, and Navy Board for the master and boatswain.

This little sketch of naval administration gives some idea of the haphazard and illogical forms which it had grown up in, and it is easy to make fun of the undoubted weaknesses of the system, but it should be remembered that it maintained at sea the largest fleet in Europe, and that in an age when no more demanding or technologically advanced task was presented to government than keeping ships of war operational. It is arguable that naval administration in the eighteenth century was in certain respects more efficient than it has ever been since. On 1 January 1763, at the worst season, and after seven years of world war, the Navy Board was able to report that more than three-quarters of the ships in the Navy were either at sea or ready to put to sea at once.[28] Nearly two centuries later, during the Second World War, the Navy does not appear to have been able to match this figure.[29] The evidence for the Victualling Board is equally impressive.[30] All in all, it seems that the naval administration, eccentric and in places arthritic though it clearly was, served the Sea Service remarkably well. Undoubtedly it was wasteful, and would not have shown to such advantage if it had been short of money, but that in itself was a tribute to a system which had found means to tap the nation's wealth without recourse to Parliament.

CHAPTER II

Shipboard Life

A WORK AND PLAY

To anyone coming upon it for the first time, the life of a ship was extraordinary. On first being 'registered in a wooden world', one entered a peculiar society, with its own manners, dress and language, all equally unexpected to an outsider. 'Nor could I think what world I was in,' one boy remembered of his first going to sea, 'whether among spirits or devils. All seemed strange; different language and strange expressions of tongue, that I thought myself always asleep or in a dream, and never properly awake.'[1] Many things in this curious life were always quite different from life ashore, but most things afloat themselves varied depending on whether the ship were at sea or in port. To weigh or drop anchor made a revolution in the internal affairs of every ship, suddenly altering the rhythms of daily life. The first question which must therefore be asked of the seaman's life is how often he was at sea. Fortunately it can be answered, for the Board of Admiralty, shrewdly aware of the limitations of human nature and the many things which might tempt captains to linger in port when they were supposed to be at sea, caused returns to be compiled from which it is possible to state exactly that from 1757 to 1762 (that is for the major part of the Seven Years' War) the number of days British men-of-war spent at sea was 43 per cent of their total time in commission.[2] The average ship, in other words, spent more than half her time in port. Moreover the largest ships, with the largest crews, were the least often at sea, so that the average man spent perhaps even less than 43 per cent of his time at sea (though the large ships in port were also the most likely to have lent men to

37

ships at sea). The life of the seaman had at least as much to do with time in port as with time at sea. 'In port' must be understood; it meant at anchor in some reasonably secure road, such as Spithead or the Nore. Only a small proportion of those in port were actually in harbour, for entering harbour was an awkward operation only undertaken if really necessary, usually to go into dock. The rest lay at anchor, often miles from the shore, cut off from it by weather too bad for boatwork and not entirely safe from the perils which attended all seafaring. Nevertheless, ships in port, and their crews, were in a fundamentally different and easier situation from those at sea, and overall, they were in a majority.

This average concealed wide variations. The biggest and the smallest men-of-war were least often at sea – three-deckers at one end of the scale, and bomb vessels, fireships and the like at the other – for in their different ways these were the least seaworthy and the most specialized vessels in the fleet. The third and fourth rates (those with between forty-four and eighty guns), the majority of the ships of the line, were at sea 41 per cent of their time, while the fifth and sixth rates (including the new 'frigates' then just coming into service) spent almost exactly half their time at sea, and the smaller cruisers, the sloops (the larger classes of which were still generally called 'frigates' by the more conservative), were just more often at sea than in port. These variations in the time at sea of different sizes of ship were compounded by considerable variations between different parts of the world. In home waters and the waters around northern Europe in general, men-of-war spent only 39 per cent of their time at sea, while in the Mediterranean it was 57 per cent. On the North American and East Indies stations too, though the actual times at sea were only 35 and 44 per cent, the real sea-time in the cruising season was higher because navigation was made impossible for part of the year by the winter in one case, and the typhoon season in the other. Perhaps the ships operating in home waters were the least efficient because the weather was worse, or because the largest and smallest types were concentrated there. A cynic might point to the proximity of England, home and beauty to leeward, and the well-equipped dockyards inviting the minor defect. Whatever the reason, on overseas stations, where it was much more difficult to keep ships in repair, they nevertheless spent much more time at sea, especially if they were cruisers. These hard-worked little ships were sometimes at sea more than three-quarters of all their time. Between September 1760 and October 1761 the *Antigua* sloop in the Leeward Islands was under way 78 per cent of her time, and in the following six months, under a different captain, 79 per cent. From April to October 1761 the *Merlin* sloop at Jamaica was 78 per cent of her time at sea. The *Pallas*, a new 36-gun frigate in the Mediterranean, spent 577 days (79 per cent) at sea between July 1760 and June 1762. By any standards, and especially by the standards of modern warships, these ships, and their officers and men, were working extremely hard.

In any case it is proper to describe first the sailor's life at sea, for it was this which defined his profession and gave rise to most of its peculiarities. At sea all men-of-war kept two watches; that is to say that the seamen and landmen, servants and petty officers of each part of ship were divided into two parties, the starboard and larboard watches, and that not less than one whole watch was on deck at all times, night and day. Each watch lasted four hours, except for the two two-hour dog watches between four and eight in the evening, which made the number of watches in the day an odd number and so ensured that the duties of each watch continually varied. The changing of the watch marked the passage of time aboard ship, where no clock would run. A petty officer, usually the quartermaster of the watch, kept a half-hour sandglass; when it turned, he rang the ship's bell, and at eight bells the watch changed. The whole cycle of the sea day, seven watches or twenty-four hours long, began at noon when the officers took their sights and plotted the ship's position, so that the calendar at sea was always twelve hours ahead of that ashore. This was strictly a sea and not a nautical peculiarity; ships in port, freed from the requirements of navigation, reverted to the civil calendar. The 'watch was set' at sea at the start of the First Watch at eight in the evening, which was, literally, the moment of 'lights out' when the watch coming off duty went to sleep until midnight. Then the other watch were able to sleep until four when the whole ship's company was roused. At sea all those in watches therefore had only four hours' sleep at most, and were liable to be awoken at any moment if an emergency required the watch below to turn out and bear a hand. The same applied to the idlers or daymen, who normally enjoyed an uninterrupted night's sleep, but were equally liable to be summoned by the pipe for all hands if their strength was required for pulling and hauling. This was quite often necessary in the frigates and sloops where the seamen were a much smaller proportion of the ship's company than in line-of-battle ships.[3] Even in larger and better manned ships, lack of sleep was a constant hardship of the sea life for everyone in watches, mitigated by whatever chances might be snatched of sleeping by day, or the occasional still tropical night when an indulgent officer might let part of the watch sleep on deck.[4]

For the officers the burden varied greatly according to the size of ship. Usually the master and the lieutenants took it in turns to be officer of the watch, which was tolerable in a second rate with six lieutenants, but in a sloop with one meant that he and the master were standing watch and watch like the men, and with even less chance of rest during the day. In practice, in smaller men-of-war the boatswain and gunner often stood watches, which must often have increased the commander's burdens. Even with experienced officers any prudent commander would expect to be called whenever the wind changed or anything untoward occurred; with young or untrustworthy officers, of whom there were naturally a good many in wartime, his worries multiplied. In settled weather, well clear of the land, a captain might enjoy uninterrupted nights, but in other circumstances he might have to keep the deck for days and nights at a stretch. Almost the only people aboard ship who could usually expect to sleep through the night were the non-seamen officers, the surgeon, purser, chaplain, carpenter and marine officers, who stood no watches and were not expected to turn out when 'all hands' was piped.

Life at sea in a man-of-war was arduous, but it was much easier than life in merchantmen in peace or war. Seamen everywhere stood watches at sea and accepted them as a natural part of their profession. The owners of merchant ships paid no more hands than they needed; the ratio of tons to men varied from fifteen or twenty to one in coasting trades down to only ten tons a man in West Indiamen and even less in slavers.[5] Men-of-war, by comparison, manned on a scale governed by the number of guns to be fought, carried crews in the ratio of one to every two or three tons.[6] It is true that they had a much larger proportion of non-seamen than merchant ships, but in 'tons per seaman' they enjoyed a substantial advantage over even the most heavily manned merchantmen. The more men in proportion to the size of the ship, the less work for each. Life in men-of-war may have been arduous, but we never hear of men dropping exhausted from the yards, or dying with fatigue at the pumps, both of which are reported from merchantmen of the period.[7]

For the seamen, the actual work of the ship involved much pulling and hauling, for of course all manoeuvres depended on manpower. The topmen had to go out on the yards whenever sail was to be made or handed, and worked aloft on all the ceaseless work of maintenance and repair. This was the common occupation of ships' companies during the day when not actually working the ship – the seamen working on the rigging, the carpenter and his crew on the hull and spars, the sailmaker and crew on the sails, and the armourer, who acted as the ship's blacksmith, on ironwork. Night and day men were posted aloft as lookouts – it was common practice to relieve the man who first sighted something, as a reward, but to continue double time those who allowed something to be seen first from the deck.[8]

Besides the common work of the ship, certain tasks required the united strength of all the seamen if not of all hands. Weighing anchor was one; scores or even hundreds of men needed to strain around the capstan for hours to bring in the huge anchors and clumsy hempen cables, and against any considerable wind or tide it was impossible. Hoisting in the longboat, which weighed several tons, likewise called for all the manpower available, and the use of the mainyard as a derrick. Many men-of-war, especially the smaller ones, tended to leave their longboats behind when they cruised in home waters, partly for this reason. In calm weather the small sloops with sweeps and rowing ports could, and sometimes did, row for hours – perhaps the most exhausting of all labour at sea. Large ships might in similar circumstances be towed by their own boats. The *Aquilon* 26 (i.e. a ship of 26 guns), chased in light airs by a French seventy-four, escaped by rowing twenty-six hours non-stop. Captain Hervey in the Mediterranean, sighting what he

41

took to be French ships in the distance, pulled for seven hours in the boats (leaving his ship behind), only to find that they were neutrals, and the labour had been in vain.[9] This sort of exhausting toil, and disappointment, were a part of the seaman's working life.

The time not occupied in the essential work of the ship might be employed in training. With wartime ships' companies containing a large proportion of landmen and ordinary seamen in addition to the usual boys, formal instruction in seamanship was necessary. The boatswain and his mates could teach the young men such essentials as knotting and splicing, but much of the work, and especially work aloft, could only be learnt by practice. Admiralty orders of 1758 required landmen and boys to be exercised aloft daily, the boys on the topgallants and the mizzen topsail, the smallest sails, and officers were urged to 'endeavour to raise an emulation in them, to outdo those of other ships'.[10] This could be done in port, but no amount of sail drill in port was a substitute for the real thing, and 'river discipline' (meaning the best state of training possible before putting to sea) was not to be depended on.[11] For young gentlemen it was considered indispensable to work aloft with the topmen. Some were killed,[12] but the survivors grew up finished seamen, and knew what they were ordering their men to do. To have as a 'sea-daddy' a steady topman like Joe Moulding, captain of the foretop of the *Panther* in 1782 who looked after the young James Gardner, was a great asset to a future officer.[13] 'Captain Mackenzie', another young gentleman wrote, 'has been so kind as to put me in one of the tops at sea, which will be very advantageous to me.'[14] For officers and ratings alike, seamanship could be learnt only by experience, and keen captains like Augustus Hervey would take their ships to sea simply to train the people.[15]

Gun drill was in some ways even more important, for there was no natural practice to be had apart from action. Accordingly the Admiralty strongly encouraged flag officers to have their squadrons exercise great guns and small arms as often as possible, and the order was generally obeyed. Boscawen's squadron crossing the Atlantic in 1755 drilled daily, and Admiral Smith commanding in the Downs ordered his captains to drill as often as possible without waiting for orders.[16] It was the same with Mostyn, Knowles,

Pocock, Osborn and Hawke, who are all mentioned encouraging gun drill, and doubtless with other flag officers.[17] Even privateers, notoriously slack in their organization, occasionally exercised at the great guns.[18] The exercises themselves consisted chiefly of going through the drill of loading, running out and firing the guns as quickly and reliably as possible. Accuracy at any range was quite outside the capability of the pieces, and there was little attempt at target practice, though Boscawen encouraged it, and the Ordnance Board experimentally issued gunlocks to a proportion of some ships' great guns with a view to improving accuracy by enabling the gun captain to judge when to fire more exactly than was possible with the traditional linstocks.[19] Small arms were also exercised, and another drill which was sometimes practised – once a week in Admiral Smith's divisional system – was fire fighting, and specifically the use of the 'fire engine', the portable fire pump which was kept on the quarter deck.[20]

In port the work of the ship was generally lighter than at sea. The actual physical labour of fitting a ship for sea and hoisting in ballast, stores and guns, or conversely stripping a ship to be docked, was considerable, but men could look forward to an unbroken night's sleep, with Sundays and holidays off except in an emergency,[21] and a good deal of relaxation. At single anchor some ships kept three watches,[22] but when securely moored most seem to have abandoned watches altogether. The crews of the guard ships, who spent their entire time in port, pulling boats and working aboard other ships, had an easy time and were much envied in peacetime, though in war many of them opted for the more exciting and profitable life at sea.[23] Not that boatwork was a sinecure; ships often lay miles from harbour and boats' crews were expected to pull long distances. When Thomas Slade, the Surveyor of the Navy, visited Portsmouth and the vicinity in 1756 to view ships building, he was taken from Buckler's Hard to Itchenor by a boat from the commissioner's yacht. The men 'had a hard row of it, they having from leaving the yacht to their getting to the ferry in Southampton rowed full twenty-two miles'.[24] It could be dangerous, too, for ships' boats would not float if swamped or capsized, as they easily could be in an open road. Captain Hamilton of the *Lancaster* was drowned in Spithead in December 1755 when his barge capsized.[25]

Men in port were not usually expected to work on other ships, nor to do the work of the dockyard. On overseas stations like the West Indies where the dockyard staffs were too small, and in the opinion of sea officers too idle, to do all the work by themselves, ships' companies did work ashore, and were paid extra for doing so; 'no seaman works here', Commodore Douglas reported of Antigua yard in 1762, 'but what do it voluntarily, and paid two royals a day when they do'.[26] Work, however, was not the only or even the most prominent feature of life in port. Strangers who found their way on board warships at anchor were impressed not by the sight of disciplined teamwork, but by bustle and confusion. 'I was surprised at the number of people, men, women and children ... There were also shops and stalls of every kind of goods, and people crying their different commodities about the ship as in a town. To me it appeared a little world ...'[27] This was the *Royal George*, but any large ship at Spithead for some time would have presented a similar appearance, if indeed there was not more organized entertainment. When the *Panther* paid off in 1782 the ship's company gave a grand supper, with the lower deck illuminated and jigs and reels all night.[28]

Music and dancing were a part of life in wardroom and mess throughout the Navy. In Boscawen's flagship as they sailed westward across the Atlantic in the mild spring of 1755 the men danced nightly to fiddle, fife and drum. It reminded the admiral as he wrote home to his wife of country dances with her in former years.[29] Even in the rather unlikely situation of a press tender we hear of a mixed set of pressed men, volunteers, press gang and tender's crew dancing on the hatch cover on a sunny summer's day.[30] Some ships had bands of a sort,[31] and privateers, for recruiting purposes, went out of their way to provide music. The *King George* of Bristol in 1746 had two horns, two flutes, a drum, a fiddle and a Welsh harp.[32] Music, however, was not always an asset aboard ship. It was fashionable in the 1750s for young men to be able to play the flute, and as is the way with fashionable accomplishments, many attempted the instrument and few mastered it. One of the ways marine lieutenants made themselves very unpopular was by playing the flute and singing in the wardroom when their watchkeeping messmates were trying to sleep.[33]

A less troublesome fashion of the time was backgammon, which officers played a good deal.[34] Officers and men alike fished when they had the chance. Every ship had an outfit of fishing tackle, including hooks and lines for issue to the men.[35] It was also possible to hang out baited hooks for gulls,[36] or indeed to shoot at them. The purser and lieutenant of the *Isis* spent an idle afternoon at anchor in Gibraltar Bay in 1763 potting at seagulls with a musket over the taffrail.[37] There were occasional boisterous ceremonies, particularly on crossing the line, when those who had never crossed paid a forfeit of 'pound and pint' or 'bottle and pound' (a bottle of spirits and a pound of sugar, to make flip) on pain of being ducked from the yardarm.[38]

Perhaps the least noticed of all recreations at sea was reading. How many men would or could read is difficult to say. Many were undoubtedly illiterate, probably more than the average for their class, but there are chance references to men off watch reading in their hammocks,[39] and very likely it was common. In 1746 the Navy Board objected to a letter of attorney on behalf of a ship's company because fewer than half had signed it. This was complained of as an unreasonable test, and perhaps it was, but twelve years later 169 men of the *Weymouth* signed a petition on behalf of all their shipmates, which was nearly half of the total without officers, and fifty-eight of the ninety officers and men of the *Firedrake* sloop signed a power of attorney.[40] How many of those who could sign their names were functionally literate for everyday purposes one cannot say, but a proportion must certainly have been. Among the officers, though there were ill-educated and even semi-literate men, some literary interests were coming to be regarded as proper, if not indispensable. Admiral Smith recommended to a young officer Rapin's *History of England*, 'to be read with the notes and without skipping the *State of the Church*, because I think it very material for a young man to be first acquainted with the history of his own country'; admirable advice, which might profit naval officers today.[41] Rapin's history is fifteen volumes in octavo. It may be doubted whether every young man had a copy in his sea chest, but reading of some sort was probably one common way in which both officers and men passed what time they had to spare from their work.

B THE DANGERS OF THE SEAS

Seafaring was an exceptionally dangerous profession. Men-of-war were certainly safer than merchant ships, for they were larger, better found and better manned, but even the best ships were often at the mercy of wind and current. Square-rigged vessels, which included all but the very smallest in the Navy, could point no higher than six points off the wind, and made so much leeway that it was frequently impossible to make ground to windward. In February 1758, for example, a captain reported from sea that he had been beating up Channel for four weeks trying to make port.[1] Ships therefore spent a great deal of time at anchor waiting for a fair wind, and the Downs, the great anchorage inshore of the Goodwin Sands, was often crowded with hundreds of sail waiting for a fair wind to carry them down Channel. Much more serious was the position of a ship closing the land in thick weather, which could easily find herself embayed, unable to weather the headlands on either side. In this case there was no hope but the anchors. Warships carried at least seven anchors, all very large, but they were not very efficient and the cables often parted, so it was dangerous to trust in them – dangerous, but frequently unavoidable. The *Ramillies*, lately Hawke's flagship, was embayed on the Devon coast in 1760 through the master mistaking his landfall. She anchored, but the anchors came home. Over a period of many hours, she dragged slowly nearer the cliffs of Bolt Tail, all on board helplessly watching their fate, until at last she struck. Twenty-seven men survived out of nearly eight hundred on board.[2] In similar circumstances five of the East Indies squadron were wrecked in one night in February 1761, two of them with almost all hands, and many of the remainder lost their masts.[3]

All ships had sometimes to trust in their anchors, and very often they had to cut away their masts to reduce the windage aloft. This drastic measure was almost a commonplace; a gale in January 1762 forced seven ships in Plymouth Sound to cut away their masts in a single night, plus five which drove ashore and two which dragged foul of one another.[4] This was a major cause of the very high consumption of masts and cordage which was one of the most serious limiting factors in naval strategy. Cutting away masts was a desperate and dangerous operation, though not so dangerous as losing them by accident. In October 1763 the *Milford* pitched away all her masts at once, losing seven men dead and twenty-nine injured.[5] Most dangerous of all was for a ship to lose her ground tackle. The French *Belliqueux* returning from Canada was badly damaged by storms and blown helpless up the Bristol Channel, not even knowing which channel she was in. Her officers and men probably owed their lives to being promptly captured.[6]

The acute danger of a lee shore, the nightmare of every seaman, could often have been avoided if it had been easier for ships to tell their positions, and, just as important, the position of the land, with any accuracy. Using a Davis or Hadley's quadrant,[7] a skilful officer could fix a ship's latitude to within ten miles or less, but even this left plenty of room for error, and not all officers were skilful, nor the sky always clear for observations. A passenger in a Dutch merchantman sailing from Cadiz to Ostend in 1743 was alarmed to discover after a fortnight at sea that the two mates differed 150 miles in their latitude, one placing the ship north of the Scilly Isles, the other south.[8] Navigational standards were rising,[9] and they were probably higher in the Navy than in merchantmen, but it was quite usual to make landfalls scores or even hundreds of miles in error. The safest course was to get into the right latitude and cautiously run the latitude down to the coast, but in wartime this was dangerous since the enemy had only to wait in the latitude of the obvious landfalls for prizes to fall into their arms.[10] British ships did this off Ushant, and French privateers likewise cruised off the Windward Islands in the track of westbound shipping. Even if one did run down a known latitude, there was no guarantee of a safe landfall. One of the troop transports coming from North America to Barbados in 1761 mistook St Lucia for her intended destination – an error of 160 miles in longitude. A few years earlier another merchantman was nearly wrecked on Bermuda, 300 miles out of her reckoning.[11] It was not only merchant ships which made such errors. In November 1758 Commodore Keppel sailed with a small squadron for West Africa. After only seventeen days at sea, being then by their reckoning more than 350 miles from land, the *Lichfield* leading the squadron ran onto the coast of Morocco, and the other ships were only just saved.[12] It is not surprising that it was proverbial among seamen that it was better to trust a good lookout than a bad reckoning.[13]

The difficulty of fixing a ship's position with accuracy was compounded by the lack of trustworthy charts on which to plot it. If the land were not accurately laid down the most skilful navigator would have difficulty making his landfall, and even Dutch and French charts, which were rightly reckoned better than English, were far from reliable.[14] After the battle of Quiberon Bay, British ships using charts in the *Neptune François*, the official French collection, found they required extensive correction. British men-of-war chiefly used charts on long ocean passages and on overseas stations. In the East or West Indies there was no avoiding the use of a chart, however inaccurate, but around the coasts of Britain they relied on pilots, as they always had done. Pilots were troublesome, incompetent, and very expensive: 'the insolence and ignorance of these fellows occasion frequent delays and inconveniences to the Service'; they often refused to sail when they could have done and ran ships aground when they need not have done, but it was universally accepted that they could not be dispensed with.[15] There was no coastal passage, however short and well-known, which a man-of-war's officers were trusted to undertake on their own. The ignorance of officers in general, and masters in particular, of their own coasts was extraordinary. It was nothing odd that the *Rose* frigate was nearly lost on the coast of Ireland, mistaking Galley Head for the Old Head of Kinsale, none of her officers knowing the waters at all, or that the charts and pilots of Harwich were reported equally erroneous;[16] for many officers Portsmouth and Plymouth were almost as unknown. When

Cotes's squadron returned from the West Indies in 1760 he had to anchor in Sandown Bay, 'his master not being well enough acquainted to bring the ship to Spithead'.[17] The unsuspected perils of Portsmouth and its approaches claimed several ships during the war. The fine seventy-four *Invincible* was wrecked on the Dean Sand in 1758.[18] Three years later the *Dorsetshire* was run on the Horse Sand, provoking the port admiral to order the masters attendant out to sound the channels, 'which I propose they should do several times by way of refreshing their memories, this being the second great ship they have run ashore lately'.[19] Various new shoals were discovered, but not all of them, for four months later the *Portland* was run very hard on the Middle Ground off Ryde.[20] All these ships were attempting the well-known passage up to Spithead round the eastern end of the Isle of Wight. To take a squadron through the Needles Channel, as Keppel did in 1754 only a year after the *Assurance* had been wrecked there on an uncharted rock, was much more daring, and it seems that nobody ever attempted the Loo Stream Channel, though a survey of it was made in 1759.[21]

The story was much the same at Plymouth, where the navigation was intrinsically more difficult. Though the Hamoaze was a very fine natural harbour, the passage to the Sound was narrow and tortuous, and the Sound itself offered little safe anchorage. Still, by 1755 when the *Vanguard* hit an unsuspected rock in the Cremyll Passage,[22] the masters attendant had been taking men-of-war through it for sixty years. In October 1760 a pilot wrecked the *Conqueror* on St Nicholas Island the same day that the *Magnanime* touched an uncharted rock in the Sound – perhaps the same rock that the *Hampton Court* hit two years later.[23]

When pilots knew so little of their own coasts it is not surprising that senior officers were less than clear about the geography of the British Isles. A captain found it necessary to explain to the Admiralty where Sunderland and Blyth were, while a Sussex man assumed that the flag officer in the Downs would not have heard of Newhaven.[24]

When charts and pilots were unreliable and often unobtainable, when navigators had great difficulty in fixing their positions, and ships were incapable of clawing off a lee shore in many conditions of wind and sea, all seafaring was attended with innumerable perils. Only a madman or (more often) a drunkard would court danger deliberately. It is all the more striking that two of the greatest British victories of the Seven Years' War were won by notably sane and sober commanders who deliberately ran their squadrons into great danger in pursuit of the enemy. At Quiberon Bay Hawke committed his ships to a stern chase to leeward in a rising gale. Ahead of them in the gathering darkness of a winter afternoon lay a dangerous coast of which they knew very little. Even without battle damage, their chances of anchoring, or of beating offshore in the teeth of the gale, were slender. Hawke's entire plan depended on following the French closely into a safe anchorage and completely defeating them in the process. He risked everything on the seamanship of his captains, on the gunnery of their ships, and, not least, on the French knowing their own coast well enough to lead him to safety. If Hawke's squadron had been wrecked, and Conflans's had survived, the way would have been open for the intended invasion. Probably no British admiral has ever risked battle in such dangerous circumstances, and no one who saw the 'gallant and swift-winged Hawke' go into action (the Aeschylian phrase is from a seaman of a frigate in company) ever forgot that day.[25]

Hawke's decision was taken, as it had to be, alone, without planning or consultation, as an instant reaction to the sudden development of affairs at sea. By contrast, the attack on Havana was a scheme long matured and carefully prepared, carried out in fine weather with no interference from the enemy and with none of the drama of Quiberon Bay, but it involved navigational risks nearly as great. The great port and fortress of Havana, then the strongest and richest place in Spanish America, lies on the north or leeward coast of the island of Cuba, whose length, lying roughly northwest and south-east, points directly into the prevailing southeasterly winds. Any ship approaching Havana had to sail down the length of the island on one side or the other, and in practice virtually all navigators took the southerly passage, where there was deep and open water. They then passed through the Yucatan Passage, rounded Cape San Antonio and beat up the north coast to Havana.[26] This was a distance of more than two hundred miles nearly dead to windward, and any large squadron could be relied upon to take a week, probably several weeks, to cover it, giving ample time for watchers on the shore to report its advance to Havana. With some reason, the Spaniards relied on having warning of any attack.

On the opposite shore of the island, a wide expanse of reefs and islands stretches for hundreds of miles north and east to the Bahamas. Even today, though accurately charted, the Great Bahama Bank is accessible only to small boats with local knowledge. There is, however, one deep channel through it, the Old Bahama Channel. Including the Nicolas Channel which prolongs it, it is 250 miles long and in places less than ten miles wide, lined on both sides by hidden reefs and low sandy cays virtually invisible even in fair weather. Though the coast of Cuba is to be seen in places to port, in the whole passage there is no natural sea mark. The Spaniards, who had charted it, thought it too dangerous for large ships, and were confident that no British squadron could or would attempt it.[27]

Only this approach, however, would allow an invasion fleet to approach its objective undetected and fast, from the windward side, and Anson decided to risk it. Attempts were made to get pilots from the Bahamas, but those supplied were soon found to be useless. The *Trent* sloop, intended as a marker, was placed by one of these pilots 135 miles out of position. The success of the passage was largely due to Captain Elphinstone of the *Richmond* frigate who went ahead to survey the channel, left parties on the cays to mark it, and returned to guide the fleet. Pocock made the most careful disposition of his huge force, and decided to pass the narrowest part of the channel by night, guided by fires lit by Elphinstone's shore parties – a daring choice, but in the end completely successful. Though the passage of the Old Bahama Channel was methodical and undramatic, carried out in fine weather and without fighting, it ranks as one of the riskiest feats of navigation of the age. It was carried out in the old style, for though Pocock had a Spanish chart which Anson had given him, and in the event found it accurate, he did not rely on it.[28]

In 1762 navigation remained more an art than a science, and perhaps more guesswork than art, but it was improving rapidly, and a good deal of official and unofficial effort was devoted to it. The best known and most important advances were the methods of 'finding the longitude', that popular phrase for an impossibility, like squaring the circle or perpetual motion. In the long run Harrison's chronometer, first tried at sea during the Seven Years' War, was to be the most successful means of fixing longitude, but chronometers were, and remained for many years, very expensive instruments which masters could not afford to buy. More serviceable was the method of lunar distances made possible by the work of the German astronomer Tobias Meyer of Göttingen, which required advanced mathematics, but no special instruments. Meyer's lunar tables were first published in 1755, tried at sea by Captain John Campbell in 1757 and 1758, again by the Reverend Neville Maskelyn on a voyage to St Helena in 1761, and published to an English-speaking audience at the end of the war in his *British Mariner's Guide*.[29] Well before this, however, the news had diffused through the Navy. Less than a year after Meyer's original publication that unstudious, not to say illiterate, young officer Lieutenant John Elliot was able to write home to his father from sea that he had no news, 'only the discovery of the longitude by a Hanoverian ... The observation is simple and easy, but the calculation is extremely perplexed.'[30] Before the end of the war this difficult calculation was already being taught in the mathematical schools which specialized in preparing boys for the Navy and the merchant service.[31] At the same time improved instruments were being developed, including Knight's azimuth compass, and the sextant, which was partly invented by John Campbell.[32] Seamarks were receiving attention, both simple devices like whitewashing Sandown Castle as a leading mark out of Sandown Bay and laying a buoy on Bembridge Ledge,[33] and expensive novelties like the new stone lighthouse which was being built on the Eddystone during the war. A serious study of navigation was becoming accepted as a normal part of the good officer's duties, and not simply a speciality of masters. Admirals and captains ordered abroad obtained charts and sailing directions, and consulted the logs of ships which had been there before: 'we frequently when we are going voyages where we have never been get journals out of the public offices for our guide and direction'.[34] Commodore Frankland, who wrote this, reported dangerous variations in marking the log line, and consequently in reckoning distance run: 'The *Winchester*, by allowing only forty-two feet to a glass of thirty seconds, overrun her reckoning by near a hundred leagues between Madeira and this island [Barbados].'[35] He asked for an Admiralty order fixing the length of the log line. This was an example of a new interest in precision and reliability in navigation. Another was official sponsorship of research into magnetic variation, and official collection of corrections for charts.[36] A zealous captain like Augustus Hervey would take the opportunity when visiting foreign waters to learn the navigation (he hired a pilot from his own pocket on the coast of Italy in 1753)[37] and an Admiralty order of 1758 required all masters to make surveys and notes of any uncharted waters they might visit.

These developments were the forerunners of many which were to improve navigation very greatly in the next fifty years, and reduce the Navy's heavy losses from shipwreck. This was not, however, the only peril of the sea. Fire was an acute danger in wooden ships filled with highly combustible stores. Rear-Admiral Broderick's flagship the *Prince George* was burnt at sea on passage to Gibraltar in 1758. The admiral himself was an hour in the water, and only 256 were saved out of 721 on board, in spite of the efforts of other ships in company.[38] Losses like this were inevitable when few sailors could swim,[39] and the modern swimming strokes were undeveloped. If ships drove ashore, it was common for no one aboard to be able to swim through the surf with a line – or, as in one case, no one but the pig.[40] When the *Lichfield* was wrecked, sixty out of a ship's company of about 350 could swim,[41] and this seems to have been about the highest proportion that could be hoped for. Those who survived shipwreck might find themselves, like the *Lichfield*'s company, among hostile natives. Survivors, if any, of ships lost at sea were in a worse position. When the slaver *Luxborough Galley* was burnt on passage home from the West Indies twenty-three men took to the boat, without food or water. Seven survived to be picked up by a Newfoundland fisherman, having lived off the dead bodies of their shipmates.[42] The future Commodore Boys was one of them, a lucky man in a profession in which perhaps one in two died unnaturally.[43] His brother officer

Captain Stancombe supported a request for sick leave in 1761 with an account of how he had narrowly escaped when his ship was burnt under him, broken his skull in a fall, and frostbitten his ears conning his ship among icebergs. Men were drowned falling overboard or capsizing in boats, they were killed falling from aloft, struck by lightning on deck, or suffocated in the noxious vapours of the hold.[44] Of those who went down to the sea in ships, very many never returned.

C THE VIOLENCE OF THE ENEMY

Warships were built to fight, though they did so infrequently even in wartime, and fighting was the supreme test of the internal organization of a ship. Each officer and rating was allotted his quarter (his station in action) by a quarter bill posted up in the ship. Quarter bills differed somewhat according to captains' opinions and the size of ships, but in general principles all were much alike. The captain himself commanded from the quarter deck, attended by one or two midshipmen to carry messages. With him were usually the master, one or more mates, and one or more quartermasters at the wheel. The boatswain, his mates and a party of seamen handled sail and repaired damaged rigging. Unless in chase ships often fought under reduced canvas, but it was vital that damaged rigging be knotted or spliced at once because if the ship became unmanageable she would be at the mercy of an enemy still under command. Most of the seamen and landmen manned the guns below, and the lieutenants were also there in charge of one deck or side of a deck each, with the remaining midshipmen and mates under them. The boys were attached to the guns' crews, one or two to each, to fetch powder from the magazines.[1] For safety's sake only a small amount of powder was kept by the guns, and the cartridges, which were vulnerable to damp, were not filled long in advance. In action therefore the gunner and his mates worked in the handling chamber above the magazine making up cartridges and placing them each in a leather case with a close-fitting lid. These were passed out through double doors hung with wet baize to keep out sparks, and carried by the boys to the guns. A well-organized ship's company would have only the minimum amount of powder in transit from the magazine, on the disengaged side if possible. The *Thunderer* in 1761 suffered thirty killed and fifty injured in a powder explosion in action at night; the boys in their enthusiasm had brought up too much powder, and in the darkness it was not noticed.[2] The carpenter and his crew attended to damage to the hull, especially to shots 'between wind and water', which had to be plugged promptly before they caused serious flooding. In order to allow the carpenter's crew to get at these holes narrow passages, the 'wings', were left free along both sides of the orlop deck, outboard of the store rooms and cable tiers. Either in the cockpit at the after end of the orlop, or on a platform in the hold completely below the waterline, the surgeon and his mates attended as best they could to the wounded, assisted sometimes by the chaplain and any women on board. The marines lined the rail on the poop, quarter deck and forecastle, and sometimes climbed up into the tops, to lay down musketry fire on the enemy's decks. It was their job especially to repel boarders or to lead a boarding party if necessary.

Boarding was a recognized tactic, but not a common one. Privateers with large crews and rather inadequate gun armament found it a convenient way of attacking, or threatening to attack, short-handed merchantmen which they did not wish to damage, but it was a bloody and desperate expedient against a man-of-war whose company were still steady and under command. The great majority of actions, between both squadrons and individual ships, were essentially artillery duels, terminated by the escape or surrender of one party. It was accepted that a ship too badly damaged to escape, and with too many killed or wounded to be fought effectively, could and should strike her colours. One of the notable aspects of the Seven Years' War is that British ships were victorious in a quite disproportionate number of actions in which the forces were more or less evenly matched. It is a matter of some interest to determine why this was so. No suggestion was ever made by British sea officers that French officers and men were inherently cowardly – on the contrary, there were many examples of conspicuous heroism among them. They were sometimes presented as worse seamen, but in a simple gunnery duel this did not necessarily matter. In some actions, notably Quiberon Bay and Lagos, misjudgements by the French admiral or his subordinates allowed the British squadron to defeat them in detail, but this sort of error was not peculiar to the French, and played no part in many actions. French ships were in general somewhat larger and longer in proportion to their number of guns, which made it easier to fight their lower-deck guns in a seaway, and rather more lightly-built, and consequently vulnerable.[3] It is true that we hear of French seamen running from their guns in action, but British seamen could do that too,[4] and in either case it was clearly the symptom and not the cause of impending defeat.

Whatever factors may have affected individual actions, the prevailing factor in most cases was undoubtedly gunnery, and this may be divided into three components: accuracy, target, and rate of fire. Though British guns' crews did sometimes practise shooting at a target,[5] most actions were fought at short range and the guns were not capable of great accuracy, so it is difficult to see how either side could have gained any real advantage in this way. More significant is the target at which they fired. French ships are traditionally said to have fired high, on the up roll, to disable the enemy's masts and rigging, while British ships fired low, on the down roll, to batter the hull and kill the gunners. This cannot have been anything like a national policy, for the choice was available only to a captain with well-trained guns' crews, and it was in practice a decision to be taken on tactical grounds. To fire high was the logical choice of the commander who desired to disable a superior enemy and then escape, or then close with an advantage of manoeuvrability. To fire low was to aim to finish the action as quickly and decisively as possible. There certainly were actions in which French ships fired high, as evidenced by suffering heavier casualties themselves, and inflicting damage largely aloft,[6] but British ships could fire high when it suited them, as did Captain Douglas of the *Unicorn* when he found himself in action against superior forces, and aimed 'to cut as much as could be of his rigging with one broadside pointed high on purpose'.[7] Moreover one could alter one's policy as the action developed. Captain Young of the *Intrepid*, one of the most heavily engaged ships at the battle of Minorca, reported that the French had begun by firing high as he approached, but fired low when they came to close quarters: 'latterly they left off firing at our rigging and hulled us every time. I had fourteen shot between wind and water, and many through both sides.'[8] In the absence of reliable information about every action, it is impossible to say if the French consistently fired high, but they would have been unwise to do so in close action, and the proposition must be doubtful.

Nevertheless, in too many cases to be accidental, French ships suffered far heavier casualties in action than their British opponents. Some examples of single-ship actions may be given in the form of a small table:

British	Casualties (killed + wounded)	French	Casualties (killed + wounded)
Monmouth 64 (guns)	30 + ?	Foudroyant 80	134 + 142[9]
Bellona 74	6 + 28	Courageux 74	240 + 110[10]
Achilles 60	2 + 23	Comte de St Florentin 60	106 k. + w.[11]
Badger 14	0 + 8	Escorte 16	55 + ?[12]
Dorsetshire 70	17 + 60	Raisonnable 64	110 + 220[13]
Tartar 28	4 + ?	Duc d'Aiguillon 26	60 k. + w.[14]
Boreas 28	1 + 1	Sirène 32	80 k. + w.[15]
Lively 20	2 + 0	Valeur 20	38 + 25[16]
Trent 20	1 + 5	Bien Aimé 20	20 k. + w.[17]
Fortune 18	1 + 6	Marie 26	12 + 13[18]

These are remarkable discrepancies between more or less evenly matched ships, and none more remarkable than that in the action between the *Monmouth* and the *Foudroyant* off Cartagena on the night of 28 February 1758, one of the most famous of all single-ship actions (though the *Foudroyant* did not strike until another ship came up). The weight of broadside of the two ships was 504 lbs. against 1222 lbs. (and the French pound was 8 per cent heavier).[19] The ratio of destructive power was thus 2.6:1 in favour of the French, but they lost 4.5 killed for every one dead in the *Monmouth*. This was an extraordinary fight in every way, but it, and the others in the table, still have to be explained, and the only possible explanation seems to be a much higher British rate of fire. Reporting his victory at the first battle of Finisterre in 1747, Anson wrote that 'I could plainly perceive that my ships made a much hotter fire, and much more regular than theirs.'[20] Unfortunately British officers do not seem to have timed their guns' crews, and such evidence as survives is not very informative. At the second battle of Finisterre in 1747 the *Defiance* fired seventy broadsides in five hours, during which she was not continually engaged. In taking the *Duc d'Aiguillon* the *Tartar* fired forty-two broadsides in an hour and twelve minutes, which if she fired continuously meant better than one broadside every two minutes.[21] However if she really fired full broadsides she probably was not firing continuously, when the regularity of broadsides rapidly broke down into individual firing. By comparison Collingwood in 1805 had his ship firing nearly one broadside a minute – but this was extraordinary by any standards, and probably could not have been sustained.[22] On shore, at the siege of the Morro Castle, the artillerymen were astonished to find the naval battery firing three times as fast as the army believed possible, but this was still only nine rounds an hour, far slower than could be obtained at sea.[23] With no useful averages of either British or French rates of fire little more can be said than that the French certainly spoke of British gunnery with respect ('les Englois ont fait des merveilles, leur cannon a été servicé comme de la musqueterie'),[24] and if it was not superior gunnery which accounted for such high French casualties in equal combat, it is difficult to guess what was the cause. Certainly the effects of a full broadside could be severe, though hardly ever as terrible as the two broadsides from the *Royal George* at Quiberon Bay which sank the *Superbe* without a single survivor.[25] The chaplain of the *Royal George* reported that on this occasion French gunnery was as bad as British was good, and his ship's situation

> would have been lamentable, if the enemy had pre-
> served any degree of composure, or fired with any sort
> of direction, but their confusion was so great, that of
> many hundreds of shot, I do not believe that more than
> thirty or forty struck the ship.[26]

This account strongly hints at the underlying cause of victory, whether effected by gunnery, seamanship or courage, which is discipline and training. When it came to battle, ships' companies who knew their ship and their officers, who together had endlessly practised what they would have to do in action, were at an enormous advantage over ill-directed bravery. Men who would lie quietly by their guns being fired at until they were given the order to fire back, as they did in Boscawen's flagship at the battle of Lagos, or clear away and hoist out their boats while in action amongst a heavy and confused sea, as Keppel did at Quiberon Bay in an attempt to save the men of the *Thésée*, were stiffened not simply by animal courage, but by thorough training and confidence in their commanders.[27]

By contrast, there were many reports of French crews in 'uproar and confusion' in action. When the *Alcide* struck to Boscawen's squadron in 1755 discipline disintegrated so fast that her own men had plundered £7600 in government money before the British boats could get aboard.[28] When the *Diadème*, a French warship with captured British troops aboard, ran aground in the West Indies,

> at this very time the French seamen behaved in so dis-
> orderly and mutinous manner that their officers put
> arms into the hands of the English prisoners to keep the
> Frenchmen in obedience. I mention this fact [Admiral
> Pocock remarked drily] as an extraordinary instance
> seldom to be met with.[29]

As for French officers, one may quote the bitter verdict of one who had served at Quiberon Bay:

> Tout le resumé de cette affaire est qu'il y a peu d'obeis-
> sance et beaucoup de valeur à la droite, grande confu-
> sion et ignorance dans le centre, et mauvaise manoeuvre
> dans la gauche, et ni habilité ni tête dans le tout.[30]

If there was a British 'secret weapon' at sea, it was not good gunnery so much as the high state of discipline of which that was a
symptom.

D HARDSHIPS AND COMFORTS

The sea life was hard and dangerous, and many observers would
have agreed with the master of a merchantman who, after eight
days and nights of struggle against a gale, eating raw meat for
want of fire, exclaimed that 'a man had better be a fish than a
sailor, excepting the little time he is on shore'. He that would go to
sea for pleasure, the proverb had it, would go to hell for a pas-
time.[1] No doubt few men went to sea for pleasure, but for whatever reason they found themselves afloat, they found the
discomforts of life aboard ship more or less severe depending on
their standard of comparison. For a young gentleman or noble-
man, brought up in a comfortable house with servants to command, with clean sheets, warm fires and good food, the inevitable
privations of a man-of-war might have appeared grim. This was
one of the reasons often stated for the necessity of catching officers
young; only a boy was sufficiently tough and adaptable. For a poor
boy, bred up perhaps in a cramped and leaky cottage, life on a
snug lower deck with hot food daily, clothes and medical attention
provided, lifetime employment at a substantial rate of pay, and
prospects of some sort of pension,[2] was probably not unbearable.

Conditions on board ship were governed by a number of factors of which the most important was space. A new 74-gun ship of
the line such as was being built during the war was about 165 feet

long internally and 45 feet in beam. She carried her main armament on two decks, and so was called a two-decker, but she
actually had three internal decks running the length of the ship.
The great majority of the ship's company of six or seven hundred
men berthed on the second of these three decks, called the gun or
lower deck.[3] They slung their hammocks from the beams of the
deckhead, which is to say that they lay fore and aft, each hammock
with fourteen inches width, according to regulation, which in
practice meant twenty-eight inches, since the hammocks were
slung starboard and larboard watches alternately, and one watch
would always be on deck. In reality the allowance might be more
or less than the regulation amount depending on the size and internal arrangements of the ship in proportion to the number of her
men. Always the men were crowded, except the petty officers who
were allowed more space. By day the hammocks were lashed up
into a sausage shape and stowed in the netting troughs which lined
each side of the quarter deck and forecastle, and in action protected the men from small arms fire somewhat in the manner of
sandbags. At least in ships operating the divisional system,[4] a proportion of the hammocks were scrubbed regularly whenever the
weather permitted drying them, and spare hammocks were kept to
replace those in the wash.[5]

The men ate their meals on the gun deck, each mess of six with
a table either hinged from the side or slung from the deckhead
between the guns. On this deck in fact they passed much of their
life on shipboard when not actually working. At sea the gunports,
which were less than six feet from the waterline, had to be kept
closed, and the only light and air came down the main hatch. Even
with the assistance of windsails in fair weather to direct a draught
below decks, it must have been close as well as dark, but no doubt
it was true then, as it was a century later, that the men 'got all the
light and air they had any use for in the fore or main top, and preferred that their messes should be what they called "snug"'. Men
from communities like St Ives, where in later years the vicar
claimed that the smell of fish was sometimes so bad as to stop the
church clock, were probably unmoved by the proximity of
unwashed humanity.[6]

One of the worst discomforts at sea was damp. In storms 'the spray of the sea raised by the violence of the wind is dispersed over the whole ship, so that the people breathe, as it were, in water for many weeks together'.[7] If the weather were too severe to light the galley fire there was no means of drying anything, so the men would have to sleep and work in wet clothes. Since there was often no fresh water to spare to rinse out clothes which had been soaked in salt water, and salt naturally absorbs moisture, seamen's clothes must have been permanently slightly damp. This was unpleasant enough in a warm climate, and there was no means of heating the mess decks. In June 1755, off Cape Breton Island, Boscawen noted that he and all his men had chilblains from the cold; in the winter of 1759, with the sea frozen sixty miles offshore, many men in the North American squadron died from frostbite.[8] It was generally reckoned very difficult to keep square-rigged ships at sea in Canadian waters in winter:

> The running ropes freeze in the blocks, the sails are stiff
> like sheets of tin, and the men cannot expose their hands
> long enough to the cold to do their duty aloft, so that
> topsails are not easily handled.[9]

Even in less extreme conditions, the life of the seaman was always arduous, but it is unusual to find either officers or men making much of the weather as a hardship. Rodney, something of a valetudinarian, complained that 'nothing in nature is so disagreeable as hard weather at sea',[10] but most people took it for granted.

What upset the men very much was getting wet in their hammocks from rain or spray leaking through the deck above. This was not common in line-of-battle ships, but it was a constant problem in French prizes and in the smaller frigates and sloops. These were much more lightly-built ships, the French designs very long and shallow, and in a seaway they worked badly, so that the seams opened and leaked.[11] The captain of the *Tartar's Prize* reported that she urgently needed strengthening with an internal deck, 'or at least a few beams, besides a standard or two upon deck to support her extreme long delicate body, which labours and opens so immoderately in rolling'.[12] Moreover the smaller ships, especially the prizes, were much more crowded than the larger, and some of the former privateers, built for short voyages in which the comfort of the crew might reasonably be sacrificed for speed, were unsuitable for prolonged cruising. The men of the *Flamborough's Prize* petitioned in most pitiful terms:

> ... beg leave to represent our hard case on board this vessel where there is not the least conveniency for the number of men on board, not having room to eat our victuals below, but is obliged to mess upon the open deck in all weathers, and great part of us are glad to lie on the cables and casks, though as many as can turn in and out two in a hammock; and when we are at sea, if it blows but a reef in the topsails, the hatches are obliged to be battened down and then we are glad to fly to the boats to eat our provisions; and when we go off the deck to our rest we are obliged to strip our clothes off before we go down, let it blow or rain ever so, and then to creep on our hands and knees to our hammocks, and we are almost devoured with vermin by stowing two in a hammock and so close, not having more room for two than is allowed for a single man. We humbly hope your Lordships will take our hard case into consideration and let us have some other ship ...[13]

This complaint, and others like it, was endorsed by the senior officers who came to investigate.[14] In the *Flamborough's Prize* 'the captain, lieutenant, master, surgeon and purser all lie in the same cabin, which is so low that a tall man can't sit upright in it', while Admiral Holburne reported that the *Escorte* sloop had only five feet between decks aft and three feet forward, 'even the captain's cabin a perfect doghole'.[15] It is hardly surprising that desertion was always worse from small ships than from large.

Even small men-of-war, however, had a great advantage over merchantmen, whose holds were naturally filled with cargo, leaving the minimum possible space under the forecastle for the men. Though warships had much larger crews, they could berth them on decks unencumbered except by guns. There is a significant phrase in a recruiting advertisement for the Bristol letter-of-marque *Hercules*, claiming 'her accommodations for officers and men superior to most private ships of war, and not inferior to his Majesty's frigates',[16] from which we may infer that most armed merchantmen did not equal the standard of a small man-of-war.

Since the men berthed on the gun deck, which had to be cleared quickly in the event of action, they could not keep many personal possessions there. Their sea clothes could be bundled up in their hammocks,[17] but those who had sea chests would usually have to stow them on the orlop or in the hold. Not everyone owned a chest, which was a substantial trunk, and implied considerable possessions to put in it, but most regular deep-sea sailors probably had or shared one.[18] In it they kept their clothes, particularly their best shore-going rig, never worn at sea. Though there was no uniform for ratings in the Navy, seamen wore extremely distinctive clothes which marked them at once from any other trade. They themselves spoke of their 'short clothes' and the landman's 'long clothes'. Men ashore wore long coats and waistcoats reaching nearly to the knee, over tight breeches and stockings. Seamen wore short 'bum-freezer' jackets, generally blue, red waistcoats and checked shirts with a scarf or handkerchief loosely knotted round the neck.[19] These clothes were 'short' because they stopped at or just below the waist, leaving no loose skirts to endanger a man working aloft. Instead of breeches they wore a garment then quite unknown to landmen, unless they happened to have a nautical dictionary to hand: 'Trowsers, a sort of loose breeches of canvas worn by common sailors.'[20] For boat work they sometimes wore a canvas 'petticoat' or divided 'petticoat breeches'. These clothes made seamen instantly recognizable, and anyone who adopted them was likely to be taken for one. A press gang in Shropshire, momentarily without their officer, seized a passing Irish collier just because he had a checked shirt in his pocket.[21] Conversely, the first move of the successful deserter was to find a suit of long clothes to disguise his profession, and those who made it their business to encourage desertion always had long clothes ready for the purpose.[22] Except for disguise, seamen scorned to wear landmen's clothes, and their best clothes were more elaborate and fancy versions of their working rig, with white duck instead of canvas trousers, silver buckles to their shoes, brass buttons on their jackets, coloured tape along the seams, and ribbons in their hats.

From 1748, commissioned officers and midshipmen, alone of all on board ship, had a uniform – or to be exact, two uniforms, a dress and an undress, or informal, suit. The uniform, adopted at the officers' request, helped to distinguish the commissioned officers from the rest and to emphasize their status. Its extension to midshipmen, who were only ratings, marked their semi-official standing as would-be commissioned officers; to a degree it was more important to be travelling hopefully towards a commission than actually to have arrived at a warrant. Uniform was one possible form of clothes 'suitable for a gentleman', or 'befitting a quarter-deck officer', those imprecise but important expressions of an invisible social distinction. It was certainly not the only form, not just because commissioned officers frequently did not wear uniform, and almost never wore it correctly,[23] but because many of those with an unquestioned right to walk the quarter deck, such as the master and his mates, had no uniform to put on. The further they were from port, and the further from an admiral's eye, the more informally officers dressed. One captain even possessed a pair of striped cotton trousers – but that was in India.[24] On board a flagship more attention was paid to the niceties, which made it an expensive appointment for a young officer.[25] The uniform itself, dark blue with white facings and a profusion of gold lace, was handsome, but officers complained that it was extremely difficult to keep the full dress presentable, since the lace dirtied the white cloth, and the brimstone used to dress the cloth damaged the lace. The undress uniform, on the other hand, 'is only a common blue frock (such as almost every person wears) without anything military to distinguish it, and of consequence, creates not the least respect, either at home or abroad'.[26]

The conditions in which the officers berthed varied approximately according to rank, with admirals and captains faring best.[27] The actual arrangements differed a good deal in ships of different age and size, and between flagships and private ships. In the case of a new seventy-four not carrying an admiral, the captain's cabin occupied the after part of the space under the poop, with a stern gallery to himself and two quarter galleries, one of which was fitted as his lavatory. Forward of the great cabin was a smaller sleeping cabin for the captain, and a space known as the coach, which served as an ante-room or dining cabin. From the coach and sleeping cabin doors led out onto the quarter deck on either side of the wheel, and here also were two small cabins, one of which was usually an office for the captain's clerk, and the other a sleeping cabin for the master to use at sea, so that he would never be far from the deck in emergency. The commissioned officers berthed below the great cabin, in the space at the after end of the main deck called the wardroom, which was partitioned off from it by a light bulkhead. Down each side between the guns were a number of small cabins, usually six in all, made of timber before 1757, but of canvas by Admiralty order of that year, so that they could be triced up during the day, and when clearing for action.[28] By tradition the first lieutenant had the aftermost on the port, and the master the aftermost on the starboard side,[29] beyond which a door gave access to the two quarter galleries which housed the wardroom officers' lavatories. In terms of space their cabins were not much better than a petty officer's berth, with barely room to keep a sea chest and sling a hammock or cot, but they did have one benefit increasingly prized by the upper classes of the age, privacy.[30]

The warrant and inferior officers berthed elsewhere. The boatswain and carpenter usually had cabins under the forecastle, a favoured position (often occupied also by the sick bay) since the galley stove below kept them warm in winter, and the gun ports, well above water, could be opened to admit light and air in hot weather. It had another advantage, particularly for the sick, which was proximity to the heads. Forward of the forecastle, on a platform built over the bowsprit and the head (whence the name) were the crew's lavatories. There were two semicircular 'roundhouses' offering some privacy to the warrant, inferior and sometimes petty officers, and four or six other seats in the open air, all discharging straight into the sea.

The purser and surgeon berthed on the orlop deck, the lowest of all above the hold, which was below the waterline and lit only by candle lanterns. Here were store rooms, sail lockers and the cable tier, and aft on the orlop, on either side of the space called the cockpit, were the purser's and surgeon's cabins. In theory they were the only ones who berthed on the orlop, but in practice the quiet and space attracted others, if they could get permission. Women and children often slept down here, and idlers like the steward, schoolmaster and cooper escaped the rough and tumble of the mess decks.

The remaining warrant and inferior officers occupied the gunroom, which was simply the aftermost part of the gun deck, screened by a canvas bulkhead. In the extreme corners of this space a couple of small cabins might be built, one of which was the gunner's, but the sweep of the tiller under the deckhead made it impossible to do more otherwise than sling hammocks along the sides. As in the wardroom above there was a table at which the warrant and inferior officers ate. The inhabitants of the gunroom included the older midshipmen and mates, the surgeon's mates, and sometimes other inferior officers. Social standing had a lot to do with the often delicate division between wardroom and gunroom, and officers like the chaplain, purser, surgeon and even marine lieutenants, whose pretensions to gentility were insecure, might sleep or mess in one or the other according to luck and circumstances. An even sharper social distinction marked those who used the heads from those with access to the wardroom quarter gallery, and in 1758 an unhappy chaplain wrote an ironic poem lamenting his failure to secure this privilege.[31]

Most officers were effectively limited in what they could take to sea to the contents of a sea chest, but a captain could furnish his cabin according to his taste and pocket, and an admiral was virtually obliged to keep up some decent state, though there were wide variations. Boscawen wrote of his junior, Rear-Admiral Mostyn's new ship 'fitted like a modern palace. Mine is strong and plain like an old country hall.'[32] A well-to-do officer could carry a good deal of furniture to sea. Captain Tiddeman of the *Harwich* sailed for the East Indies in 1750 with, among other things, one large and one small bedstead, twelve dining and two leather chairs, a settee, two large tables, two escritoires, three bookcases, three chests of drawers, six more chairs and a table, two tea chests, four clothes and china chests, six pictures of the king and the royal family, a looking-glass in a gilt frame and a large quantity of plate.[33] Captain Johnstone of the *Hornet* sloop shelved his cabin from deck to deckhead; 'more like a bookseller's shop than the

captain's apartment in a man-of-war', a visiting officer remarked.[34]
A newly appointed commander, like John Elliot in 1757, had a lot
to collect; 'I'm in a manner married and setting up house, or more
properly, ship,' as he wrote to his mother, thanking her for a
timely present of linen.[35] It was possible in the great cabin to enjoy
the luxury of a portable stove, though its effect in so large and
draughty a space cannot have been very great.[36]

Captains and admirals enjoyed a degree of ease which vastly
exceeded anything available to their officers and men, but many officers accepted at sea conditions much more cramped, cold, damp
and uncomfortable than those they were accustomed to ashore.
For the sons of the poor, on the other hand, the spartan conditions
of a crowded mess deck may well have been better than home, so
that by the standards of the age, sea life was a leveller of the advantages which money could buy.

E   CHILDREN AND ANIMALS

If there was one thing which sharply distinguished life in eighteenth-century men-of-war from the disciplined regularity of a
modern warship, it was the presence on board of large numbers of
children and animals. A line-of-battle ship might have on board
fifty or more boys aged from six up to eighteen. They had work to
do, especially the older boys, and they might receive some formal
instruction, for many of the bigger ships had a schoolmaster, but
they undoubtedly spent much of their time as children do, in play.
This was certainly how one seaman remembered his first going to
sea at the age of twelve: 'we were always together, and a great part
of our time was spent in play'.[1] We must imagine children playing
as a constant feature of life at sea, skylarking in the rigging, playing hide-and-seek about the decks, and engaging in elaborate and
dangerous practical jokes, such as to

hang up hammocks so as to let poor boys fall down –
one of the most wicked things that could be done on
board. All these things I took to very well, for we served
our poor schoolmaster in this manner in the after hold
when it was clear of casks, which trick had like to kill
him, so that he was bad for a month or more.[2]

The author of these reminiscences, who went to sea at eight, was
not surprisingly often in trouble, and remembered with feeling
Monday morning, 'market day at Plymouth', when the boys were
whipped, but he also spoke of the kindness of his elders, of the
'lady of the gunroom' (the youngest inferior officer) who was told
off 'to see I went to bed in good hours', and the midshipmen and
quartermasters who 'began to learn me to call names, which was
the first rudiments of that university, which I soon learnt at that
age'. This was one of the basic reasons why it was necessary to go
to sea in boyhood, to learn the ropes. There was a lot to be learnt,
and it had to be mastered before a boy had grown to manhood if
youthful strength and quickness were to be matched by experience
and confidence. The presence of children, especially very young,
was a source of some trouble as well as disruption. Men had to
look after them, to see that they washed, to lift them into the hammocks which they could not reach:

he gave him particular order to be very careful of me as
being so young, for me to lay with him, and he to keep
me clean, reminding him I was but a child, and to be
tender of me, nor to let me be as little as possible out of
his sight.[3]

It is probable, however, that children were less numerous and
less troublesome aboard ship than animals. Every ship had animals
of many kinds aboard. First and most numerous were the fauna
native to the wooden world, 'where rats, scorpions, centipedes and
all manner of venomous animals devour us'.[4] Rats were always
present, and always hungry. Whenever stores of any sort were
missing, for good or bad reasons, and had to be accounted for, the

standard explanations were 'lost overboard' or 'eaten by rats', and there was virtually nothing which could not plausibly have gone one way or the other. Rats often ate through casks in the hold, and were quite able to eat through the side of the ship. In the bread room of the *Peggy* sloop in 1756 'it was found that the rats had pared the whole breadth of a plank in the counter ... to a mere shell', and in 1763 Captain Laforey of the *Levant* reported apologetically that his ship had suddenly become so leaky that he feared the rats had eaten through her bottom, again.[5]

There were other animals brought aboard as pets, dogs the most common. They could be a source of dissension, for no first lieutenant looked kindly on an animal which fouled his clean decks – or worse still his cabin – and no one cared for animals which stole their food.[6] Monkeys and parrots were less trouble, except that they often died. They were not always on board strictly as pets, for the demand for exotic birds and animals in England was high, many people had commissions from wives or sweethearts to bring one home, and others simply intended a profitable sale in the London bird market.[7] Rare plants also found a ready market in England, which seamen were well placed to supply. Even more exotic animals than apes were sometimes found aboard ship. Captain Forrest took a French ship with a bear aboard, and one of the early captures of the war was a French East Indiaman laden with scientific collections made for Monsieur Réaumur, the president of the French Academy of Sciences, among which was an elephant.[8] The collection was released as private property, but the elephant died before it could reach France. A more successful voyage was enjoyed by the two tigers which Captain Augustus Hervey (never a man to do things by halves) kindly carried from the Dey of Algiers to the Emperor.[9]

The majority of the livestock on board, however, was not exotic. Cattle and sheep, pigs and goats, hens and geese were carried to sea in great numbers for fresh meat. Apart from freezing, the eighteenth century knew no means of preserving meat other than by salting and pickling, a sophisticated process requiring complex plant and highly trained staff, which could not possibly be carried out aboard ship.[10] There was no intermediate point between flesh in cask and flesh on the hoof, so for health's sake ships carried as many beasts as they could. In October 1760 the *Somerset*, a 64-gun third rate, sailed from Messina with supplies for her squadron including sixty oxen, and in the following January the *Elizabeth*, a ship of the same size in the Indian Ocean, had not less than seventy-one head of cattle on board. Admiral Hawke thought it reasonable that ships of the line sailing from Plymouth in winter should carry forty sheep and a dozen oxen each.[11] The accommodation of all these beasts in ships already very crowded, the fodder they consumed and the dirt they produced, must have created formidable problems, but they were a part of everyday life for officers and men in the eighteenth century.

Cattle were supplied by the Navy as part of the regular diet, but pigs, goats, hens and geese were usually bought by officers and men out of their own pockets. The fowls lived in coops, but goats roamed freely about the ship, where their habit of eating bread from the bread bags hung up by each mess made them unpopular.[12] Those who had the most money were naturally in the best position to buy livestock, but it is quite untrue to say that it was a prerogative of the captain and the wardroom officers. Any sensible captain would much rather see his men spend their money on food than on drink and women, which were the likely alternatives. No doubt a mess which proposed to buy a pig or two would have been wise to ask the first lieutenant's permission, but there was no reason why he should refuse, considering how much of a farmyard the ship was likely to be already.[13] Captain Tiddeman sailed for the East Indies in 1746 with a goat, half a dozen sheep, four hogs, a sow in pig, six and a half dozen fowls and thirteen ducks.[14] Captain Clements left Leghorn in 1763 with four dozen fowls, three dozen pigeons, five sheep, two geese and a dozen ducks.[15] The eighteenth-century Navy combined the disciplined efficiency of a man-of-war with large elements of the playground, the farmyard, and the travelling circus.

F DRINK

'Grog, the *sailor's* best friend, and the *main support* of the British Navy': thus a satirical pamphlet,[1] and it hardly exaggerated. In 1735 the annual consumption of gin in England was over five million gallons.[2] By the time of the Seven Years' War this was declining, but drunkenness remained an almost universal failing, and nowhere more so than in the Navy. 'We made him welcome,' one seaman wrote, 'as all Englishmen do their friends, damnable drunk.'[3] Officers drank as much or more than their men, the only difference being that gentlemen were expected to keep sober at sea, or at least on watch. The amount of alcohol officers took on board was prodigious. In the *Monarch* in 1756 after she had taken some prizes laden with wine, the purser was selling claret at a shilling a gallon. A mess of four warrant officers took two gallons a day. The surgeon indeed

> hinted that in a flagship and in the road to preferment, we should be cautious of conduct and behaviour so as not to offend against the laws of prudence and sobriety, and as the admiral was a strict disciplinarian he paid great attention to the conduct of the inferior officers[4]

– but this was Rear-Admiral Savage Mostyn, aptly named in the opinion of his subordinates for the 'extreme of tyranny and despotism', a man who would not even walk the same side of the quarter deck as his flag captain. Standards were less stringent elsewhere. The mate commanding the *Industry* tender on the Jamaican station took on board fourteen gallons of rum to sustain him for a short passage, besides his share of the common stock.[5] Captain Clements of the *Argo* took advantage of a visit to an Italian port in 1761 to restock his cellar, after which he made the following inventory:

Messina: 1 butt, and 3 kegs containing 40 gallons each
Port: 2 hogsheads

Cyprus: 2 kegs, 1 demijohn and 2 bottles
Champagne: 6 dozen bottles
Burgundy: 12 dozen bottles
Claret: 12 dozen and 7 bottles
Frontenac: 6 bottles
Montepulciano: 1 chest
Florence: 8 chests and a half
Malvasia: 2 chests
Rum: 1 dozen and nine bottles
Beer: 3 dozen and six bottles[6]

In 1749 the captain of the *Harwich* in the East Indies had on board:

Madeira: 2 pipes, 2 puncheons and 2 hogsheads
Arrack: 1 puncheon, 3 hogsheads, 1 half-leaguer and 4 third-leaguers
Rum: 27 gallons 2 quarts in bottle and cask
Brandy: 20 gallons[7]

That is to say over six hundred gallons of spirits, and nearly as much wine, though some of this was for private trade rather than personal consumption.

It is hardly surprising that there are references to officers 'eternally drunk', or a midshipman discharged for 'sottishness and neglect of duty'.[8] It seems remarkable that officers managed, on the whole, to stay sober when they had to be, except perhaps that the prospect of drowning concentrates a man's mind wonderfully.

There was of course no question of denying the men their liquor. Particularly zealous officers tried to regulate the suttling of spirits aboard their ships,[9] but it was an all but hopeless task. Officers often gave their men spirits from their own supplies as a reward for work well done.[10] They did not 'splice the mainbrace' in the fashion beloved of novelists, for there was no official issue of spirits in the Navy. Men drank beer, except on long voyages when it ran out and on foreign stations where it could not be had. Then they drank watered wine, or as a last resort, watered spirits, usually rum in the West Indies, arrack in the East Indies, and brandy elsewhere.

Everybody knew that drink was a factor in crime, most often

73

the chief factor, but it was virtually impossible to do much about it. If libertymen came on board drunk some captains put them in irons, but the regulations of Admiral Smith's divisional system went as far as most officers thought it reasonable or possible to go; the midshipmen of the watch were to 'see all men they find far gone in drink, put in their hammacoes'.[11] If riotous they were to be confined until sober and then punished. Drinking as such was not a crime; the midshipmen were not

> to interrupt the men in mirth and good fellowship, while they keep within the bounds of moderation, the intention of it being to prevent excessive drinking, which is not only a crime of itself, but often draws men into others which when sober they would most abhor.[12]

Even excessive drinking was only a slight offence, and no man who was peaceably drunk would normally be punished for it; but in this as in all things, there was a great difference between the standards obtaining at sea and in port. At anchor most people could get drunk and most did; at sea some did, but the man who could not turn out when his watch was called, in a condition to hand, reef and steer, was very likely to be flogged. The last fling of a ship's company came when they were paid just before sailing, and even the best captains were likely to find their ships disabled for up to twenty-four hours after pay day.[13] 'We are now in a great hurry for sailing,' Keppel wrote to Anson in January 1747/8, 'and I in a sad pickle, with my whole ship's company drunk.'[14] It was the same with prize money, as was reported of the *Achilles* in 1762: 'the men in great confusion, having the day before received fourteen pounds prize money, and could not get their anchors up to save the tide'.[15] Once at sea ships became relatively sober, which is perhaps the only reason why the Service survived the quantities of alcohol which were drunk aboard ship.

G   SWEETHEARTS AND WIVES

The sea service was hard on women, as it is still. Those officers who married, often late in life, had to inflict and to endure prolonged separation from those they loved. 'The parting was very severe,' wrote Captain Samuel Hood, 'I did not think it would have affected me so much, but I find I love my sweet wench better than I thought.'[1] In spite of all difficulties, there were many happily married officers, whose tender letters home to their wives form one of the most evocative records of the naval life of the period.[2] It is impossible not to be moved by the last letter written from Gibraltar Bay in September 1744 by Captain Samuel Faulknor of the *Victory* to his 'dear Fanny' just before he sailed for home, a letter written under a clear premonition of death.[3] The *Victory* was wrecked on the Casquets; Admiral Sir John Balchen, Captain Faulknor and all on board died. Some officers managed to bring their wives out to foreign stations, which was neither easy nor safe in the eighteenth century. Captain John Harrison, flag-captain to Pocock, commanding the East Indies squadron, had his vivacious and pretty wife at Madras, where she was the toast of local society.[4] Other married officers – too many others, in the Admiralty's view – were tempted to linger with their wives when they should have been at sea. Captain Richard Watkins damaged his career by staying ashore in Barbados with his new wife when he was ordered to sea. He died a poor man, but still deeply in love.[5]

Many other officers were bachelors who sought their pleasures elsewhere. Senior officers who are known to have kept mistresses or left bastards include Lord Colvill, Augustus Hervey, Commodore Pye, Rear-Admiral Steevens and Rear-Admiral Keppel.[6] Captain Edward Wheeler, a colourful officer whose outspokenness got him into trouble on occasion, left for posterity a ringing declaration that

> the *children of love* are more naturally and properly the
> heirs of your inheritance than those of the modern

75

Smithfield or Newmarket matches, or the unwished-for
consequence of dull conjugal duty.[7]

Most officers were more discreet, though Commodore Pye, something of a naval grotesque who aroused mingled amusement and
contempt, lived openly in Suffolk Street with the wife of a customs
officer, their relationship cemented by the debts owed the commodore by her husband and father.[8] Away from home, the Navy
offered its officers the possibilities always more open to visitors
than to settled members of a community. It was said of one of
them, as it could have been said of many, that 'there is nothing permanent in these attachments; the exigencies of the Service come to
his rescue and he is free to hunt in pastures new'.[9] The surgeon of
the *Coventry* relates a story of John Robinson, the master of that
ship, a man so fat that he proved on his wedding night to be effectively impotent; he tells of the first lieutenant's horror at this 'disgrace to his Majesty's ship *Coventry*, whose fair fame in this line
had never been blotted, and whose officers had always distinguished themselves in every port both in England and in Ireland'; and of the latter's heroic night's work vindicating her
reputation.[10]

There were women at sea as well. From time to time they were
carried quite legitimately: a colonial governor or notable given
passage with his wife, perhaps, or at the other extreme of the social
scale Hannah Giles, nurse in the *Apollo* hospital ship, who in 1749
was ordered a passage home from the East Indies in the *Harwich*.[11]
It was not unusual for a few wives, usually of the warrant or inferior
officers, to live on board ship. The practice was officially tolerated
in peacetime, and certainly survived in time of war. The women
were not borne on the ship's books, and made their own arrangements with the purser for victualling, but there are chance references to what may well have been a widespread practice. The cook
of the *Ocean* had his wife aboard in 1761, the boatswain of the
Liverpool had a woman (possibly not his wife) with him in 1759,
and in 1755, just before the war began, Captain Arbuthnot earned
a mild reprimand for giving the wives of his boatswain and master
a passage to Virginia.[12] There were a number of useful tasks
aboard ship that such women could do, but it was understood that

they should be plain and elderly, for a young woman would have been altogether too disruptive.

No such restriction was applied by those officers who carried loose women to sea with them. Authority was prepared to turn a blind eye to this in peacetime, particularly on foreign stations. In the Mediterranean before the war Augustus Hervey had a woman aboard for some time, and in 1765 both Lord Colvill commanding the North American station, and the Admiralty, showed marked reluctance to investigate an anonymous claim that his commanders were carrying lewd women to sea.[13] Captains were obviously in the best position to indulge themselves in this way, but other officers did so as well, such as Lieutenant Pike of the *Baltimore* sloop in 1750 who had a 'Miss Nancy' aboard.[14] In time of war officers were supposed to have their minds on other things, and senior officers were less tolerant. Lieutenant Maltby commanding the *Dorset* cutter was in trouble in 1760 over his women, and Captain Cuming of the *Blandford*, who had two women in succession on board with him, might well have suffered likewise had he not first been dismissed the Service on other charges.[15] Some such story probably lies behind the discovery of a woman's body sewn up in a hammock in the bread room of the *Defiance*; she had come on board, it was alleged, without the officers' knowledge, and later died.[16]

One other category of women at sea which should not be omitted is the women disguised as men so popular in eighteenth-century romantic fiction. Surprising as it seems, it was possible for a woman to keep her secret in a crowded mess-deck with little privacy. At least one case can be documented: William Prothero, a private marine of the *Amazon*, who was discovered to be a Welsh girl of eighteen who had followed her lover to sea.[17] There is also a curious reference in the memoir of an officer who was recruiting in Shropshire. When the *Scorpion* sloop was lost with all hands,

> among them were five or six Shrewsbury lads and one woman; this brought much weeping and wailing from parents and relatives to headquarters, and rather dampened the ardour of such young fellows as were inclined to enter.[18]

One can see why; unfortunately he says no more about the woman.

It was convenient to some opponents of the press to speak as though all those pressed into the Navy were married men torn from the arms of their wives and children, and it suited the men themselves on occasion. It was more plausible to demand pay for a starving family than for a drunken spree. Modern historians have proved somewhat credulous of this improbable tale.[19] Seamen alone were liable to impressment, and deep-sea sailors were overwhelmingly young single men. Fifty-three per cent of all able seamen in the Navy, and not less than 85 per cent of ordinary seamen and landmen, were aged twenty-five or under. This was less than the mean age of marriage in England, and probably much less than the age of marriage among the poor.[20] The petty officers and idlers, who were generally older, undoubtedly included more married men, but the trades in which married seamen were most likely to be found, like the East Coast coal trade in which whole communities earned their livelihood, were also the most heavily protected from the press.[21] There is no direct evidence of the proportion of men who were married, but the indications are that it was a minority. Of 1512 men killed in action during the war, 329 (including some killed in accidents) left widows or orphaned children to claim bounty.[22] If all claimed who were entitled to, then less than a fifth of those who were killed had been married. Of 1407 officers and men of a sample of ships who died during the war, and whose next of kin is stated in the ships' pay books, 355, or one-quarter, left widows.[23] A small and haphazard sample of ninety deserters whose captains gave descriptions of them contained seventeen married men, or just under one-fifth.[24] This group may of course be untypical of the Navy as a whole, but only a cynic would suggest that married men had less incentive to desert than bachelors.

The provisions of the 1758 Navy Act, which offered an improved means of remitting ratings' pay to their families, give further evidence. In a sample of nineteen ships' pay books, fewer than 5 per cent of the men made any remittance at all, and of these only just over half were to wives, or to women of the same surname who might have been wives.[25] Most officers used other means of transmitting their pay to their families, but even so the figure of about 2 per cent of ships' companies making remittances to wives must understate the proportion married, and it may be that many remittances to kinsmen were actually for the use of wives.

This raises the question of what exactly was meant by marriage. It seems probable that many 'wives' were not legally married, certainly not in the terms of Lord Hardwicke's Marriage Act. 'One can find a rag of a wife anywhere,' as a Scots sailor put it.[26] When the *Magnanime* was docked in September 1756 her men were accommodated in a hulk and not allowed leave, but their wives were permitted to visit. Out of 750 on board, 492 produced wives,

> who all declared themselves married women, and were acknowledged by the sailors as their wives. Where or when they were married was never enquired, the simple declaration was considered as sufficient to constitute a nautical and temporary union, and which was authorised by long established custom as practised time immemorial in his Majesty's Navy.[27]

Wives like this could be had in every port, and make it difficult to draw a useful distinction between wed and single. Even officers indulged themselves similarly, if we may judge from the fact that between 1750 and 1770 at least twelve officers died leaving two widows each to claim pensions, besides one enterprising woman who claimed in respect of two naval husbands to whom she had been married at the same time.[28]

The evidence suggests that the proportion of the officers and men of the Navy who were permanently married was no more than a fifth or a quarter, disproportionately concentrated among the officers, petty officers and older seamen. The majority of ships' companies were young men without ties, and it is hardly surprising that when given leave with money in their pockets, they tended to spend it unwisely. Captain Wheeler, whose opinion on love and marriage we have already quoted, reproached his men in these terms:

> I have observed too, whenever ye get any money paid,

> ye do not act with it like rational creatures and lay it out
> on clothes and necessaries, but ye throw it immediately
> away on dirty whores and in stinking gin.[29]

Cases of venereal disease ran, on average, at over 8 per cent of complement a year, and in some ships over 20 per cent.[30]

The probability that three-quarters or more of ships' companies were not married raises a question beloved of some modern historians, the incidence of homosexuality. It has been suggested that there was a 'rash' of cases during the Seven Years' War.[31] There appear in fact to have been eleven courts martial for sodomy during the war, of which four led to acquittals, and seven convictions on lesser charges of indecency or 'uncleanliness'.[32] This does not seem a remarkably large figure for a seagoing population which was for most of the war seventy or eighty thousand, but the crime was strongly abhorred and very difficult to conceal aboard ship where there was so little privacy. A ship at sea was about the most difficult possible place to commit sodomy, and moreover it was almost the only crime in the Navy for which the death penalty was often awarded.[33] Officers had the most privacy, and there were some cases among officers which never came to trial; the purser of the *Newcastle*, for instance, 'detected in some things not so decent to name', deserted before he could be arrested, the surgeon of the *Mermaid* was discharged for some indecency stopping well short of the crime specified in the Articles of War, and Captain Churchill of the *Canterbury* buss, confronted with a complaint from one of his men, denied it, and shot himself.[34] A more prominent case was the court martial in 1762 of Captain Henry Angel of the *Stag*, who was arrested by his officers, but acquitted on a conflict of evidence. The record of the trial suggests that his brother officers were glad to find an excuse to avoid convicting a respected officer on a capital charge. Angel at once resigned his commission, and begged his commander-in-chief to represent him as favourably as possible – which does not read like a consciousness of innocence.[35]

All these cases, however, add up to a very insignificant total; a score or so of known instances, over a period of nearly nine years during which at least a hundred thousand individuals must have served in the Navy. It is difficult to believe that there can have been any serious problem with a crime so much detested, but so seldom mentioned. If senior officers were concerned about it, they gave no hint of the fact in their correspondence. Everything suggests that it was an insignificant issue, and there was reason why it should be, for when ships spent more time in port than at sea, and women freely came on board even when leave was not given, men had a good deal of opportunity (though doubtless less than they desired), to indulge in orthodox pleasures. The eighteenth-century Navy was largely populated by young single men of vigorously hetero-sexual inclination, with a relatively small proportion married, but very few indeed who were not interested in women.

CHAPTER III

❦

Victualling and Health

A FOOD

Few things were nearer to the sailor's heart than his stomach. A century after Pepys said it, it was as true as ever that

> Englishmen, and more especially seamen, love their bellies above anything else, and therefore it must always be remembered in the management of the victualling of the Navy that to make any abatement in the quantity or agreeableness of the victuals is to discourage and provoke them in the tenderest point, and will sooner render them disgusted with the King's service than any other hardship that can be put upon them.[1]

The happiness and health of the Navy were greatly dependent on its victualling, and yet of all the administrative difficulties of getting a fleet to sea, this was probably the most intractable. In order to feed men at sea food had to be preserved for months, often for years, but the best methods available of preserving were expensive and unreliable. There were severe limitations on what sorts of foodstuffs could be preserved at all, which posed further problems in an age which was beginning to appreciate the importance of a varied diet, and in particular to understand scurvy as a dietary disease.

To meet these problems, an extremely expensive and sophisticated machine had been developed. With the precarious technology of food preservation only relentless attention to the quality of the raw materials and the accuracy of the processes could ensure a reliable supply to the Navy. The actual foods issued by the Victualling Board, in the standard weekly ration, were as follows:

	Bread	Beer	Beef	Pork	Pease	Oatmeal	Butter	Cheese
Sunday	1 lb.	1 gal.	—	1 lb.	½ pt.	—	—	—
Monday	1 lb.	1 gal.	—	—	—	1 pt.	2 oz.	4 oz.
Tuesday	1 lb.	1 gal.	2 lbs.	—	—	—	—	—
Wednesday	1 lb.	1 gal.	—	—	½ pt.	1 pt.	2 oz.	4 oz.
Thursday	1 lb.	1 gal.	—	1 lb.	½ pt.	—	—	—
Friday	1 lb.	1 gal.	—	—	½ pt.	1 pt.	2 oz.	4 oz.
Saturday	1 lb.	1 gal.	2 lbs.	—	—	—	—	—[2]

The bread was in conventional loaves in port, and at sea a sort of biscuit, carefully baked and packed in bags at the Victualling Office on Tower Hill and its branch establishments at Portsmouth and Plymouth. The beef and pork were likewise processed at the Victualling Office, salted and pickled in cask. Casks were also the means of packing all the other commodities, including cheese and butter, which were unusual in not being processed by the government, but supplied by contractors under a six-month warranty. Besides the items specified in the rations, the Board issued flour, suet, raisins and vinegar, all in cask, some stockfish (dried cod), and oil instead of butter for ships sailing for warm climates. The quantities issued to the fleet between 1750 and 1757 of the commodities packed by the victualling organization (that is, excluding butter and cheese) were as follows:

Bread	54,642,437 lbs.
Beer	110,049 tuns
Brandy	351,692 gals.
Beef	4,498,486 lbs.
Pork	6,734,261 lbs.
Pease	203,385 bushels
Flour	6,264,879 lbs.
Suet	809,419 lbs.
Raisins	705,784 lbs.
Oatmeal	138,504 lbs.
Vinegar	390,863 gals.
Stockfish	166,943 lbs.
Oil	71,668 gals.[3]

These are formidable quantities, and only the last two years of the period were a time of war, with the Navy mobilized. At the height of the war in 1760 the Board bought, among other things:

Wheat	33,600 qtrs.
Pease	11,700 qtrs.
Hops	4,300 cwt.
Flour	34,100 cwt.
Biscuit	41,400 cwt.
Malt	35,500 qtrs.
Beef Oxen	96,700 cwt.
Hogs	32,400 cwt.
Butter	9,500 cwt.
Cheese	22,200 cwt.
Vinegar	500 tuns[4]

These figures imply a rate of consumption twice or thrice that of 1750–1757.

If when casks were opened aboard ship the contents were found to be decayed a survey had to be held on them by a panel of ship's officers in order that they should be condemned as unfit to eat, and the purser receive credit for them. The officers had no interest in concealing any deficiency, and the purser had some interest in exaggerating it, so we may accept the quantities condemned as a fair measure of the reliability of the Victualling Board's methods. In the period 1750–1757, the proportions condemned were as follows:

Bread	0.3%
Beer	0.9%
Brandy	nil
Beef	0.06%
Pork	0.03%
Pease	0.6%
Flour	0.3%
Suet	0.1%
Raisins	0.1%
Oatmeal	0.9%
Vinegar	nil

Stockfish 7.9%
Oil   0.4%[5]

With the exception of stockfish, there was no item of which as much as 1 per cent was condemned, an astonishing fact considering the limitations of technology and the hazards to which the full casks were exposed after issue.

These results were achieved by great care in the manufacturing process (backed by continual experiment and development) and by using only the most expensive ingredients. The Admiralty declared 'their intention that the seamen should be supplied with the best of everything in its kind',[6] and in general they were. Care was taken to turn over stocks so that issues were as new as possible. Two years was regarded as the maximum time beef or pork in cask could be kept in store, and even at the end of a long supply route, the *Elizabeth* at Madras was unlucky to receive in April 1758 a cask of beef which had been packed as long ago as October 1755.[7]

There was a particular problem with cheese and butter. The Navy had always issued Suffolk cheese, a thin, hard and durable variety, but practically inedible. There were frequent complaints against it, and in 1758 the decision was taken to switch to Cheshire and Gloucester cheese, even though they were considerably more expensive, and probably did not keep so well.[8] Since the Victualling Board did not issue cheese, it kept no figures of the quantities condemned, but there were frequent complaints about cheese, and a distribution system at the mercy of wind and weather was not always able to get the cheese and butter to the ships before the six months' guarantee had expired. If cheese did decay it smelled very badly, and according to the climatorial pathology then in favour among medical men, foul air was not merely unpleasant but the carrier of disease. Captains therefore had reason to worry about decayed cheese 'which might, by its nauseous smell, be liable to cause an infection'.[9]

The diet supplied by the establishment was plain and very restricted in its range, but it provided more than sufficient calories for hard physical work.[10] All food was cooked in a large 'copper' set in a brick hearth, or in more modern ships, in an enclosed iron stove.[11] It was possible to bake or roast on a small scale, for the officers or the sick, but the ship's company as a whole had all their dinners boiled. By the standards of the poor naval food was good and plentiful. To eat meat four days a week was itself a privilege denied a large part of the population, if only because in many parts of the country firing was too expensive for the poor to cook every day.[12] For the same reason many did not eat a lot of vegetables, for most vegetables in common use were roots or green plants like cabbages, which were not eaten raw. The seaman who had a hot dinner daily, with beef and beer, bread and cheese, and sometimes vegetables and fruit, was eating well by his standards, and it seems he knew it, for in an age when seamen could and did complain freely, it is remarkably difficult to find them grumbling about the food (cheese perhaps excepted). It is sometimes said that seamen were extremely conservative eaters, rejecting any novelty however good for them.[13] It is certainly true that there was a riot in Haslar Hospital the day Dr Lind introduced porridge for breakfast instead of bread and cheese, that Captain Cook occasionally had trouble forcing his men to eat fresh food, and that the sauerkraut which became one of the commonest remedies for scurvy was not popular[14] – but an Englishman may be permitted to observe that an aversion to pickled cabbage is not necessarily the mark of unreasoning conservatism. Many vegetables were then novelties in England, including the potato, and yet the seamen took to them with enthusiasm, and complained when they did not get them.[15] It was the same with fruit; when a shipload of apples reached Hawke's squadron off Brest in September 1759 it was immediately plundered by the men before the pursers could take any account of it.[16] In foreign ports the men bartered beef and bread for fruit and vegetables.[17] The 'portable soup', a form of dried beef stock first introduced for the sick, and usually made up in a broth with vegetables, was well received.[18] What the men did not like was the foreign substitutes for their regular diet which sometimes had to be served on overseas stations, such as chick peas, or flour and yams in lieu of bread.[19]

Because the connection between scurvy and diet was understood by experienced seamen, if not by the medical world, the Navy went to great expense to provide ships in port and at sea with fresh vegetables, fruit, and fresh meat.[20] The livestock so often carried was a part of this effort, and an elaborate logistical organization, extending all over the world, ensured as far as humanly possible that men had to live continually on salt provisions only on long ocean passages.[21] Even frozen beef was supplied to the North American squadron wintering at Halifax.[22] These efforts were successful in reducing scurvy from a permanent disaster which crippled or destroyed whole squadrons, to a minor irritant of no operational significance. To what extent the seamen appreciated this benefit of their diet is difficult to say, but there is no doubt that its food was one of the attractions of the Navy. Monotonous and basic though they now seem, the seaman's meals were by his own standards good and plentiful. Even with modern dietary knowledge, it is possible to guess that with a reasonable proportion of fresh provisions the men of the Navy probably ate something nearer a balanced diet than many of their contemporaries ashore.

B   PURSERY

'The dark and mysterious nature of pursery' was something little known to most sea officers. They appreciated from experience that 'industry and unweariedness ... is necessary to the purser's office on a ship's fitting out in time of war',[1] but this was not at all the same thing as understanding the business themselves. Young commanders who found themselves commissioned to the little sloops (no more than eight guns or eighty men) which were not allowed pursers, so that they had to do it themselves, counted themselves lucky to find some experienced man prepared to take on the job in exchange for its profits.[2]

The job of a purser was unique, and in many ways highly invidious. He discharged several different functions, both official and unofficial. Firstly he was responsible for the victuals issued by the

Victualling Board, but unlike other warrant officers, he was not simply answerable for any unusual loss or wastage, but accountable for the entire value of the stores for which he was responsible. In order to recoup himself he had to keep a very detailed and complex account of the consumption of every officer and man for each day. This was based on the ship's muster, which purser and captain kept jointly, and upon which was founded the pay book.[3] In spite of his name, however, the purser had no official funds in his keeping and had nothing to do with paying the ship's company. In addition to victuals, the purser had to supply at his own expense fixed quantities of 'necessaries', that is, various consumable stores such as coal and firewood (for the galley), candles, lamp oil, hammocks and bedding. He was credited on his accounts for those consumed by the ship, and those issued to individual men were charged to their wages on the pay book. He issued slops (clothes) on much the same basis as victuals, except that he received them from a clothing contractor, and after 1758 from the Navy Board. He was by custom obliged to provide as a private merchant tobacco for sale to the men, and it was common for the purser to act as a banker for his shipmates.

The key to a purser's survival in all these activities was credit. Simply to take up his warrant he had to give large sureties (£600 for a first rate, down to £200 for a sloop)[4] and in each of his capacities he had to spend large sums of money in the hope of very distant returns. The best basis for a purser's career would have been an independent fortune, but of course no man possessed of a good fortune wanted to risk it in so dangerous and thankless a career as pursery. In practice, the purser sought credit, and he was lucky to get it on easy terms from friends.[5] The most obvious and dangerous sources of money were merchants in dockyard towns, who would expect in return the purser's contracts for necessaries and tobacco to come to them at favourable rates. The purser who had fallen into such hands might easily find himself forced to transact business at a loss for fear of having his bonds foreclosed and being thrown into jail. Imprisonment for debt was a recognized hazard of pursery, so much so that the Admiralty was prepared to allow the sufferers to act by deputy. This was a privilege denied any other officers, even flag-officers' secretaries, who were permitted to hold purser's warrants, but only for their own ships, or ships out of commission in the Ordinary.[6]

The first duty of a purser on appointment, and sometimes his first failure, was to provide his ship with the quantity of necessaries fixed for her rate and the number of months she was ordered to store for. He was allowed an advance of 'necessary money' calculated according to a complex formula, but the advance did not equal the expense, and only two-thirds of it was payable in cash, the rest being a credit on his accounts, available in cash only at 25 per cent interest. There were also various other small payments on account like 'adz money', 'drawage' and lading charges.[7] During the ship's commission the purser was expected to renew her supplies of necessaries as often as required. Providing his vouchers were faultless and authenticated by the captain, he was credited on his account, not with the actual cost of the necessaries, but with a fixed price set by the Navy Board. If real prices were higher or the purser forced to make a disadvantageous bargain, he stood to lose. If necessaries were damaged or destroyed by any cause, including shipwreck or enemy action, the purser received no compensation.[8] Only necessaries actually consumed and properly attested were paid for.

The purser did not have to pay for the ship's provisions, which were his most important responsibility, but he was charged on his accounts with the value of them, and received credit for the standard ration multiplied by the number of men in the ship's authorized complement for the accounting period. He also received credit for any victuals he returned unused, but the price he received as creditor was always lower than the price he was charged as debtor – for example, three halfpence a pound for bread issued, but only a penny farthing a pound as returned.[9] In order to be repaid for the victuals actually consumed the purser had to keep a victualling account of extraordinary complexity. Every officer and man was allowed the standard ration, but he was not obliged to eat it, and he was entitled to credit for whatever he did not consume. Officers and (less easily) ratings could arrange with the purser to eat all, part or none of the standard ration, and they could change their minds as often as they pleased. Those who had provided themselves with private stocks would take part or none of the purser's victuals until their own provisions ran out and they had to revert to the naval ration. The purser's account or mess book was kept monthly, and divided into the six-man messes in which the men ate. Every month men could change messes if they wished, so the composition of the messes was never fixed. If the whole ship's company were put on short allowance (usually 'six to four', meaning two-thirds) they were allowed a payment, known to the sailors as 'pinch-gut money', calculated by an elaborate formula.[10] The keeping of a precise daily account of every man in a constantly-changing ship's company over months or years was an administrative nightmare, and the least discrepancy could be disastrous:

> One or two days' neglect of all or any of these, will not only prove burthensome to the memory, but in the end turn to a heap of confusion, and the least omission will cause an objection in your certificates which without very good reasons will not be removed.[11]

If the standard rations alone had been issued, the accounting problems would have been severe, but what made things much worse was that the purser was frequently issuing substitutes for the usual articles. Especially in hot climates, the Navy had to provide other foodstuffs, and an elaborate table of equivalents gave their value in terms of the standards. Here are a few of these equivalents:

1 pt. wine *or* $\frac{1}{2}$ pt. arrack, rum or brandy = 1 gal. beer
3 lbs. flour + 8 oz. suet *or* 3 lbs. flour + 8 oz. raisins + 4 oz. suet *or* 2 lbs. suet = 1 piece of beef
2 lbs. potatoes or yams = 1 lb. bread
4 lbs. rice or stockfish *or* 1 gal. wheat = 1 gal. oatmeal
1 qt. calavances [chick peas] = 3 pts. oatmeal *or* 1 qt. pease
1 pt. oil = 1 lb. butter[12]

and so on through many permutations. This was difficult enough, but often the purser had to issue foods not listed on the table. When fresh beef was served he had to try to ensure that the oxen were butchered as nearly as possible in the standard 4 lb. pieces. If fresh vegetables or fruit were available, or local produce of any sort, he had to buy them from his own pocket and compensate himself by making equivalent savings in the standard ration. Most perplexing of all were the occasional special provisions issued by the Navy whose accounting status was unclear. Sometimes these were 'free gifts' for which the pursers were not charged, but it was rash to assume so. The pursers of Hawke's squadron blockading Brest took the vegetables shipped out to them as a free gift, and only discovered their mistake when it was too late to make corresponding savings.[13] The status of the 'portable soup' caused particular difficulties; it was issued by the Sick and Hurt Board to the surgeons for the use of the sick, and if the rest of the men had any the two officers, and the two boards, had to account to each other.[14]

Pursers were accountable not only for the victuals themselves, but also for the casks and bread bags in which they were issued.[15] To clear space in the hold empty casks often had to be 'shaken' into their constituent parts, and the Victualling Board laid down exactly how many hoops and staves belonged to each size of cask. The purser was allowed a limited wastage, but anything over that was charged to his account. This made the ship's cooper a rating of great importance to the purser, and both he and the steward who assisted the purser in the issue of food and kept the rough mess book, were in practice found by the purser and paid by him extra above their wages. Dishonesty or incompetence in either of them could ruin a purser, and it was necessary to pay heavily to get reliable men. In the early years of the century it was claimed that a steward's pay of £2 to £4 a month would have to be supplemented by at least another £5, and the cooper's by £3. In addition a steward's mate and cooper's mate would be needed in larger ships, and the cooper's tools had to be supplied.[16]

The cooper's workmanship directly affected the wastage of victuals from damaged casks which was of great financial consequence to the purser, but he had a still more important task, to oversee the issue of beer. Men at sea, like men on shore, did not drink water, which was unpleasant and unsafe. The ships carried a great deal of water, but if possible it was used only for cooking, and much of it occupied the 'ground tier' of casks in the bottom of the hold, which was part of the permanent ballast and only started in emergency. On long passages and on foreign stations men drank watered wine (in the proportion of 8 to 1) or watered spirits (in the proportion of 16 to 1),[17] but in home waters they drank beer alone, and the length of time a ship could stay at sea was effectively measured by how long her beer would last. This made the consumption of beer an important operational factor, but it was even more significant to the purser's finances. The 'ration' of a gallon of beer a man a day was in practice no more than an estimate of consumption, for by ancient custom the men drank as much as they pleased. One of the cooper's jobs was tactfully to see that beer was not wasted without appearing to stint the men. When beer was wasted or drunk to excess it was a reliable sign of an unhappy or disorderly ship. Even in a happy ship, 'wives' and visitors in port expected to drink the purser's beer as freely as their men did, and a purser could lose heavily by a stay in port, especially if leave were refused but visitors permitted.[18]

Quite apart from misfortunes like these, the purser was exposed to continual losses from the accidents of daily life; of bread

> by its breaking and turning to dust; of butter, by that part next to the firkin being not fit to be issued; of cheese, by its decaying with mould and rottenness and being eaten with mites and other insects; of pease, oatmeal and flour, by their being eaten by cockroaches, weevils and other vermin, and by that part at the top, bottom and sides of the cask being so often damaged, as not being fit to be issued; besides the general loss sustained in all these provisions by rats, which is very great . . .[19]

Rats could not only 'destroy most part of the dry provisions on board', as was reported from the *Amazon* in 1761, but were easily capable of eating through casks.[20] Even if they did not consume all the contents, the leakage of pickle from beef or pork would allow the remainder to spoil. Casks were often damaged in handling, and in very hot climates they had to be spiled (pierced) to prevent them bursting. Sometimes casks of beer or other liquid were deliberately started in malice or by the mischief of small boys, to harm the purser.[21]

The purser's losses from all these and a thousand other causes were continuous and largely unavoidable. He had three ways of recouping himself. Firstly, if a whole cask or casks of provisions were spoiled they could be condemned by a panel of officers, and the purser would then receive credit as though they had been consumed. It is often alleged that pursers tried to serve the men rotten victuals in order to line their own pockets, but to do so required the connivance of all the officers and the silence of all the men, and there was very little chance of either. In theory, the purser had an interest in the opposite process, getting good victuals condemned which he could then serve to the men and make a hidden saving. I know of no instance in which this was discovered to be taking place, and it would have required the acquiescence of most of the officers, but it could have happened, for the men did not suffer by it and would not have complained.

Condemning food by survey allowed the purser to break even, to receive credit in his accounts for the same value as the stores had been issued at. In addition there was one general allowance for all wastage and loss. The purser was permitted, by ancient custom rather than regulation, one-eighth of all issues. This he took by serving dry provisions by a fourteen-ounce pound, and beer by a 'purser's quart' of thirty-five fluid ounces.[22] In return for his eighth, the purser was expected to stand all ordinary wastage and loss. Beef and pork received short weight from contractors were allowed only if the contractors agreed. Butter and cheese condemned out of warranty were never allowed. Stores of all sorts eaten by rats, washed overboard, burnt or thrown overboard in clearing for action were allowed only by special order in very exceptional circumstances. Even in cases of shipwreck the want of correct paperwork would invalidate any claim. When the *Blandford* was taken by the French and thoroughly looted her purser was allowed nothing for his losses. No wastage of wine, spirits or oil was ever allowed. If victualling stores were used for the ship – vinegar for disinfection, for example – a purser might, but would not necessarily, be allowed a credit. Only very rarely did the Victualling Board make exceptions to its rules. Nicholas Brooke, purser of the *Ferret* sloop, who while his ship was careening hired a storehouse which burnt to the ground, was given credit for his lost stores, and at least two lucky pursers during the Seven Years' War were allowed livestock lost, or thrown, overboard. If a ship were lost, and the purser's books and papers lost with her, he was very likely to be ruined. In order to minimize this risk pursers tried to have their stores surveyed whenever possible, in order to make up and pass accounts up to that date and expose themselves as little as possible.[23]

Besides his eighth share of all dry issues, a purser's only recourse to cover his losses was 'savings'. To compensate for extra provisions issued he had to save on the consumption of something else sufficient to make up the value. If food was lost or wasted, if beer was drunk at over the established rate, the purser had to find savings to compensate himself. A dishonest purser in league with his captain and far away from an admiral to whom the men could complain might succeed in defrauding them of some of their legitimate rations, but this was never easy or common. The crime was too obvious and it was too easy for the men to complain. The captain and purser of the *Blandford* in 1758 (after her return from France) tried to save rum in exchange for fresh beef and other provisions received at Carthagena, but the lieutenant of marines, who spoke Spanish, discovered that they had been not a purchase, but a gift from the Spanish authorities. Henry Nelson, purser of the *Sunderland*, defrauded the ship's company of a day's fresh beef, but they at once detected the loss and complained; Nelson was court martialled and dismissed the Service.[24] A purser had to be foolish or desperate to steal food from vocal mouths, but he had to find his savings nevertheless. The superstitious sailors, watching the great albatrosses following their ships in southern latitudes, week after week on motionless wing, saw in them the souls of pursers long departed, haunting their former ships in a sleepless search for savings.[25]

The purser's function as a supplier of slops was less troublesome, and offered some chance of an illegal profit. So long as the bales of clothes actually contained the purported quality and quantity (it was because they frequently did not that the Navy Board took over the supply) it was relatively easy to issue them, charging the recipients the set prices on the ship's pay book. Though vulnerable to rats, clothes were less liable to decay than food, and the accounting procedures were more straightforward than most the purser had to deal with. They offered the dishonest man the chance to make an extra saving by 'selling' slops to men who had died or deserted and were no longer present to complain at the imposition.[26] The purser made a hidden saving of slops, and the next of kin (in the case of dead men) or Greenwich Hospital (in the case of deserters) received less in wages. How common this practice was is difficult to say, since it was and is difficult to detect. The money to be made by it varied more or less with the size of the ship's company and the length of the commission, since it was rash to sell too much to any one man and invite awkward questions in the Navy Office.

Exactly the same fraud could be practised with tobacco, with the difference that the purser laid in his own stocks as a private merchant, but sold at a fixed price, and charged the recipients on the pay book as with slops. His chances of a legitimate profit depended on the price he had to pay for his supplies, but he was a monopoly seller with a good market, and no doubt usually gained. As a private merchant the purser had to sell tobacco by a sixteen-ounce pound, but there was an obvious temptation to substitute the weights used for issuing dry provisions. Henry Nelson of the *Sunderland* was guilty of this, and so was at least one other purser. Like all frauds which immediately affected the men, however, it was very difficult to conceal from them, and consequently very dangerous. It was much safer to sell modest amounts of tobacco to dead men and deserters. The surgeon likewise could profit from the departed, with the purser's connivance, for he received fifteen shillings from the wages of every man treated for venereal disease, and the dead or deserted were in no condition to complain of the scandal, or the cost, of a fictitious treatment.[27]

All the money that a purser made by his official duties was made in the form of paper credits which could only be cashed when his accounts had been passed. It will be evident just how complicated was the paperwork he had to provide, and the slightest discrepancy would stop the accounts. It was not unusual for accounts to take many years, and very large sums in expenses, to pass. One hundred pursers' accounts were paid in the year 1759, on average twenty-seven and a half months after the end of the commissions to which they referred. The shortest delay was six months, and the longest fifty-seven years.[28] The will of Samuel Furzer, a purser who died in 1762, could not be proved until 1773 when his last set of accounts at length passed the Victualling Office. Furzer was a successful purser and prize agent whose widow was comfortably off (and remarried),[29] but there were many others less fortunate. Even when a purser had passed his accounts he was paid his credit not in cash but by a Victualling bill payable 'in course', that is to say in numbered sequence, after a delay which varied but could be ascertained in the financial press. Victualling bills bore interest at 4 per cent after six months, and could be sold at a discount to brokers who dealt in them, but the purser was left with the option of further delay or less money. The course of the Victualling was rising a year in 1758, and reached twenty-two months in 1762. The discount was between 5 and 10 per cent in 1760 and 1761, and rose to 12.5 per cent at the beginning of 1762.[30] The only money that a purser was allowed in cash on passing his accounts was his tobacco money and his actual wages. For everything else he had to wait for his balance bill – if he had any credit to wait for. Many pursers actually made a loss and owed the Navy money at the end of their commissions. Alexander McPherson, admiral's secretary and purser in succession of the *Montagu, Plymouth, Sandwich* and *Cumberland*, lost money on all four, and was only permitted to draw his pay as a special concession, on giving large sureties.[31]

The position of the purser without McPherson's advantages was thankless. Whether honest or dishonest, his chances of making money were precarious and the risks high. Business ability and method were indispensable, but without luck and credit they would count for nothing. Socially and psychologically the purser was isolated, a natural target for the suspicion of his shipmates, the complaints of the ratings and the oppression of the captain. Depending utterly on the captain's signature to his vouchers, he was in a weak position to resent it if, say, the captain's hogs were fed on his pease and oatmeal. A purser might be a popular man himself,[32] but he had to overcome the unpopularity and weakness inherent in his position. Because he was friendless and suspect, his opportunities to defraud his shipmates were poor. It was the commanders of small sloops, acting as their own pursers, who were in a position to attempt the kinds of frauds so often attributed to pursers. No purser could tell the men, as Captain Long told the crew of the *Wolf* sloop, that 'it was better that we should lose half a pound than him to lose ten shillings'.[33] Even for a captain, judge in his own cause, this was dangerous, for the men could and did complain to higher authority.

A purser's real chance of wealth and success lay not in his official duties but in private business, in broking, moneylending and agency. He acted in these matters very much as 'men of business' did ashore, and like them he needed ability, contacts and credit to succeed. Pursers often acted as bankers, making advances to their brother officers, who also had to wait for their pay. Richard Drakeford in 1740 was lending officers money at 5 per cent or somewhat less, and acting as agent for about 2.5 per cent. These were not excessive profits, but Drakeford did much better out of prize agency. He was agent for the *Lennox*, one of the captors of the *Princessa* in 1739. The prize was worth over £19,000, split between three ships and the admiral. As agent Drakeford had to make various initial payments in legal fees, wages to the *Lennox*'s men for unloading their prize (not part of their duty) and to the yard officers to superintend, but compared to pursery, this was a relatively painless way to earn a percentage of a large sum, and happy was the man who could get it.[34] Pursers were not often this lucky, for Navy Office or Admiralty clerks and dockyard officers were better placed to ease the prize through the many legal and practical difficulties which awaited her, but those few who rose to be flag officers' secretaries were almost certain to receive at least the admiral's agency if not the squadron's. The most successful pursers, like the most successful officers of all ranks, were those who followed captains who became admirals, and among them there were a few who reached wealth and eminence. Anson's secretary Philip Stephens became Secretary of the Admiralty and died a baronet. Boscawen's secretary Charles Brett also reached the Admiralty Board. Francis Gashry, son of a Huguenot refugee, became secretary to Sir Charles Wager, married his niece, and moved in turn to the Sick and Hurt Board, the Admiralty Office, the Navy Board and finally the Ordnance Board.[35] People like these, however, were really well-connected men who held purser's warrants because they were already secretaries, not humble pursers who had gained that rank. Brett, for instance, was the son of a commissioner of the Navy; one of his brothers was a captain and the other was clerk of the cheque at Portsmouth.[36] Men of such origins did not make a career as pursers, but those who did become pursers and prospered – as many did, in spite of everything – generally did so, like them, as 'men of business', trading on their connections and their credit as bankers and agents, for the rewards of pursery itself were slender and precarious.

c SICKNESS AND HEALTH

Few boys who grew up in seaport towns in the 1730s and 1740s could have failed to know the mournful ballad of 'Admiral Hosier's Ghost', which told the tale of the disastrous Caribbean expedition of 1726. In two years a squadron of 4750 men lost over 4000 dead, including the admiral and his successor, seven captains and fifty lieutenants.[1]

> 'Think what thousands fell in vain
> Wasted with disease and anguish,
> Not in glorious battle slain.'

It gave a whole generation of sea officers a dread of serving in the West Indies, and not unreasonably, for many senior officers of the middle years of the century had personal experience of losses on this scale. Boscawen had been a young lieutenant in Hosier's squadron, and in a single commission his ship had lost six commanders. Hawke, as captain of the *Portland* in the Leeward Islands in the 1740s, lost in three years his boatswain, surgeon, master, cook, purser and two successive gunners.[2] Any extended

98

operations in the West or East Indies, especially operations inshore in the West Indies, carried grave risks of fever. The siege of Havana in 1762, though in the end successful, cost very heavy losses because it ran into the rainy season.[3] English Harbour, the dockyard at Antigua, was reckoned fatal to the crews of any ship that lay there during the hurricane season, from yellow fever. All experienced officers knew the dangers of anchoring close under a weather shore, especially to leeward of a marsh.[4] Unfortunately a safe anchorage to windward of land was almost an impossibility, and they often had to risk fever to avoid shipwreck.

It was no wonder that service in the West and East Indies was unpopular with many, but the heavy losses on several well-known expeditions should not lead us to exaggerate the real risks of ordinary service. In the 1740s Bristol merchantmen were losing only slightly more than average (5.5 per cent a year against 4.5) on voyages to the West Indies, and it has been calculated that at the same period British men-of-war in those waters were losing about 6 per cent of their authorized complements a year dead from all causes.[5] Allowing for the usual turnover of ship's companies, the mortality as a percentage of the population exposed would have been lower. By eighteenth-century standards this was not a disastrously high death rate, and it fell as ships' companies became 'seasoned' to the climate. An experienced officer like Rear-Admiral Cotes, re-appointed to command at Jamaica in 1757, gathered his old ship's company from his previous commission not only as his followers, but because as seasoned men they would suffer much less from fever. Two years later, when Bompar's squadron appeared in those waters, Cotes was pleased to find his men healthy while the French, newly arrived from Europe, were very sickly.[6] This was one of the disadvantages of the French policy of sending flying squadrons out on particular missions rather than keeping a squadron permanently on station.

In all climates, and especially in heat, there were obvious precautions to be taken against disease, one of which was not working the men too hard, and if possible preventing them from drinking.[7] A good example was given by Captain Lucius O'Bryen, who commanded the seamen landed to assist in the attack on Fort Royal, Martinique, in 1762. Over a thousand men hauled for three miles up and down precipitous, rocky and overgrown slopes twenty 24-pounder guns (weighing two and a half tons each), three 13-inch mortars and twenty howitzers, all with their ammunition.[8] O'Bryen stopped all work between ten in the morning and three in the afternoon, the men resting in the shade, and then working in the cool of the evening. With this careful handling and the favourable season (it was January), there were no serious losses, even from a land operation in the West Indies, the most unhealthy of all eighteenth-century theatres of military operations. Disasters such as befell Hosier were avoidable, and usually avoided, and the fear of the fevers of hot climates, though certainly not idle, was probably exaggerated.

Scurvy was in some ways a more serious, certainly a more widespread problem. Relatively few men actually died of scurvy except on very long ocean passages, but it effectively limited the time a squadron could stay at sea, and thus directly affected the efficiency of the Service. No strategy of blockade, or any other which depended on keeping squadrons at sea for long periods, was possible in the face of endemic scurvy. The difficulty was to find a cure. Much has been made by medical historians of the work of Dr James Lind, the great naval physician who first provided experimental proof of the antiscorbutic properties of oranges and lemons, and the Admiralty has been freely castigated for not adopting this remedy at once. In fact Lind's celebrated controlled trial may well have occurred by accident, and he does not appear to have appreciated its importance himself, or to have made it very clear to his readers.[9] The value of lemons against scurvy was itself a commonplace known amongst seafarers for generations, but the fruit was only one among very many remedies, good or bad, which neither the naval nor the medical world had any scientific method of sifting. Moreover lemons were scarce and expensive in northern Europe, and the obvious method of preserving them incidentally destroyed the vitamin.

Fortunately, there was a general understanding among sea officers that scurvy was a dietary disease, caused either by the presence of something harmful in the sailor's diet, or by the absence of something essential, and in either case curable by fresh victuals. Under Admiralty order from the spring of 1756 the Victualling

Board began to issue fresh meat and vegetables to ships in port, both in home waters and abroad.[10] The effects were immediate. Boscawen, at sea that summer commanding the Western Squadron, was amazed to keep the sea for twelve weeks.[11] But this improvement was insufficient to sustain a strategy of permanent close blockade of Brest such as was developed during the Seven Years' War. Anson was seriously worried by scurvy when he commanded the Western Squadron in 1758,[12] and in the spring of 1759 the Admiralty ordered the squadron to be victualled at sea by transports sent out for that purpose. This was a momentous order, perhaps the first adoption on a large scale of the practice of 'replenishment at sea' on which modern navies heavily depend. During the summer the fresh victuals began to be sent out to Hawke's squadron. There were considerable practical problems to be overcome, not least in the deep-laden and leewardly merchantmen actually beating up from Plymouth to the blockading station dead to windward, but the practical effects were very striking. Hawke's great victory of Quiberon Bay was fought on 20 November 1759, on which day there were fewer than twenty men sick in a squadron of twenty sail. As Lind remarks,

> It is an observation, I think, worthy of record, that fourteen thousand persons, pent up in ships, should continue, for six or seven months, to enjoy a better state of health upon the watery element, than it can well be imagined so great a number of people would enjoy, on the most healthful spot of ground in the world.[13]

As Lind implies, it is quite possible that scurvy was actually less prevalent in Hawke's squadron, and other British squadrons throughout the world, than it was on shore. Scurvy was endemic in many areas ashore, especially among the poor, and new recruits to the Navy were sometimes rejected as chronic scorbutics. Even among sea officers, drawn from classes generally better fed and more likely to be eating the newly fashionable green vegetables and salads, it was not unknown.[14] Captain Geary, who grew salads at sea and presumably ate them ashore, was 'not very well, with a scorbutic complaint' at his home in Surrey in June 1761, and Captain Bover of the *Raven* sloop asked to be relieved of his command in 1757 because of inveterate scurvy.[15] Often scurvy must have been latent, in a sub-clinical and undetected form. There is a revealing mention in a letter from Lady Anson to her father, of a visit her husband had received

> from Captain Rodney and two or three more of the captains returned from Louisbourg ... whose company was so offensive from the state of their health, as to make it but just possible to bear the cabin with them, not even almost after they were gone.[16]

Bad breath and rotting teeth are early symptoms of scurvy.

Nevertheless, the general issue of fresh meat and vegetables, costly and troublesome though it was, largely eliminated scurvy as an operational problem during the latter years of the war. Unfortunately we lack complete hospital musters for the war years, but the returns from sick quarters (including the contract hospitals) for 1757 and 1758 are indicative. In this table are shown the numbers of sick received at Deal and Plymouth, the number of them suffering from scurvy, and the number of scurvy patients who died.[17]

	PLYMOUTH			DEAL		
	Sick	Scurvy	Died	Sick	Scurvy	Died
1757 1st Qtr.	566	145 = 26%	7 = 5%	367	57 = 16%	2 = 4%
1757 2nd Qtr.	523	211 = 40%	10 = 5%	327	23 = 7%	1 = 4%
1757 3rd Qtr.	168	49 = 29%	2 = 4%	430	42 = 10%	1 = 2%
1757 4th Qtr.	264	61 = 23%	2 = 3%	360	28 = 8%	3 = 11%
1758 1st Qtr.	390	59 = 15%	6 = 10%	263	36 = 14%	0
1758 2nd Qtr.	161	23 = 14%	1 = 4%	142	33 = 23%	1 = 3%
1758 3rd Qtr.	n.a.	n.a.	n.a.	115	17 = 15%	0

These figures need to be read with caution, particularly as they do not include the naval hospital at Plymouth, but they do suggest that scurvy was declining both absolutely and proportionately, and that it was less of a problem at Deal, where the patients came mostly from ships operating in the Channel with fairly frequent opportunity to get fresh provisions in port, than at Plymouth where many men were landed from the ships of the Western Squadron after weeks or months at sea. Unfortunately we do not have figures which would illustrate the effects of sending fresh food out to the squadron at sea from the summer of 1759 onward. In spite of good progress, authority was by no means complacent, and the Sick and Hurt Board continued to experiment with anti-scorbutic diets, more or less successfully – less, in July 1762, when they were directed 'not to proceed any further in making experiments of the regimen lately proposed to eliminate the scurvy, its effects having upon trial [been] found to be fatal'.[18]

No amount of trials could have eliminated the exhausting and debilitating nature of service at sea. For officers as well as ratings, the Navy was a profession for young men. An officer like Captain Henry Harrison, who had received his first commission in Queen Anne's reign and was still at sea in 1755 when into his seventies, was regarded as something of a wonder. As port admiral at Plymouth the following year, he was reported as carrying out his duties 'with surprising activity and diligence for one of his years'.[19] On the other hand Captain Salt of the *Hornet* was relieved of his command in 1758 on account of deafness, gout and senility, though he was apparently not yet fifty, and Captain Cornwall of the *Emerald* had to resign his command from gout in 1760 at the age of twenty-eight.[20] Generally the oldest men serving afloat were the warrant officers and the senior admirals, in both cases because it often took long service to rise so far. Admiral Osborn in the Mediterranean was seventy-two when he was incapacitated by a stroke,[21] but Boscawen died in the same rank at only forty-nine, and few of the admirals serving at sea during the war were past their fifties. Keppel first hoisted his flag at thirty-seven, Rodney at forty, both having been commodores beforehand.

There were certain illnesses incidental, though not unique to naval service which afflicted many, young or old. The gravel was a common consequence of too little water and too much alcohol.[22] Seamen aloft often ruptured themselves as they hung over the yards to hand sail. The strain of long service among the same unvaried circle of faces, especially in wartime, produced a number of cases of madness. At least three lieutenants became insane during the war, and in the previous war, in 1741, Admiral Haddock commanding in the Mediterranean broke down completely and returned 'melancholy distracted'.[23] This was an extreme illustration of a principle known to all, that health and happiness were closely linked. Lind remarked that pressed men were especially liable to scurvy because of their discontent, and even Boscawen, a man of strong rather than subtle intelligence, thought that a high sick list was attributable to the fact that 'dread of going to the West Indies, as well as the regret of being pressed, hangs heavy on many'. Officers knew that rest and leave, 'to recruit their health and strength', were essential to sickly men.[24]

Sickness was dangerous to the Navy not so much from the absolute losses of men dead, as from the temporary loss of men ill, most of whom recovered. When seamen were in acutely short supply, even a small proportion ill had a serious effect. Among ships in home ports in January 1757 5.6 per cent of complements were sick, but this figure appears to have fallen thereafter: to 3.9 per cent in July 1757, 3.4 in January 1759, 2.3 in July 1759, and 3.7 at Christmas of that year.[25] Most of these men undoubtedly recovered, some giving strong evidence of it, like Andrew Kelly of the *Bideford*, sent home invalid from Jamaica, who escaped from Haslar Hospital. 'As he was capable of getting over a wall twelve foot high', the Agent remarked drily, 'I think he may be able to do duty.'[26] From August 1755 to February 1763 Haslar, the biggest and most important of the naval hospitals, lost 3067 patients dead.[27] In the five years from 1753 to 1757, 1002 men died in Haslar, which was 7.6 per cent of those admitted, and in addition 924, or 7 per cent were discharged unserviceable.[28] Undoubtedly Haslar had more than its share of acute cases, and consequently deaths, and it seems safe to suppose that the proportion of the sick who died in the Navy as a whole was lower.

It is more difficult to estimate the actual number of deaths. Five thousand men died ashore in the first three years of the war,[29] which implies over 12,000 deaths throughout the war if this rate remained constant. Most observers thought the Navy became much healthier as the war progressed, but it also became larger, and moreover these figures appear to exclude deaths at sea. If one guesses that the Navy's deaths from all causes other than combat or drowning were about 15,000 in the seven and a half years of the war, that represents just over 1 per cent a year of the total number employed at sea.[30]

Even if this rough estimate were to represent only half the true figure, it would still emphasize the remarkable achievement of the Navy in keeping its ships healthy during the war. It seems very likely that Lind was literally correct in claiming men-of-war as being healthier than communities of similar size ashore. They were manned largely with fit young men, and isolated from shore diseases. There was no risk comparable to that faced by soldiers, say, in Hilsea Barracks, which in 1759 was reported as infected with smallpox, dysentery and typhus.[31] The Navy was acutely dependent on, and conscious of, the health of its men, and by the standards of the day remarkably successful in preserving it.

D   CLEANLINESS

From the Venetian ambassador in 1696 to Napoleon on his way to St Helena, foreign visitors were invariably impressed by the cleanliness of British men-of-war. A French clergyman in 1777 described the English as 'a people to whom cleanliness is a kind of instinct'. Conversely, British officers were often unfavourably struck by the dirtiness of French ships which they went on board.[1] Augustus Hervey thought the *Comète*, which he met at Lisbon, 'a dirty little frigate', though she was commanded by Bidé de Chézac, a distinguished officer at the time engaged in an important series of scientific observations.[2] It is probable that hygiene in French ships had considerably declined from the days of Colbert seventy years before, and it was certainly greatly inferior to that of British ships. To this was attributed in part, the much worse health record of the French navy. The French custom of burying the dead in the ballast must have been particularly unfortunate.[3]

The connection between dirt and disease was made because of

the climatorial pathology which was the prevailing medical theory, and which taught that infections were transmitted by foul air. It therefore seemed to be of great importance that ships should smell sweet. It was for this reason that Edward Ives, physician to the East Indies squadron,

> made it my principal care to keep them [fever patients] as clean in their persons and berths as possible, and to purify the air around them as much as lay in my power.[4]

The object of cleanliness was to purify the air, and cleaning the ships, or the men, was a means to that end. Fresh air was the real essential for health. It was said with approval of Captain Rodney of the *Dublin* that he

> always took the greatest pleasure in keeping her clean in the highest degree, not even permitting the seamen to dine between decks when the weather would suffer them to eat above deck.[5]

In all ships it was routine to wash the decks frequently; in the *Prince Edward*, commanded by William Cornwallis in 1765, the upper deck was washed daily, the lower deck at least twice a week, and the sides morning and evening. Indeed an experienced naval physician like James Lind, though well aware of 'filthiness being a chief source of infection and cleanliness an excellent preservative', was worried that so much washing of decks endangered the men by making the air damp, which in his view was the main predisposing cause of scurvy.[6]

The search for clean air also led to the widespread use of ventilators to purify the air below decks. The simplest form was a windsail, a canvas scoop rigged on deck to direct a draught down the main hatch, but this had little effect below the gun deck. To reach the foul and stagnant air of the hold artificial ventilation was needed, and the need was a real one, for without it the hold could be fatal to those who had to work there. Boscawen lost three men suffocated when the bilges were opened to pump them out. After that experience he became a strong advocate of ventilators, and specifically the type invented by his wife's kinsman, the distinguished scientist Dr Stephen Hales. Hales's ventilator was a hand-powered mechanical air pump which forced air down into the hold through tubes. In 1756 these ventilators were ordered to be installed in all ships of twenty guns and upwards, and captains were enjoined to see that the pump was worked for a period every watch. The system was also used to ventilate hospital wards. A rival scheme, Sutton's Tubes, depended on ducts led through the galley where they were heated in order to create a draught. This does not seem to have been so successful.[7]

It was well understood that any serious outbreak of contagious disease afloat required the ship to be stripped and disinfected. There were various ways of doing this, but the method proposed by a conference of captains at Portsmouth in 1758 was as comprehensive as any: the ballast was to be taken out, the hold washed with fresh water and clean ballast put in. With the ship completely battened down and caulked, fires were to be lit in the hold and between decks and trains of gunpowder flashed off several times. Finally the deckhead was to be washed down repeatedly with warm vinegar and smoked with 'pitched loggerheads'.[8] The effect of all this would at least have been to purify the air, and this was the chief object aimed at.

Next after the cleanliness of the ship came the cleanliness of the men, and more particularly of their clothes. Efforts were generally concentrated on clothes because the men's opportunities for washing themselves were limited at sea; there was little fresh water to spare, soap was ineffective in salt (and an expensive luxury) and there was no suitable place to bathe. We hear of a commander with a bathtub at sea,[9] but it is doubtful if this was a common convenience even among officers. Clothes were an easier target, and a more important one, for dirty clothes were rightly suspected to be the bearers of gaol fever and other infections, and were often burnt to destroy them.[10] Admiral Smith's divisional system of 1755 required the men to shift their linen twice a week,[11] and it seems probable that in well-run ships during the war this was the practice as well as weather and circumstances would allow. Washing clothes at sea was not easy; in the absence of soap 'chamberlye' (urine) was used as a detergent, and the clothes rinsed in fresh water if there were enough available.[12]

The Navy's greatest problem was in dealing with new recruits in ragged, dirty and probably infected clothes. There was every reason to wash and reclothe them, and this was often ordered to be done as soon as they were entered on a ship's books, and could have the value of the slops charged to their names. The trouble was that they might by then have been several months aboard a tender, filthy and in rags, and it was too late to ward off infection when they had joined their proper ship. Until then, however, they were not legally entered in the Navy, which meant not only that there was no easy means of charging the cost of the clothes to them, but, much more serious, that there was no legal means of keeping them in the Service. Since clothes could very easily be converted into money, clothing new recruits on shore amounted to a payment to encourage them to run away at a stage at which there were no legal and few enough practical means of stopping them.[13] The Marine Society, which initially outfitted its recruits as soon as they were accepted, found that this caused heavy desertion, and was obliged to leave them in their own clothes until they were safely afloat.[14] Faced with the same choice between possibly infected men and no men at all, the Admiralty reluctantly chose the former. Volunteers, including volunteer prisoners of war (a particularly dangerous source of infection), could be clothed to the value of their bounty, but pressed men, and prisoners of war returned by cartel from France, presented an apparently intractable problem. In October 1758 Lind received into Haslar Hospital some men who had not changed their clothes since June. It was, as he said, shocking, but the difficulty was to find a means of avoiding it, and it was not overcome during the war. In 1762, at the suggestion of Commodore Gordon, a hulk was fitted out in the Medway to receive convalescent patients from hospital and prevent them carrying fever back to their ships.[15] Some extension of this system to new recruits was probably the best answer, but it would inevitably have slowed down the recruiting service at a time when men were desperately needed, and it is easy to see why it was not at once adopted.

In spite of this failure, the Navy's attention to cleanliness was impressive. To an extent it was misplaced, for clean air is not so closely linked to health as clean bodies and clean clothes, and the ships might actually have been healthier if less attention had been paid to scrubbing the decks and sweetening the air, and more to the men. Nevertheless, it was a great strength of the Royal Navy that it did regard dirt and disease as closely linked, even if the nature of the connection was misunderstood. Captains were liable to be blamed for keeping dirty ships if typhus broke out on board,[16] so any officer of average professionalism or ambition had good reasons for attending to the cleanliness of his ship and his men.

E   HOSPITALS

The traditional way of caring for sick men landed from ships was to put them in sick quarters, which meant rooms rented from local landladies, who undertook to feed and care for their patients. As a system it had the advantages of cheapness and flexibility. No capital was required, and facilities were provided only when and where they were needed. From every other point of view sick quarters were a disaster. The landladies had no incentive to look after their patients, and it was impossible for even the most active doctor properly to treat and supervise patients scattered in garrets all over the town. Those with contagious diseases rapidly communicated their infections to the townspeople. What was worse, lodging-house keepers were often tavern-keepers as well, who encouraged the sick (if they needed encouragement) to drink their way to the grave, often selling their clothes for liquor on the way. Tavern-keeping was traditionally combined with 'crimping', so those who recovered were quite likely to be sold to merchantmen. A great many of those sent to sick quarters either never recovered or never returned.[1]

Consequently naval opinion by the early 1750s was unanimous in preferring a hospital. Naval hospitals were usually run by contract, whereby the contractor furnished premises and non-medical staff, being paid by the number of patients he accommodated. The

Sick and Hurt Board provided furniture and equipment and appointed the medical staff. A hospital run on these lines was greatly superior to sick quarters, and like them it did not have to be maintained in times and places where there was no demand. The sick, being concentrated, could easily be supervised and tended, and at the same time infectious cases could be isolated in different wards, rather than being mingled, often two or more to a bed, as in sick quarters. This was the system on which all naval hospitals were run in 1755, but in spite of its advantages the Sick and Hurt Board was dissatisfied with it. Dr Maxwell, one of the members of the Board, made a tour of inspection of the hospitals at Plymouth and Portsmouth in February 1756, and on viewing the overcrowding and dirt at Plymouth, commented, 'the contracting for hospitals [is] always to be avoided, for from the lucrative views, the contractor will endeavour to crowd his hospitals'.[2] Further from the Board's eyes, the situation was often worse. In the hospital at Cobbs Cross on Antigua, where the steward kept a punch house at the main gate and the sick men's messmates were freely allowed to bring them rum, 'great outrages have been committed thereby, as well to the scandal of the Service, as to the damage and terror of the inhabitants and neighbours'.[3] Doubtless it did the patients no good either.

The first remedy for such evils was then being built on the outskirts of Gosport: the new naval hospital of Haslar, begun in 1745 and completed in 1761, though its first wards were occupied in 1754. For many years the largest brick building in Europe, and one of the most costly projects undertaken by the Navy in the eighteenth century (it cost over £100,000, nearly double the cost of the Admiralty itself, or enough for three battleships), Haslar stands to this day as an impressive testimony to the importance which the Admiralty attached to caring for the sick. Haslar was the prototype of a new regime in treating sick seamen, under professional care, in buildings designed for the purpose, carefully isolated from the temptations of drink and desertion.[4] It was followed by a new naval hospital at Stonehouse, near Plymouth, begun in 1758, finished in 1762, but partly in use from 1760. Although the new hospitals continued to be supplemented by contract hospitals at other ports and overseas, and to a limited extent by sick quarters, they represented a large and very important advance in the care of the sick, both administratively and medically.

The new hospitals were very fully provided with drugs and medical equipment,[5] and carefully applied the principles of hygiene which were not so easily adopted at sea. All patients arriving at Haslar were stripped, their clothes burnt or disinfected, themselves washed in tubs with hot water and soap and put into 'hospital dresses' (a sort of shift or nightshirt) which were regularly changed. A series of diets for different conditions was provided, the standard including soft bread, beef or mutton, vegetables, broth, and 'milk pottage' for breakfast.[6]

The Sick and Hurt Board was concerned to provide the best medical staff. Their most famous choice was James Lind, appointed as Physician of Haslar in 1758, but his colleagues, now forgotten, seem generally to have been conscientious and able, and the Board tried to keep them that way by raising their salaries and forbidding private practice, as well as by treating seriously any complaints, such as that which led in 1756 to the dismissal of the Surgeon of Plymouth Hospital.[7]

As an additional safeguard, senior sea officers were ordered to inspect the hospitals regularly. It must have been a tiresome chore for the captains to have to take it in turns to make daily inspections, but the evidence suggests that they took it seriously. Captain Duff visited Haslar in June 1755, at a time when the hospital's permanent officers had not yet been appointed, and the few wards open were being run by a local contractor. Some of the sick complained of being neglected, and when Duff confronted the contractor, he 'treated the affair in a ludicrous manner and told me the complaints of common seamen were not to be regarded'. Captain Duff's indignation is plainly expressed in his report, and it was shared by his brother officers. Port admirals like Lord Colvill made it their business to make surprise visits to the hospitals to see that all was in order.[8]

The Navy during the Seven Years' War certainly had some way to go in applying to the full all that was known about hygiene and the care of the sick, but the new hospitals at Haslar and Stonehouse were model establishments unmatched in Europe, and it is difficult not to be impressed by the seriousness and clarity of purpose with which both Admiralty and Sick and Hurt Boards worked for the health of the Navy, and the very large sums of money which they were prepared to spend to cure the sick and keep the well in health.

CHAPTER IV

Ratings' Careers

A JOINING THE NAVY

Before one can say why men joined the Navy, it is necessary to ask why boys went to sea at all, for relatively few ratings seem to have joined the Navy in childhood to make a career of it. A large proportion of the officers' servants were young gentlemen, and the remaining boys were almost certainly too few to provide all the men the Navy needed, even in peacetime. In any case it is quite unrealistic to think of the Navy as something which seamen could join in the modern sense, a body inviting boys to enter and make a career for much of their working lives. Neither in law nor in fact was it possible for a rating to 'join the Navy' in that sense, for only commissioned and warrant officers had any permanent connection with the Navy as a service beyond what they gained as members of a ship's company. A man entered for wages on the books of a King's ship had joined the King's service until he was discharged or the ship paid off, but in constitutional theory and in everyday practice, he was primarily a member of a ship's company and not of the Navy as a whole. Men joined a King's ship or a merchant's as opportunity or preference suggested, and they moved easily from one to another. In peacetime the Navy was, from the point of view of the seaman in search of employment, simply a collection of ships differing somewhat from the usual in their conditions and ethos, but offering a job like any other. There was no identifiable class of man-of-warsmen, there were simply seamen working at the moment for one particular employer. The same was true of the non-seamen. The Navy employed a higher proportion of idlers than merchant ships, and to the extent that they were a specialized class they were more distinctively naval, but in practice many idlers were simply older seamen who had learnt a new skill or found a less arduous position, and who, had they not been in the Navy, might have been working ashore.

It is clear from the ships' musters that in peacetime the Navy found nearly all the men it needed from those who were already able seamen or skilled in their trades. There were some ordinary seamen, and even the occasional landman, but the Navy had no need to make much effort in peacetime to train adults. It was quite different in wartime, but it looks as though in peace the Navy may have been a net consumer of trained manpower, drawn from the merchant service.

In either service, seamen had to learn their trade from boyhood if they were to attain the skill born of experience before they lost the vigour and agility of young manhood. With some exceptions among coasting trades like the East Coast coal trade, deep-sea sailors were overwhelmingly young men, in Britain and in all other countries.[1] The nature of their calling required it. The earliest demographic information from censuses, in the late eighteenth and early nineteenth centuries, shows the typical seaman aged between twenty-two and twenty-four, with seven years' experience at sea.[2] The same picture is painted by a list prepared in 1762 of neutral seamen made prisoner of war who were willing to serve in the Navy. Most were in their early twenties, hardly any as old as thirty, and from their stated experience, many had been at sea from the age of five or six, and virtually all from ten or twelve.[3] Of the fourteen crew, including the mate, boatswain and carpenter, of the *Deepsea* brigantine in 1755, the oldest was aged twenty-eight, and the mean age was below twenty-three.[4] They were probably typical of a peacetime merchantman's crew.

If men went to sea as boys, the first question to ask is why. The main part of the answer is undoubtedly economic necessity, or opportunity. There was nothing unusual in the eighteenth century in people beginning their working lives at ten or twelve, and for the boy growing up near the coast seafaring was an obvious calling. It was highly paid by comparison with agricultural wages, and for many it was probably the best job they could hope for. Nevertheless, the sea was a unique and in many ways forbidding prospect. It was not only a hard and dangerous life, but it took a boy away

114

from family and friends in a peculiarly stark and uncompromising way. One thing which drew boys to go to sea in spite of all was undoubtedly the romance of it. It may be that boys had always longed to go to sea, but the outlook of the eighteenth century was especially encouraging to them. Among all classes there was an increasing interest and pleasure in the created world for its own sake, in the beauties of nature and the curiosities of foreign parts.[5] Foreign travel was undertaken for the first time as a pleasure in itself rather than a means to an end. In this new, outward-looking world of curiosity, the sea was attractive as a highway to the new sights and experiences of distant lands. For the first time men joined the Navy to see the world. 'A tender mother, among the inferior ranks of people,' wrote Adam Smith, 'is often afraid to send her son to school in a seaport town, lest the sight of the ships and the conversation and adventures of the sailors should entice him to go to sea.'[6] This is the view from university, but there really were many like Thomas Finley the butcher's boy who longed to go to sea,[7] or William Spavens, growing up in Cleethorpes and watching the ships:

> I thought sailors must be happy men to have such opportunities of visiting foreign countries and beholding the wonderful works of the Creator in the remote regions of the earth; I thought of nothing but pleasant gales and prosperous voyages.[8]

It may have been, as Dr Johnson thought, a 'perversion of the imagination', but many boys and men wanted to be sailors.[9]

It remains to be explained why seamen, having in many cases already learned their trade in merchant ships, chose to join a man-of-war. Partly the reason must have been simple economics. If the supply of seamen roughly equalled the demand, there should in theory have been men faced with the choice of unemployment or a King's ship. In practice it probably was not so very often, for there was no national market even for so mobile a labour force as seamen. Wages and conditions varied greatly from port to port, and several of the dockyards where warships fitted out lay some way from the large commercial ports, so that there was no reason why a surplus of men in, say, London, should be translated into a supply at Portsmouth or Plymouth unless seamen made a decision to travel thither to join a man-of-war.

The reasons why a man might choose to enter a warship – apart from the question of wages, of which more later – were several. Firstly, as we noted earlier, life aboard a man-of-war was relatively easy. Taking the simple but expressive measure of tons per man, English merchantmen trading in European waters generally had a ratio of between ten and twenty tons a man (the higher ratios in the larger ships), and West Indiamen ten or fifteen tons a man. In coasting trades up to thirty tons a man was considered reasonable. In a line-of-battle ship, by comparison, the ratio was under three tons a man. Admittedly men-of-war had a higher proportion of idlers than merchantmen, and higher in small ships than in large, but even in the large sloops, which were the worst manned, the number of tons per seaman was only nine at the most.[10] This is a crude but effective measure of the amount of work which had to be done. Moreover it is possible that merchantmen suffered more than warships from wartime shortages, at least in crude numbers, though the dilution of skills must have made more work for the seaman in either service. Life could be very hard in short-handed merchantmen in wartime. When the *Blandford* was lying in St Mary's Road, Scilly, on 28 October 1758,

> a ship came in from Malaga, which had been out so long that her bottom was quite green and her sails and rigging bleached white. The crew were so emaciated with continual fatigue and their strength so much exhausted that they could scarcely hold themselves on the yards, and one of them was so weak that he fell from the mainyard as the ship came into the Sound.[11]

There were old seamen in the Navy (a man of sixty-four was discharged in 1759 after forty years' service), but it would have been unthinkable in a man-of-war to have a man of fifty-six still working aloft, as there was in the *Julius Caesar* of London in 1761.[12] In peace or war, the Navy was the place for a seaman who wanted a relatively easy life.

It seems probable that another advantage of service in the Navy was the food. We have already seen that the naval diet was

116

good and plentiful by the standards of the day. It is much more difficult to get evidence from merchant ships, and difficult to generalize from what there is, since there is no reason to suppose that the practice of one master or owner was typical of all. There certainly were complaints of short and poor victuals in merchantmen, of food stopped from the sick to force them to work, and the absence of any equivalent of the naval short-allowance money.[13] It is significant that the cost of victualling a merchantman has been calculated as about seventeen shillings a calendar month.[14] For the purposes of the Navy Estimates the equivalent in the Navy was reckoned at nineteen shillings a lunar month, but the real cost was about 23s. 6d. in 1715, and probably at least 25s. by the 1750s.[15] The Victualling Board bought in very large quantities, and at the keenest prices (the Navy generally paid at least 12 per cent below usual wholesale prices)[16] so that it probably got better value as well as spending 60 per cent more on each man. It is difficult to believe that so much higher expenditure did not produce more and better food.

Discipline in merchant ships was generally slack, and mutinies or even murders were not infrequent.[17] Whether this laxity was attractive or repellent rather depended on temperament, but it was certain that the powers of a master were very great, and the victim of ill-treatment was in a far worse position than in a man-of-war, where there was an authority to appeal to which took seriously the welfare of its men.[18] The only hope of an aggrieved merchant seaman was an action at law, which was hardly easy for a penniless illiterate. Robert Barker, carpenter of the *Thetis* slaver of Liverpool, was put in irons by the master and so maltreated that he lost his sight. He was rescued by Keppel's ship the *Torbay*, whose officers befriended him and whose ship's company made a collection for him. On his return to England he won £26 damages from his master – not a large compensation for blindness, but better than most men in his position managed.[19]

All these were reasons why men might prefer the Navy to merchant ships, to which might be added medical treatment, compensation for wounds, injuries and death, and the opportunity of a pension in old age.[20] The most telling advantage of all was perhaps the prospects of advancement, of which more later, but in order to be attracted by this or any other long-term advantage it was necessary that the seamen should rationally assess their future prospects in either service. Had they been sober married men in middle age, seamen would doubtless have done so, but being giddy young bachelors, they seldom did. The common thread of every informed description of the sailor's character is imprudence:

> Our seamen are like froward children not knowing how to judge for themselves, but on account of their great use to the nation, are to be cherished as the first born of a fond parent.[21]

'The multitude of these men are wholly illiterate,' another officer wrote,

> their ideas wild, confused and indeterminate as the elements they have to combat with; their dispositions naturally generous, though turbulent; fearless, or rather thoughtless of consequences (from being inured to hardship and danger), they will run every risk to satisfy the caprice of the moment.[22]

Seamen were genuinely a peculiar class, isolated by their profession from the bulk of their fellow-countrymen, living in particular quarters of seaside towns, speaking a language of their own, 'a people of a distinct nature in themselves, for the most part divest of common knowledge of things ashore'.[23] No analysis can do justice to them which attributes their actions simply to rational calculation. It would undoubtedly have been easier for sea officers to man and control their ships if seamen had been less turbulent and eccentric, but in practice that was the price to be paid for skill and daring.

B FOLLOWINGS AND ADVANCEMENT

'hif your honer would be Cind A Nuf to Right to the Lords of the Admirtle to get your Ould Ships Compeney We All Would be glad to go A Long With your honer A gain.'[1] In these words, which we need not doubt were their own, fourteen men who had formerly served under Captain Mackenzie of the *Sunderland* wrote to him in March 1757. Petitions of this sort were an everyday occurrence in the Navy, usually from men who wanted to be with an officer they already knew, but sometimes asking to serve with one known only by reputation.[2] Whenever possible authority tried to grant these requests, for they were not simply a peripheral matter of satisfying private wishes as far as was consistent with the needs of the Service; they touched directly the central loyalties which bound the Navy together. Just as men did not join the Navy as a whole, neither did they love it as a whole. Their loyalty was precisely concentrated on their shipmates, and their obedience was specifically to their officers. Officers could and did express devotion to the Service, to abstract concepts of duty and honour, but ratings attached themselves to the concrete reality of their friends, their officers and their ship. Captain Forrest explained it thus:

> Every officer has his particular forms of duty; those men are so well acquainted with mine, that they might be better with me than with another commander till experience brings them in. Their good behaviour has been such as to gain my affection, and I do believe that I have not less of theirs, which makes us very unwilling to part with each other.[3]

It was of the utmost importance to the Service that men should as far as possible serve under the officers they desired. The Admiralty knew well that an unhappy ship is never an efficient ship, and moreover, that if men were forced to serve with officers they disliked, there was every chance that they would run away to follow others more popular. We shall see that the authority of the Admiralty and of senior officers was weak, and rested more on persuasion than force. It was essential that men like Captain Mackenzie's followers should be gratified in their wishes, because that was the only practical way the Service could be carried on. All captains would have echoed his opinion of the importance of

> that confidence and affection of the people I have under my command, which every man who has the honour of commanding one of his Majesty's ships would be glad of acquiring in peace, much more so in war.[4]

It was much more valuable to have a settled and happy ship's company than to have a good ship. The ambitious Captain Augustus Hervey of the *Hampton Court* 'never liked her, but kept her on account of my people', and Captain John Elliot for the same reason declined the offer of a larger ship in order to keep his experienced company.[5]

When captains did change ships they hoped to be able to take with them their followers, or as many as possible. 'I hope it is not desiring too much', one wrote,

> to have leave to remove a few men with me into whatever ship I may have, for without some to begin I can trust, we shall make a poor figure in setting out. I only ask for twenty, and shall then leave this sloop completely manned.[6]

Until the 1756 edition the Admiralty's printed instructions actually gave commanders a right to take a specified number of followers with them on 'turning over', but that was then restricted as a right to the captain's servants.[7] Nevertheless, more was almost always asked for and often granted, always on the understanding that the men would be replaced by the same number in return. The ideal was to turn over an entire ship's company, and the Admiralty was even prepared to approve the dangerous idea of swapping two complete ships' companies at sea in order to keep officers and men together.[8] This scheme was not fully carried out because some of the officers and men professed to be fonder of their old ship than of their captain. This seems to have been an unusual reaction, but the *Monmouth* was a famous ship, and she was ordered in to refit, with the prospect of leave for those who stayed in her. The result was the splitting of a settled ship's company, which the Admiralty had striven to avoid, and which was usually intensely unpopular with the men. Any suggestion of drafting men away from their ship would arouse an instant protest, such as that reported by Captain Clive, whose men 'are come to the cabin door most earnestly imploring that I would write to their Lordships to reverse this order'.⁹

When captains or admirals changed ships they were not often lucky enough to be able to take the entire ship's company, but it was always the ideal they hoped for:

> I received yours acquainting me their Lordships ... had resolved to remove my captain and officers ... and that they are likewise pleased to consent to my removing as many of the petty officers and men out of the *Marlborough* as I shall desire, which I am much obliged to their Lordships for, and do desire to remove the whole, as it has been the constant practice lately for the flag officers to do so ... Were I to choose any in particular of the Marlboroughs they would certainly be the best, and the rest would go very much dissatisfied. I have taken great pains to discipline and make them a tolerable ship's company, which was very bad when I had them first. I can't help saying it would be a little hard to be the first instance of losing my people; in what a light must I appear to them, and indeed to the whole officers.¹⁰

As Admiral Holburne indicates, securing one's old followers was not only a means to an efficient and contented crew, but also a main support of an officer's credit. The senior officer who could not get his men when he asked for them was not worth following. Usually they did get the men they asked for, so long as they were not asking for too many, and the documents abound with examples. 'There are some seamen left on board the *St George* who have sailed with me many years, and are very desirous of going with me again,' Admiral Saunders wrote, and Lord Colvill asked the Admiralty 'to indulge me with fifty of my old shipmates from the *Northumberland*'.¹¹ When Rear-Admiral Steevens shifted his flag in 1759 seventy petty officers and 259 seamen applied to follow him, and were allowed to do so.[12] There were even followers on land. Captain Patrick Baird spent the first part of 1755 on the Impress Service in Norfolk, and when he was rewarded for his thankless work with a command, his press gang asked to go to sea with him.[13]

There could be losses as well as gains from the constant exchange of men. Bad men as well as good might be keen to follow a good captain, as Augustus Keppel complained: 'All my Maidstones are not come, but all the worst, worthless rascals are.'[14] If a swap were not carefully and impartially supervised, a captain might receive worse men than he sent. The usual practice was for officers from the two ships to pick alternately, but one might know the men better than the other.[15] Moreover it was possible for an unscrupulous or simply optimistic captain to claim the allegiance of good men who found the proposal less attractive than he did. Sometimes two captains fought over the same men, each claiming them as followers.[16] One popular captain with many genuine followers who manufactured connections in order to poach good men from his brother commanders and dispose of worthless ones, was Rodney.[17] Successful captains like him whose ships were already well manned were not likely to be granted all their requests for followers, for however healthy it was for the Service that men should have the officers they chose, it was necessary that even unlucky or unpopular commanders should have a proportion of able seamen.[18]

A settled, efficient ship's company was a precious possession, which both deserved and required careful nurture. A captain or admiral who had, or wished to have, a following had to look after his men. He had to spend time and trouble, and the time and trouble of his agent or banker, to get his men the prize money and back pay they were due.[19] If they fell on hard times, they looked to their patrons for protection. Benjamin Gregory, a deserter condemned to death, was reprieved at the intercession of Admiral Holburne whose follower he had been, and Commodore Keppel, having a vacancy to fill for a cook (always chosen from disabled men), appointed one 'who received his hurts with me in the *Torbay*'. When followers grew old or ill, they looked to their patrons to get them superannuated or pensioned.[20]

The most important service a patron performed for his followers was to promote them. Perhaps many men served with particular officers simply because they liked them, but anyone with even limited ambition looked for officers who would be able to reward merit. Any captain could on his own authority raise a deserving man to a petty officer's rating, which was by no means a negligible ambition in itself. Beyond that, warrant officers were invariably chosen on the recommendation of captains or admirals. The officer who had shown himself to be a reliable judge of men had excellent prospects of being able to advance his followers, and that in turn drew good men to serve him, and advanced his own career.

It is not too much to say that good followers were the foundation of an officer's success. Even the most senior officers took great pains to look after their people. In the middle of the war, after nearly ten years at the Admiralty, Anson himself was taking a personal interest in the careers of individual ratings.[21] The more senior the officer, the greater his power to reward, and the stronger the attraction of serving him. In a rough and ready way, a free market in talent ensured that flagships were always the best manned, and justified the invariable practice of all flag officers in filling vacancies among warrant officers from their petty officers. The gunner's mates of the flagship were the most likely candidates to be made gunners, and likewise with all the other mates.[22] The petty officers of private ships therefore hoped to be taken into the flagship and so be placed within reach of a warrant. A recommendation of Rear-Admiral Geary demonstrates the process well:

> I have given an order to Benjamin Serjeant my gunner's mate to do the duty of boatswain of the *Sapphire* till further order; he has been my gunner's mate three years and is a sober good seaman, has passed his examination for gunner of a third rate upwards of two years, and I beg to recommend him to their Lordships' favour, as I believe he will make a very good boatswain. Captain Strachan is very desirous of his being his boatswain, as he has sailed with him several years.[23]

Three years was a short time to have followed an admiral; Lord Colvill in 1762 asked confirmation of a boatswain's warrant for a man who 'has been mostly with me since the year 1743'.[24] There were many who had followed particular officers all their working lives.

Francis Perry, acting boatswain of the *Namur*, was described in 1756 by Admiral Hawke as 'a good man whose sole dependence is on me'.[25] This hints at the weakness of a follower's position, vulnerable to any reversal of his patron's fortunes. The death or disgrace of an officer would cause his followers to scatter at once in search of those better able to help them. Moreover there were some officers who broke the established convention that the best leaders were also the best patrons. However able a captain, if he acquired the reputation of a bad judge of men his recommendations were likely to suffer. George Rodney was the most notable example of a brilliant officer, rapidly advanced for his professional qualities, but found by experience to be untrustworthy. In November 1759 he asked for some followers, who were transferred to him, and one was soon after made a boatswain. Within four months this reliable old follower, a petty officer with Rodney upwards of twelve years, proved to be useless and continually drunk.[26] This sort of débâcle would naturally damage an officer's credit and undermine his attraction as a patron.

An inability to attract good men was a fatal weakness in the career of an officer, however brilliant, for successful patronage was the key to a successful career, the principal means by which a reliable ship's company was cemented, and one of the strongest of the social forces within the Navy. Like electrons in ceaseless motion around one another, neither colliding nor parting, the officers and men of the Navy were bound together by invisible but tenacious bonds, of which the relationship between followers and leaders, together with that between shipmates, were the strongest.

c PAY AND CREDIT

Low pay is usually offered as one of the main reasons why the Navy in the eighteenth century suffered difficulties in recruitment, and that indeed was the view of some observers at the time,[1] but the proposition has not always been examined as closely as it should be. Some modern authorities even appear unsure what the actual rates of pay in the Navy were.[2] In fact, an able seaman received twenty-four shillings a month, an ordinary seaman nineteen shillings, and a landman eighteen shillings. From each was deducted sixpence a month for Greenwich Hospital, and a shilling for the Chatham Chest, of which sixpence actually went to the Chest, fourpence to the chaplain and twopence to the surgeon.[3] The net rates of pay were therefore 22s. 6d. for an able seaman, 17s. 6d. for an ordinary and 16s. 6d. for a landman, or £14 12s. 6d., £11 7s. 6d. and £10 11s. 6d. a year respectively, since men were paid by a month of twenty-eight days.

This last needs to be emphasized, since some writers have assumed pay by the calendar month. It is quite clear from the pay books that they are wrong, but it is worth digressing for a moment to examine the reasons which led even so rigorous a scholar as Daniel Baugh astray on this point. He refers to a letter written in 1780 by Admiral Pye, then commanding at Portsmouth, about a recent mutiny in which men had demanded to be paid by a twenty-eight day month, and had made good that right at a court martial.[4] Pye told Lord Sandwich that 'I believe there are few if any precedents where seamen have been paid but by the calendar month'. This was an astonishing statement, for the Navy had always been paid by the lunar month; all the ships under his command were paid thus, and he himself had received his pay by the lunar month in every ship in which he had ever served before reaching flag rank. It is true that Pye ('Goose Pye' as he was known among junior officers) was an ignorant and clownish person of few professional talents, whose career had nearly been ended in 1758 by court martial.[5] (He seems to have been saved only by the absence of Anson and Boscawen at sea, allowing him to deploy his excellent political influence on the civilian members of the Admiralty Board and counterbalance Admiral Forbes, the sole remaining sea officer.)[6] It still seems extraordinary that he should have known so little about the basic administration of a warship after more than half a century in the Navy.

The wages earned by an able seaman are one obvious reason

why boys should have wanted to go to sea, for in an age when a ploughman might earn £3 or £4 a year, an able seaman's pay was attractive.[7] Even a landman's pay was more than many country-men might earn, especially in the poorer parts of the three king-doms. Moreover, because all seamen's wages were paid at long intervals they often represented quite large sums when they came. In warships, which in wartime were generally paid just before sail-ing, it was common for men to have a great deal of cash with them. A seaman of the *Falkland* in 1760 had sixteen guineas besides small change and two gold rings, a man in the *Anson* that same year had fourteen guineas, and in 1757 a man aboard another ship had nearly £20 stolen from him. Richard Skinner, seaman of the *Northumberland*, who died in Plymouth Hospital in 1762, left about £25 in wages. He probably did not have this on him in cash, but it was a problem in hospitals that patients brought large sums in money and jewellery like rings and shoebuckles, which the nurses were tempted to steal. One man arrived at Haslar with forty-three guineas in his pockets.[8] This enforced saving was a dis-advantage to a man with dependants, but it may well have been something of an attraction to the unmarried who had no need of a regular income.

There is no doubt, however, that since the naval wage rates had been established in 1653 pay in merchantmen had risen. To what extent the Navy was at a disadvantage over merchantmen in peacetime is difficult to say with confidence, for wages in merchant ships varied from time to time, from trade to trade and from port to port. Ralph Davis, using figures chiefly derived from London ships, suggests that wages for an able seaman were about twenty-five shillings a calendar month in the mid-century; evidence from Bristol suggests that the figure there was about thirty shillings. In wartime these figures rose rapidly, but unevenly. During the war London wages were apparently anything up to sixty or seventy shillings a month for an able seaman, but in Bristol they rose only to thirty-five shillings, and there were probably equally wide dis-crepancies between other ports.[9] In 1760 a cooper's mate at Cork was offered seventy shillings a month on a voyage to the West Indies, and sixty to Quebec. In the West Indies, where the demand for European seamen was always high, men might be offered anything up to £40 for the voyage home to England, or thirty guineas and twenty gallons of rum.[10]

Clearly the Navy in wartime could not compete with these wages, but it still retained certain financial advantages. Volunteers joining the Navy in wartime could expect a bounty offered by proclamation, and paid on joining in addition to two months' advance wages. By 1759 the bounty for an able seaman had risen to £5, so that one who volunteered could expect over £7 in cash when he joined his ship.[11] Advances could be had in merchantmen also, but less easily, and without bounty. Men-of-warsmen sometimes earned extra wages, for example by rigging other ships, or working in the colonial dockyards, both of which were considered beyond the line of duty.[12] In warships the monthly pay came net of fixed deductions of 1s. 6d. and nothing else (apart from the cost of slops and tobacco sold to the men). In merchantmen the crew was liable to arbitrary deductions on account of damaged cargo; they paid sixpence a month to Greenwich Hospital and got nothing in return for it; on Atlantic voyages they often received part of their wages in debased colonial currency; and above all they were not usually paid unless the voyage was completed.[13] If the ship were wrecked, or simply sold abroad by a dishonest owner, the men stood to receive nothing. In the Navy men were entitled to pay for as long as the ship was in commission, which in the case of shipwreck was until the conclusion of the obligatory court martial on the captain or surviving officers.

The gravest weakness of the merchant seaman's position was the risk of being cheated by an unscrupulous master. The system of pressing at sea out of inward-bound merchantmen (see Chapter Vc) offered particular temptations to masters to encourage their men to flee ashore to some nearby coastal port to escape the press – and to leave behind their wages. The master then engaged some local fishermen or boatmen to bring his ship in, and complete a voyage made, in effect, almost entirely without labour costs. When press officers did come aboard masters sometimes tried to get rid of their men unpaid. It was one of the basic duties of a press lieutenant to see that all those he took received their wages in cash or by ticket, and if masters made trouble the Admiralty solicitor would be instructed to sue for the pressed men's wages.[14] The Navy was an effective refuge for oppressed merchant seamen, which of course made it unpopular with dishonest masters of merchantmen. One of their tricks was to save wages by maltreating their men in the hope that they would desert in a foreign port. The seaman's best answer to this was to enter on board a King's ship, and return the next day with a lieutenant to demand his wages and sea chest.[15] A variation on this allowed a crafty man-of-warsman with leave to enter a merchant ship, claim advance wages, and then return to his proper ship where the master would have extreme difficulty in recovering the advance.[16] On the whole, however, the existence and power of the Navy offered the merchant seaman no more than some chance of countering an oppressive or dishonest master, and to that extent, some counter to the high nominal wages of merchantmen in wartime.

It has been suggested that privateers were particularly attractive because 'the wages were comparable to those paid by the merchants, and in addition each crewman could expect a much larger share of prize money than his counterpart in the Navy'.[17] There may have been some truth in these assertions among colonial privateers; in the West Indies, for example, privateers were said to pay £3 sterling a month, and at least one American privateer, the *Sturdy Beggar* of New York, was offering a far more equitable distribution of prize money than obtained in the Navy,[18] but there is something very odd in the suggestion that privateer owners, who naturally took their profit from the prizes, were able to distribute more to their crews than the Navy, which gave the captors the entire value of what they took.

The actual situation in privateers owned in British ports during the Seven Years' War appears generally to have been that the owners took half the value of any prize, and in addition charged agency and commission of perhaps 5 per cent each.[19] The commander's share was 8 per cent, so the remainder of the ship's company shared 32 per cent of the value of the prize between them, divided up in shares. There was no fixed number of shares, but it was commonly about double the number of men. The officers received between eight and twelve shares each, able seamen one to two, and boys from a quarter to one share.[20] In a privateer of 200 men and 400 shares, an able seaman with two shares was receiving

0.16 per cent of the value of each prize.

In warships the entire value of the prize was distributed to the captors in the proportion one-eighth to the commander-in-chief, one-quarter to the commander (plus the flag officer's eighth if the ship were under private orders), one-eighth to the master and the lieutenants, another to the other warrant sea officers, another to inferior and petty officers, and the remaining quarter to 'private men', seamen and marines.[21] In a 28-gun sixth rate with 200 men, the same as our illustrative privateer, there were 141 men to share the quarter, so that an able seaman took 0.18 per cent of the value of each prize – marginally more than in the privateer.

Of course in reality much depended on the size and luck of the captors. The average privateer was smaller than our illustration – something under 200 tons, or the equivalent of a fourteen-gun sloop with 110 or 120 men,[22] but the average man-of-war was certainly larger, and the 'private man's' share of any prize taken by a man-of-war fell as the size of the ship, and consequently the number of persons sharing the quarter, rose. Privateers could concentrate on taking prizes without the distractions of other duty, though the smaller they were, the less likely to come by prizes of great value, which were obviously the best defended. It was therefore by no means certain that the privateersman would actually make less prize money than the seaman in a King's ship, but it would be very rash to assume the converse.

What is more, privateersmen received no wages, and the cost of their victuals and medical treatment was deducted from their prize money when it was paid.[23] Pursuing our comparison of the situations of an able seaman in a privateer of 200 men and one in a warship of the same size, we can say that the latter received wages and victuals worth £30 17s. 6d. a year (valuing his victuals at 25s. a month). Simply to earn as much as this the privateersman would have to share in prizes worth nearly £19,300 a year, before taking any account of what prizes the man-of-war might take. Clearly the seaman who entered a privateer in preference to a King's ship was taking a financial gamble against long odds, and it is no surprise to find that British privateers were extremely short of seamen.[24] It is difficult to believe that many men can have chosen privateers in preference to the Navy for the money.

They could have been tempted by 'letters of marque', by which was meant armed merchantmen engaged in their usual trades which had taken out a letter of marque in order to be able to profit by any chance capture which fortune might throw in their way. These paid the usual wage rates, 'an advantage that privateers have not', as one recruiting advertisement mentioned,[25] and offered shares in a prize fund of one-quarter of the prize's value. The chances of making a fortune were clearly poor, but all prize money came in addition to high wages. A peculiar system, midway between British privateers and letters of marque, was used by the numerous privateers of Jersey and Guernsey. They paid shares of a prize fund of one-third of the value of the prize, but the shares were exchangeable for wages at the rate of four livres a month for each share. This allowed the seaman to choose how much he wished to gamble on his ship's fortunes.[26]

The method of paying men-of-war had remained essentially unchanged since the days when ships only put to sea for the summer. When a ship ended her commission, and in principle not before, the pay books having been made up,[27] the commissioner of the yard and his clerks came aboard with money in cash to pay the entire ship's company. By the 1750s the system had been complicated in various ways, but it remained generally true that no rating, and officers only to a very limited extent, could draw their pay in cash before the ship paid off. All those discharged from the ship before then (and ships discharged 50 per cent of their companies a year on average)[28] received only a ticket for their wages, encashable on board on the day of paying off, and thereafter at periodic 'recalls'. These tickets could be assigned, and there was a flourishing trade in buying tickets at a discount. The seamen got cash when they needed it, but often at a usurious discount (five or six shillings in the pound in 1757). Many ticket brokers were merchnats or innkeepers, but pursers often bought them, and sometimes captains. This was dangerous to the seamen, whose best defence against ticket brokers was for the captain or commissioner to force them to accept a lower discount when they presented the tickets at pay day.[29]

Seamen sent to hospital were in a particularly difficult position, for if they were discharged as unfit for service while still borne on the books of their own ship, since sailed, they might wait for years before they received even a ticket. So might those discharged cured into another ship in the absence of their own, so that they had to serve as supernumeraries for victuals only until they met their old ship again. These evils were effectually remedied by a new system in 1756, which required all men discharged to hospital for more than a week to be removed from their ship's books and given a ticket for their wages to date.[30]

Meanwhile several efforts had been made to limit the abuses of the ticket system. The Navy Act of 1728 forbade any assignment of unpaid wages, and required that ships in home waters should be paid two months' wages every six months, and those overseas have opportunity to name attornies at home to receive their pay at similar intervals.[31] The 1758 Navy Act enacted that a common seaman or inferior officer could revoke an assignment of wages in any form simply by appearing in person at 'the pay' and demanding his wages.[32] This was a remarkable, if not unique, legal provision, allowing one party unilaterally to abrogate a binding contract. Moreover by the 1728 Act seamen in men-of-war could not be arrested or imprisoned for debts of less than £20, so the ticket broker had limited chances of recovering money laid out on a ticket. Buying tickets, especially for under £20, then became a risky business. Samuel Robinson, landlord of the Haunch of Venison on Portsmouth Common, bought a £21 ticket for £14 15s. in 1757, only to encounter another of the risks of the trade when he discovered it was forged.[33] Quite apart from this hazard, it seems likely that after 1758 the ticket broking business became much less attractive.

The 1728 Navy Act for the first time provided a means for men to remit money to their families, either when the ship was paid (in home waters), or at the same six-monthly intervals abroad. Unfortunately there were still considerable weaknesses in the system. Apart from the difficulty of paying ships as often as the Act required, it was difficult for the seamen to find honest and inexpensive attornies. This problem was exacerbated by a well-meant measure of 1707 forbidding Navy Office and dockyard clerks to act as agents, which simply threw the seamen into hands less scrupulous, less expert, and less easily supervised. This was repealed in

1751 when the clerks were permitted to act for a fixed commission of threepence in the pound (1.25 per cent), and thereafter their names appear frequently in the pay books.[34]

Nevertheless, payment by attorney always involved some expense and legal formality, and many seamen preferred to avoid it. Admirals and captains would often make remittances for their men, as Boscawen did for some Cornishmen in his flagship in 1755: 'several of them have been with me to-day to desire me to send their wives their advance money, which I have done by Mr Veale'. The same thing happened the following year:

> Our men have been paid, and, what is very extraordinary, have paid into my hands £563-9-0d to send to their wives all over Britain. Remark, not one Irishman.[35]

Boscawen sent the money by Mr Child his banker; one got a better class of attorney by speaking politely to a senior officer, and probably a cheaper one.

Remittances were only useful to those who wished to send money home. The great majority of ratings were unmarried young men, who felt a more pressing need for cash in hand. Captains were sympathetic to this, especially if, knowing their men, they thought the money might be laid out on something useful like clothes or provisions. Often captains acted as bankers, lending their men money on the security of their wages – a fragile security, under the terms of the 1758 Act, but presumably captains chose their clients with care.[36]

This helped the rating with an understanding commander and a steady character, but there must have been many others. The principal object of the 1758 Navy Act was to benefit them by enforcing more frequent paying of ships. Instead of the rather unrealistic provisions of the 1728 Act, Grenville's Act (as it was often known, from its chief sponsor) required ships in home waters to be paid a year's wages every eighteen months, and forbade the Navy Board to appropriate money voted for wages to any other purposes. In practice the urgent need to safeguard the Navy's credit still tempted them to do so, and the practical difficulties of paying ships at fixed intervals in wartime still gave them opportunity, but the spirit of the Act was followed to a considerable extent. Anson's Admiralty Board had been pressing the Navy Board for some time to pay ships more often, and in this matter welcomed the support of the Act.[37] Requests from ships' companies or smaller groups of men to be paid were generally received favourably, and it was the practice to pay men turned over from one ship to another.[38] The Admiralty was insistent that even supernumeraries not yet entered on a ship's books for wages, and consequently not yet able to receive pay even though they were earning it, should in the end receive what they were due. In the case of some sickly Irishmen sent from Cork in February 1763 just as the war was ending and discharged at once, the Admiralty ordered the port admiral to be sure that they were paid for their time in service, even though they had never been borne for wages on any ship's books. Some eighteenth-century commentators, followed by modern historians, thought that supernumeraries not yet entered for wages – and the least useful recruits might remain in this situation for months – were earning nothing, which was not the case.[39]

The great disadvantage of paying men more frequently was that it made them difficult to handle, and was supposed to tempt them to desert. Many senior officers maintained that putting money in men's pockets simply encouraged them to run away and spend it, and indeed there were obvious reasons why it should have done, so money was withheld to keep a hold on the men.[40] When men were paid before going on leave they were not usually paid up to date; two years' wages was considered an adequate security.[41] The weakness of this approach was that it appealed to the self-interest of a notoriously improvident class of men, and in any case wages owed could be converted to credit, and thus, at a discount, to cash.[42]

The usual practice was for ships to be paid just before they sailed, lying in an outer road well away from the shore. Even there boats would crowd round the ship, spirits would come aboard, and the ship would be disabled just when she was supposed to be getting to sea; 'the ship being just paid and in such confusion', as one report put it.[43] It is not certain to what extent more frequent paying of ships did encourage desertion. It probably had some effect,[44] but certainly any admiral of Anson's day would have laughed at the hysterical denunciations of Lord St Vincent fifty years later:

> the discipline and subordination of the Navy was shook
> to the foundation by the Grenville Act (framed *ad cap-
> tandum vulgus*), which transferred the command of the
> fleet from the officers to whores, landlords, crimps and
> lastly to United Irishmen ... Unless that fatal Act is
> repealed, and another of a very different form substi-
> tuted, the British Navy is no more.[45]

One of the provisions of the 1758 Act which was most strongly
urged at the time, and has been most highly praised since, was its
new mechanism by which men might remit money to their relatives, free, via government channels. It suited the politicians to
speak as though every seaman had a family and a settled home,
and very exaggerated claims have been made for the use made of
the new remittance system. The *Gentleman's Magazine* of 1759
claimed that the ship's company of the *Dorsetshire* had sent home
£16,000 – remarkable news, if true, for that sum represented over
two years' gross wages, without deductions, for every person on
board. The actual figure was £106.[46] In fact, very few men made
use of the new system. In seventy-two ships which were paid at
Plymouth in 1759 and some of whose men made remittances, only
665 men, or 3 per cent of their authorized complements, made any
remittance, and this takes no account of ships which made no remittances at all. In a sample of nineteen pay books, those making
remittances were 4.6 per cent of the ships' complements a year,
and the sums sent represented 5.6 per cent of the net pay of the
ship. Just over half the payments were to wives, or to women of
the same surname who might have been wives.[47]

Clearly, remittances were not attractive to the majority of seamen, no doubt because so few of them had family ties. For the
minority who did, however, the 1758 Act established a free system
with a minimum of legal formality, within the capacity of unlet-
tered users. It was necessary only for the man to sign a legal instrument, a 'will and power' in common parlance, naming the
beneficiary of his remittances. A good example of the system at
work is given by this letter, written from the village of St Winnow
near Lostwithiel by the mother of William Burnett, ordinary sea-

man of the *Burford*, to her daughter-in-law:

St. Twinow, December 2nd 1759

Dear Child

You know that my Son made me will and powr, but since that he is married to you, for that reason I freely resine all right and title to you, as being his wife, my sons will and Power you know is in your own keeping, so you may do just as you please with it, for it is of no use to me. May all happiness atend you boath which is the Prayers of your affectionate Mother

Ann Burnet

to Mrs Sarah Burnet in New Church Lane, nigh Martingate, Plymouth.[48]

This letter survives because it had the desired effect; the pay clerks pinned it to the back of the pay book as their authority for paying Burnett's remittance to his wife.

The proportion of men who needed or wanted to make remittances was small, but the Act was nevertheless an advance, for it made the Navy more attractive to married men, and gave it an advantage which the merchant service did not possess. If married men had been more common at sea it might have answered one of Grenville's hopes in significantly easing the manning problem.

There is no doubt that prize money figured far more in the seaman's mind than remittances. Small though the 'private man's' share of a prize was, it meant a lot to him, and it shaped the popular image of the sailor. Men did not often fry gold watches on Portsmouth Hard, as the crews of the *Favourite* and *Active* were able to do in 1762, but it was the sort of thing which stuck in the memory.[49] In 1780 the young James Gardner, a schoolboy destined for the Navy, witnessed some French prisoners being landed on Gosport beach and handed over to a party of soldiers, while the Gosport girls sang this song:

> Don't you see the ships a-coming?
> Don't you see them in full sail?
> Don't you see the ships a-coming

135

With the prizes at their tail?
Oh! my little rolling sailor,
   Oh! my little rolling he;
I do love a jolly sailor,
   Blithe and merry might he be.

Sailors, they get all the money,
   Soldiers they get none but brass;
I do love a jolly sailor,
   Soldiers they may kiss my arse.
Oh! my little rolling sailor,
   Oh! my little rolling he;
I do love a jolly sailor,
   Soldiers may be damned for me.[50]

The hope of prize money was always good for morale: 'You can't think how keen our men are, wrote Boscawen in 1756, 'the hopes of prize money makes them happy, a signal for a sail brings them all on deck.'[51] Even better than hope was reality, especially on overseas stations where ships could not be paid, and prize money was the only cash the men could hope for. Senior officers went to great lengths to get them prize money and distribute it widely.[52] It was one reason why the larger ships in the West Indies would man and send out private tenders, the property of their captains. There were excellent operational reasons to do this – they were the best counter to French privateers – and of course the officers profited from the prizes, but they were conscious of the importance of sharing the tenders' takings among the men of the big ships who would otherwise get nothing.[53]

Prize money could also be used as a reward for some particularly gallant action. In September 1759 Augustus Hervey led his ship's boats in a characteristically daring and flamboyant attack, cutting out a French schooner from under the guns of the batteries of Camaret, near Brest. Both Hervey and Hawke, the commander-in-chief, gave up their shares of the prize money to the boats' crews, which increased their gains by 150 per cent.[54] Prize money was a species of property, and the rights of property were highly regarded in the eighteenth century. Captains were scrupulous in getting their men's permission for anything affecting a prize in which they had an interest. Augustus Hervey, having taken a little tartan in the Mediterranean not worth the trouble of keeping, sold her back to her master 'with the consent of my officers and people'. Another captain asked whether his men wanted to insure their money for the voyage home from the West Indies, or stand the risk. A prize agent had to have a power of attorney signed by a majority of the ship's company before the Navy Office would allow him to pass the captors' accounts.[55]

Even without prize money, the wages paid seamen in the Navy, taken in the context of their security, were by no means unattractive in the 1750s. The latter part of the century, however, was a time of rising prices and wages. In 1768 seamen in the Thames successfully went on strike for a rise from 32 s. to 40 s. a month,[56] and by the time of the American War naval wages were well behind even peacetime wage rates. In wartime they always had been, and men were undoubtedly tempted to leave the Navy to earn more elsewhere, but it is not likely that this was a principal reason for the Navy's shortage of manpower. Though the common seaman would be lucky to make his fortune in the Navy, the wages, and the chances of advancement and prize money, together made the Service a real attraction for the poor boy without education or expectations.

D   LEAVE

There is a popular impression of the Navy in the eighteenth century as a sort of floating concentration camp, and part of this picture has inevitably been the assertion that in wartime the Navy granted leave seldom or never.[1] If life on board was so unpleasant, if most of the men had been forced into the Service and hoped to escape, it naturally followed that leave could not have been granted, because the men would have run away as soon as they had the chance. The alleged unpleasantness of life in the Navy, and the alleged lack of leave, support each other. If the evidence shows, as it does, that leave was frequent and widespread, it severely undermines the credibility of the traditional interpretation.

Leave in wartime usually came in one of two forms; general leave for an entire ship's company to be absent for a time between a week and a month, and short leave for a day or a few days, given to individuals, to groups or to a watch. General leave was given by the Admiralty, usually though not only in particular circumstances which gave men a strong claim to expect it. The admiral or captain concerned would be consulted on the trustworthiness of his people – a delicate point, for an over-optimistic report, falsified by the event, would do an officer no good at the Admiralty, but on the other hand it was desirable that men should have leave, not only for their health and happiness, but for the credit of an officer among his followers. A temporizing reply, like Admiral Broderick's, was one possible answer:

> I never had any complaint of their absenting themselves from their duty when the ship was cleaning at Gibralter, but ... I cannot take on me to be answerable for seamen's keeping their words, but ... I hope if their Lordships indulge them with leave, they will have so much gratitude to return to their duty, after the expiration of the time given them.[2]

If men had been promised leave it was difficult to refuse them in any case, for a senior officer's honour pledged to his men was not lightly to be broken. Nor was it easy to refuse a request if other ships in similar circumstances had been granted leave.[3] Authority naturally encouraged people to return from leave by emphasizing the risks they ran by not doing so, and by requiring them to leave behind some security against their return – the sea chest and bedding of a recently pressed man were judged insufficient. But leave was given even when the Admiralty knew men would desert.[4] It was obvious to every thinking officer that men needed leave, if only 'to recruit their health and strength':

When the *Sunderland* came into the harbour, the ship's
company were then, through sickness and fatigue, in
such a situation that it was thought necessary by Vice-
Admiral Knowles as well as the captain, to give them
leave to range about a little, otherways a great many
more must and would have died.[5]

This motive for giving leave was especially strong in the case of
ships returning from long commissions abroad, which was one of
the circumstances in which leave was regarded as almost a right.[6]
Men returning fron the tropics could expect leave regardless of
their reliability – although, as we shall see, being from settled
ships' companies such men were anyway likely to be among the
most trustworthy. 'There is no danger of their leaving the ship,'
Captain Forrest reported of his men, home from Jamaica in 1759,

as the few that were suspected were left on board the
Royal Anne, and I don't suppose their Lordships meant
to confine the others there after so long a voyage; and
were they to have a few days' leave ashore here after the
ship is cleared it would be an encouragement to them.[7]

Leave was also given to returning prisoners of war exchanged by
cartel, and to the survivors of shipwrecks, like that of the *Lyme*,
lost in the Baltic in October 1760. The survivors of the *Lichfield*,
who endured more than a year of slavery after she was wrecked on
the coast of Morocco in November 1758, received not less than six
weeks' leave on their return, which appears to have been the longest leave granted by the Admiralty during the war.[8]

A particular means of granting leave was the bargain often
made with the men of returning East Indiamen. They were in a difficult position, for their ships were valuable and always heavily
escorted, so that they had little chance of escaping the press, but
after years away from home, with their 'adventures' of mer-
chandise to sell, they had an urgent need of leave. The obvious and
usual solution was to volunteer on condition of being allowed
some leave. This practice may well have been officially encouraged
by the East India Company, and was certainly attractive to all concerned on grounds of humanity and efficiency. The Admiralty

either ordered or approved such arrangements freely.' 'I am confident the public service will benefit by it,' Captain O'Bryen wrote of
one such agreement he had concluded,

> as they'll be well recruited in health after their tedious
> voyage from Canton and Limpo, and will be quite reco-
> vered of the scurvy which they all have, more or less, in
> their blood.[10]

The problem was of course to enforce such agreements, for only a
fool like Thomas Pye would trust an unsupported promise to return.[11] One method was for the men to sign a paper withholding
half their wages due from the East India Company until they
returned from leave, but the Admiralty found by experience that
such a contract was unenforceable at law, and instead required
that volunteers from Indiamen be entered and mustered before
going on leave, so that at least they were legally in the Service and
liable to be treated as deserters if they did not return. Sometimes
they did not, but all through the war such agreements were being
made nevertheless, for in practice the benefits, even the necessity,
of giving leave outweighed the inevitable losses.[12]

Leave was often given to ships' companies which were paid off
and turned over complete to another ship. Usually they were mustered on board their new ship, or some ship, before going on leave,
in order to ensure that they were legally obliged to return.[13] When
their new ship was to commission at another port men were sometimes given their 'conduct money' (travelling expenses) and told to
report there at the conclusion of their leave. When the *Princess
Louisa* paid off at Sheerness in April 1760 and her men turned over
to the *Modeste* at Portsmouth a cutter was ordered to carry their
sea chests and bedding round so that they might travel unencumbered. A similar arrangement was made in 1759 when some men
newly arrived in Portsmouth from the West Indies, and so entitled
to leave, were lent to bring the *Centaur* round to Sheerness, 'upon
condition they shall be allowed fourteen days' leave to return to
Portsmouth, and conduct money'.[14]

Sometimes when men were sent on leave it was not yet decided
where they were to serve, in which case they would be advised to
look out for advertisements in the newspapers for directions. In an

age when many seamen were illiterate and newspapers were expensive and of only local circulation, this seems an unreliable method, but the Admiralty used it regularly and appears to have found it satisfactory. It was employed to summon back men who had overstayed their leave ('advertise the *Mars*'s men that if they do not return to their ship directly they will be apprehended as deserters') and the Admiralty Office kept a list of the London papers in which the advertisements were inserted: the *Gazeteer*, *Daily Advertiser*, *Public Advertiser*, *Evening Advertiser*, *Whitehall Evening Post* and *General Evening Post*.[15]

Although the Admiralty habitually gave leave as a matter both of policy and necessity, it could not in wartime grant every request. Leave was refused to ships under sailing orders, to some, though not all men recently pressed into the Service, and to a ship of a squadron the rest of which had not had it, and would be jealous of any favouritism.[16] Leave was also sometimes declined by the men themselves. When the *Marlborough* paid off in September 1761 Admiral Durrell ordered a month's leave 'to all such as chooses that liberty to go and see their friends', while 'whatever number of men who have no friends to go to' were to help rigging other ships.[17] This must be a rare appearance of that inconspicuous figure, the provident and thrifty seaman, who preferred to earn money in rigging wages rather than spend it on the town.

Admiralty leave to whole ships' companies was frequently given, but it must have accounted for only a small fraction of the opportunities of leave available to the typical rating. Much more common than long leave by Admiralty order was leave for a day or two to a watch, a group of men or to individuals, granted by the captain when the ship was in port. This was part of the ordinary routine of the Service, and though it appears less often in official documents than long leave requiring Admiralty sanction, it was in fact much more frequent. We have seen that ships spent more than half their time in port, and there were many opportunities when men could be spared for a night or two. Captains were expected to use their discretion in such matters without bothering flag officers, though they could get into trouble for granting leave too freely.[18] The most common opportunity for leave was when ships came into harbour to dock and clean. The ships of the Navy were not yet

coppered, and had to have their bottoms scraped at regular intervals; the Navy Board's standing order required cruisers in home
waters to be docked, if possible, every six weeks, and the line of
battle ships usually came in three or four times a year. The yards
were remarkably efficient, and could dock, bream, scrape and pay
a third rate in two tides, working night and day.[19] They had to
work fast because the larger ships could only dock on the spring
tides, so the whole process of cleaning a ship, preferably several
ships in succession, had to be done in no more than a few days. If
there was too much work to complete in that time, the ship would
have to be 'neaped' in dock until the next spring. These month-
long stays in dock, when there was little for the ship's company to
do, were a good opportunity for leave, and all but the most untrustworthy men could hope for it. Even if a ship were in and out of
dock in twenty-four hours she would still be in port for a long
time, for ships had to be laboriously lightened to enter the dock by
landing guns, stores and tophamper. This required a lot of work,
some of it ashore in the dockyard, but there was usually opportunity to spare men for a while, and policy as well as humanity
suggested doing so, for men who had worked hard and behaved
well looked on a run ashore as their due, and it was far better to let
them go with leave than have them run away without.[20]

Ships came in to dock or to replenish stores at Plymouth, Portsmouth or Sheerness, for the upriver yards were difficult to get to,
and dealt in building and large refits. All these yards were fortified,
with guarded gates, and Portsmouth and Sheerness are on islands,
so there was very little chance of men let ashore for the day escaping. They might and often did get drunk and not return, but it was
not difficult to send out a patrol or two under reliable officers or
petty officers to round up one's men.[21] This sort of thing hardly
counted as breaking leave, and officers were extremely casual in
their attitudes to those who returned late. Lieutenant Thomas Lee
was acting in command of the *Royal George*, guardship at Portsmouth in the summer of 1760, and gave his men two days' leave,
fifty at a time. One man who failed to return was offered pardon
ten days after he was supposed to be back, and again a fortnight
later, and was only finally punished when a patrol brought him
back more than a month after his two days had expired.[22]

It was more difficult to give short leave overseas, where the risks of losing seamen were greater. Moreover there were no docks on foreign stations, and ships careening needed their own men to assist the weak staffs of the colonial yards. Nevertheless leave was given in foreign ports, at least to trustworthy men. Captain Middleton of the *Anson* gave some of his men leave in Barbados, and Rear-Admiral Steevens had to stop the leave given to his squadron in Bombay in April 1761 because 'great irregularities are committed by a number of seamen being suffered to ramble about on shore when they are not on duty'. On the coast of Sardinia Captain Hervey 'let the people all go on shore in different parties to refresh themselves and play about'.[23]

Ships in home waters, particularly in the Channel, often used the system of pressing men at sea out of inward-bound merchantmen as a disguised method of giving leave. The pressed men had to be replaced by others to navigate the ship in, and they obviously had to be men who could be trusted to return. They would receive a ticket of leave from their captain to cover the time needed to reach port and return overland. With a reasonable margin to allow for the vicissitudes of navigation this could provide a week or two ashore, and captains answered requests for leave by sending their men away pressing, so as to be lent in lieu and find their way ashore. Men lent in lieu in this way were often delayed on passage and overstayed their tickets of leave, which tempted others to prolong their leave, knowing it would be difficult to fault an excuse when they returned. As an alternative, some tried to alter their tickets to extend their time.[24]

Tricks like these are among the many things which make it very difficult to define what is meant by desertion from the Navy. Many men went adrift from their leave who were subsequently found, or returned by themselves, and attitudes to returning on time were less than rigorous. In individual cases it was often hard to say when a man passed from being overdue to being presumed a deserter. No one doubted, however, that some men would desert, and it is possible to give some idea of what proportion did so. When the *St George*'s men had leave in August 1758, twenty-three out of about 350 men failed to return. The company of the *Hornet* sloop had a month's leave on returning from the West Indies in

October 1759, and three out of about 110 men went missing. Admiral Smith was concerned to discover that thirty-three of the men of his former flagship had gone adrift from leave, out of about 600.[25] In these cases of general leave given to entire ships' companies, between 3 and 6 per cent failed to return. From the Admiralty's point of view, such losses were not trivial, but they were not sufficient to offset the benefits, indeed the necessity, of giving leave. Men had to be given leave, not only for their health and happiness, and consequently for the efficiency of the Service, but simply to attract seamen when they were desperately needed. The fact that 94 to 97 per cent of the ships' companies mentioned returned from their leave makes a nonsense of the idea of the Navy as a floating concentration camp, and one of the reasons why men did return to their ships when they might have run away is undoubtedly because all but a small minority of troublemakers could expect leave at intervals. The Navy was a reasonable employer, which gave its men considerable liberty, and lost only a few in the process. Had it given less leave, it might well have lost more men, for in this as in so many other respects, the Navy kept the services of its ratings not by the exercise of an authority which was in reality very weak, but by offering attractive conditions and opportunities.

CHAPTER V

❈

Manning

A THE PROBLEM

There was no difficulty in waging war at sea which caused the Navy so much anguish as manning. In almost every aspect of wartime operations, the problem of finding and keeping men was the first obstacle to be met, and the last to be overcome. It was undoubtedly the gravest weakness of the Navy as a fighting force, and might easily have been decisive in war if the French had not suffered the same problem.[1] Unfortunately, we still lack any useful analysis of how the Navy was manned. There are some official statistics, but they are not very informative in themselves, and positively misleading to the careless reader. Some historians who have examined these figures have indeed become thoroughly perplexed by them, and it is necessary to digress somewhat to look at them in detail.

An account of the number of men recruited into the Navy (distinguished as volunteers or pressed men) and of those lost to it (distinguished as discharges, desertions, and deaths from various causes) was called for by the House of Commons during the debate on the 1758 Navy Bill, and presented in January 1759. This covered the three years from Christmas 1754 to Christmas 1757, and it shows, among others, the following figures:

	1755	1756	1757
Recruits	31,126	19,758	19,682
Volunteers	9,943	4,662	5,765
Pressed	7,843	4,815	4,295

The problem is obvious; only 57 per cent of the recruits were shown as either volunteers or pressed men. Some extremely fanciful explanations have been proposed for the origins of the remaining 43 per cent,[2] but the solution is actually straightforward.

The House of Commons in fact asked for three different statements: of the numbers of men pressed and volunteered, of the cost of recruiting them, and of the numbers pressed at sea and the names of the ships from which they had been taken. The language of the resolutions is vague, and it is not certain if the Commons clearly understood what distinctions they meant to draw between the three requests.[3] What is clear is that after seven months of work, and an expenditure of £1200, the Navy Office was able to supply figures for the first two, but professed itself unable to produce any figures for the third, for want of materials in the office. Evidently the Navy Board understood the last request to refer to something different from the first two, and it seems to follow that the figures they did produce must cover only part of the recruiting effort.

Reading the detailed statement of expenses produced in response to the Commons' second request leaves no doubt that it refers to the cost of the Impress Service ashore (and afloat in creeks and rivers). This service was administered by the Navy Board, which was well able to total the salaries and expenses of the officers and men concerned, the cost of rewards for bringing in stragglers, of conduct money, of the cost of chartering tenders to transport the recruits, and of victualling their crews. All these expenses except the cost of tenders were attributable solely to the Impress Service ashore, and only for this could the Navy Board produce any distinction between volunteers and pressed men, using the muster books of the rendezvous or headquarters of each impress district.

Pressing at sea by warships, on the other hand, or by tenders manned by man-of-warsmen, was outside the Navy Board's purview, and occasioned no attributable expense, except part of the cost of chartering tenders, which were employed as required on recruiting at sea, transporting men recruited ashore, or other miscellaneous transport duties. There was indeed no way the Board could produce any detailed figures for the men raised at sea, or the cost of raising them. Moreover the cost of the Impress Service, which the Commons no doubt supposed, as modern historians have supposed,[4] to represent the cost of impressing men, actually represented the total expenses of a service which spent only part of its effort on impressment.

There is no doubt that the Navy Board's figures for pressed men and volunteers include only those recruited ashore. Moreover they profess to be what the Commons asked for, the totals of able and ordinary seaman and landmen. By this it seems probable that the figures actually meant ratings in general, for the clerks had no means of knowing how captains would rate their new recruits when they received them. They evidently do not include officers and servants, nor, probably, any of those who joined ships without passing through the hands of the Impress Service.

It is fairly certain that the Navy Board arrived at its total number of men taken into the Service as seamen or landmen from the weekly statements returned by captains and senior officers, which contained crude totals of new recruitment, sufficient to yield a rough idea of progress. It would not have been easy to distinguish ranks and ratings, or source of recruitment, and men raised overseas must have been included very late if at all. But these were the best figures the Navy Board possessed, and from them it compiled the mean numbers borne and mustered for each month and year.[5] It is not surprising that these figures do not very closely relate to those for the product of the Impress Service in the first three years of the war.

In 1763 the House of Commons received a statement showing the number of men raised during the war (184,893), remaining in service (49,673), killed in action (1,512), and died, discharged or deserted (133,708). Leaving aside the number of those killed in action, which could easily have been compiled from slain lists, it is evident that one of these three figures is the product of the addition or subtraction of the other two.[6] It should have been possible to produce a total of the number of men still in service from the weekly returns of 'state and condition', and it would have been possible, though laborious, to add up the numbers borne on every muster or pay book returned on a ship paying off since the beginning of the war, to give the total number of entries during the war. More likely total recruitment was also derived from the weekly returns. Subtracting the number remaining from those recruited would give the number of discharges from all causes. It certainly cannot be that these figures represent individual men, for there was no central manning record, and no possible means of determining how many times particular men had been entered in different ships, nor even how many times re-entered in the same ship. How plausible they are as totals for entries and discharges is difficult to say. It appears that ships on average discharged from all causes about half their companies each year.[7] Applying this to the mean numbers borne in the Navy as a whole in each year,[8] suggests that the total number of entries should have been about 340,000 rather than 185,000. It is possible that the figure of 50 per cent turnover a year, though a fair average of ships, may be too high for the Service as a whole, since the largest ships, with the largest crews, had generally the lowest turnover.

What is more, that 50 per cent includes discharges into other ships, which is almost certainly not true of the figure of 17,795 discharged in 1757 from all causes, including desertion, out of a mean of 63,259 borne in the whole Navy during that year,[9] making a turnover of only 28 per cent. If this figure were typical of every year of the war the annual mean numbers borne would imply about 208,000 entries during the war, which is not impossibly far from 185,000. Moreover it should be noted that that total purports to be of seamen and marines. If it really excludes officers, which seems doubtful in view of the labour needed to isolate them in the statistics, the discrepancy of 23,000 entries is largely accounted for. It is probable that the truth will not be certainly known until the musters are seriously analysed; meanwhile it is well to remember that the Navy Board had more incentive and more opportunity to provide the House of Commons with some impressive-seeming statistics, than actually to get them accurate.

The reason why the Commons were interested in how many men were recruited for the Navy, and at what cost, was no doubt the same reason that the 1758 Act was passed. Many observers in the eighteenth century believed, and not a few since have believed, that the supply of seamen was so large as to be virtually infinite, and the Navy's recruiting problems arose solely from its unattractiveness to seamen.[10] Pamphleteers proposing novel means of manning the Navy, of whom there were many, generally concentrated on making the Service more attractive in the confidence that the seamen were there if only they could be tempted to serve.[11] Modern studies have been written in a very similar vein, concluding that a want of political will to pay seamen in the Navy more highly, or to institute some scheme of conscription analogous to the French *inscription*, condemned the Navy to struggle on with the inefficient, costly and distasteful system of impressment. The most recent work on the subject concludes simply that higher pay and limited service would have been the 'real solution' to the manning problem.[12]

This is surprising, because eighteenth-century government had figures available (from the Sixpenny Office, which collected a levy on the pay of merchant seamen for the support of Greenwich Hospital) suggesting that on the eve of the Seven Years' War, when the Navy had only 10,000 men, the merchant service employed about 34,000.[13] Since by 1760 the Navy had expanded to over 85,000, and merchant ships were apparently employing more rather than fewer men than before the war, there was an apparent deficit of about 80,000 men, or nearly double the total employed before the war. One might have thought that this was sufficient to account for all the Navy's problems.

In fact it is probable that these statistics made the situation seem even worse than it was, for the returns from the Sixpenny Office understated the true number of merchant seamen. It has been calculated that there may have been as many as 80,000 seamen and fishermen outside the Navy before the war, of whom at least 60,000 were needed in wartime. In addition many men were employed in privateers, possibly more than 20,000 in 1757, though privateering from British ports declined steeply thereafter, with only a brief resurgence when Spain entered the war in 1762.[14] These figures suggest that wartime demand for seamen, from all services, exceeded supply by no more than two, rather than three to one – still an adequate explanation for all the Navy's difficulties.

Since there were not, and never could have been, enough experienced seafaring men to man the Navy, its recruitment problem resolved itself into three parts: in competition with the merchant service it had to find as many seamen as possible, it had to recruit landmen to make up the numbers, and it had to reduce wastage as far as possible. Pressing was a partial solution to the first problem. Only seamen, or more specifically 'seamen, seafaring men and persons whose occupations or callings are to work in vessels and boats upon rivers' were liable to be impressed. It was neither legally nor practically possible to press anyone who did not fit this description, and suggestions to the contrary are quite wrong, at least as relating to the mid-eighteenth century.[15] It is true that pressed landmen are occasionally to be found in ships' musters, but they can be accounted for either as watermen and river boatmen, who were liable for impressment but effectively quite unskilled in seafaring, or as landmen pressed by constables and magistrates.[16] The importance of the press to the Navy lay not so much in its numerical contribution as in its selective ability to take skilled seamen, the class the Navy stood most in need of.

The press was highly distasteful to all, but it was accepted by everyone who had any experience of the subject as an unavoidable necessity. 'No man who had the least spark of humanity but must be very sensible of the hardships in impressing seamen,' one officer said, and a press lieutenant, intercepting some escaping men,

> could not refrain from shedding the sympathetic tear myself. Is it not a hard case to act a part so repugnant to one's nature and temperament? But would it not be the worst of acts to eat the bread of one's country and betray its most material interests? For, however unconstitutional it may be to deprive this useful class of people of their liberty above all others, it is an act of necessity that can not be dispensed with, and whoever coolly considers the nature of the thing will soon be convinced that it is the mode, and the only mode, that upon an emergency will or can humble the arrogance and insolence of the House of Bourbon. Seamen were now much wanted, and seamen were to be procured at all events to bring affairs to a happy crisis.

> Such are the methods frequently made use of to obtain seamen for the Service in this land of liberty. It seems

shocking to the feelings of humanity ... It is a hardship
which nothing but absolute necessity can reconcile to
our boasted freedom.[17]

These three quotations are similar in tone, but though the first two
come from officers, the last is the opinion of a seaman who had
himself been pressed into the Navy. Impressment was universally
accepted as an evil, but to nearly everyone concerned, even perhaps for the seamen themselves, it was a lesser evil.[18] Everyone
could and did condemn it, civil authorities ashore often worked
actively to frustrate it, but no one cared to replace it. In the political climate of the day, bills proposing even a mild element of compulsory registration were denounced as tyranny worthy of Genghis
Khan or the Spanish Inquisition.[19] Even if the theory of conscription had been acceptable, it is doubtful if the practice would have
been much less chaotic and unjust than impressment, given the
extreme shortage of seamen. All registration schemes, including
the French *inscription*, depended for fairness and effectiveness on a
supply of seamen sufficient to provide for each man a regular
rotation of duty broken by periods of freedom. If the necessary
surplus of men were not available, which it never was, there was
no alternative to indefinite service. If the men disliked indefinite
service, which they did, there was no alternative to compulsion.
Compulsion in turn made the Service odious and repelled volunteers, so worsening its difficulties and increasing its dependence on
the press.

The Navy had to meet this situation in various ways. It recruited large numbers of landmen to make up the numbers of each
ship's company. It distributed the product of the press 'so that the
ships may be as equally manned as possible', and commanders did
not find themselves, like Captain Clements of the *Actaeon* in
February 1758, with only a dozen men 'capable of getting on a
yard when under double-reefed topsails'.[20] Another palliative
measure was lending men from ships in port. Since the typical ship
spent less than half her time in commission at sea, the scope for
this was theoretically large, but in practice being in port seldom
meant lying idle; ships awaiting a fair wind, or taking in stores, or
stripping for the dock, could hardly spare any men. Moreover it

was bad in principle to break up settled ships' companies to meet short-term exigencies:

> it is to be wished that every ship should form a regular ship's company, which will be much broken into if we go on borrowing and lending.[21]

Nevertheless men were lent, especially the inevitable floating population of men returning from leave, hospital or pressing, or for some other reason detached from their ships. In midwinter, to judge from some figures for 1757 and 1759, ships then in home ports had lent between 7 and 8 per cent of their men (that is, of those borne, presumably including supernumeraries belonging to other ships). In the summer of 1757 over 17 per cent of the much smaller number then in port had been lent, but two years later, in July 1759, that figure had fallen to under 12 per cent.[22]

   Expedients like this were palliatives, most useful to meet short-term needs. In extreme emergency very large numbers of men could be borrowed in this way. In November 1759 Admiral Holburne commanding at Portsmouth learnt that the French invasion fleet was at sea some days before he received the news of Hawke's great victory over it. Fearful that Conflans might elude the pursuit, Holburne ruthlessly stripped every ship which could not be got to sea at once to man every one which could, and in twenty-four hours had assembled a respectable battle fleet. The Admiralty highly approved his 'zeal, despatch and circumspection . . . never more necessary than at this juncture'.[23] But what would answer in an emergency was no solution to the general problem. There was no single solution to that, but the double effect of the press to bring in the necessary minimum of skilled seamen, and volunteers to make up the numbers, was successful. For all the difficulties and delays of manning, it is rare to find a ship in home waters obliged to put to sea below her established complement, and there were occasions, as in the winter of 1760–1761, when it was reported from Portsmouth that 'we are not now in distress for men', or even that there was an embarrassing surplus.[24] The story of the manning of the Navy during the Seven Years' War is one of protracted difficulty rather than failure.

B VOLUNTEERS

The recruitment of volunteers was the basic method of manning the Navy. In peacetime it was almost always the only method necessary, and even in wartime there were always many men willing to volunteer. The problem was that there were not enough of them, and in particular not enough seamen among them.

It is extremely difficult to say with certainty what proportion of the men of the Navy were volunteers. Individual ships' companies show percentages varying between one- and two-thirds,[1] but the ships' musters distinguish three main means of recruitment into a ship: volunteers, pressed men and men turned over from other ships. To modern eyes accustomed to the idea of men joining the Service as a whole, the category of 'turned-over' seems anomalous, but it reflected both the legal and the real situation in the eighteenth century, when a man could be said to have joined the Navy only as a side effect of his joining a King's ship. It mattered far more how long a man had been in his present ship, than whether his last had belonged to the King or a merchant. For the historian, the turn-overs, who in wartime often formed a large part if not the whole of a ship's company, make it difficult to arrive at a clear idea of the proportion of volunteers to pressed men. In the first three years of the war, the Impress Service ashore raised rather more volunteers than pressed men, but we do not have figures for pressing at sea, certainly the most important source of impressed seamen, nor for officers, servants and marines, probably the largest group of volunteers. Moreover the figures for the Impress Service do not distinguish seamen from landmen. In the eighteen months from January 1759 to June 1760 the rendezvous at Hull collected 313 men, made up thus:[2]

	Able	Ordinary	Landmen	Totals
Volunteered ashore	41	35	32	108
Volunteered afloat	4	3	0	7
Pressed ashore	90	46	2	138
Pressed afloat	30	18	0	48
Pressed by magistrates	3	7	2	12
Totals	168	109	36	313

There is no way of knowing how typical these proportions were of an Impress district at that stage of the war, and strong reason to think that the situation changed as the war progressed. The sums paid in bounty to volunteers for each year of the war were as follows:

1755	£16,803 0s. 0d.
1756	£16,335 10s. 0d.
1757	£11,676 10s. 0d.
1758	£9,406 0s. 0d.
1759	£12,767 10s. 0d.
1760	£8,868 0s. 0d.
1761	£4,312 10s. 0d.
1762	£16,121 10s. 0d. (including arrears)[3]

This cannot be translated into numbers of men, because able seamen received more than ordinary seamen and landmen, but as the rates of bounty rose at intervals during the war, it is obvious that the number of volunteer seamen declined steeply, which is what one would expect as the overall shortage of seamen developed.

In ordinary times, when supply and demand were more or less in balance, there was seldom any lack of volunteers for the Navy. This was true of the opening months of the war, and even as late as 1757, when merchantmen were offering up to £40 a man for the voyage to England, a warship at Charleston, South Carolina, reported no lack of volunteers. In December of that year a sloop touching at Oporto found English seamen there keen to enter the Navy.[4] We have already seen some of the reasons why they might have wished to join a King's ship regardless of higher wages elsewhere. Less work, better food and the chance of prize money were doubtless among their considerations. Patriotism may have played a part, though on the whole eighteenth-century patriotism expected its reward, and public opinion did not think it any nobler to join the fighting services simply because the country was at war. One certain temptation was the excitement, real or imagined, of active service in wartime. Guardships, which in peacetime offered the most comfortable and sought-after berths in the Navy, suffered greatly on the outbreak of war as all the best men seized a chance to transfer to a sea-going ship.[5] It was said of one in 1776 that

> she is as well manned, my Lord, as the situation of a guardship under the temptation of active service going on under her boltsprit for these eighteen months past would admit.[6]

Apart from the working of the Impress Service ashore, of which more later, it is difficult to say much about the mechanisms by which volunteer seamen were recruited. It appears to have been largely a matter of individual contacts, as it must have been, for seamen were by the nature of their profession scattered individuals if not individualists, seldom to be found in any social unit larger than a ship's company. Seamen volunteers could usually be found only in ones and twos, so that even in peacetime it was a slow and often troublesome business to build up a ship's company.[7] The volunteers might in principle be available, but it was not necessarily quick and easy to collect them. It was this which gave a decisive advantage to the commander with a good following, even in peacetime. The more and better the seamen who would seek him out on hearing that he was commissioning a ship, the more fortunate he was.

When it came to recruiting landmen, as most captains had to do in wartime, the situation was different. Landmen were recruited by the Impress Service, but most officers preferred to recruit directly if they could, and almost invariably they looked first to their own home districts. This was especially true of officers drawn, as so many were, from the landed gentry, and it seems to have been truest of all of those from the remoter and poorer parts of the three kingdoms, where no doubt the pay and opportunities of the Navy were most attractive to the landless labourer. The first reaction of an officer learning that he was appointed to a ship was often to send home for men:

> Lieutenant Bover, on his being appointed to the *Buckingham*, wrote to a friend of his at Wells in Norfolk, to enter as many volunteer seamen as he could.[8]

As this quotation shows, seamen as well as landmen could be found in this way by those who were fortunate enough to have connections in seaport towns and villages, like Captain Warwick of the *Jason* in Falmouth and Captain Baillie of the *Tartar's Prize* in Dublin. In 1755 Captain Porter of the *Prince Frederick* raised fifty keelmen and seamen in Newcastle.[9] The most striking instances, however, are of landmen recruited, sometimes in large numbers, from officers' home districts, if not from their ancestral estates. This was so common a situation that people tended to assume that any landed gentleman captain would have at least some followers from home. During the siege of the Morro Castle at Havana in 1762, the army requested the assistance of any former miners who might be in the ships, to help driving the sap. It at once occurred to Keppel, commanding the inshore squadron, that Pocock's flagship the *Namur* was the obvious source: 'your own ship is the most likely to be able to furnish, as she did belong to a Cornish chief, Admiral Boscawen'.[10] A Cornish admiral meant Cornishmen, and Cornishmen meant miners. When Boscawen commissioned the *Torbay* in 1755 he had fifty-five of 'my Cornishmen', 'stout fellows, but all landmen', besides a hundred Scots raised by one of the lieutenants.[11] The same story could be repeated many times for officers from all parts of the three kingdoms and beyond. Captain Saumarez raised men in Guernsey, Captain Lobb (a Cornish follower of Boscawen's) around Mount's Bay, and Captain Douglas, MP for Orkney, in those islands.[12] In July 1768 Captain O'Bryen of the *Solebay* had, among 104 men whose birthplace is stated in the ship's musters, not less than thirty-two from his own county of Cork, and a further seven from the neighbouring county of Kerry.[13]

An even more striking example is the *Elizabeth*, commissioned at Portsmouth in January 1778 by Captain the Hon. Frederick Maitland, a younger son of the Earl of Lauderdale. The able seamen and petty officers of the ship came from all over Britain and Ireland, indeed all over the world, with no strong concentration from any one county except Fife and Midlothian. Apart from these Scotsmen, their connections with Maitland, if any, were undoubtedly the personal ties of seamen followers to their patron. Among the ordinary seamen and landmen, the new recruits to seafaring, the situation was completely different. More than 70 per cent of them came from Fife and the neighbouring counties about the shores of the Forth and Tay: Angus, Kincardine, Perth and the Lothians. More than a quarter of the entire ship's company came from the single county of Fife, around the estates which Maitland's wife brought him.[14] It would hardly be too much to say that officers like Captain Maitland carried their tenantry to war much as their ancestors had done centuries before.

This was not the only way that landmen might be recruited, for ratings as well as officers had friends and relations whom they might persuade to join them. The *Belleisle* commissioned at Plymouth in March 1777 with a ship's company drawn from many different parts, including two Frenchmen born in the island from which she took her name. There is no indication of any significant territorial recruitment by any of her officers. Roughly half the able seamen, petty officers and idlers came from nine counties: in descending order, Devon, London, Cork, Cornwall, Lancashire, Kent, Dublin, Northumberland and Dorset. There is nothing surprising in these counties individually – all were maritime counties with seaports and seamen – but their distribution was distinctive, for there were few men from several counties strongly connected with the Navy, and none at all from Hampshire or Sussex, which must have made the *Belleisle* all but unique. It is therefore significant that the ordinary seamen and landmen came from the same counties, and in virtually the same proportions, as the experienced men. Out of a total of 211 men whose place of birth is stated, only nineteen newcomers came from counties unrepresented by experienced men, and fifteen of those were the only pressed ordinary seamen aboard.[15] Since the *Belleisle* sent out no recruiting parties apart from one to London, it is difficult to see what persuaded men to make their way to Plymouth from places as remote as Northumberland and Dublin to join a ship they had probably never seen, unless it was the seamen already in the ship sending to their home districts to encourage their friends and connections to join them.

It seems probable that personal connections of one sort or another played a crucial rôle in recruiting volunteers, but there were many who came to join the Navy without necessarily having any acquaintance with individual officers and men. This must have been the case with the many foreigners who were willing to serve. There were men from every nation under heaven in the Navy, sometimes swept up in the press, but more often volunteers. Cretans, Danes, Italians, Portuguese, Swedes, Hanoverians, Americans of every colony and every colour, they appear in almost all ships' musters.[16] Men, both Britons and foreigners, deserted to the Navy from every organized service in Europe; from the army and the militia,[17] the East India Company's ships and army,[18] from the Dutch army, navy and East India Company,[19] the French navy, the Austrian army, and even the Prussian East India Company.[20] Prisoners of war, both French and neutral, often volunteered to serve, as did British prisoners in similar circumstances in France, but the French were in a worse position, for so many more had been made prisoners that many had no hope of being exchanged by cartel, and no other means of getting out of prison than to volunteer as seamen or marines.[21] Neutral seamen were welcome in the Navy, but Frenchmen, not surprisingly, proved unreliable, and by 1762 no more were being accepted.[22] Some Spaniards who had volunteered as neutrals, and then found themselves transformed into enemies when Spain entered the war, were by a humane Admiralty order paid off and sent home in a neutral merchantman.[23] Men often volunteered for or deserted to the Navy from British merchantmen, including the transports whose crews were protected from the press.[24] The Havana expedition was nearly paralysed at the outset by the number of men who ran from the transports to serve in the Navy. Men even deserted the marines to become seamen, losing wages and risking punishment to do something which was officially encouraged anyway.[25]

One source of willing volunteers which made a small but not insignificant contribution to the Navy was the debtor's prisons. With the notable exception of smugglers, criminals were almost never accepted,[26] but debtors for sums not over £20 could be released to serve in the Navy under the provisions of an act of 1706, and as there were usually about 2000 people in prison for debt in England and Wales this was not a negligible source of recruits. During the war of 1739 to 1748 the Admiralty solicitor paid

£624 4s. 10d. in legal expenses for clearing a total of 487 men out of gaol, and the process was continuing throughout the Seven Years' War.[27] No man would stay in gaol who had contrivance enough to get to sea, where he could enjoy more room, better food and commonly better company, besides many other advantages.[28]

Another minority which contributed usefully to manning the Navy was blacks. In America and the West Indies there were many black seamen, slave and free, and they were evidently quite common in the Navy,[29] though it is impossible to establish any figures, as they were not officially distinguished in any way. The Navy's attitude towards them was liberal by the standards of the societies from which they had come, and it is easy to see the attractions of a world in which a man's professional skill mattered more than his colour. Some black seamen chose to remain in the West Indies, turning over to other ships when theirs were ordered home. John Hutton and Peter Lewis, two black seamen of the *Jamaica* sloop in 1757, had served continuously on the Jamaica station for twenty-two years.[30] Many others followed their ships wherever they served, like the black seaman who was the principal prosecution witness in a court martial for sodomy held at the Nore in 1761. This was almost the only crime in the Navy for which the death penalty was both awarded and executed, and the accused, understandably desperate, objected to the witness 'as it was never known that a black should swear against a Christian'.[31] The reaction of the court to this gives an indication of officers' views of colour. They took the objection literally to be to a pagan giving evidence under oath. The black man having shown that he was a Christian (Commodore Keppel was his godfather) and understood the meaning of an oath, the court accepted his evidence and proceeded to convict on it. These officers' willingness to hang two white men largely on the evidence of a black is an interesting illustration of the Navy's relatively liberal outlook on questions of colour.

This attitude did not extend to a questioning of the institution of slavery. Some officers were slave-owners themselves, either because they were planters, like Captain Forrest in Jamaica,[32] or because they took slaves to sea. Commodore Douglas in the Leeward Islands manned his private sloops partly with slaves, some of whom were free Negroes and mulattoes made prisoner of war and condemned to slavery.[33] This was a practice both sides indulged in, but British officers protested strongly when their own men were enslaved.[34] There was more to this than a simple double standard, for French practice was different in important respects. On both sides in the West Indies privateers were little better than pirates, the universal enemies of mankind. To encourage blacks to engage in this sort of warfare seemed to the British dangerously near to encouraging that general assault upon white society in the islands, a slave rebellion – a prospect equally disastrous for either side. So they reacted fiercely when they took black or mulatto seamen out of privateers. Their own men, on the other hand, were serving in King's ships, fighting a regular war by the conventional rules which posed no threat to the fabric of society, and it seemed to their officers that they were as entitled to the amenities of civilized warfare as their white shipmates.

Some British officers went so far as to carry their own slaves to sea in the King's ships,[35] but this was best done under disguise, for naval opinion in general and the Admiralty's in particular inclined to regard a man-of-war as a little piece of British territory in which slavery was improper. In the East Indies in the 1740s Captain Tiddeman of the *Elizabeth* concealed some of his slaves under false names in the muster, thus:

> George Wright, Ordinary = Coffee
> Edward Hughes = Webb
> Richard Jones, Trumpeter = Soboir
> Stephen Wright, Ordinary = Black Will
> James Quelch, Trumpeter = Quashey
> John Williams = Black Jack[36]

In rare cases when owners claimed back from the Navy slaves whose ownership was beyond dispute, the Admiralty was prepared to release them, as it did in the case of some slaves impressed: 'these negro slaves shared the same fate with such free-born white men as we could pick up at a very critical time'.[37] But the owner of William Stephens, a Maryland slave, was refused, for the Admiralty evidently felt that as a volunteer he deserved protection, besides being an experienced seamen, and too valuable to lose.[38] The same line was taken with slaves fleeing from enemy plantations, and even from those of the East India Company.[39] Their Lordships' attitude is well illustrated by the tale of William Castillo, a slave seaman who in 1751 was serving in a merchant-man trading out of Boston, commanded by James Jones. Fearing that he was to be sold ashore, and much preferring the seafaring life, Castillo persuaded the master to buy him. Jones made him his apprentice, and promised to emancipate him when his wages had made up his purchase price, but five years later, tired of waiting for freedom, Castillo ran away. In 1758, in Portsmouth, he was unlucky enough to meet his former owner, by then the master of the *Northumberland*, who arrested him, put him in an iron collar on board his ship, and threatened to sell him in Barbados. In this condition Castillo wrote to the Admiralty begging its protection. Their Lordships' rection was vigorous:

> Acquaint Admiral Holburne that the laws of this country admit of no badges of slavery, therefore the Lords hope and expect whenever he discovers any at-tempt of this kind he should prevent it; and that the Lords desire to be informed how Castillo is rated on the ship's books.[40]

They wanted to know how he was rated in order to be sure that he would receive his own wages as an able seaman, not hand them over to his master as an officer's servant. They had no objection to a prime seaman being pressed into the Service, but once in it he was entitled to the same consideration as any other man. To anyone bred on the plantation, this must have been a refreshing world of relative equality.

There remained various other sources of manpower which the Navy was able to tap. Returned prisoners of war exchanged by cartel were one, though so many found means to get ashore before they could be collected by the Navy that they represented an ad-dition to the nation's stock of seamen rather than the Navy's. In the Leeward Islands the squadron depended heavily on returned prisoners, and Commodore Douglas found that his efforts to in-jure the French by sending captured privateersmen to England caused his own squadron to suffer as much as the enemy.[41] In home waters guardships and others were able to recruit some volunteers from Greenwich Hospital.[42] One of them was Andrew Ferguson, a man of nearly seventy, who overestimated his strength:

> Thinking I was able I was willing to serve his Majesty again as long as I could anyways under honourable Captain Rodney, hearing he was so good a commander, which I always found, which made me more willing to serve under him, and am greatly sorry that I cannot serve him no longer.[43]

A supply of rather younger recruits was found in 1756 by Lord Harry Powlett, who took poor boys from the streets of London and clothed them at his own expense to add to his crew. This is said to have given the idea to Jonas Hanway to found the Marine Society, a practical charity which took destitute (but not, it should be noted, criminal) London boys, gave them clothes and some elementary training, and sent them to sea either in the Navy or in the merchant service.[44] In the course of the war the Society sent into the Navy 10,625 boys and men, at least 5 per cent of the Navy's total recruitment during the war, and a most effective example of Christian charity for the poor of London. Boscawen considered that 'no scheme for the manning of the Navy within my knowledge has ever had the success of the Marine Society'.

Sometimes the Admiralty was able to come to agreements with towns which offered to raise men in return for freedom from the press, or for a ship assigned to protect their trade. The Bristol Society of Merchant Venturers had a regular arrangement of this sort, with two ships assigned to the Bristol Channel 'except in cases of the greatest emergency'. The senior officer at Plymouth in 1756 got into trouble for borrowing one of them.[45] Boscawen offered a ship to Philadelphia on similar terms, but she was declined.[46] Elsewhere town councils, like that of Hull, added extra money to the official bounty, or groups were active like the 'gentlemen of Cornwall' who raised ninety-six men for the Savage sloop in 1759.[47] In such cases patriotism was probably mixed with the hope that it would be rewarded with more protection from enemy privateers or the press gang.

Volunteers were the first and the fundamental means of manning the Navy. Seamen were obviously the most valuable, but landmen 'mix very well with seasoned ships' companies, though the captains do complain of them'.[48] Naturally commanders always hoped for seamen in preference to landmen, but as Captain Wheeler put it:

> Nor will I ever keep (knowingly) a dissatisfied man in any ship with me, if he were the best seaman in the world; I would rather have a willing and contented landman, who with a little time, and his own endeavours, I could make a seaman of.[49]

The difficulty of knowing how many volunteers there were is compounded by the impossibility of telling how many 'volunteers' had only offered themselves to escape the press. The Admiralty had to reprove officers for accepting 'volunteers' and paying them bounty *after* they had been pressed. This cost the Crown money, but it saved the officers trouble, and avoided any risk of the pressed men claiming protections.[50] Admiral Smith, who was given to exaggeration, claimed that 'seven out of eight take that name [volunteer] only for the bounty, and are as improper to be trusted as those who appear as pressed men in the weekly account'.[51] This sounds most unlikely, and in any case rather misses the point, for if it was ever true that volunteers liked the Service and pressed men hated it, it ceased to be true very soon after men joined their ships. It was not unknown for pressed men who had petitioned for release to have changed their minds and decided to stay by the time an answer came from the Admiralty, and it was equally true that volunteers often changed their minds and deserted.[52] It is therefore to an extent misconceived, as well as very difficult, to estimate the proportion of volunteers in the Navy. What is certain is that they were numerous, and indispensable to the prosecution of the war.

C IMPRESSMENT

There are few aspects of eighteenth-century history which have aroused more passion and less accuracy than the press gang. It was odious to all who knew it, it had no defenders except as a cruel necessity, and to condemn it was easy and popular. It was, and is, tempting to offer facile condemnation rather than workable alternatives. But the political reality of eighteenth-century England was that the very forces which made the press so unpopular also made it inevitable. Englishmen prided themselves on their liberties, by which as a rule they meant the rights of local authority against central. Government found it extremely difficult to enforce its will in the provinces,[1] and was itself controlled by a House of Commons in which independent members held the balance of power. Its commands were executed, or not, by an unpaid magistracy whose political obligations were almost entirely local. The Navy, and consequently the press, was pre-eminently an instrument of central government, and potentially of 'tyranny'. For many Englishmen it was a patriotic duty, or at least a political necessity, to oppose the unpopular actions of government, and above all to oppose any extension of government's power to control and regulate. Thus, in the midst of war, public opinion and the law still worked strongly to hamper the Navy. Even men who were most in favour of the war were active in damaging the Navy's capacity to fight it. To modern eyes this seems illogical and hypocritical, but that was the reality with which the Navy had to live. The Admiralty had seen too many schemes of conscription or registration damned as instruments of despotism to have any more hope of a system less arbitrary, less brutal, and in truth less despotic, than the press.[2] Though it bore harshly, erratically and inefficiently, it bore largely on an inarticulate and politically weak group, and the alternatives proposed seemed to threaten more powerful interests. So the Admiralty was obliged to make the best of an extremely unsatisfactory job.

There were two entirely different circumstances in which pressing took place, having hardly anything in common beyond the legal position. At sea recruiting was done by men-of-war, or tenders belonging to them, out of inward-bound merchantmen within soundings. The recruits were almost all seamen or seafaring men, and most were probably pressed rather than volunteers. On land recruiting was done either by parties sent out by particular ships, or by what came to be known as the Impress Service (the term was not yet universal during the Seven Years' War, but it is convenient to use it).[3] This organization dealt in all forms of recruitment, both of volunteers and pressed men. In fact it had three functions of broadly equal importance: recruiting volunteers, pressing, and acting as a police force to control straggling and desertion.

The Impress Service was disposed under captains or commanders, sometimes called regulating captains, appointed one to each district (in principle each county made a district) with a number of lieutenants under them. Each captain, and sometimes each lieutenant, established a headquarters or 'rendezvous', invariably in an inn, where he solicited recruits and lodged them – in the case of pressed men, imprisoned them.[4] Most Impress districts were centred on a seaport where one or two tenders would lie afloat to receive men and convey them to Portsmouth, Plymouth or the Nore. These tenders might have a cutter or boats attached to recruit in the stream and the offing. Each lieutenant had a 'gang', ideally of seamen, but sometimes of local toughs engaged for the purpose. Seamen were preferable because they could and did persuade people to volunteer, which mere violence would never do, and unlike a local gang, they would not be afraid of their neighbours' reprisals if violence were needed.[5] In the case of lieutenants sent up by their own ships to open a rendezvous, usually in London, the gang was always composed of their shipmates, which gave the best prospects of recruiting volunteers, for seamen were much more likely to enter for a particular ship of which they heard well than for the Service as a whole. When it came to recruiting landmen, there was nothing like a real sailor with his romantic tales and his exotic appearance to lure the raw countryman away to sea, and press officers brought their gangs to fairs and markets, or sent them into the countryside at the end of the harvest, with this object.[6] A lieutenant of the St George sent to Salisbury on a report of seamen there,

> met with no success in pressing, but seventeen entered
> voluntarily with him for the *St George* and five for the
> *Prince George*. Of the former ten are seafaring people,
> and the remainder able-bodied landmen.[7]

To encourage and retain good men in the gangs they were well paid, if specially recruited, or received extra allowances if belonging to a ship. The officers likewise received substantial allowances and large expense accounts. All this made the Impress Service costly, though estimates of the cost of each man pressed vary widely, not to say wildly, and are nearly all based on the misconception that the costs of the service could be attributed solely to impressment.[8] For officers the high pay was an incentive to accept service ashore. One lieutenant who had a pension for the loss of an arm calculated his earnings as an Impress officer from half-pay, pension, Impress allowance and subsistence as 14s. 6d. a day (more than the captain of a third rate), plus 10s. for each able seaman raised, and all lodging and travelling expenses. His full pay at sea would have been 4s. a day (plus 5s. pension), with no opportunities for an agreeable time among female society.[9] Moreover it was not true at that date that the Impress Service was only for failed officers. It was regarded as active service, and indeed the lieutenant who had lost his arm applied for the job partly to establish that he was not disabled: 'it was ... putting to the test, whether or not their Lordships looked upon me as a pensioned officer incapacitated for further service'.[10] Many of the Impress captains were young and energetic officers who looked forward to a command as the proper reward for their labours. George Peard was reportedly given command of the *Savage* sloop for raising 150 men, and James Smith, midshipman of the *Hampton Court*, actually proposed a bargain: 200 men for his commission as a lieutenant, or 50 for a first lieutenancy of marines (a revealing index of the standing of marine officers).[11] Their Lordships prudently declined to give the commission until they had received the men, but apparently did not disapprove the principle. Many commanders served for a while as Impress officers before resuming their sea careers, and some promising captains like John Bover, who suffered from constant scurvy, chose shore duty from personal preference.[12] There was some scope for employing elderly or less fit officers, but a regulating captain had a demanding job calling for character and ability. It was not for the feeble or the hesitant.

It has been said that Impress officers were easily corrupted, and their position certainly gave opportunities for blackmail, but the only such accusation made during the Seven Years' War was against the lieutenant commanding a press tender – a duty which did tend to be the repository of the least useful officers.[13] What was often complained of against regulating captains was their alleged willingness to accept recruits of very poor quality. They had an obvious incentive to take an optimistic view of the health and strength of potential recruits, since their efficiency was being judged by the numbers they raised, and an equally good motive for taking an optimistic view of the skill of those they accepted, as they received a bounty of ten shillings for each seaman but only five shillings for each landman.[14] There were particular complaints of men sent from Bristol and Gloucester:

> The sending such men is aggrieving the subject, embarrassing me to dispose of them, of no use to the public, a great expense to the government, and tends to no other purpose than to make their numbers raised appear considerable to their Lordships.[15]

Sea officers were good at colourful description of the poor quality of their recruits:

> numbers being invalids, incurables for various diseases, blind, lame, ruptured, and the rest the dregs of the earth, having been refused by all the ships they've been offered to,[16]

but they too were not disinterested. It suited them to make the most of their difficulties with 'landmen, very ordinary seamen and invalids',[17] in the hope of getting good seamen instead, or at least of gilding their achievements and excusing their failures. One need not therefore take their complaints against the regulating captains quite literally, though there really was a permanent residue of unemployable recruits, many from the Impress Service, who were refused by every captain who saw them

> as they say they are full if bad men; if good, they find room. So the poor fellows go as supernumeraries from ship to ship and belong to none. There are many in this situation; the men serve for nothing, and it makes the greatest confusion.[18]

The disposition and employment of Impress Officers and their gangs varied greatly according to their circumstances. The hapless lieutenant attempting to recruit at Poole with a gang of two[19] was clearly less well placed than his brother officers in Shropshire at the same date, where Captain Harman had his rendezvous at Shrewsbury and his officers carefully disposed about the country:

> Lieutenant William Smith visited Welshpool and Ludlow, Lieutenant John Becher was stationed occasionally at Kidderminster, Bridgnorth and Newport, and Lieutenant Charles Henley, as he had not yet learned to ride a live horse, was constantly at head-quarters.[20]

It was exceptional, however, for a gang to exceed a dozen men, and these three officers with their little parties represented a very thin coverage of the county. In November 1762 when Harman's successor broke up his rendezvous he reported having raised sixty men in eight months. At the beginning of the war recruiting ashore was much easier, and at King's Lynn Captain Patrick Baird raised 410 men between February and May 1755, in spite of lukewarm co-operation from the local authorities.[21]

Their attitude, in this and most other districts, was crucial to the Impress Service's success. It was customary, though not legally necessary, for officers to get their press warrants 'backed' (endorsed) by local magistrates, which many refused to do.[22] This was only the beginning of the officer's difficulties. It was rare to find a mayor of any seaport who would offend his electors to help the Navy, and in many towns and cities the magistrates used every legal and illegal means to frustrate recruitment. The Lord Mayor of London was publicly thanked for defeating the press; the mayor of Gravesend threatened to imprison the press officers, and the local justices refused to attest sworn statements of what he had said.[23] Liverpool was violently opposed to the presence of the Navy even in search of volunteers, and the mayor let it be known that he would throw the officers in prison before any man would be pressed in his town; 'there's not a seaport in England where a man fights so much uphill to carry on the Impress Service as at Liverpool'. The mob damaged the rendezvous, murdered several supposed informers, nearly killed the regulating captain, and completely cowed the town council – which, ironically enough, had to be rescued from corn rioters by the Navy.[24]

Though impressment itself was unquestionably legal, the threat to imprison officers and their gangs was not idle, for magistrates frequently disposed of these unwelcome arrivals under colour of law. In Massachusetts a couple of men on leave were imprisoned as a reprisal for pressing at sea, and in Southwark an entire gang was imprisoned after a fight with privateersmen.[25] In Bristol, where the local authorities were usually quite co-operative, Captain Graves found himself pressing during a by-election, when every voter had friends.[26] He took a man out of the crew of a ship arriving from Virginia, but the Recorder ruled that he was no seafaring man, and Graves and his lieutenant were condemned to pay £250 each in costs and damages. Graves was lucky; he was a successful captain and could afford to pay. Peter Rawlings, the lieutenant of the gang, was still in gaol six years later, by this time insane, and his wife and children starving. Even in Plymouth, a town as susceptible to Admiralty influence as any in England, a magistrate who was also Agent for Sick and Wounded, a lucrative office in the Admiralty's gift, did not hesitate to imprison officers for attempting impressment.[27]

Everywhere the work, not only of the Impress Service, but of the Navy as a whole was constantly harassed by vexatious litigation. Captain Pascal at Cowes, who had pressed some seamen and released them on seeing their protections (certificates of exemption from the press), was sued for false imprisonment for the short time they were in his hands. The Porter of Portsmouth Dockyard was prosecuted for obstruction for preventing strangers entering the yard. In the West Indies Captain Taylor was arrested at the suit of merchants whose trade with the enemy he had interfered with.[28] In virtually all such cases the courts were flagrantly biased, and it was not unusual for damages of hundreds or even thousands of pounds to be awarded.[29] False charges of murder were brought against gangsmen and convictions secured in defiance of the evidence, while gangsmen themselves, as a result of a famous case in 1743, could be killed more or less with impunity, it being held that a press warrant empowered only the officer it named and no one under his orders, so that resistance to a gang was legitimate self-defence.[30] In all these cases the Admiralty would defend its people, and even pay their fines, providing it was convinced that there had been no breach, however slight, of the terms of the press warrant. Pressing remained, however, a dangerous occupation, and when there was so little chance of an unbiased judge or jury, and so much risk of further inflaming public opinion, the Admiralty was reluctant to go to law in any but the clearest cases.[31]

In one respect, however, magistrates found the press useful. It presented an excellent opportunity to dispose of paupers, idiots, cripples, vagabonds and petty criminals. Very few of them were seamen, and there was no legal justification for pressing them, but as the magistrates were the law in their districts, they were not perturbed by that.[32] Their main difficulty was in persuading the Navy to take their offerings. Impress officers were obviously susceptible to pressure, and could sometimes be induced to take the less hopeless cases, but they were very likely to be sent back by the first flag officer who saw them. The marines were more tolerant, and the Recruitment Act in effect permitted impressment for land forces, so a considerable number were recruited in this way.[33]

In no part of the Sea Service were criminals ever accepted, and an attempt by London magistrates in 1759 to dispose of a notorious gang of pickpockets, the Black Boy Alley Gang, was firmly countered. Nothing more quickly destroyed the mutual trust of a happy ship's company than the presence of a thief among them, and it was the one crime for which a prime seaman might be discharged without hesitation.[34]

The only felony which was acceptable in the Service was smuggling. Smugglers were fine seamen and perfectly reliable if sent to a foreign station, well away from their old associates. Sometimes they were rated petty officers. Many of these smugglers were simply taken at sea and pressed without ceremony, but others were discharged from gaol to the Navy.[35] In one case a captain was frustrated in getting some smugglers from Rochester Gaol by the Customs officers releasing them. Little as Customs men liked smugglers, they hated the Navy more, and took pleasure in interfering with its operations as much as they could, such as by arresting men-of-war arriving from abroad and placing them in quarantine, or hindering the movement of naval stores on the grounds that they might be dutiable.[36] In fairness to the Customs men it must be said that in their case conventional anti-militarism was sharpened by the knowledge that the sea officers were themselves inveterate petty smugglers.

Apart from smugglers and debtors, the Navy admitted nobody from prison. It is necessary to emphasize this to counter the hyperbole which was sometimes passed for fact. It has been claimed that the press was so indiscriminate that the Navy was manned by 'the most gigantic collection of human freaks and derelicts under the sun'.[37] Edward Thompson – 'Poet Thompson' as he was known – an officer whose literary aspirations were chiefly expressed in poetic licence, claimed of the *Stirling Castle* when she arrived at Spithead in February 1756 that out of 480 men, 'two hundred and twenty-five were the pressed refuse of gaols and the scum of the streets'. As Thompson was then a midshipman in that ship he has been taken as a reliable witness, but from the ship's muster it is evident that there were only 115 pressed men aboard, and not one who can be identified as coming from prison.[38]

The actual means by which a gang could impress men, assuming the civil authorities allowed them to press at all, were limited. It was out of the question for a gang of six or a dozen or even a score of men, armed only with sticks, to rush through the streets seizing anyone they met; most would not be seamen, and anyone liable to impressment could slip away without difficulty. 'Whoever indeed considers the cities of London and Westminster', Henry Fielding complained,

with the late vast addition of their suburbs, the great

171

irregularity of their buildings, the immense number of lanes, alleys, courts and by-places, must think that had they been intended for the very purpose of concealment they could scarce have been better contrived. Upon such a view, the whole appears as a vast wood or forest in which a thief may harbour with as great a security as wild beasts do in the deserts of Africa or Arabia.[39]

What was easy for a thief was easy for a seaman. It is ridiculous to suggest that honest citizens, unconnected with the sea, were afraid to walk the streets for fear of being swept in by the press, for the press was quite unable to 'sweep' the streets of any sizeable town.[40]

What an Impress officer did was to set up his rendezvous in an inn near the docks. In London, pressing was confined to the riverside suburbs, and it was sufficient for a seaman threatened by the press to retire from Rotherhithe to Hoxton, and to put on long clothes for his visits to the City.[41] Suitable rendezvous were the Horse and Groom in Lambeth Marsh, the King's Head in East Lane, Rotherhithe, the City of Rotterdam in St Katherine's, or the Black Boy and Trumpet at St Katherine's Stairs.[42] Here the lieutenant would lodge his gang, receive volunteers, and discreetly collect information, and from here the gang would set out in the evenings to raid taverns where seamen were gathered. Since it was all but impossible to try pressing in the streets, and very dangerous to enter private houses without a search warrant (that would have been a very quick way to get thrown into prison), raiding taverns was the best means of pressing ashore. In March 1757, for example, Lieutenant I'Anson of the *Achilles* joined forces with John Taylor, mate of the *Royal Sovereign*, and with their joint gang numbering forty, surrounded the Black Spread Eagle in Tooley Street where privateersmen were drinking. At first the operation went well, until the commander of the privateer arrived with reinforcements armed with cutlasses and pistols; in the ensuing fight one privateersman was killed, and the entire gang, officers and all, was put in prison. There they might have remained indefinitely if Taylor had not escaped and written to his captain reporting their situation.[43]

If raids like this were to succeed, they needed to be carefully planned and based on good intelligence. One of the uses of a lieutenant's expense account was to obtain information, for there were many who, for a consideration, would point out where seamen could be found. Many indeed would do it for their private satisfaction; men were pressed by the malice of rivals in love or law, of relatives eager for an inheritance, or jilted sweethearts, unhappy wives and enemies of every kind.[44] Masters often contrived to get their apprentices press'd, which spared them the necessity to feed, clothe or educate, and gave them a good income, since by registering the indentures at the Navy Pay Office they could claim the apprentices' pay. Some of these apprentices were experienced seamen as old as twenty-four, and it was so obviously inequitable and impolitic to make them serve without wages that the Navy was in the habit, unjustified in law, of forcing the masters to take only part of the wages, 'it being notorious that many of these people are drove to sea by the cruelty and ill-usage of their masters'.[45]

It is an open question to what extent Impress officers used crimps to recruit. On the whole crimps were the enemy of the Navy, but if it were mutually profitable some trade might well have taken place. The determining factor would have been money, and it is this which makes one doubt if such bargains were often struck, for the lieutenant had only ten shillings to offer for an able seaman and, at wartime wage rates, merchantmen could almost certainly outbid that. On the other hand the rewards for recaptured deserters were higher, and crimps sometimes did take advantage of them.[46]

Besides raiding taverns, one other way of pressing, or recruiting volunteers was available to the Impress Service. Most regulating captains had a cutter or at least a few boats attached to their tender for work afloat in the river or harbour, and for pushing far enough out to sea to prevent men escaping ashore before they reached port.[47] As we see from the case of the Hull rendezvous, this could be quite a productive approach. It also saved any difficulties over keeping the pressed men, who could be delivered straight on board the tender and be held there until she sailed. This was the usual arrangement for men raised in port, but Impress officers working inland had either to march their recruits in a body, or send the pressed men handcuffed by wagon. Even volunteers might be treated this way: 'as my volunteers proved nearly as ungovernable and obstreperous as the pressed men, I kept them handcuffed, two and two, all night and the next day's march,' recalled Lieutenant William Owen.[48]

Only a very foolhardy Impress officer would deliberately press men who did not use the sea, but it was possible to make mistakes, especially when working afloat. A good many men were taken who should not have been, including men from other men-of-war, who either could not prove they had leave, or fell into the hands of unscrupulous officers anxious to increase their numbers without asking questions.[49] Foreigners serving in British ships, who were not always easy to tell from native subjects, were often pressed, and there was a regular correspondence with foreign ambassadors reclaiming their nationals. Passengers and travellers by sea were sometimes brought in – in one case a party of Irish priests and seminarians, later released.[50] Quite often the press took freeholders or other men of substance, and consequently of political weight. These men might well be liable to the press, but it would have been most unwise to have kept them. Usually they were released on finding a seaman to substitute for them, which in effect meant a money levy sufficient to induce a man to enter in their stead. (In the marines it meant literally this; the sum of six, later ten, guineas would buy out a recruit.)[51] This request by Commodore Frankland MP is typical of many:

> Roger Talbot esq. my other member for the borough of Thirsk has desired me to solicit the release of one George Middleton, a young fellow of a hundred pounds per annum in his neighbourhood, who was impressed last July at Scarborough.[52]

The political costs of keeping people like this far outweighed the benefits, especially as they were seldom among the best men. As it was said of a Scots freeholder, 'his service on board ship will not earn the bread he eats, being entirely a stranger to the sea, and too old and clumsy to learn'.[53]

When the civil power often opposed the press as much as it could, it was not to be expected that seamen themselves would always submit tamely to it. Riots and fights ashore were common-

place, and pitched battles occurred between incoming merchantmen and the Impress service's cutters or boats. Men confined in
tenders before they were delivered to the fleet several times mutinied and seized the tenders. It is obvious enough why men disliked
the press, and in an age when rioting was a common means of
popular protest, it is not surprising that it was a common weapon
against the press gang. It is nevertheless interesting to examine in
detail those fights of which something is known, because they appear to have a factor in common. In every case the attacks were led
or instigated by deserters from the Navy. The same seems to have
been true of mutinies in tenders, and was very probably true of
attacks by privateersmen, who were often deserters.[54] This suggests that the Navy's much-publicized deterrent punishments for
desertion, which in fact were hardly ever applied, may have helped
to make deserters desperate, and willing to resist the press by force
of arms. This was certainly the opinion of Captain John Fortescue,
the experienced regulating captain at Liverpool. Many ships of
that port were slavers or West Indiamen, which regularly returned
with deserters tempted by twenty-five guineas for an Atlantic
voyage, 'which encourages all the men to leave their ships in the
West Indies, and then they are desperate when they come here for
fear of being discovered as deserters'.[55] If Fortescue was right the
Navy would have been better advised to have advertised its real
leniency towards desertion rather than its theoretical severity.

Fortescue's men working afloat in the Mersey were in a particularly difficult position, for they often had to board incoming
ships which were heavily armed and ready to fight. Guineamen
and West Indiamen might carry anything up to fifteen six- or nine-
pounders on a broadside, with crews of up to eighty men prepared
to use them. A boat's crew, or even a cutter, stood a poor chance
against such odds; many ships forced their way past without much
difficulty, and some killed and wounded boats' crews which tried
to stop them. There was no remedy in law, as Fortescue found
when he brought an unsuccessful suit against the men of the *Tyrrell* for firing on the *Hawk* sloop and killing one of her men.[56] In
one celebrated fight, however, the Navy was successful. In July
1759 the *Vengeance* 28, was lying in the Mersey when the Green-
land whaler *Golden Lyon* came in. Whaling men were partly pro-

tected by Act of Parliament, and there was initially no trouble in boarding her and mustering her crew, but hidden below were the men of another whaler which had been lost in the ice. With their ship sunk their protections were valueless, and they rose suddenly, took the officers prisoner, threw the gang overboard and fired into their boats. The *Vengeance* slipped her cable and pursued the *Golden Lyon* up the river, firing blanks at her, but to no effect. The *Golden Lyon* reached the docks, where the officers were released and the whaling men dispersed. There the incident might have ended as many had done before, but Captain Nightingale of the *Vengeance* was a determined man, and though pressing ashore in Liverpool was reckoned impossible, he organized a raid that night, surprised the men of the *Golden Lyon* renewing their protections at the Custom House, and carried off seventeen of them, firing over the heads of the pursuing mob. Nightingale flogged several of the men who had fired on his boats.[57]

The practice of lodging pressed men and volunteers in a tender was safer and more convenient than keeping them ashore, but there was a risk of the pressed men trying to seize the ship. In two cases such mutinies succeeded: the *Tasker* in 1755 on passage from Liverpool, and the *James & Thomas* in 1760 sailing from Newcastle to the Nore. In both cases the lieutenants in command were unequal to the task; Robert Sax of the *James & Thomas* had completely lost his nerve, and Ezekiel Cosentine of the *Tasker* was 'drunken and unfit for service anywhere'. The *James & Thomas* was retaken by her escorting sloop, but the *Tasker* was brought into a bay where many of her men escaped ashore.[58] What is interesting, however, is that more than forty of the pressed men declined the opportunity of freedom and placed themselves once more under Cosentine's orders. These men had not yet joined the Navy either legally or practically; they had had no opportunity to experience the excitements of active service or the comforts of a settled ship's company. They had simply been confined for some time in a tender, in circumstances which might have tried the patience of the most enthusiastic volunteer. Yet it seems that many of them were sufficiently reconciled to the Navy to prefer to remain in the Service into which they had recently been forced. This was not an unusual reaction. Pressed men often accepted their situation with

remarkable speed, and for every mutinous tender there were probably several which were 'so regular, and behave so well', that they
needed little supervision.[59] It is interesting that men who had been
pressed into the Service and petitioned for release, or whose
friends petitioned for them, had sometimes decided to stay by the
time the petitions were investigated.[60]

In order that the tasks most essential to the country and the
war effort should proceed in spite of the press, many seamen, or
classes of seafarers, had certificates of exemption known as 'protections'. One of the Impress Captain's most delicate duties was to
scrutinize these protections when presented, detect the numerous
forgeries, and release the owners of those which appeared to be
genuine. Protections were of two kinds: those granted by Act of
Parliament, and those granted by the Admiralty.[61] Parliament protected the masters and chief mates of all merchantmen over fifty
tons, apprentices within their first three years at sea, and landmen
in their first two. Fishermen, whaling men and colliers had special
provisions. The Admiralty, or the other boards under its authority,
protected privateers, transports, dockyard workmen and the crews
of all sorts of vessels in government service. These Admiralty protections were usually valid only when afloat; seamen ashore could
legally be taken, though it was ruled that men aboard ship in an
enclosed basin, fitting for a foreign voyage, were protected.[62] The
complications of administering this system of protections would
have been great even if it had been operated with scrupulous
honesty; in fact it was the vehicle for every kind of fraud and manipulation. Shipowners who could obtain protections had secured
the perfect instrument to reduce wartime wage rates, and they happily engaged in widespread forgery of apprentices' indentures, protections for 'foreigners' and protections for riggers and other
shipyard workmen which were valid ashore and could be used
with a ship's protection to give complete coverage.[63] In the Downs,
and all along the south coast, protected fishermen, watermen or
pilots came off to bring safely into port merchantmen whose own
men had fled ashore to escape the press. When the merchants of
Poole secured the right to allow their men to work ashore on their
protections the port became a haven to which seamen came from
all over southern England.[64]

Given the indiscriminate nature of the press, some system of protections was unavoidable, but of course the number grew inexorably. In 1741 there were said to be 14,800 valid protections issued; by 1757 this total had risen to nearly 50,000.[65] If this figure is reliable, more than half the seamen in the country were protected, which made the Navy's manning difficulties quite insuperable. At its most desperate moments, therefore, the Admiralty would authorize a 'hot press', ignoring all protections not backed by Act of Parliament.[66] A hot press had to be organized in secrecy, to catch the protected seamen unawares.

One of the obvious disadvantages of this and all other pressing was its deterrent effect on volunteers. It not only presented a poor image of the Navy, but set practical obstacles in the way of volunteers. Seamen in inland parts were afraid to come to volunteer for fear of being pressed on the way, and losing the bounty.[67] When seamen did volunteer, one factor was almost constant, that they volunteered for a named ship, one no doubt where they had friends, or of which they had heard well. When tenders full of men arrived, the recruits were always distinguished according to which ships they were for:

> The *Arundel* brought in thirty volunteers for the *St George*, twenty-eight for the *Newcastle*, one belonging to the *Yarmouth*, one to the *Seaford*, three to the *Lancaster*, four for the *Prince George*, five for the *Dunkirk*, and fifty-one not belonging to any ship, all of which I have distributed to the ships at Spithead.[68]

This was an important reason for a seaman to volunteer rather than take his chance of being pressed, for the volunteer usually had his choice of ship, but the pressed man went where he was sent. The same may often have been true of landmen, but perhaps for them the attractions of a service of which they knew little were joined by the repulsions of home – poverty, boredom, the narrow world of rural society, or domestic strife. One press officer tried to dissuade a man of substance from volunteering, but the latter insisted:

178

the poor fellow had to hint that at home 'the grey mare was the better horse'. Indeed he was not the only man in the course of this service who flew to me to get rid of termagant wives.[69]

One of the principal functions of the Impress Service was only indirectly connected with recruiting. The Navy's manning difficulties would have been greatly increased if there had not been an incentive for men on leave to return, if it had not been made difficult for deserters to move freely, if protections had not been liable to scrutiny. The press gang acted as a naval shore police force. Gangs were sometimes stationed essentially as road blocks, to prevent the free movement of deserters along major highways. One was stationed at Canterbury in 1756 for this reason, to cover the road from the Downs to London. The hot press of that year in London was completed by road blocks on the roads out of town. In this case they were manned by marines, and the Admiralty was always keen to replace seamen in static posts by soldiers or marines if possible.[70] When the gang was recruiting as well as controlling movement, however, there was no good substitute for seamen. In inland parts, where seamen were even more conspicuous than usual, the press gang was in a good position to hear of and pursue deserters, like the seven men caught by Lieutenant Owen on Clee Hill in Shropshire, after a long chase across country. These men were returned prisoners of war who had seized their cartel and escaped ashore at Portland. They were making their way across country to Liverpool, 'thinking themselves perfectly safe while they kept aloof from the seaport towns'.[71] It was an important function of the Impress Service to falsify that sort of expectation.

Another was to act as some sort of counter force to the Navy's most persistent domestic enemies. There was no question of pressing landmen, but some troublemakers were, or could be squeezed within the category of seafaring men. Among those impressed to stop their activities were men suspected of spying and of aiding prisoners of war to escape, those detected selling grog to the sick, and those who concealed deserters. The abusive or violent master of a merchantman might lose his mate or apprentice.[72] Breaking a Parliamentary protection was dangerous, but the Admiralty was

179

able to use the threat of removing or breaking its own protections to put pressure on recalcitrant local authorities. Sometimes unusually troublesome privateersmen were pressed.[73] The hope of every senior officer was to find means of pressing the crimps, but they were too wise to go afloat or offer any appearance of being seafaring men.[74] Thomas Rogerman of Portsmouth, who imprudently issued advertisements bearing his name, was taken, as was another at Kinsale, but such a coup was seldom possible, and the most that could be hoped for was to frighten the more timid:

> Mr Mears who secreted the *Edgar*'s men is a tailor and lives upon the Point – good for nothing – we shall frighten him at least.[75]

It was possible in principle to use the press to recruit in the colonies, but in practice there were acute difficulties. In America and the West Indies the colonial authorities believed themselves empowered to forbid pressing, and as local interests suffered from a scarcity of seamen, they generally did so.[76] It took an officer of unusual tact, or a situation of unusual desperation, to secure leave to press ashore, but it was occasionally done in the West Indies, and Admiral Holburne was able to press at Halifax, where there was no colonial assembly.[77]

It was at sea, however, that impressment was at its most productive. Only at sea could seamen easily be found, with little chance of evasion or disguise. By long custom and Admiralty order, only inward-bound British merchantmen within soundings could be stopped and boarded;[78] the men taken out had to be replaced by others to carry the merchantman to her intended port. Short-handed merchantmen could not safely be left without men in lieu, so pressing at sea could only be done with a supply of reliable men who could be lent to a merchant ship with a reasonable prospect that they would return – or of useless men who could be lent with the unspoken hope that they would not. Pressing at sea was done by men-of-war in the Channel and Western Approaches, or by tenders manned by parties from a man-of-war and sent out specifically to press.

The great advantage of pressing at sea was its selective ability to provide good seamen, the class of which the Service was most acutely in need. What proportion of those recruited at sea were pressed is difficult to say, not least because many men would 'volunteer' when certain impressment was the alternative. There certainly were volunteers to be had at sea, as in the case of the East Indiamen we have noted, and the enthusiasm of one party in 1755 ('as soon as we heard that there was a demand for men in his Majesty's service we all entered aboard of the first tender that fell in with us'[79]) may be genuine, but it seems probable that the majority of men raised at sea were pressed. One good source of volunteers was foreign ships stopped at sea. Captains were instructed to demand all British seamen out of foreign ships in time of war, and often they found these men eager to escape their situation and join a King's ship.[80]

It was quite possible for a good man pressed at sea to step straight into a petty officer's berth, or even straight onto the quarter deck. Pressed men rated midshipman, or given warrants, were not unknown,[81] and there was nothing to stop a pressed man rising as high in the Service as any other. The ship which manned a press tender generally kept the men she raised – if good, as an incentive, if bad, as a punishment.[82] The good men were worth keeping, so it was worth rating a good man as highly as he deserved, lest he find means to go elsewhere. John Stevens, mate of the *Neptune* snow, was pressed in 1755 because of some ill-timed abuse of the press officer by her master.[83] He petitioned either for his discharge, or to be allowed to serve in the *Elizabeth* whose captain offered to rate him midshipman. Whether there were any commissioned officers who had been pressed is not certain, though it could have happened. John Campbell, Hawke's flag captain who died a vice-admiral, is said to have been brought in by a press gang, but as a volunteer. 'Poet' Thompson claimed to have been pressed out of an Indiaman, but his claims are never to be depended on.[84]

In spite of the opportunities the Navy offered, men at sea were often as willing to oppose the press with force as those on land, and as on land, it seems often to have been deserters who led them. The officers of merchantmen which opened fire on press tenders or men-of-war would profess to have been powerless to prevent them, but they had such strong financial reasons to wish their men ashore before the end of the voyage that they doubtless did not assert their authority with much enthusiasm. Several pitched battles occurred. One in which the hapless Robert Sax was involved led to the death of three men in the *Britannia*, a merchantman which fired on his tender and was only subdued by force of arms.[85] Several similar incidents occurred, and men on both sides were killed.[86] In these cases the officers concerned were usually court-martialled for murder, partly because the Admiralty regarded the death of a man very seriously, partly because if the officer had acted properly, an acquittal might safeguard him against a civil trial for murder with no chance of an impartial verdict.[87]

Incidents like this were the most dramatic of all the many unpleasantnesses surrounding the work of the press, but it is important to keep them in perspective. Pressing at sea or on land was for the most part a humdrum affair calling for little if any violence. On land, pressing was only part of the duties of officers and men who were much occupied in recruiting volunteers. There was a holiday element in being sent pressing either by sea or by land; it was a welcome relaxation from the unvarying round of shipboard life and offered the prospect of rambling about on shore. Among those recruited, it was not always easy to distinguish pressed men from volunteers, and before they had been long in the Service, sometimes before they had joined it at all in any legal sense, it was impossible to say that all pressed men were all unhappy, or indeed all volunteers happy. It is easy to over-stress the differences between the two classes. For many practical purposes the distinction between them was so difficult to draw, and so weak an indicator of behaviour, attitude or usefulness, that it is best for the historian to consider the recruiting service ashore and afloat as a unified system, applying various interlocked means to the same object of manning the Navy.

D COMPETITION

The Navy's manning difficulties have often been distorted by being seen in isolation, as though the supply of manpower was limitless and only the demerits of the Service explained its difficulties. In reality the problem was that the Navy was trying to draw a quart out of a pint pot, and moreover that others were trying to draw from it at the same time. There was intense competition for men between the Navy, the merchant service and privateering. As the State declined to become involved in regulating this competition, it developed into an unrestrained battle in which all three services supplemented their intrinsic attractions by force, fraud and money. In this struggle the Navy had both strengths and weaknesses. Its superior conditions of service and the prospect of prize money drew large numbers of volunteers, and the press gang brought in others. It lost men to crimps and to higher wages elsewhere, but there is some reason to think that of the three sea employers, the Navy was the strongest, and probably the largest. Warships usually put to sea fully, if not perfectly, manned. They were not obliged to recruit a large proportion of foreigners, nor to rely on boys and old men, as some merchantmen were.[1] The height to which wartime wage rates were driven, at least in London, is telling evidence of the extreme scarcity of men in the merchant service.

This shortage of men was a great encouragement to the crimps, as dealers in a scarce and valuable commodity. They made it their business to entice seamen from their ships and sell them to the highest bidder.

> It is well known a set of people called crimps constantly attend upon our hospitals to entice the seamen as they recover to desert the Navy and enter on board some merchant ship or privateer (the latter more frequently in time of war), first debauching them with drink and then bribing them with money.[2]

This was one simple method, but there were others cheaper and even more effective. The crimps were often tavern keepers, who took in seamen who had been paid off and encouraged them to spend themselves into debt, when they would be offered the alternatives of gaol or a ship, or imprisoned first and sold off to a good bidder later. The publican took the seaman's advance money, and sometimes a lien on his wages or a cash payment from the shipmaster as well. Simplest of all the crimp's methods was to make a man drunk, hit him over the head and carry him unconscious aboard. 'The crimp is worse than the deserter,' Admiral Holburne pronounced, 'and ought to be hanged in his stead, as many a man is decoyed away by them that never intended it by being made drunk.'[3] Means like this were used to steal men from any and every ship, but the Navy was an obvious target, especially as a source of prime seamen and petty officers. Crimps like Thomas Gater of the King of Prussia's Head in Shadwell were well known to authority, but the law was all but powerless against them. At worst crimping was only a misdemeanour, punishable by a small fine. Local merchants like Mr Carver in Gosport or Mr Ross in Cowes, supplied men along with other articles a ship might need.[4] At Liverpool,

> here is a nest of women crimps, that make it their business to draw and inveigle all the sailors that put their foot on shore, and then sell them to the merchants for three pounds a month with two months' advance, which encourages desertion from all his Majesty's ships, and I verily believe three parts of the sailors out of this town are deserters from the men-of-war.[5]

At Gravesend the landlord of the Ship, having a sick man-of-warsman lodging with him, 'endeavoured to persuade him to enter for one of the Indiamen, but on his refusal, informed against him'. Even Indiamen were not above crimping out of the Navy; George Shooter, mate of the *Delaware*, was detected buying man-of-warsmen at ten guineas each in 1759.[6] Many crimps specialized in getting men out of hospital, for bored convalescents were particularly easy to tempt with alcohol.[7] Sick quarters were especially dangerous in this respect, and the new naval hospitals of Haslar and Stonehouse, with their high walls and tight organization, were designed to make this all but impossible.

A 'Wapping landlord' (to use a naval term more or less synonymous with 'crimp') could sell men to any bidder, perhaps even to
Impress officers, but in a high proportion of cases where the information is given it was privateers which were the crimps' principals.
It has been said that 'the difficulty of manning the King's fleets and
the constant enticement of seamen by privateers can only be
explained by the presumption that privateering was the more attractive service'.[8] This was neither the only nor the most likely
explanation, for seamen were not wholly free agents, and the
crimp was no more a friend of liberty than the press gang. The frequent, indeed desperate efforts by privateers to seduce seamen
from the Navy suggest how extremely short of seamen they were.
Only the most reckless gambler would join a privateer for money,
and in the absence of enough of them, privateers had to depend
heavily on foreigners, landmen and criminals. If the small number
which took out Mediterranean passes were typical the proportion
of foreigners in privateers' companies was 22 per cent in the first
year of the war, 41 per cent in the second, and 75 per cent, the
maximum permissible by law, in the third, by which time privateering from British ports was anyway in steep decline.[9] A detailed
study of seafarers of Bristol, one of the main privateering ports,
shows that alone of Bristol ships privateers were obliged to recruit
largely from inland parts where no seamen dwelt.[10]

It is easy to see why privateers were so desperate for a minimum of seamen, and would stick at nothing to get them. The Navy
was not the only sufferer, for privateers seduced men from merchantmen, and indeed from each other, but it was the obvious
source of skilled manpower, and it was not unusual for privateers
to be discovered with several deserters from the Navy aboard.[11]
Privateers anchored at Cowes expressly to pick up men from the
warships at Spithead.[12] In 1757, when the shortage of seamen was
not yet at its worst, the officers of the *Hawke* privateer were offering advances of eleven guineas to try to lure men into their ship.[13]

Privateers were well known as a haven for all sorts of criminals, their discipline generally weak, and the ships' companies
often troublesome ashore or afloat.[14] Instances of mutiny and even
murder at sea were not unusual. Some privateer officers were men
of bad character if not, like John Patrick of the *Fame*, 'little better
than a madman'.[15] In home waters the smaller privateers were

simply smugglers,[16] and in the Mediterranean and West Indies the letter of marque, on both sides, was often a slender cover for piracy. In the West Indies,

> the atrocious conduct of these privateers have brought stain upon the nation's character. Rapine was their view and our allies have felt the effect of it; Dutch, Danes and Spaniards were equally the object of their spoil.[17]

At Gibraltar 'the privateers in general, fitted out in this part of the world, are little better than pirates'.[18] The cruelty of privateers was a byword, so that when the master of a packet was questioned about a French ship which had stopped him, he could assert with confidence that she must have been a man-of-war, because of the officers' uniforms, 'and the civil treatment he met with'.[19]

In the face of these abuses the government was cautious to the point of pusillanimity. A few pirates are said to have been hanged, and two letters of marque were revoked, those of the *Fame*, and of the *Sampson*, which fired into a warship's boat at New York and killed four men.[20] Otherwise little or nothing was done. In the West Indies, 'the privateers' people are very riotous; even on shore they assemble and break open the gaols, and press the men from the merchant ships'.[21] At home, the crew of the *King of Prussia*, two known pirates among them, defied the Navy and terrorized the population of Dartmouth, but the law officers advised that such conduct was insufficient to justify action against them.[22] It is difficult to endorse the opinion of an older authority that privateersmen were 'the flower of British seamen'.[23]

There was competition for men not only from other ships but also from the army, whose manning difficulties were considerable. Officers were ready to steal men to make up their regiments, and no keener to weed out the obvious seaman from among their recruits than sea officers were to spot the soldier among theirs.[24] Probably the Navy gained more from the army than it lost, for soldiering was not attractive to anyone bred in the freedom of a sailor's life – as the case of Charles Collings, a follower from boyhood of Captain Cornish, indicates:

He was seduced in his liquor to enter for a soldier in Lord Robert Manners's regiment, where he continued about a twelvemonth, but not liking a soldier's life, being bred a sailor, deserted.[25]

Besides the competition of those who were concerned to get men from the Navy because they needed them themselves, there was also the opposition of those who made it their business to frustrate naval recruitment from principle, or private interest disguised as principle. The same motives which led magistrates to fine and imprison press officers led others to mount legal assaults on naval recruitment, and especially on impressment. In 1758 a bill to extend the provisions of *habeas corpus* to impressed men passed the Commons and only failed in the Lords. Although designed to make impressment for the army impossible, had it become law it would have forced a partial demobilization of the Navy in the middle of the war.[26] To modern eyes this seems a curious way to govern the country, but it demonstrates the passions roused by the subject, as well as the extent to which Members of Parliament were divorced from practical acquaintance with the realities of public administration.

Though the bill failed, some judges were willing to grant a writ of *habeas corpus* if even the faintest doubt existed as to the legality of taking any particular pressed man. This seems to have been a new tactic; at least it astounded the experienced commander-in-chief at Portsmouth, Admiral Holburne, when he encountered it in October 1758:

An extraordinary thing happened to-day to Captain Hollwall of the *Deptford*. A *habeas corpus* writ was given him ... It's a very unusual thing in our service, and I could wish a stop might be put to it, as here's a fellow upon the Common would take every man out of our ships if he can, the same that was arresting the masters of the transports.[27]

The writ was soon followed by another, put up by a crimp 'in order to get so much by the Run for the landlord'. 'I am sorry any of these sort of things creep into the Navy, as it may be of bad consequence, and may be made use of by every Wapping land-

lord.'[28] These writs became sufficiently common for the Admiralty
to issue a circular instruction to all captains on how to deal with
them (send the man up to the Admiralty under guard). They were
also used, more legitimately, to retrieve foreigners who had been
accidentally pressed.[29]

In the event the use of writs of *habeas corpus* proved to be only
a minor irritant to the Navy beside the sustained and intense competition for men which it faced from merchantmen and privateers.
In the competition all parties used violence and intimidation to
some extent: the Navy by the press gang, in circumstances limited
by law and custom; merchantmen, and even more so privateers, in
circumstances limited only by opportunity. To the extent to which
either method was able to affect the distribution of manpower, the
seamen (it was almost entirely seamen who were the victims of
both) were not free agents, and their movements into or out of the
Navy tell us nothing about their inclinations. In fact seamen were
free agents to a considerable extent even in wartime, but they
never moved in an unconstrained, neutral environment in which
personal preference alone dictated where they served. They were
constantly drawn and repelled by the violent currents set up by
unregulated competition between the Navy and its rival employers
of manpower afloat.

E STRAGGLING AND DESERTION

The manning problem had to be addressed in three ways: by finding volunteers, by pressing, and by preventing wastage. In both
gains and losses, the men themselves were partly free agents whose
wishes affected the Navy's fortunes, and partly the objects of
manipulation by others, either the Navy itself or its rivals for manpower. Many men who had apparently deserted the Service, in the
formal sense that they had missed three consecutive weekly musters and been marked 'run' on the ship's books, had in reality been
kidnapped or lured away when they were not masters of themselves. Nevertheless it seems unlikely that these were more than a

minority of those who were made 'run'. A larger, though still unquantifiable number undoubtedly consisted of people who were legitimately ashore and failed to return for other reasons. All over the world men were ashore in great numbers, on short or long leave, landed as boat's crews, working parties or press gangs, lent in lieu of men pressed out of merchantmen and left to find their own way back to their home port, or sent overland to join a new ship. Apart from a small minority of habitual deserters, impressed smugglers and men awaiting court martial, any man in the Navy could count himself unlucky if he did not at least occasionally get a run ashore, particularly when all ships had to be docked or careened several times a year. There were always many men on leave, and there was usually a small proportion who failed to return and were 'run' on their ships' books. It is easy to assume that these men were 'deserters' in the full sense of the word, men who had deliberately fled the Service intending never to return.

This was not an assumption made by any informed contemporary. Sea officers who were at all careful of language applied the word 'deserter' only to men who had been, or might plausibly have been, accused under the XVth or XVIth Articles of War of deserting the Service. Merely being 'run' on a ship's books was no more than a precondition of being a deserter. Even men who had clearly deserted their ships were not necessarily deserters in this sense, for we shall see that deserting one's ship by no means certainly implied deserting the Service. At the court martial of some men of the *Blast* bomb vessel in 1760, who had beyond doubt wilfully deserted their ship, one of the accused asked his captain, who had witnessed them pulling away in a boat, 'Did you think that we were determined to leave his Majesty's service?' Cautiously the captain replied, 'I cannot tell.'[1] He was wise to do so.

The term usually employed in the eighteenth century to describe men absent from their duty in culpable, suspicious or simply unexplained circumstances, was 'stragglers'. This evocative term, vague and comprehensive, covered the multitude of sins, errors and mishaps which might befall seamen ashore. Very often men were delayed in return by simple physical causes; by bad roads and bad weather, by illness or accident, by arrest for debt, or simply by death.[2] Men lent in lieu who were longer than expected on passage often found that their tickets of leave had expired before they even landed. All these men were liable to be arrested by soldiers, parish constables or press gangs, all eager for the reward payable on bringing in a straggler. Even those whose tickets of leave were in order were at risk, for tickets could be forged or manipulated. Seamen were easily identified at sight, and those in hope of a reward were naturally tempted to assume the worst (or from their point of view, the best) whenever they met one. There were many who really had overstayed their leave, either unintentionally or deliberately, profiting by the many good excuses which the latecomer could offer.[3] Men were always returning, or being returned to their ships, overdue from leave, and sometimes after they had been 'run' on the books, but they were seldom either spoken or thought of as deserters. The usual, and almost always the only, punishment for straggling was to be charged the reward paid to whoever had made the arrest – in effect, a fine of a few pounds.[4]

Besides straggling, there was another category of absence, equally ill-defined and equally common, known as 'rambling'. When ships came into harbour to dock it was virtually impossible to prevent the men going ashore if they wished, and captains seldom tried. They put their untrustworthy men aboard another ship and did not worry unduly about the rest.

> As to keeping the men on board the ships in the harbour fitting, it is almost impossible. The St George has the most absent, but the captain does not think any of them will desert, and believes most of them are here upon the spot.[5]

Though the Admiralty was not always happy to hear it, experienced flag officers like Admiral Holburne at Portsmouth mentioned with little or no concern such information as that 'the Happy is in the harbour and her people straggling about'. When the men were needed again, patrols would be sent out for them. It was usually not difficult to find out in which tavern one's shipmates had been drinking and rouse them out.[6]

A great many men are ashore from the ships, particularly from those in the dock, but I have sent drums and advertisements through the town for them immediately to repair to their duty, and I hope it will have the desired effect, for I have at the same time given them to understand they will be taken up as stragglers and deserters tomorrow.[7]

This makes the distinction between rambling and straggling explicit. Straggling was mildly culpable, but rambling was regarded by senior officers as perfectly legitimate. It was a grievance they complained of, that rambling seamen were often arrested and charged as stragglers, which moved Admiral Osborn to suggest a formal zone of immunity about two miles around Portsmouth Dockyard, bounded by a line connecting the Commodore Brown at Forton on the Fareham road, the White Hart on the Stoke road, and the Coach and Horses at Hilsea Green:

> Some of them have not been absent from their ships more than three or four days, and taken up within two miles of the town. It were therefore to be wished they had certain limits assigned them to ramble in, and the soldiers' liberty of taking them up were more confined, for at present I fear they watch their opportunity to lay hold of the seamen when they see they are drunk and not sensible where they are, and very probably may themselves tempt them out for the sake of the reward for bringing them in again.[8]

Osborn's scheme was not approved, but the fact that it was seriously put forward by an experienced senior officer is indicative of official attitudes.

If seamen did take advantage of their freedom to run away, there were still severe obstacles in their path. Even in a landman's long clothes they could be recognized from their gait and their weather-beaten complexions. One deserter, confident in his disguise, was alarmed to meet an old woman in the street in the first town he came to who said to him, 'Young man, are you not afraid of the soldiers?' In the countryside inland, away from the main roads, a seaman was a conspicuous oddity likely to be talked of for miles around.[10] Most absentees did not get so far, and were found easily. Francis Lanyon of the *Royal George*, who was finally looked for after stretching two days' leave to over a month, was recovered from his home, the prominent Gosport bawdy house kept by his wife. Only a hopeless optimist could have supposed that that address was unknown on board.[11]

The distinctions between rambling, straggling and desertion were vague, but they could if necessary be specified. At Halifax on 28 May 1758, shortly before sailing to attack Louisbourg, Boscawen issued general orders to his squadron warning that

> All seamen taken up by the patrol on being on shore contrary to order, will be paid for as stragglers, and the same charged against their wages, and also punished if they otherwise misbehave.[12]

The rewards were fixed at ten shillings for a straggler and thirty for a deserter, defined as anyone more than twenty-four hours overdue, and the latter were threatened with court martial. The circumstances were unusual – in a foreign port, on the eve of a major expedition – and Boscawen's attitude towards straggling was more rigorous than most officers'. There was also an element of bluff in the threat of court martial, for a charge of desertion against a man missing less than three weeks would have been difficult to sustain. Even in these regulations, however, there is no question of punishing stragglers (unless they 'otherwise misbehave') except financially. In ordinary circumstances captains sometimes waited months before they 'ran' an absentee on the ship's books,[13] and anyone who returned with a reasonably plausible excuse, and managed to avoid being arrested on the way, stood an excellent chance of escaping any punishment. At some periods during the war there were proclamations in force offering a pardon for deserters, so men could return with guaranteed impunity.[14]

Beyond the wide penumbra of ramblers and stragglers, some of whom had been 'run', but hardly any of whom were deserters in the strict acceptance of the word, there was a large number of men who had deliberately left their ships without permission, but not permanently. Men often ran away, generally drunk, and then thought better of it. They ran to visit their families and then returned, and in one case they ran to escape an outbreak of small-pox aboard.[15] Men sometimes ran for a 'run ashore', to take the leave they felt they had been unjustly denied. In one noteworthy case the men gave warning of their intention by putting on their best shore-going rig, their white duck trousers gleaming in the shadows of the lower deck.[16] This makes it unlikely that they were proposing to leave the Navy, for these clothes were very well adapted for charming the girls, but a more disastrous choice for the serious deserter, concerned to conceal his profession, could scarcely be imagined. Richard Burmingham, a seaman of the *Bristol*, ran in 1748 to visit his family only to find his ship had taken a rich prize in his absence. Being a Petworth man, he enlisted the aid of the Duke of Richmond to try to get his 'R' taken off.[17] All these men were in a sense deserters, but it is clear that they were far from the traditional stereotype of the wretched seaman fleeing the intolerable misery of naval life.

So too was Daniel Tyrrell, able seaman of the *Wasp* sloop in 1755, who was thus described by his captain:

> The man is one of the best men I have – very sober, diligent, has been absent to London with leave and punctually returned to his time, and has been extreme active and instrumental in raising most of the men I have, and is always employed in the boat, and never absents himself from his duty.[18]

This paragon of seamanlike virtue was a deserter from the *Medway*. There was a large traffic in desertion from one ship to another. Men ran from small ships, especially the cramped and leaky sloops, to the relative comfort and less strenuous work of a ship of the line. The *Wasp*, Tyrrell's rather surprising choice, was

> like all the small sloops built in the last peace to prevent smuggling ... They are really very bad vessels to cruise all weathers, and so sure as a seaman is trusted on shore from any of them, he runs away.[19]

An officer could be cashiered for receiving a deserter from another ship, but the temptation not to enquire too closely into the origins of able volunteers was strong, and the captains of sloops often had occasion to complain of their brother officers permitting, or even encouraging this traffic: 'If they are suffered to run from small ships and go on board of large ones unpunished it will be very difficult for us to keep our people.'[20] Even an admiral felt it necessary 'to convince their Lordships [that] their leaving her was not by my connivance', while at least one captain was apparently arranging for men who had run to him to receive their wages for their former ships, which amounted to a direct incentive to desert.[21] Sometimes men even ran to join the marines.[22]

Another motive for running from ship to ship was financial. Since volunteers were entitled to a large bounty, there was a temptation to desert in order to volunteer for another ship, and repeat the process as often as one dared. It was dangerous, for authority regarded desertion for financial reasons as far more serious than anything else except serving the enemy,[23] and it was easy to run into an officer who remembered you, but on the other hand there were severe difficulties, legal and moral, in a court martial convicting a man for desertion who was then actually serving in one of the King's ships. The attempt failed in the case of Barnaby McGinnis who was suspected of this crime, because it was impossible to fault his claim that he had been left behind by his former ship by accident, and entered another from simple willingness to serve.[24] If a man had made no money by desertion, either because he had received no bounty or because he had forfeited more in wages when he was 'run', authority – in this case Admiral Holburne – was inclined to treat the issue very lightly:

> You have not mentioned what should be done with the marine now in confinement ... I think as he left more wages than he received bounty, he might be released and go to his duty.[25]

Probably the most frequent motive of all which tempted men to run from one ship to another was the desire to be reunited with their former shipmates. The cohesion of a settled ship's company was by far the strongest force which bound the Navy together, and officers and men were at one in intensely disliking any idea of breaking one up. If men were drafted away from their ship or their captain, their first reaction was often to run straight back. If newly turned-over men deserted, it tended to be assumed that this was where they had gone: 'as they formerly belonged to Captain Digby in the *Bideford* . . . I dare say they are gone to the *Dunkirk*' (which Digby then commanded).[26] In a particularly striking case, some of Captain Nightingale's former shipmates actually wrote to him aboard his new ship the *Flora* announcing their intention to rejoin him, which they did. Some of these men were court-martialled, but as with other men who had run from ship to ship, it was very difficult to convict them, and after their acquittal the Admiralty tacitly admitted defeat and returned the rest to the *Flora*.[27]

Nothing more effectively undermined the morale and cohesion of a settled ship's company than the suggestion that they might be broken up; it was a quick way to encourage desertion. Even an order to lend men might raise a virtual mutiny. Captain Hervey of the *Monmouth* had to abandon the delights of the London season in a hurry and go down to Rochester to promise 150 of his men that they were only being lent to the *Temple* to help fit her out, and would return to their own ship before she was ready for sea. When the men of Commodore Cotes's squadron were given a month's leave on returning from the West Indies in 1756, they were told to watch the newspapers for an announcement of where they should report for duty, and carefully promised that each ship's company would be kept together.[28]

If this sort of undertaking were not made, or not believed, the results were usually disastrous. When the *Yarmouth* came home from the East Indies in 1760 her entire company was ordered leave. In practice they did not all leave at once, but over a period as the ship was stripped for the dock. Just before Christmas, when there were only a hundred or so left on board, a rumour spread that on their return they were to be sent to the guardship *Princess Royal* at the Nore, with the implication that they were to be split up into drafts for different ships. At once all the remaining men ran, and the commander-in-chief at the Nore pointed out to the Admiralty that it was unlikely that those already on leave would return once they heard the rumour. The Admiralty's reaction was to print advertisements in the newspapers informing the men that the story was false, that they were intended to serve together and form the crew of the new 74-gun *Arrogant*, then just about to be launched at Harwich, and that if they would report for duty at Sheerness, they would be victualled aboard one of the hulks until their new ship was ready. The effect was remarkable: 375 officers and men were either on board the *Yarmouth* in December or on leave from her. Of these at least 340 men, excluding officers, subsequently reported for duty.[29] It would be hard to find a more striking instance of the degree to which loyalty to shipmates kept seamen in the Navy, and the fear of new men, strange faces and other minds drove them away.

The other side of the same coin was that newly formed ships' companies, or men newly come aboard, were the least settled and the most likely to run away. It was a commonplace among officers that new recruits, volunteers as well as pressed men, were not to be trusted on shore until they had settled down. The captain of the *Dragon*, called upon to account for some desertion from his ship, could 'only impute it to the natural levity in seamen and the mixture of which a new ship's company is mostly composed of'.[30]

The accuracy of this sort of observation can be tested by analysing ship's musters and observing how and when men deserted. It will be obvious by now that not all men 'run' on the books were wilful deserters from the Service, or even from their ships, but the relationship is sufficiently close to provide useful evidence of the circumstances in which men were prone to run away. Much of what one finds by studying Run lists is unsurprising. Men ran in home ports and in the Americas, above all in the West Indies: places where there was temptation and opportunity. In the East Indies, where there was nowhere for a European seaman to go, very few went. It is equally unremarkable to find that more men ran from small ships than from large, for we have seen why they were unpopular. Nor is there anything odd in the finding that captains of known brutality suffered higher desertion than good and humane officers.[31]

There is, however, one very striking fact: that the propensity to run was in inverse proportion to time in the ship. The vast majority of men who ran did so soon after they had joined their ships. More than half ran in their first six months aboard, three-quarters within their first year. By the time a man had been in the ship eighteen months, the chances of his running were negligible. This was true regardless of the actual rate of desertion. It was true of small ships as well as large, of good officers and bad, and in every part of the world. It was as true of pressed men as of volunteers. Most interesting of all, it was true of men turned over from other ships. Among the others there were no doubt many men already familiar with life in the Navy, but they cannot easily be identified. Those turned over were by definition already familiar with life aboard a man-of-war; if they showed the same tendency, it cannot have been because naval life as such struck them as an unpleasant novelty; it must have been the transition from one ship to another.

This supports the other evidence which all points to the importance of the ship's company as the basic social unit of the Navy. In an ideal world, no ship's company would ever have been broken up, but kept up to strength with reinforcements as necessary. Even then there would inevitably have been unsettled and unsettling newcomers constantly coming aboard, and in practice in wartime the rate of turn-over as men left the ship and others came to replace them varied from 20 to over 80 per cent per annum (the higher figures in the smaller ships).[32] The Admiralty was very conscious of the importance of keeping shipmates together, but the inevitable demands of wartime operations and the acute shortage of seamen all combined to force a much greater degree of change than it wished, and that in turn encouraged desertion.

Captains themselves were not above encouraging desertion when it suited them. Every ship had a few of the King's hard bargains whom the officers longed to be rid of, and it was easy to arrange to leave them behind 'by accident' in the hope of getting better men to replace them. Men were so often left behind by genuine accidents that it was easy for captains to play this sort of game.[33] The Admiralty was aware of it, and quick to accuse officers whom it suspected of wilful carelessness. Officers were always held responsible when their servants deserted, and charged for their rewards.[34] A prudent commander-in-chief like Admiral Broderick, organizing a panel of captains and surgeons to examine men whom the medical authorities of Haslar Hospital proposed to discharge as invalids, assured the Admiralty that 'I have likewise taken care that none of the men belonged to the captains who were to be examiners'[35] – this to remove from them the temptation to dispose of their least useful men. The Admiralty itself was constrained in 1762 to tell the commander-in-chief at Plymouth that they 'would not have ships supplied with men that are just come from another port, because it will be an encouragement to captains to leave their men behind'.[36]

When all has been said to discount the traditional stereotype of the wretched seaman fleeing the intolerable misery of naval life, it remains clear that many, perhaps a majority of those 'run' on their ships' books, actually intended to leave the Service. It is difficult to speculate about their motives for doing so, but the most obvious temptation to leave a service which, even in wartime, offered many advantages over merchantmen, was undoubtedly money, and this was considered by some contemporaries as the chief cause of desertion. We know of men, particularly among the minority who were married, who were seduced by higher pay elsewhere, but it seems to have been regarded by officers as an exceptional and mitigating circumstance.[37] All officers, however, agreed that paying men increased desertion. For this reason ships were paid only just before they sailed, and the wages were always well in arrears. The 1758 Navy Act prescribed a maximum arrears of six months, but in practice that was administratively impossible even if the officers had thought it desirable.[38] It is difficult to discount the united testimony of experienced officers that putting money in men's pockets encouraged them to run away and spend it.[39] There is statistical evidence to support them, for in the first three months of 1757 1.9 per cent of the 18,770 men with more than a year's pay due deserted, but 4.1 per cent of the 27,279 with less than a year's pay owing.[40] There seems no reason to doubt that this quarter was typical of the war as a whole. It must be said, however, that those least often paid were predominantly in overseas squadrons whose opportunities and temptations to desert were in some cases less, in others more, than prevailed at home, so it cannot be assumed that there is a simple statistical link between frequent pay and frequent desertion. Nor is it clear whether such a link would show the seamen as provident savers, whose 'growing bank' of wages caused them to serve cheerfully,[41] or reckless spenders for whom cash in hand was an irresistible temptation for a spree ashore. Contemporaries firmly believed the latter, and there is no doubt that seamen often left behind far more in forfeited pay than they could have hoped to make up in years of service at the highest rates in merchantmen.[42]

The historian must always be wary of assuming that seamen, any more than other classes of men, were always rational and calculating. In the nature of their profession, seamen were trained to act fast on their own initiative, and many certainly deserted on the spur of the moment, perhaps with no very coherent motives. Officers regarded this as far less culpable than the planned escape, and courts martial often asked whether deserters had taken their clothes, which was a convenient indicator of a planned escape. The intelligent author of a rare lower-deck memoir frankly admits that he deserted, from the Navy and the East India Company in succession, on a whim, losing his possessions and nearly his life. Another was reported by his captain as having run 'not so much with intention to defraud or avoid service as from wantonness and want of thought'.[43]

Sea officers were not on the whole introspective men, and it is unusual to find them reflecting on the motives which led men to desertion. One thoughtful officer who has left us an opinion on the subject was Philip Carteret, who commanded the *Swallow* on Wallis's expedition of 1766. At Madeira he lost eight men who swam asore, almost naked, on their own account 'only to get a skinful of liquor, and then swim back to the ship'. This was very likely, as they had left their clothes, and having recovered them, and seeing them contrite, Carteret pardoned them:

> A gentle whisper of satisfaction was instantly heard through the ship's company, and never were people happier or better pleased; one would have thought that some great fortune had happened to them all; and indeed I was amply rewarded for this indulgence, for these poor fellows were of infinite service to me, as will be seen during the course of the voyage, and always discharged their duty with cheerfulness.

Let no man suffer an opportunity of doing a benevo-
lent action to escape him. The failings of brave men
should be treated with kindness; there was neither
malice nor want of honour in their conduct, they were
only hurried away by the violence of their passions,
which they now very sincerely repented. Unawed by
fear, to which they were strangers, and without giving
themselves time to think what might be the consequence
of their rash behaviour, they boldly took the resolution
of going on shore, and daringly put it into execution.
This is the true genius of our British sailors; a noble
spirit indeed, which ought carefully to be nursed and
encouraged, and which when rightly managed commands our respect.[44]

This incident happened in peacetime, and it is important to
realize that desertion was not an exceptional reaction to wartime
service in the Navy, but a normal part of life in an extremely mobile profession. In peacetime, when it was easy to get a discharge
with a ticket for one's wages, men ran away frequently.[45] They ran
from merchant ships at least as much as from men-of-war, even
when they were not running from one to another, and they did so
in peace as well as war.[46] In the latter part of the nineteenth century more than a fifth of merchant seamen sailing from St John,
New Brunswick, deserted in the course of each voyage;[47] it would
not be surprising if the rate in British ships a century earlier was at
least as high. Privateers suffered as well; the St George of London
lost 5 per cent in a short cruise, and the Liverpool privateer of that
port is said to have lost all but twenty-eight of her 207 men on the
prospect of serious action.[48] Transports, which offered the attractive combination of wartime wage rates and protections from the
press, suffered desertion in spite of it.[49]

Seamen belonged to a highly mobile profession, and were in
the habit of coming and going as they pleased. They valued their
accustomed freedom to ship where they would, for shorter or
longer voyages, and resented attempts to tie them down to unlimited service.[50] This was the Navy's great disadvantage in wartime, for the shortage of seamen was such that it could not avoid

200

unlimited service, and the men knew it. Once it had recruited its men, introduced them to a ship's company and given them time to settle down, it could generally win their loyalty, but in the meantime the temptations and pressures to desert were very high. They affected volunteers and pressed men alike, in fact the evidence gives no strong grounds to argue that their propensities to desert differed by much;[51] what mattered was their attachment, or lack of attachment, to a cohesive ship's company. At one end of a scale of social stability were captains like Edward Hughes who could claim that

> In the course of three years I have had the honour to command the *Somerset*, her company have never been refused going on shore in port wherever she has been employed, and no desertion nor any complaint till that of these newcomers.[52]

At the other end were prisoners of war returning from France, perhaps the most unsettling possible situation, who seized their cartels so frequently that their 'desertion' rate must have approached 100 per cent.[53]

The prevention of desertion can be seen as a sort of game, played by elaborate unwritten rules, in which the recruits' object was to regain their liberty, and the Navy's was to keep them long enough to win their loyalty. Common humanity, operational necessity and the unwritten rules of the game gave men many opportunities of escape, and however serious desertion was as a problem for the Navy as a whole, authority moved slowly and reluctantly to punish individuals. The Admiralty never accepted that firearms could legitimately be used to prevent desertion except in very extreme circumstances, and on the two occasions during the war when men were shot attempting to escape, those concerned were at once court-martialled for murder (partly, in the event of acquittal, to protect them from the vengeance of a civil court).[54] The penalties for desertion were almost entirely financial, and it was extremely difficult to get oneself court-martialled for it. Out of a possible total of about 36,000 instances of desertion, it can be shown that 254 men were court-martialled, of whom thirteen were acquitted, nine found guilty on lesser charges, 176 sentenced to be flogged, and fifty-three to hang. Of these most were pardoned, but it is possible that as many as a dozen may actually have been hanged, mostly for desertion aggravated by other crimes.[55] If desertion had not been too frequent, or conversely if men were very scarce, but chiefly from simple humanity, authority was extremely reluctant to execute deserters.[56] Courts martial were remarkably willing to accept, if not propose, the excuse of youth and inexperience in mitigation.[57] They accepted some very improbable excuses, such as the tale of the man who 'took a walk to see a friend' and got lost, or the man arrested by the guard at Portsea Bridge who claimed he thought it was the dockyard gate (four miles away at the other end of Portsea Island).[58] The risk to a deserter of being court-martialled was extremely small, and of being hanged was infinitesimal – which perhaps explains why even Court Marshall, able seaman of the *Torbay*, tempted fate by deserting her.[59]

One reason why courts martial for desertion were rare is that in many cases they were legally impossible. This was one rule of the game which was written down, in the Articles of War, which held that men were only in the King's service when actually borne for wages on the books of a ship. Men recruited by the Impress Service and transported in tenders were not yet in the Navy, and if they ran away nothing could be done to prosecute them.[60] The same applied to men more than one month in hospitals at home, who then ceased to receive full pay. There was some hope that the men did not realize this, and the Admiralty was careful not to expose the weakness of its position by rash prosecutions.[61]

At the end of the war the game was concluded by the issue of sweeping orders to the Navy Board to take off the 'R's from all deserters except the most serious cases, chiefly those who had run more than once, or run for money, so that in the end even the financial penalty of forfeiture of wages was removed from many. The Navy Board was sternly cautioned to treat the men properly, 'that they may not be put to any unnecessary or unusual expenses whatsoever'.[62] This tenderness for the welfare of men guilty of a capital crime was very characteristic of the spirit in which the

Admiralty approached the problem. The men too, knew how to play the game. When a party broke out of their ship alongside at Portsmouth and escaped out of the yard before the porter could close the gates, they paused outside to give three cheers before dispersing into the town.[63]

Desertion was an elaborate game played by relatively humane rules, but its results were of the utmost consequence for the country. It is both important and difficult to determine how many men the Navy actually lost by desertion. In the first three years of the war the totals were 4310, 3339 and 4647 respectively, that is 12.8 per cent, 6.3 per cent and 7.3 per cent of the mean number of men borne in each year. In 1760 there were 5743 cases of desertion, or 6.7 per cent of the mean number borne in that year.[64] These figures suggest an annual loss during the war of about 7 per cent, which agrees well with an independent calculation of losses from ships in the West Indies during the previous war, and is not inconsistent with the losses of individual ships whose musters have been analysed.[65] A desertion rate of 7 per cent applied to those years whose real total is not known would give a total number of desertions during the war, 1755–1762, of 40,470. It is known that desertions in 1757 represented 36 per cent of discharges from all causes, and the return made to the House of Commons in 1763 stated that from 1755 184,893 seamen and marines had been employed, of which 49,673 remained in service and 133,708 had been discharged from all other causes.[66] Allowing for 35,124 already demobilized from the maximum strength of the previous year, this gives 98,584 discharges from all causes, of which 36 per cent is 35,490. It seems likely, therefore, that there were between 36,000 and 40,000 cases of desertion, in the sense of men 'run' on their ships' books, during the Seven Years' War.

It must be emphasized that these must be cases of desertion, not individual deserters, for no means existed of identifying individuals, and there is no doubt that the same men figure more than once in the statistics, both of recruitment and discharge. The barriers which the Navy erected to prevent men leaving it in wartime were always fairly permeable, and it never lost its character as one very large, but not isolated, employer in a highly mobile profession. Desertion was always a serious practical problem for the

Navy, the prevention of which made all sorts of daily operations far more vexatious than they would otherwise have been, but it was fundamentally tolerable as long as recruitment could keep pace with it, for men escaped only to rejoin the same pool from which the Navy replenished its manpower. The more detached flag officers realized this, and took a philosophical view:

> I always thought it better to risk the losing three or four in the hundred [from leave] than to confine the majority, which not only gives the greatest discontent to the men, but frequently occasions sickness among them, and it [is] certainly more for the good of the Service that a man should run rather than die by sickness. Run men may be catched again for the Service; if not, the trade has them, and more may be impressed from the trade.[67]

In many ways this is the most useful view of the problem of desertion and the Navy's response to it: a successful endeavour to regulate and keep within bounds a traditional liberty of the seafaring life which could not be reconciled with the Navy's wartime needs.

CHAPTER VI

———⊗———

Discipline

A OBEDIENCE AND COMMAND

The Icelandic language is said to have one hundred and fifty words for the cod's head,[1] from which one may judge its importance to Icelanders. The eighteenth-century Navy, by contrast, lacked even a single word for discipline. The word 'discipline' itself was known well enough, but in ordinary usage it bore a sense much nearer to its Latin original than to its modern English sense. Sometimes people used it in something like its modern meaning,[2] but generally they used the word as a rough equivalent to the modern 'training'. When they spoke of 'river discipline' they meant the best state of training a ship's company could achieve before she actually put to sea; when they did set sail captains talked of getting their men into a state of discipline in exactly the sense that modern officers speak of 'working up' their ships to efficiency. When Rodney in 1780 complained of the failure of some of his captains to follow his signals, 'an inattention which ought not to have been shown by an officer who had been bred in the good old discipline of the Western Squadron',[3] he was referring to the thorough training in fleet manoeuvres which he, and they, had received under Anson thirty-five years before. If people did try to talk about discipline as it is nowadays understood, they had to resort to clumsy and vague circumlocutions about 'subordination' or 'authority'.

This observation is of more than linguistic significance, for when men lack a word for something it is safe to assume that they do not often think and talk about it. If eighteenth-century sea officers had worried about discipline in their service, they would certainly have developed at least one word or phrase to express it. In fact they gave it very little thought. This was not because they were untroubled by indiscipline; in the eyes of a modern officer, the discipline of the mid-eighteenth-century Navy would appear lax to the point of anarchy. Insubordination in every form and from every rank and rating in the Service was a daily part of life. Where modern officers expect to command, mid-eighteenth-century officers hoped to persuade. The fact that this did not alarm them was partly because it was a feature of Service life to which they were completely accustomed, and no different from the weakness of civil authority on shore. Much more, however, it reflected an unconscious belief in the stability of society, ashore or afloat. English society in the middle years of the century was, or at least seemed to be, fundamentally secure and almost static. Those in positions of power or authority, and those without either, felt themselves far more bound by mutual ties of dependence and obligation than separated by divisions of class. Forty years later, at the time of the great naval mutinies of 1797, officers and ratings spoke and acted as though they perceived class interests at work which united lower deck and quarter deck against each other. At the time of the Seven Years' War it is difficult to find any such sentiments. However often they were troubled by individual men or groups of men, officers never behaved as though they felt threatened by ratings as a class. The men for their part frequently found reason to complain about particular officers, but always assumed that officers in general would support their legitimate grievances. Naval discipline was by modern standards feeble and anarchic, but it rested on a fundamental stability which no longer exists. Disorder was tolerable then, as it would not be now, because order did not seem to be essentially threatened. The officers and men of the Navy in the 1750s and 1760s were the last generation to be unconscious of the class structure in which they moved. Their problems of discipline were all problems of detail, which carried no implications for the basic stability of the system. Particular cases always remained particular, without producing any general threat to the discipline of the Service as a whole. For this reason discipline never presented itself as a generalized issue or unified concept, merely as a host of individual incidents, trifling or serious, among the daily affairs of the Service.

It is easy to think of discipline as a code of behaviour imposed by external authority and maintained by force, as it often is. Discipline of this sort existed in the Navy in the eighteenth century only in a limited and subsidiary form, riding on the back of the real, natural discipline of the Service. This was something inherent in the nature of seafaring, and common to ships and seamen everywhere. It owed almost nothing to the authority of officers, and almost everything to the collective understanding of seamen. A ship at sea under sail depended utterly on disciplined teamwork, and any seaman knew without thinking that at sea orders had to be obeyed for the safety of all. This was not a matter of unquestioning obedience – those working aloft in particular had to exercise a great deal of initiative – but of intelligent co-operation in survival. No one who had ever been to sea needed to be told this, and it is rare to find the fact remarked on except by observant landmen who found themselves at sea,[4] but it is implicit in the remarkable contrast which is everywhere to be seen between ships at sea and ships in port. In port, and even more on shore, seamen were notoriously riotous and insubordinate. Once the anchor tripped and the last libertymen sobered up, they became a different breed of man, alert, intelligent, and obedient. This was not because the officers suddenly recollected their duty, it was because the prospect of drowning concentrates a man's mind wonderfully.

Ships in port, either in harbour or in a secure anchorage like Spithead, were like little towns without a police force. Authority spoke with a very small voice on board them. In Portsmouth Harbour in 1749 the Master Attendant of the yard was complaining that the guardships' men under his orders shamelessly plundered the ships they were working on, and stopped for their dinners precisely at noon even if it meant leaving ships adrift in the stream. The officers of guardships thought twice before venturing below decks; Lieutenant Jahleel Brenton, a visiting officer who was unwise enough to go below in the *Royal Sovereign* in 1758, was very nearly murdered by a drunken seaman whom he ran into in the gloom.[5] This man too was a visitor from another ship, and the large number of strangers of either sex who were generally aboard ships in port made it even more difficult to maintain order.

At sea, by contrast, even weak or unpopular officers seem to

207

have had no trouble obtaining obedience, for any seaman realized that disobedience was dangerous. This discipline was purely functional, and existed only to preserve the ship's company in safety. It owed very litle to the officers, even though officers were in practice essential to take decisions and to navigate the ship. It was a function of necessity as seamen understood it – or, in some circumstances, misunderstood it. If shipwreck or fire threatened their survival, discipline almost always disintegrated, and the officers were powerless to preserve it. In most of these cases, men's chances of safety would have been greatly improved by keeping their heads and following their officers' orders, but it was a rare and outstanding captain who could keep his men sober and obedient in such a crisis.[6] When the *Prince George*, Admiral Broderick's flagship, was burned at sea in 1758, the greater part of her crew was lost, although there were many ships in company, because of panic.[7] Few officers could hope to maintain any authority in such circumstances, for their authority was a fragile and artificial addition to the natural hierarchy of an ordered ship's company, and most unlikely to survive its destruction.

There is nothing remarkable in this, for in the mid-eighteenth century authority in general was weak. In the absence of a police force even great men were often at risk from mob or individual violence.[8] Sea officers were no different in this respect, for the Admiralty never hoped to sustain their authority off duty ashore, and was reluctant to become involved even if they were attacked by ratings when on duty. Officers who sought sympathy in such cases had to make it clear that they had been in uniform and identifiable as officers, and had offered no provocation, but even so they were likely to be told that their Lordships declined to act 'as what hath happened was done on shore'.[9] Officers who bothered their commander-in-chief with requests for a court martial just because they had been stoned, or 'beat and abused very much' coming off from Portsmouth Point by men from other ships, were likely to get a short answer, for the Navy was not a profession for milksops.[10] As far as the Admiralty was concerned, it was no matter for interference if a petty officer beat up a warrant officer from another ship, when both were off duty.[11] This was an obvious restraint on misuse of authority, for officers had cause to fear the consequences of unpopularity ashore. Lieutenant Ralph Dundas, the 'severe' First Lieutenant of the *Coventry* in 1763, left her two days before paying off to get a head start, but all in vain; a gang led by a gunner's mate caught up with him in Cheapside and beat him severely.[12] In one case when two men stabbed Lieutenant Hicks of the *Maidstone* outside the main gate of Sheerness Yard, a court martial was held, but this appears to have been an almost unique example of official interference.[13] For the most part, officers ashore and off duty were on their own.

Nor was personal violence the only threat they had to encounter. The law, which befriended the enemies of the press gang, was equally available to the rating with a grudge, and officers were frequently prosecuted by their men. Persons awaiting court martial, or even awaiting sentence, prosecuted the captains who confined them for false imprisonment. A master who found a seaman asleep on watch (a capital offence under the Articles of War) and shook him by the collar to wake him, was prosecuted for assault.[14] Cases like these were often undertaken by lawyers like 'Powell at the Vine at Portsmouth (who I am told gets his bread there by undertaking these kinds of suits)'. It was he who had the boatswain of the *Somerset* thrown into prison. That officer had received a complaint from the coxswain of the pinnace about William Welshman, a troublesome member of his boat's crew, who had broken two oars. The boatswain reprimanded the offender, who replied with abuse. The boatswain struck him with his rattan, whereupon Welshman followed him about the ship shouting further abuse, went ashore, and fee'd Powell the lawyer to complete his revenge. 'He is a very good officer', Captain Hughes reported apologetically, 'and acted as is customary in his station, with humanity.'[15] All the Admiralty could do in such cases was to instruct their solicitor to defend the officers. It was quite impossible to prevent the suits being brought.

The Articles of War, as revised in 1749, stated specifically that offences committed on shore were cognizable at court martial as if they had been committed at sea,[16] so that the Admiralty might have taken a stronger line in at least some of these cases if it had felt it advisable. In many circumstances, however, its legal position was insecure. It has already been noted that persons not borne for full pay on the books of one of H.M. ships were not liable to naval discipline. This included not only new recruits, but also the crews of the hired tenders which conveyed them. 'Hired armed vessels', which were chartered merchantmen commissioned into the Navy and employed as convoy escorts, were liable to naval discipline, but they were in practice little different from the hired tenders, and it is not surprising that their crews, especially foreigners among them, sometimes rejected the Navy's authority.[17]

In spite of legal weaknesses like these, the fragility of authority in the Navy was not primarily the fault of the law. It was a feature of society in general, to which the Navy conformed. The peculiar nature of seafaring gave to ships at sea a natural cohesion unknown ashore, and perhaps permitted the Navy a legal code which, as we shall see, was remarkably lenient by the standards of its day, but the Navy remained a part of British society, its officers and men drawn from the body of the population, and partook of its ideas and ideology. Whatever they might feel about their own service and their own cases, officers genuinely shared the common distrust of too much governmental, and especially military, power. Admiral Rodney was very much a stickler for his own authority, but when he was sent the prospectus for a proposed naval charity school which emphasized that the boys would be brought up in principles of the strictest obedience to authority, he scribbled firmly in the margin: 'Those who are put over us if they act their part right, we ought to reverence. If they do not I say *no*. None of your passive obedience and non resistance, especially among the seamen.'[18] The easy-going and informal discipline of the mid-eighteenth-century Navy was not simply something forced on authority by its inability to act more firmly, it was to an extent the conscious choice of people who believed that that was the right and natural way to behave, and would have ordered things so even if they had had alternatives.

Some modern writers have represented the Navy as a strictly ordered, hierarchical society, brutally repressing the slightest deviance and entirely controlling the public and private lives of its personnel – in short, what sociologists call a 'total society'.[19] It will be clear by now, and clearer still in due course, how far this fantasy is from the facts. In reality, when brutality occurred, it tended to destroy naval discipline, which rested on unstated consent, not force. Ill treatment, especially capricious and arbitrary ill treatment, made for disordered and dangerous ships. The most famous case in the mid-century of a cruel captain was that of Captain the Hon. William Hervey of the *Superb*. Though he was a fine seaman, the ship was completely dismasted not long before the court martial which finally broke him, and well before that she was notorious for indiscipline. 'There is no government in that ship,' the commander-in-chief reported; 'the men run away with the boats and won't obey their officers. Something must be done or that ship is lost to the Service.'[20] 'Government' – that is, discipline – was the condition upon which survival at sea and success in war depended. If officers like Hervey had been common, or behaviour like his tolerable, the Navy could never have become an efficient fighting force.

B   VIOLENCE AND HUMANITY

The eighteenth century was the age of benevolence, an age in which Christian virtues were almost universally approved, and not infrequently practised.[1] The man who helped the needy, protected the weak, and used power with justice and mercy was respected, if not always imitated. In this, as in most other matters, the officers and men of the Navy accepted the values and attitudes of the community from which they came. Almost all of them were Christians, and though their degree of active commitment to a life of faith varied from devotion to indifference, they were no more untouched by the moral climate of their times than any other class of men. It is necessary to make this obvious statement because one would have to believe, if one believed some authors' accounts of life in the Navy, that the majority of officers were monsters of cruelty.[2] In fact, as we have seen already, they had strong practical reasons for showing consideration to their men, for in many ways an unpopular officer was at a severe professional disadvantage compared to those who could attract able volunteers. A brutal officer was, of necessity, an inefficient officer, distrusted by the Service for reasons both moral and practical.

At the same time, the eighteenth century was an age in which personal violence was more common than it is now. Flogging was a frequent punishment for both children and adults, and even in the highest levels of society fights, brawls or duels were not unusual. People were more accustomed to settle affairs with a blow than now seems proper, and the Navy was no exception. Captain Augustus Hervey, as polished a sophisticate as any in the Service, punched his steward in the mouth in anger, while Captain Charles Middleton, an officer of real piety and a future First Lord of the Admiralty, kicked one of his warrant officers in the backside.[3] The fact that this sort of behaviour was possible bespeaks the different standards of a different age, but there were standards nevertheless, well understood and precisely defined. The brutality of a William Hervey was quite unacceptable to naval opinion,[4] and three commanders were dismissed the Service during the Seven Years' War for cruelty or oppression: Edward Clarke, Thomas Smith (who by coincidence succeeded him in command of the same ship, the *Jason*), and Penhallow Cuming of the *Blandford*.[5] It is clear from these cases that cruelty did exist, but equally clear that it was not tolerated.

Between an officer like William Hervey, whose sadistic caprices strongly suggest that he was unbalanced, and one like Captain Samuel Faulknor, who made his men 'do their duty like brisk lads' but absolutely forbade his officers to strike them, lies a broad range of behaviour. There is no doubt that in practice officers did vary greatly in the degree of violence which they employed. Faulknor, in two years commanding the *Windsor*, three times had men flogged (two of whom admitted they deserved it), and three times struck men himself.[6] There were probably few officers who used less violence than that, and many who used more, but the degree of violence which was acceptable was clearly defined by public opinion on the lower deck, and articulated at courts martial on charges of cruelty. In one such case one of his men remarked of

Captain Alexander Campbell of the *Fortune* sloop that 'sometimes he would strike a man in wearing or tacking and other occasions, but never barbarously'. Otherwise he was very mild, 'if in fault any way he was too much so, nor was he used to drub or drive the fellows'.[7] Much the same attitude appears in a petty officer's opinion of Lieutenant Teague of the *Penguin* sloop:

> If things were not done properly, the lieutenant would beat the people, sometimes severely. He was otherwise always very tender and kind, by taking care of the sick and giving people liberty. He has given them grog at his expense to encourage them in their duty.[8]

An enquiry into the conduct of an officer of the *Albany* reported that

> We could not find that he had any ways treated the complainants with cruelty, but at sometime had struck them with a small rattan, when slack in their duty. The officers and rest of the sloop's company declared they never knew him severe in the execution of his duty.[9]

The cooper of the *Juno* complained that Lieutenant Wood had assaulted him. On enquiry, the commander-in-chief reported that the lieutenant had indeed struck him with a small stick, but it had been well deserved, the cooper being 'a very idle, drunken, insolent fellow'. Another admiral exonerated Lieutenant Birt of the *Captain*, who had given a leave-breaker twelve strokes with a 'bargue sterrer' (presumably a burgoo – or porridge – stirrer).[10] All these comments appeal implicitly to an accepted standard of violence. Whether the officers complained of had really not exceeded it is perhaps less interesting than the very similar attitude shown by all the witnesses, both officers and ratings.

In cases which called for it, naval public opinion could be quite exact about what constituted acceptable violence. Striking an elderly landman with a broomstick in the urgency of a chase, though not well thought of, was insufficient to secure a conviction at court martial. The use of a boatswain's rattan two and three-quarter inches in circumference was not in itself considered unrea-

sonable by another court.[11] A case on the margin of acceptable behaviour was reported of Mr Crane, boatswain of the *Kennington*.
Though a good and sober officer he was 'very passionate', and had
in one case beaten a man excessively; on the other hand, the complainants were 'very much addicted to liquor, quarrelsome, sulky,
abusive'.[12] Striking a man's face was completely unacceptable.
William Russell, able seaman of the *Seaford*, a bad character who
had frequently been in trouble, was convicted of knocking down a
midshipman, but awarded no punishment, because he had first
been hit about the face, which the court regarded as a provocation
justifying the assault.[13] Also well beyond tolerable limits was the
practice of Captain Cuming of flogging men who took more than
five minutes to answer the pipe for 'all hands'.[14] This is a revealing
attitude, for all hands were only called when they were needed, frequently in an emergency in which the safety of all on board might
depend on the promptness with which the command was carried
out. It should have been possible to get on deck from any corner of
a small ship like the *Blandford* in a couple of minutes at most; in
the circumstances a modern captain might well regard five minutes
as an excessively generous allowance. Probably Cuming's cruelty
was held to lie in flogging instead of imposing a lesser punishment,
but even so it is an interesting insight into the degree of discipline
expected at sea.

In questions of civility and politeness between officers and ratings, practice varied greatly. As early as 1739 Vernon was urging
his officers to 'exercise their authority over them with dignity as
much as may be, to establish the affections of the men for the public service'.[15] From the conduct of Middleton and Augustus Hervey
it is evident that the ideal was still some way from attainment, but
elementary marks of respect were in common use. There was no
form of personal salute, but junior officers were expected to tip
their hats to senior, and petty officers and foremastmen to doff
theirs when speaking to officers in formal circumstances. Relations
between them were still more likely to be coarse and familiar than
stiff and polite, but in the majority of cases they seem to have followed a pattern of respectful informality. On the whole, Service
opinion did not see personal violence as inconsistent with close
relations between officers and men, but there was some friction on

this, as on other, points between the Navy and the marines. Marine officers were under orders not to strike their men, nor to permit them to be struck by others, and a sea lieutenant who beat an insolent sergeant of marines was reprimanded for conduct unbecoming an officer.[16] In this case the ostensible issues were underlaid by inter-service rivalry.

There was a particular reason why it was a delicate issue whether marines might be struck by sea officers – or more often petty officers. Officers and petty officers did not use personal violence indiscriminately against all ratings in all circumstances. Leaving aside for the moment the matter of deliberate punishment for offences committed, men were struck chiefly in moments of crisis – in chase, in tacking or wearing, or whatever. Those who were struck were not the seamen, who were mostly aloft and out of reach, and in any case required no encouragement to do the job which they knew thoroughly. The officers' problem lay with the inexperienced landmen in the waisters and afterguard under their immediate eye. Their collective strength in pulling and hauling was essential, but they were not expected to show much individual skill. It was, however, essential that they work in an organized and co-ordinated fashion, and it was commonly held that there was no alternative to herding them about the deck with blows, or at the least in chasing up the lazy with a rattan. The marines were among these ignorant landmen, and for practical purposes indistinguishable from them, since they wore no uniform at sea – hence the difficulty of not hitting them if such was the practice. Hence also the toleration, not to say approval, with which seamen regarded the custom, for they were not the sufferers. The able seaman viewed landmen and marines with an indifference verging on contempt, and had no great objection to seeing them chased about their duty.

The Admiralty, on the other hand, took the issue seriously. They never went so far as to forbid such 'starting', but they were anxious to restrict it as far as possible. In February 1755 they heard a report (false, as it happened) of

> a poor countryman who entered on board the *Grafton* being beat in such a manner by Lieutenant Prescott as to jump overboard, only for doing some of the ship's busi-

ness in an awkward manner, owing entirely to his inexperience. .... Such inhumanity is very offensive to their
Lordships and brings an odium on the Service whereby
many useful men are deterred from entering into it.[17]

It seems probable that officers like Samuel Faulknor who followed
the spirit of this comment were still a minority, but intelligent
effort was being applied, apparently quite independently of the
Admiralty, to improve the conditions of the people aboard ship.
Part of the problem which led officers to 'start' their men was that
they were dealing with an undifferentiated mass of persons, few or
none of whom they knew as individuals. It was extremely difficult
in the hurry of manoeuvres at sea to distinguish between stupidity,
clumsiness, inexperience and laziness, and to react accordingly.
Except in very small ships with stable companies (itself something
of a contradiction), officers could not hope to know even their
men's names.

The solution to the problem was the divisional system: an idea
like all great ideas, simple, elegant, and obvious once it had been
thought of. It appears to have been the invention of Vice-Admiral
Thomas Smith, an officer now largely forgotten, who deserves to
be held in honour for an idea which has contributed so much to the
efficiency of the Navy and the well-being of its men. Smith took
command of the Downs Squadron in 1755, and very soon after circulated the outline of his scheme, with a request for captains to
suggest detailed improvements on it.[18]

The principle of the divisional system was, and is, simply that
each of the lieutenants should take charge of a division of the
ship's company, for whose welfare and efficiency he should be particularly responsible. Under the lieutenants the midshipmen were
allocated sub-divisions. The warrant officers looked after their
own departments, and the master's mates mustered the seaman
petty officers. Each officer was responsible for the discipline and
cleanliness of his division. Smith's regulations paid particular attention to the need to wash hammocks regularly in rotation, to
muster each man's clothes twice a week to see that they had not
been lost or sold for drink, and to enforce a change of linen at each

muster. The midshipmen of the sub-divisions were to train their men in the use of the great guns and small arms, and all divisional officers were to take pains to know their men as individuals, and attend to their welfare.

It would be difficult to exaggerate the importance of this innovation. The larger grew the Navy as a whole and its ships individually, the more able seamen were diluted in wartime by landmen and foreigners, the more crucial it became that officers should handle their men in an intelligent and humane fashion. The advantages of the system were obvious, and it was soon spread throughout the Service by ships from the Downs squadron. By the end of the Seven Years' War, though not yet universal, it was widely known and approved. Influential officers like Lord Howe were early exponents of it, and by the time the young Captain William Cornwallis assumed command of the *Prince Edward* in 1765 some form of divisional system was a natural choice.[19]

The advantages of the divisional system lay in part in greater efficiency and closer control, but it was also an expression of a concern for the welfare of the ratings which officers showed in other ways. It was accepted as a moral duty by good officers to take particular care of their sick, which usually included sending them delicacies from the captain's private stores.[20] In their capacities as patrons and protectors of their men, captains exerted themselves to obtain for them pay or prize money, and if they died, their widows and orphans had friends to intercede for them.[21] This was accepted good practice, which does not of course mean that all officers conformed to it. There were always many too negligent or indifferent to do what was expected of them, but the standard which they failed to uphold was a standard nevertheless, implicitly recognized and from time to time explicitly upheld by the general opinion of the Service. It was characteristic of the age that this genuine and practical humanity co-existed with a tolerance for personal violence which would today be considered the mark of coarse brutality. By the standards of the eighteenth century, the ways in which violence was used in the Navy were generally acceptable, even enlightened, and did not contradict the real benevolence of good officers.

c CRIME AND PUNISHMENT

Any organized community, especially one in which men live and work as close to one another, and depend on teamwork as much, as they did in the Navy, is bound to encounter the need to define and repress crime. The eighteenth-century Navy experienced more problems in this than it need have done because it largely lacked a developed legal code. The ordinary law of the land was almost never admitted to run on board men-of-war, but the Service had little that was effective to put in its place. The only written body of naval law was the Articles of War, a haphazard collection of regulations and admonishments largely concerned with court martial offences by officers. They offered very little guidance to the captain facing the ordinary petty disciplinary problems of daily life. The Admiralty issued a small volume of *Regulations and Instructions relating to His Majesty's Service at Sea*, which purported to describe the duties of each officer, but did so chiefly in terms of accounting responsibilities, and said little about discipline. It did however state explicitly that no captain could on his own authority punish a man with more than twelve lashes. This at once presented a considerable difficulty. The crimes mentioned in the Articles of War and cognizable at court martial were serious ones, and courts martial were accustomed to award severe sentences for them. Moreover courts martial were extremely cumbersome instruments, difficult to organize and by no means predictable in their results. It was out of the question to summon them except in really important cases. This left many offences which seemed to be too serious to be let off with a mere twelve lashes, but could not possibly justify a court martial, nor deserve the punishment which it would be likely to award. No help was offered to the officer facing this common dilemma.

A similar problem presented itself at a lower level. A dozen lashes was not only the maximum a captain might inflict on his own authority, but pretty well the minimum which, in the opinion of many officers, justified the elaborate and time-consuming spectacle of a flogging, with the gratings rigged and the hands turned up to witness punishment. (In the naval context, the word 'punishment' was virtually synonymous with flogging.) A flogging was itself too severe and formal a punishment for many everyday offences, but a captain had no instructions as to how else he might deal with them. There were certain traditional sea punishments, for example making a man 'lord of the heads' (he had to keep them clean), but there was no general system of 'defaulters', and not much unpleasant work aboard ship which was not essential and therefore part of ordinary duty anyway. Leave could be stopped, but only if there was some prospect of granting it in the near future. For incompetence or abuse of authority a petty officer could be disrated, but there was nowhere for a common seaman or idler to be reduced to. 'Able seaman' was a simple description, and a man could not be disrated to ordinary or landman just because he had been making trouble. There was a real problem for officers to find suitable punishments for trivial offences, and it was this which led so many of them to use canes. It seemed to them, not unreasonably, to be more humane to give a quick blow and forget the affair, than to condemn a man to the delay and severity of a flogging. It was also far less inconvenient for all, it avoided disrupting the ship's routine, and it accorded with simple justice in matching the slightness of the offence with that of the punishment. As Captain Peyton of the *Prince* pointed out, if officers were to get into trouble 'for conveying now and then the lesser punishment of a stroke instead of applying to me' (for a flogging), discipline at sea would become impossible.[1]

Just the same problem presented itself in a magnified form with offences which seemed too serious to be dealt with just by a dozen lashes. Different officers solved it in different ways. Some simply accepted the large gap in the responses available to them, and realized that as a result punishments might be either more severe or more lenient than the crime warranted. Usually it was the latter, for everyone was anxious to avoid courts martial if at all possible. Rear-Admiral Mostyn (not the gentlest of officers) proposed a dozen lashes each for cases of drunkenness and mutiny to save the bother of a court martial.[2] Admiral Smith dealt with some men who had robbed French prisoners of war by flogging them in the presence of their victims, and warning them how lucky they had been to escape a court martial for theft, which would certainly have punished them far more severely. In the case of some deserters taken up a few days after others had been sentenced by a court martial to between one and three hundred lashes for the same offence, he felt obliged to ask for a trial, as 'it might seem partiality if they were dismissed with a dozen lashes only, which is, as I take it, the highest customary punishment in the Navy'.[3]

A much more common answer to the problem was to exceed the permitted twelve lashes. Just how frequently this was done is difficult to say, for though captains were supposed to record floggings in their logs, with the number of lashes and the offence, most were very careless in doing so, and either omitted the number of lashes, or omitted the fact altogether. Some, however, openly recorded numbers of lashes in excess of twelve, and from them one may say that it seems to have been uncommon for a captain to exceed twenty-four lashes. This was the case with one officer who has left us both an official log with false figures and a private journal with true figures. It does not seem that captains who did this were any less popular with their men, and some, like Boscawen, were conspicuous favourites.[4]

Just as the same argument of humanity could be invoked in these cases as in the others. If the alternative were a court martial, it seemed to many officers far better to dispose of the matter with relative leniency, informality and speed by ignoring the regulations. Occasionally the Admiralty enquired why a captain had punished a man himself for a capital offence, but generally they were happy to have as few courts martial as possible, and did not investigate too closely how they had been avoided.[5] It was extremely foolish for any rating to demand a court martial when threatened with a flogging, but occasionally some sea lawyer tried, usually with disastrous results. One marine who denied the authority of his officers and refused to accept a flogging was sentenced by court martial to six hundred lashes; a seaman who knocked down a midshipman and refused to accept twelve lashes for it received two hundred from a court martial.[6] Disparities like these make it clear why captains felt it more humane as well as more practical to exceed twelve lashes than to summon a court martial. As Captain Peyton put it in applying for a court martial on a man who had had one of the lieutenants arrested for striking him:

I told him that as he was resolved to act up to the rigour of the law with the officer, I would show him that there was a great difference between the receiving a stroke and away from an officer and the weight of the Articles of War.[7]

The weight of the Articles of War was in fact a great deal less than the Admiralty desired. Although revised in 1749, they remained a haphazard collection of regulations and admonitions, in which both offences and punishments were vaguely defined, and some of the commonest crimes were not mentioned at all. There was for example no offence of homicide other than murder, so that courts martial had to be held in many cases in which there was no suspicion of deliberate killing, and an acquittal was inevitable.[8] Although the Admiralty *Regulations and Instructions* were largely concerned with officers' responsibilities for stores and accounts, the Articles of War offered no charge of fraud, and it was impossible to court-martial an officer detected in this crime.[9] The offence of mutiny was so loosely defined that it was often used when 'striking a superior' would have been more appropriate. The punishments specified were either death, or 'such punishment as a court martial shall think fit to inflict'. In the revision of 1749 Anson's Board of Admiralty had managed to secure a considerable reduction in the number of offences for which a court was at liberty to vary a death sentence, but even so there were only eight crimes for which the death sentence was mandatory, and a further eleven for which it might be awarded. The eight were: corresponding with the enemy, cowardice or neglect of duty (three offences, defined in a vague and overlapping fashion), taking a ship over to the enemy, burning a ship or magazine, murder, and buggery.

The Articles of War had several serious weaknesses apart from their vagueness. In 1749 Anson's Board had tried and failed to remedy one of them by making officers on half-pay subject to naval discipline. The violent protests from sea officers had forced the ministry to back down,[10] with the result that an officer had only to resign his commission to escape from inconvenient situations. The Admiralty could refuse to accept his resignation, but it had no real means to prevent officers who were prepared to sacrifice their careers (or wait for their political friends to get into office) from withdrawing from active service. Another deficiency had theoretically been filled by a new clause inserted in 1749 which made offences committed on shore 'in the actual service and full pay of His Majesty's ships' cognizable as though they had been committed afloat.[11] In practice, as we have seen, 'actual service' was construed as meaning 'on duty', and even then the Admiralty was extremely reluctant to get involved.

A court martial was an unwieldy and unpredictable instrument, assembled by authority only if it seemed unavoidable, and viewed with considerable trepidation as a weapon which was quite likely to misfire. It had to be presided over by the second in command of the squadron or port, and consist of all post-captains, or failing them commanders, whose ships were then in company, to a minimum of five and a maximum of thirteen. Only serious illness duly certified could excuse a captain's presence.[12] Even the briefest trial would take a morning, and if it had a large backlog of cases, a court martial might sit for several days, during which the work of the port or station would be paralysed by the absence of all the captains. In time of war there were better things for them to be doing. On overseas stations, particularly with the smaller squadrons like that in the Leeward Islands which were widely dispersed on cruising stations, months might elapse before a bare quorum could be assembled. Moreover it was necessary to collect not only five captains, but the prosecuting officer, the key witnesses, and of course the accused, all of whom might be in different ships. Men awaiting trial at court martial often languished in irons for months without any strong possibility of an early delivery, which led their officers to apply for a pardon on the grounds that they had suffered enough. From the inconvenience to the ship of keeping prisoners under guard for long periods, and the inconvenience to the Service of trying them, such requests were usually granted. Men in irons were released if the ship went into action, and good behaviour in the face of the enemy was another useful excuse for pardoning the accused.[13]

The court martial once assembled consisted of a panel of captains, all of them legally untrained, assisted by a judge advocate

The quarter deck of the *Deal Castle*, 20, on passage home from the West Indies in 1775, by Thomas Hearn. The view is taken from outside the captain's cabin door, looking forward along the port side. Note the untethered goat, and the fowls in coops stacked behind the man at the wheel. Behind the two officers talking in the foreground some work is being done on the main rigging. At the starboard gangway (in the right background) the midshipmen have assembled with their quadrants to practise taking their noon sights. This was the most spacious and least cluttered area of deck in the ship.

A twelve-gun ketch-rigged sloop, one of those built in the 1750s for the suppression of smuggling. The figures of the crew are to scale, and this was by no means the smallest class of man-of-war.

A mess table slung between two guns, here on board H.M.S. *Victory*. The mess traps ranged on the table would be slung from the deckhead or against the side when out of use. The benches are modern, and originally the men probably sat on their sea chests.

The Surgeon's dispensary on the orlop deck of the *Victory*, next door to (and about the same size as) his cabin. Only the largest ships provided such spacious luxury.

The galley stove of H.M.S. *Victory*; iron stoves of this pattern were introduced in the 1750s. The hearth is on the right, with a spit for roasting, the door of the oven is in the side, and the lids of the cauldrons in which the ship's company's meals were cooked are visible to the left of the chimney.

A model of Cook's ship the *Endeavour*, showing her company and some of her stores to scale. The *Endeavour* was actually a merchant ship bought into the Navy for Cook's voyage, but the Navy commissioned and armed other ships like her, and there were many regular men-of-war of a similar size.

A lieutenant, by Dominic Serres.

A seaman, by Serres, wearing petticoat breeches. His waterman's cap and badge doubtless distinguishes him as a member of the crew of the captain's barge drawn up behind him.

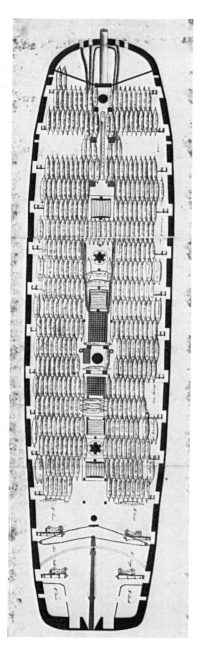

The divisional system at work: this plan of the gun deck of a ship of the line, showing the slinging of the hammocks of one watch, each hammock named and numbered, was probably compiled by a lieutenant to keep account of the men of his division. The more spacious berths along the sides belong to the petty officers, and the open space aft is the gunroom, where the sweep of the tiller overhead restricts the berths to the sides.

Anson in 1755, engraved after Reynolds.

Boscawen in about 1754, engraved after Allan Ramsay.

Keppel as a young commodore in 1749, by Reynolds. Having lost most of his hair and teeth to scurvy on Anson's voyage round the world, Keppel preferred to be painted with his hat on and his mouth shut.

Augustus Hervey in 1767, by Gainsborough, who has well caught his insolent self-confidence.

The lower deck of a ship in port, sketched about 1800, but the scene would have been much the same forty years earlier. The men have got their sea chests up from below and their 'wives' on board. The guns are still secured for sea, with their muzzles elevated to house against the upper cills of the ports, rather than run out to make more room inboard as was often done in port.

An Admiralty advertisement, from the *Public Advertiser* of 26 December 1760: it was this notice which recalled the *Yarmouth*'s stragglers.

who was usually the admiral's secretary and might have some passing knowledge of the law. Together they had to interpret the loose and contradictory language of the Articles of War, and it is not surprising that their verdicts were, taken as a whole, extremely inconsistent, and taken individually, often quixotic. Sometimes courts adopted a position of precise legalism, acquitting because the wrong date appeared on the charge, because the officer to whom the order to hold the court had been directed was absent, or because the prosecuting officer was in jail.[14] At other times they cheerfully pursued justice as it appeared to them with scant regard for the wording of the Articles. The most obvious example of this is the fact that they seldom awarded the death sentence in many cases in which it was mandatory. They were quite capable of convicting on a charge which had not actually been brought, as in the case of George Henderson, boatswain's mate of the *Magnanime*, who got in a fight when drunk and fell overboard with his opponent, who was drowned. Henderson was charged with murder, acquitted as it was evidently an accident, and sentenced to receive fifty lashes and be disrated for fighting.[15] This was no doubt questionable from the legal point of view, but it is typical of many decisions of courts martial in being more irregular than unfair. It is remarkable how difficult it is to find courts martial which, on the minutes of evidence, seem to have reached unjust verdicts – or rather, it is difficult to find them convicting the innocent, for their willingness to acquit in the face of damning evidence was surprising. The only court martial of a rating during the Seven Years' War which looks like a serious miscarriage of justice is the conviction of William Howson of the *Norwich* of desertion even though he produced a certificate from St Thomas's Hospital proving that he had been ill.[16] He was pardoned by the Admiralty. There are many cases, especially of desertion, where the court accepted improbable excuses,[17] or returned lenient sentences. The death penalty was available for the crime which actually received two dozen lashes, or even no punishment at all.[18] Courts were sometimes willing to believe that men not long in the Service did not realize that they were not supposed to run away – which perhaps was not as unlikely as it seems considering the freedom with which men ran from merchantmen.[19] It is also noteworthy that courts martial often judged the accused guilty but lunatic, or refused to try the evidently unbalanced.[20] Commodore Keppel sent up the verdict on a man sentenced to death for trying to murder him on his own quarter deck with the comment that 'I cannot help thinking that the man, who is of a melancholy and sullen turn of mind, must be disordered in his senses'.[21]

The court martial assembled to try a rating consisted of the prosecuting officer, the panel of officers who judged and sentenced, and the accused, who had to conduct his or their own defence. The rating on trial for a serious crime was psychologically and practically in a very weak position, however lenient the court might be. This, at least, was the usual position up to the moment of conviction. At that point it is possible to observe in the minutes of courts martial a subtle change in the social dynamics of the trial. The prosecutor (plus the accused's captain if he were not himself prosecuting), would be a shipmate of the accused, and other shipmates, officers or men, might be admitted to offer him a good character in mitigation. From being a contest between one or more ratings accused and many officers judging, the trial changed to one between the officers and men of one ship and the captains of the others. Officers frequently appeared at courts martial to vouch for the good characters of their men, sometimes in decidedly implausible cases.[22] It was not unusual for the prosecuting officer, having secured his conviction, to appear as a witness in mitigation of his shipmate's crime, and courts sometimes received petitions from the accused's shipmates appealing on his behalf.[23] If the accused were an officer the solidarity of shipmates was equally or more evident. Captain Vincent of the *Weymouth*, charged with cowardice in action, was supported at his trial by a petition signed on behalf of all by 169 members of his ship's company, all who could write their names, in favour of their beloved and admired captain for whom and with whom they were willing to face death. Vincent was found partly guilty, and the petition, which was as requested entered in the formal record of the trial, undoubtedly had an effect in rehabilitating his reputation.[24] A rather different form of group solidarity was that of the marines in face of the Navy, as evidenced by the petition in favour of a marine lieutenant from the men he was accused of robbing.[25]

Leaving aside all common law offences, the number of capital statutes in the eighteenth century exceeded two hundred. It has been calculated that in the 1760s about 60 per cent of those condemned to death in London and Middlesex were actually executed, or about thirty-three persons a year.[26] By comparison, the naval code, with fewer than twenty crimes for which the death penalty might be awarded, was notably mild, and the great difficulty of holding courts martial, combined with their reluctance to hang men, made it more lenient still. Of the eight offences for which the death penalty was in theory compulsory, only murder and buggery usually attracted it. Most of the other six were either very rare or difficult to define, but even with murder and buggery courts martial were quite capable of returning a verdict of guilty and not sentencing the prisoner to death.[27] In the case of crimes like desertion, mutiny or striking an officer, courts seldom awarded the death penalty. Of 254 men accused of desertion between 1755 and 1762, only one-fifth were sentenced to hang, and less than one-twentieth were actually executed, almost all for desertion aggravated by murder, repeated offences, or serving the enemy.[28] From a strictly objective point of view it was perhaps better to be condemned to death, with a very good chance of pardon and no punishment, than to receive the sentences of several hundred lashes which courts martial often awarded, for this was one aspect of naval legal practice which was at least as severe as punishment ashore. But it needs to be emphasized how rare courts martial were, and how difficult it was to be tried by one. Merely knocking down a petty officer was insufficient; in a typical incident, a drunken sailor who attacked the ship's corporal was just bidden to go to bed, and no more would have been heard had he not insisted on making a fight of it.[29]

The relative leniency and great flexibility of naval justice served among other things to protect officers and men from the vengeance of civil courts ashore, which were often available to the Navy's enemies. It was a moral duty for any officer to do his best to keep his men out of the hands of the civil courts in which they were likely to meet injustice. Thus Commodore Keppel refused to hand over to the Attorney-General of Jamaica a marine sentry accused of murder (having fired on a boat trying to come aboard his ship in

Port Royal Harbour), not only to uphold the independence of the Service, but to protect the man himself from what there was good reason to fear would have been no fair trial. In a similar case at Plymouth the port admiral unwisely allowed the coroner to hold an inquest, and the Admiralty felt obliged to let the law take its course.[30] If men did find themselves in court ashore, their officers were expected to act in their defence. Thus Admiral Holburne supported the petition of two seamen condemned to hang at Winchester Assizes, who, as he explained, had only participated in a riot against the Portsmouth whores, and in another case he allowed Captain Edwards of the *Belliqueux* leave in order to attend the trial of one of his petty officers and give him a good character.[31] Two years later he reported to the Admiralty with indignation the conduct of Captain Abdy of the *Beaver* sloop in handing over to the civil power, without even informing his senior officer, a marine who had shot an escaping deserter:

> The poor fellow for doing his duty and obeying his officer's orders sent to gaol all this time, tried, and like to been hanged – and would have been so had not by accident Lord Harry Powlett and the adjutant of marines from hence been there [Winchester], for the marine [commanding] officer here knew nothing of the matter, which if I had, I should most certainly have acquainted their Lordships of immediately, who doubtless at least would have directed officers to appear there in his behalf. I think this is such an unofficer-like behaviour that I can't help representing it to their Lordships.[32]

It is sometimes assumed that the chief or only functions of a disciplinary system is to preserve authority; in other words, in the naval context, that punishments and courts existed to protect the officers from their men. It is not self-evident that this must always be so, and from the crimes which were taken seriously, and the severity with which they were punished, it is possible to argue that preserving officers' authority was in practice a relatively minor object of naval discipline. We have already noticed the opinion of Rear-Admiral Mostyn that mutiny and drunkenness deserved a dozen lashes each. Even allowing that 'mutiny' may have meant no more than striking an officer, it seems to modern eyes a surprising equivalence, but the crimes which attracted the most severe punishment, both at court martial and informally, seem generally to have been those which threatened, not the officer's authority, but the comfort or safety of the shipboard community as a whole. The worst crime, in contemporary opinion, was undoubtedly sodomy, which often attracted the death penalty, and in one case the extraordinary sentence of one thousand lashes,[33] which if delivered all at once, rather than divided into two or more instalments at long intervals as was the practice with severe flogging sentences would have been equivalent to death. Next came murder, which was almost as rare, and after that theft, by far the most serious crime which was at all common. Because ships were paid just before sailing, men often had large sums in cash in their possession, with little privacy or security to protect it. A thief among the ship's company destroyed its mutual bonds of trust and loyalty more swiftly than anything else. Though the victims were almost always ratings rather than officers, courts martial habitually treated theft much more severely than, say, mutiny or desertion. A single court which in the course of one day tried three men from the same ship sentenced a deserter to two hundred lashes, a mutineer to three hundred, and a thief to five hundred.[34] This was a fair index of the relative seriousness of these crimes. Theft regularly attracted sentences at court martial of two to five hundred lashes, and offers an example (admittedly in very unusual circumstances) of the men complaining of the leniency by which a thief had been allowed to get away with only four hundred lashes.[35] The same attitude was shown in customary punishments. Theft was the sort of crime which could be punished by forcing the offender to run the gauntlet, a punishment which gave concrete form to the feelings of the community, and would have been entirely ineffective if the offence had not been hated by all.[36] The procedure is explained in a case involving a man of the *Royal George* guardship at Portsmouth. The first lieutenant allowed leave on condition that no one broke it,

At the same time I acquainted them if they did not re-

turn agreeably to their leave, they could not think themselves ill-used if I delivered them to their *shipmates* for
punishment, as it would rob them of their liberty. This
they agreed to.

Francis Lanyon broke leave, so Lieutenant Lee

made him walk around the deck three times with his
clothes on to show himself, and then once round without his shirt; this he did without receiving more hurt
than he would have had from a dozen at the gangway.[37]

Because Captains were unreliable in recording punishments in
their logs, it is more difficult to prove that customary punishments
also served, in general, to secure the peace of the community rather
than the dignity of the officers. Most offences are recorded in
general terms, such as 'drunkenness', or 'neglect of duty'. Being
drunk was not in itself regarded as much of a crime, so long as the
offender was peaceable and still able to do duty, and 'drunkenness'
usually implies fighting, or shirking work. This is often what is
meant by 'neglect of duty' also, and always what is referred to as
'skulking', meaning hiding below when supposed to be working on
deck. It is easy to see that all these offences made life more difficult
for one's shipmates, and it seems reasonable to assume that
punishing them would have their tacit support. A particular problem with landmen was what was sometimes referred to as
'uncleanness', which was not usually anything to do with homosexuality, as some commentators have assumed, but was the habit
of men unaccustomed to the sanitary disciplines of communal living of relieving themselves in any dark corner, rather than using
the heads. It was sometimes necessary to post sentries over the
hold to prevent this.[38] Those who found their berths fouled in this
way were naturally even less fond of landmen than they might
otherwise have been, and without doubt would have supported the
officers in punishing them. The clear impression given by the
admittedly vague descriptions of offences in ships' logs is that they
were chiefly the sort of anti-social behaviour which made life more
unpleasant, more arduous or more dangerous than it need have
been, and that they were generally punished only at sea, where

there was a real functional need of discipline. The fact was that living, and still more sailing, in the crowded and dangerous environment of a ship required a high degree of self-discipline, and those who had not learnt it, or would not learn, were a burden on their shipmates. In this, as in other aspects, discipline in the Navy appears on examination to have been largely an organic response to the nature of life at sea, overlaid with a ramshackle legal structure, and not an attempt to sustain an artificial authority by force.

D COMPLAINT AND CONSULTATION

In modern navies elaborate mechanisms are provided whereby ratings may convey complaints or suggestions to their officers without appearing to subvert discipline. The mid-eighteenth-century Navy possessed absolutely no defined means of doing this, from which it is easy to assume that complaints could not have been made without severe risk. It suited some outsiders at the time to suggest as much,[1] but the idea would have surprised anyone in the Service. The absence of any official mechanism for complaint meant in practice that any method was accepted as legitimate. In modern armed services, the freedom with which ratings of those days felt able to complain to their superiors, if not the seriousness with which their complaints were taken, would appear astonishing, not to say subversive.

The first and simplest way to complain was to go and speak to the captain – or, if the complaint was against him, to the admiral. It was not thought in the least improper for seamen with a grievance, or just a problem, to go and speak to the port admiral in person (at sea it was obviously more difficult). A man left behind by his ship at Plymouth found the port admiral breakfasting in a coffee-house and asked him how to rejoin her.[2] It was quite normal for a port admiral to find a party of men with a request or a grievance, even sometimes an entire ship's company, waiting at his front door to speak to him.[3] This was a respectable procedure, and the first thing which aroused suspicion about what turned out to be malicious complaint from Portsmouth was the lame excuse that the complainants had been 'unable to find' the port admiral.[4]

These men had gone to London to present their petition in person at the Admiralty, a custom common enough to provide a living for 'the petition writer at the Admiralty gate' who helped illiterate ratings put their grievances into writing for the Board's consideration. Others sought legal assistance in drafting their petitions.[5] For those at sea or otherwise unable to put their case in person, requests were either presented orally to the captain, or sent up in writing. Usually captains would forward them to their senior officers,[6] or direct to the Admiralty:

> I hope their Lordships will pardon this request, but as it
> has been by desire of the whole ship's company I could
> not avoid applying to their Lordships in their behalf.[7]

It was proper to speak first to one's captain, and the ship's company of the *Speedwell* were reproved for sending a petition direct to the Admiralty without even mentioning their grievance to their commander,[8] but if a captain made difficulties it was impossible to prevent messages being sent ashore, and the post was available to all. In a characteristic transaction, the outspoken Captain Wheeler of the *Isis*, an uncomfortable former French prize, vehemently opposed his men's desire to seek another ship, but pointed out that he could not prevent them petitioning, and then sent their round robin to his commander-in-chief with a covering letter strongly supporting it, and reflecting on the Master Shipwright of Chatham in terms which subsequently got him into trouble with their Lordships.[9]

Though there was no standard procedure for making complaints, there was something like a standard form for investigating allegations against officers. The commander-in-chief would send two or three junior flag officers or senior captains, who would interrogate the officers separately, examine the ship's books for traces of frauds at the men's expense or of unusually numerous desertions, and summon the ship's company as a whole to ask their views. The procedure may be illustrated by the report of an investigation into an anonymous complaint received at the Admiralty against Captain Rous of the *Success*, then at Halifax. In this case Commodore Spry took all the commanders of his small squadron to investigate:

> We first called in the commission and warrant officers and examined them particularly to every article, who all declared there was not a word of truth in the whole complaint. We then sent for the ship's books ... We then sent for the ship's company who were all on board (except one checked with leave) and appeared to be a very good one. When the complaint was read to them they seemed greatly surprised, and when we told them we were come to enquire into and redress their grievances, they to a man declared they never knew or heard the least syllable of it before, and that they never desired to sail with a better captain or officers as long as they lived, that they had never been ill-treated by either, or had any part of their provisions unjustly stopped from them, and seemed greatly exasperated against the person who had wrote the complaint ... In short the whole complaint is without the least foundation, and has been wrote (as appears by many petitions in the same hand) by one David Sutherland, now a prisoner in the common gaol of this place and under sentence of the pillory for forgery and many other frauds, because (as imagined) Captain Rous refused to screen him from the law.[10]

Reports like this offer an almost Panglossian view of relations between officers and men, and however much flag officers emphasized the strictness with which they investigated complaints,[11] it is easy to be cynical about the willingness of ratings to expose themselves by complaining in public against their officers. In fact they appear to have been remarkably uninhibited in speaking up when they wanted to. Even the sick found the energy to protest; in March 1756 Rear-Admiral Holburne, commanding at Plymouth, went on a formal visit of inspection to the naval hospital, accompanied by two senior captains and the Physician and Surgeon of the hospital – which might be thought a sufficient display of authority to deter the bravest complainant. However, as Holburne reported,

> in examining the men, many of them said the Surgeon had not been near them nor given them any medicine the time they had been there, which I thought very negligent, and could not help telling him so.[12]

As a result of this account the Admiralty ordered the Sick and Hurt Board to investigate, and the Surgeon was dismissed.[13]

This was not an isolated instance, for similar investigations on other occasions made similar reports. Thus Commodore Hanway of Plymouth, who with two other captains investigated complaints against Captain Jacobs of the *Actaeon*, wrote that 'with much concern I find myself obliged to acquaint their Lordships that great part of them appeared to us to be too justly founded'.[14] Admittedly Hanway believed that the fault was excessive zeal rather than a settled principle of cruelty, and six months before Holburne had explained a complaint by some of Jacob's marines in similar terms:

> There was nothing appeared to me like cruel treatment. I believe Captain Jacobs has been a little too earnest to learn them to be seamen contrary to their inclinations, which I have told him he was not to do for the future.[15]

No such mitigating circumstances appeared in the case of ill treatment reported of his predecessor in command by Captain Bover of the *Raven* sloop in 1757,[16] or in the complaint of poor provisions made by the ship's company of the *Nottingham* to Admiral Knowles at Portsmouth in the same year. Captain Marshall was on leave, and the first lieutenant's failure to do anything to remedy their grievance, Knowles reported, was wholly responsible for the trouble, for they made no kind of complaint of bad usage or ill treatment from any of their officers; on the contrary they frankly expressed a liking to their captain and a willingness to serve under him.[17]

These examples show that a ship's company's complaint was a powerful weapon against real oppression, which is an important reason why pursers' opportunities of corruption at the men's expense were so limited. Those who tried, like Henry Nelson of the *Sunderland*, soon found senior officers coming aboard to investigate complaints.[18] It was not only British seamen who spoke up with effect, for the complaints of French prisoners of war more than once led to the punishment of those responsible for ill treatment.[19]

The willingness of the Navy to accept complaints was obviously most tested by accusations against officers, but they were not in fact the only, or even the most common subject of lower-deck petitions. A frequent matter of complaint was the living conditions aboard the smaller men-of-war, especially French prizes and the smallest class of sloops.[20] Though sometimes supported by senior officers, these requests to be transferred to more comfortable ships were generally rejected by the Admiralty, which took the view that hardships were to be borne in wartime, and small cruisers were too much in demand to be paid off unless really necessary. Justified complaints of unseaworthiness, however, were acted on. When Rear-Admiral Rodney reported on the petition of the crew of the *Laurel* sloop, 'which I find to be true in every respect', she was paid off at once.[21] A more remarkable case occurred in the summer of 1758, when Lord Anson, the First Lord of the Admiralty, was commanding the Western Squadron with his flag in the *Royal Sovereign*. This ship had been launched in 1728, and was nominally the same as her predecessor, built in 1701, which may explain 'some prejudices the *Royal Sovereign*'s men have conceived on account of her great age and weakness'. Expert opinion in fact judged her surprisingly strong for her age, but Anson did not hesitate in the face of his men's opinion; he paid her off and shifted his flag to another ship.[22] Anson, if any man, wielded unquestioned authority in the Navy, and the fact that he at once yielded to his men's ungrounded fears is very interesting. There is room to argue whether this illustrates the weakness of all authority in the Navy, or Anson's discretion in never quarrelling with his men unless he had to, and it is true also that he was short of men and could more economically employ the *Royal Sovereign*'s in smaller ships. Nevertheless, this little incident opens a window onto relations between lower deck and quarter deck very different from those of the nineteenth or twentieth centuries.

Equally revealing are the cases in which investigation reported some fault on both sides. It is so much a matter of common experience that in real life things are seldom simply black and white, that one is inclined to trust reports which frankly portray an ordinary human situation of confusion and misjudgement, rather than malice versus sanctity. In 1746 Admiral Steuart, commanding at Portsmouth, investigated a complaint by the men of the *Prince Frederick* that they had not been getting their regular dinner hour, 'and some days they were even without any beer to drink'. He reported that there was some truth in the charge, but that it was not the result of general neglect or mistreatment, only of the extreme pressure which he had been putting on the captain to get his ship ready for sea.[23] In another case a court martial had to untangle the mutual accusations of the commander, lieutenant, purser and a seaman of the *Baltimore* sloop. Passing over some rather irregular behaviour not forming part of any charge (there was evidence that the lieutenant's woman, 'Miss Nancy', was the cause of some of the dissension), the court exonerated the commander but severely reprimanded Lieutenant Pike for beating a drunken seaman so badly that he could not work for some time.[24]

The fact that complaints were made easily and taken seriously offered an opportunity for men with a grudge to get their officers into trouble. It is not therefore surprising that there were many malicious or frivolous complaints, and the many investigations which judged complaints ungrounded are a backhanded tribute to the fairness of the system. Having seen how willing seamen were to speak up when they had a grievance one can more readily believe reports like that from Commodore Spry, and many others like it.[25] It was easy to forge signatures on a petition, and to charge the officers with ill treatment was the obvious counter-attack of a man in serious trouble ('says in his own defence the bad usage on board was the cause of his desertion, but that is of course').[26] It was not unusual for a ship's company to react as the *Success*'s did, with indignation against those who had defamed their officers, and by implication, their ship.[27] Authority too was indignant about malicious complaints, and if the authors of them could be traced within the Navy, was sometimes prepared to punish them. At least two courts martial were held on the authors of false complaints during the Seven Years' War.[28]

These trials were of course intended to deter abuses by ratings of the freedom to complain which they Navy allowed. Abuses by officers were also possible. The authors of justified complaints might get into trouble, like the signatories of a round robin whom Captain Cuming had flogged,[29] and investigations could be misled. One may suspect this of the complaint made by some of Cuming's men which was judged to be frivolous only two years before he was dismissed the Service for brutality, but even this report was qualified by references to the absence of some and the unreliability of other key witnesses.[30] In any case the obvious lesson to draw from Cuming's progress is that his conduct was in the end his ruin, which could not have been the case in a system which upheld authority at the expense of justice. It is possible that the men of the *Pembroke* who resorted to the classic complaint of the voiceless at sea, rolling shot about the decks at night, had real grievances against Captain Simcoe, but they presented a petition which was investigated by Rear-Admiral Broderick and Captain Rodney and pronounced to be the work of drunken troublemakers.[31] Perhaps these shrewd officers were mistaken, but they were certainly sincere, and all the evidence strongly suggests that miscarriages of justice in the investigation of complaints were as rare as the fallibility of human nature would allow.

Besides complaints and petitions presented by ratings to their officers, there were occasions when the officers took the lead in presenting propositions to their men. This was the case with property rights which they held in common, usually prize money,[32] but in certain circumstances it also applied to operational matters. The Navy at the time of the Seven Years' War had a good collective sense of the boundaries between duty and foolhardiness. The officers and ratings were not cowards, for the most part, but they did not believe in useless bloodshed. Officers who led their men into action against reasonable odds – which could mean quite heavy odds – did not feel any need to ask them first, but if it was seriously doubtful whether the risks were worth running, and there was time to do so, it was considered proper to assemble the ship's company and ask their opinion. This might be, for example, if a ship were attacked by greatly superior forces without chance of escape, and because it was the custom to enquire into the loss of any of H.M. ships by a court martial of the commander or surviving officers, we have good evidence of such cases. The *Penguin*, a twenty-gun sloop, found herself chased by two French thirty-six-gun frigates, which head-reached on her and ranged up on either side. Captain Harris summoned his officers and men and asked their advice whether to fight or not; they replied that they would have taken on one thirty-six, but two was too much. So the *Penguin* struck her colours without firing a shot, and at the court martial Harris was honourably acquitted, as having done everything that a good officer could do.[33] Captain Carteret of the *Stork* surrendered in similar circumstances on the advice of his men, and likewise was acquitted.[34] A lieutenant carrying despatches home in the hired cutter *Ann*, which was intercepted by a French privateer, proposed to her men that they should attempt boarding. The odds were fourteen men against about seventy, and the fourteen politely declined the invitation, so the officer sank his despatches and surrendered.[35] In all these cases, naval opinion entirely supported the officers, and there were sound military reasons to do so, quite apart from the moral argument against the unnecessary shedding of blood, for with the rapid exchange of prisoners by cartel a captured ship's company in home waters could be back in England in a month, and experienced officers and men were scarcer and more valuable to the Navy than ships.

Such considerations might conceivably apply in similar circumstances today, but we are remote from a world in which a captain in the face of the enemy could formally consult all his men on whether to fight or no, or in which a seaman in trouble might naturally go and speak to the commander-in-chief in a coffee-house. The Navy in the middle years of the eighteenth century retained a large degree of informality, even of intimacy. It was not a very large permanent force, though growing all the time, and many of its officers and men were bound to one another by ties of personal loyalty developed over many years. All of them were united by the shared experience of a dangerous profession, in which teamwork was essential to survival. In their working lives, officers and men lived close together, sharing similar discomforts and lack of privacy. Moreover it was easy for them to transcend the wide social disparities which existed as much in the Navy as in society ashore, for they accepted these divisions without thought. Those who are conscious of class feel awkward about it, but the officers and men of the 1750s and 1760s were perhaps the last generation in the Navy to be almost unconscious of class, to feel themselves to belong to a world ruled chiefly by the vertical links of patronage and personal loyalty which bound a ship's company, officers and men, together. In a sense, they still lived in a world of innocence, and one powerful expression of it was an easy informality between officers and ratings. This was not a matter of behaviour – people did behave informally by modern standards, but ratings were still expected to show common marks of respect to their superiors – it sprang from a psychological intimacy which expressed the hidden ties binding the Sea Service together.

E MUTINY

The word 'mutiny' was used in the Navy in our period in two senses, neither of which corresponds to the usual modern usage. Most often it was applied to individual acts of violent insubordination of the sort which might more logically have been described as 'striking an officer', but it was also used to refer to collective actions by whole ship's companies which approach more nearly to the modern idea of mutiny, while remaining in many respects quite unlike it. This is a matter in which most writers today may be said to belong to the Cecil B. de Mille school of history, whose notion of mutiny is of the violent seizure of a ship from her officers, on the high seas. Mutinies of this sort did occasionally occur in merchantmen and privateers, but they were virtually unknown in the Navy. The kind of mutiny which did happen, and happened quite frequently, conformed to certain unwritten rules, which if they had been codified, would have looked something like this:

1. No mutiny shall take place at sea, or in the presence of the enemy.

2. No personal violence may be employed (although a degree of tumult and shouting is permissible).

3. Mutinies shall be held in pursuit only of objectives sanctioned by the traditions of the Service.

The only cases in which these rules were broken were mutinies openly led or covertly incited by officers; genuine lower-deck mutiny invariably conformed to them, and so long as it did, authority regarded it with a weary tolerance, as one of the many disagreeable but unavoidable vexations of naval life. It called, not for punishment, but for immediate action to remedy the grievances complained of.

The Admiralty's reaction to a mutiny played by the rules is neatly illustrated by two Board minutes:

[10th March 1745/6]: The company of the *Sunderland* having mutinied and refused to go to sea with Captain Brett, resolved that Captain Crookshanks be ordered to repair down to Plymouth and take the command of the ship in the room of Captain Brett.

[11th March 1745/6]: The Lords thinking proper that the captain and company of the *Sunderland* should be parted, in regard to the present dissension between them, and the mutiny of the men, they have sent down

Captain Crookshanks to command her until Captain
Fox (for whom she is designed) who is now at sea in the
Captain returns to Plymouth; resolved that Lieutenant
Kirley be directed to get the men on board, and the ship
ready for sea, and he is to be acquainted that if any dis-
turbance happens and the men do not come to their
duty, it will be imputed to him as the cause of it.[1]

The ejection of intolerable officers was a proper and traditional
object of mutiny, and in this context, 'mutiny' and 'dissension'
were more or less interchangeable terms. Another example was a
quarrel between Captain Ward of the *Penzance* and his men in
1758; its actual causes were reported by the commander-in-chief at
the Nore to be trivial, but their Lordships informed Ward that they
were 'extremely dissatisfied' with him, and would supersede him if
they received any more complaints.[2] In both cases, the Board
assumed without question that the officers were at fault, and that
the only remedy was to replace them. The idea of punishing the
mutineers was never raised. All this was characteristic of a regular
mutiny according to the traditions of the Service.

By far the most common object of mutiny was pay, and a typical example was the mutiny of the *Bedford* in January 1761. This
ship, then at Portsmouth, had been ordered to sail for St Helena,
there to meet and escort home the annual East India convoy. This
was a voyage south of the Equator, and hence, by convention, a
'foreign' voyage before which the men were entitled to be paid.
Orders to that effect had been given, but because of a mistake in
the Navy Pay Office, unknown both to the Admiralty and to Holburne, the commander-in-chief at Portsmouth, the ship's pay
books had been sent to Plymouth, and the men were still waiting
for their money when the order came to weigh anchor. They
refused to obey it. This appears to have been the extent of the mutiny; there is nothing to suggest that the ship's officers felt themselves in any danger, or indeed that the ordinary life of the ship
was in any other respect affected. Holburne reported the mutiny
without emotion in the course of his daily letter to the Admiralty,
which ordered another ship in the *Bedford*'s place, and sent her to

Plymouth to be paid, which was quicker than waiting for the books to return overland.[3] Their Lordships' only idea was evidently to close the affair as soon as possible by removing its first cause, and again there was no suggestion of punishing the men. It is possible that Holburne had private words to say to the *Bedford*'s commander, for a little forethought on his part might have prevented the incident. In similar circumstances later in the year the captain of the *Coventry* gave the admiral a timely warning:

> Captain Carpenter is afraid the ship's company won't heave the anchor up, and don't choose to put it to trial as there is money on the road and the books are here.[4]

A series of mutinies, each with the same cause, occurred in the spring of 1763. It happened then, as it has happened at the end of wars before and since, that on the announcement of peace every man wanted his liberty at once, and there was great difficulty in manning the ships which it was necessary to keep in commission. The problem was exacerbated by some ill-judged orders from the Admiralty (at this time presided over by George Grenville, Anson being dead) to release various groups of men who had petitioned, which of course led the others to expect the same. In the *Antelope* the first lieutenant reported to Holburne that

> every man in the ship came aft in a body to him, and told him they were determined not to go to sea in her, and that they had a right to be paid off as well as other ships, that they had served the King faithfully for many years in the war, now in peace they could better themselves. At first I resolved to go off, but the lieutenant told me they seemed determined, and [I] was afraid it would avail little, that if I went matters would be carried to extremities, which I could not avoid when no persuasion would prevail with them ... I don't find that one is more to blame than another; the whole speaks, or we could have silenced a few.[5]

Similar cases occurred in other ships. Holburne and his captains dealt with them with a judicious mixture of threats (which they were careful not to carry out) and conciliation. The ships were

paid, and deserters were promised that their 'R's would be taken
off if they returned to duty. With commendable prudence, Holburne avoided committing himself to any course which might
force him to proceed to 'extremities' – that is, actually to invoke
the penalties of the Articles of War. Within a couple of months the
crisis resolved itself as the ordinary conditions of the peacetime
labour market returned, and the ships were able to find men without difficulty.

In this case, Holburne had to contend with mutineers coming
ashore and surrounding his house. ('I have had their whole ships'
companies here upon me at times.')[6] Since mutinies generally
happened in the dockyard ports where there were commanders-in-
chief or port admirals, this was an obvious and common approach
for the mutineers. There was in practice little difference between a
ship's company assembling at the admiral's door civilly to present
a request, or mutinously to present a demand. It was a matter of
interpretation, and not one of much importance when the proper
reaction was the same in both cases. Senior officers had to expect
from time to time that angry men would be at their doors demanding something, usually pay, and there was nothing to be done but
produce it as quickly as possible.[7] The difficulty in doing so was
seldom the lack of money itself, but the delays of the cumbersome
naval accounting system.

This sort of 'mutiny' ashore was only one example, and a relatively mild one, of the eighteenth-century enthusiasm for rioting.
Seamen rioted as much as anyone. There were fights with towns-
men and landmen, and fights between ships. In November 1760
Holburne stopped shore leave at Portsmouth because of the
Mayor's complaints about the riots – no doubt they must have
been really troublesome to outweigh the advantages of so many
free-spending libertymen.[8] Riots happened in eighteenth-century
society because other means of social protest were lacking, and in
the absence of an effective police force there was little to stop
them. Riots were the commonest weapon of the trade dispute, and
naval mutinies conformed to this pattern. It has been said that 'the
study of the pre-industrial crowd suggests that it rioted for precise
objects and rarely engaged in indiscriminate attacks on either
properties or persons'.[9] This was how seamen behaved, and so

241

long as they kept the unwritten rules, sea officers were too sensible to make an issue of something which they were powerless to prevent.

The only way to eliminate mutiny was to remove the grievances which gave it birth, but given that accidents, errors and delays would occur, and that many of the men in the Navy were not there by choice, it was impossible to forestall every complaint. A good captain, however, made all the difference. He would foresee and if possible redress grievances, and if trouble nevertheless occurred, his men would trust him to represent them without taking matters into their own hands. A bad captain, on the other hand, would not be able to prevent mutiny even if he were not himself the cause of it. It was important, too, not to change captains unless it was really necessary, for 'changes of captains makes great alterations on board men-of-war, both to officers and to common men, and it was then dangerous for men to speak their thoughts'.[10] A weak or lazy commander, like Burslem of the *Coventry* in 1759, who was so relaxed 'that the ship resembled a privateer more than a man-of-war', or the young and inexperienced Captain Carpenter who succeeded him, could be extremely destructive of the mutual trust of the ship's company:

> I have often compared the little feuds and jealousies that occur in many ships, as a good picture in miniature of what is experienced on a larger scale in the courts and palaces of princes, where everyone is courting the favour of a despot, and trying to undermine his rivals.[11]

A good commander, by contrast, cemented the loyalty of his men, both to himself and to the Service. Part of Holburne's problems in 1763 with the *Antelope* and other mutinous ships was that their captains were on leave, and even the best first lieutenant was no substitute: 'though the lieutenant [of the *Antelope*] is a very diligent good man and takes great pains, the captain has always the greatest weight with the people'. When Captain Falconer of the *Juno*, which was similarly affected, returned from leave, one of the ways in which he brought the situation under control was by promising to discharge some men if they would first help to fit the ship for sea, 'which', reported Holburne, 'he did twenty-five after they

242

were there [Spithead] by my approbation, as there was no breaking our words with them'.[12] No officer who did not keep his promises could expect, or deserve, the loyalty of his men.

The majority of mutinies kept to the rules, but it is equally instructive to consider the few which did not. One such was the mutiny of the *Swallow* at Plymouth in 1762. Superficially this was very similar to the case of the *Bedford*, the men refused to weigh anchor unless they were paid, but in reality the situation was different. The *Swallow* was a Channel cruiser, chasing privateers and escorting convoys in home waters, coming into port every few weeks for orders and supplies. Nothing in the customs of the Service authorized her men to expect to be paid every time they sailed, and moreover she was ordered to sea urgently in pursuit of French privateers reported in the Channel. The reaction of authority was in keeping with this breach of the unwritten rules of mutiny: swift and forceful. The leaders of the mutiny were court-martialled, and two of them sentenced to hang – which they might well have done, had not sufficient come out during the trial to make it clear that, for reasons of his own, the boatswain had urged them to it. The men had a real grievance, but without the officer's encouragement it would have been unlikely to have issued in mutiny.[13]

A more dramatic incident was the *Chesterfield* mutiny of 1748, a rare example in our period which took place, if not in the open sea, at least outside home waters. The ship was anchored off Cape Coast Castle in West Africa, the captain and most of his officers dining ashore, when Samuel Couchman the first lieutenant siezed the ship and carried her off to sea. A few days later the ship's company, led by the boatswain, recaptured her and confined Couchman, who was later court-martialled and shot.[14] It is a perplexing incident, for though he was certainly drunk, it is difficult to see what he hoped to achieve.

These two mutinies were exceptions which prove the rules by which other mutineers conducted themselves. These rules were very similar to other sets of unwritten rules by which the Navy conducted its affairs – the rules for impressment, for example, or for desertion. When other methods failed, mutiny provided a formal system of public protest to bring grievances to the notice of authority. It was a sort of safety-valve, harmless, indeed useful, so long as it was not abused. It was part of a system of social relations which provided an effective working compromise between the demands of necessity and humanity, a means of reconciling the Navy's need of obedience and efficiency with the individual's grievances. It was a means of safeguarding the essential stability of shipboard society, not of destroying it.

F   COURAGE AND MORALE

The Navy during the Seven Years' War had a real problem of cowardice. It was not so bad as it had been earlier in the century, and it was virtually confined to three ranks of officer, but it remained a source of intermittent anguish to senior officers and the Board of Admiralty, and was several times the cause of serious failures in action. This was in part because the three ranks in question were admirals, commanders and masters.[1] If the senior officers set a bad example, it was scarcely to be expected that the Service as a whole would be unaffected – indeed, it hardly helped if it were not affected, for the courage of junior officers and ratings would avail nothing if flag officers and captains would not carry their ships into action.

We need to understand what made these officers susceptible to cowardice when others were not. It seems reasonable to suggest that men are more likely to be mastered by fear when they run greater risks, when they have more opportunity for reflection on them, and when they face dangers for which they are psychologically unprepared. On all these grounds, but especially the first two, the officers whose station in action was on the quarter deck were in the worst position. The largest part of a ship's company at quarters, including all the lieutenants and most of the midshipmen, was below decks fighting the guns, where they were protected by the heavy scantling of the ship's sides. Except in prolonged and close action, their casualties were generally light, and they were continually busy, with no leisure for reflection on the risks they did run. The marines and their officers were on deck, lining the rails of the quarter deck and sometimes the forecastle, but they fired from behind a breastwork of rolled hammocks in nettings on top of the bulwarks, forming a protection similar to sandbags to chest height or higher. It was not proof against round shot, but it gave at least an impression of security. They too were very busy, and never more so than in their moment of greatest danger, in leading or repelling boarding parties. The boatswain and his crew who handled sail and repaired damaged rigging were exposed in action, but continually active and on the move. Only the quarter-deck officers were in the position of standing still to be shot at.

In order to appreciate their position it is necessary to visualize the geography of the quarter deck.[2] Its arrangement varied in ships of different age and design, but in the newer line-of-battle ships, which may be taken as representative, it was a rectangular space about twice as long as it was broad, bounded on either side by low bulwarks topped in action by hammocks in their nettings. Over these the marines fired their muskets, and behind them the light quarter-deck guns were worked. At the after end of the deck, under the break of the poop, stood the wheel and binnacle, with the way into the captain's cabin on either side of it. On these three sides the deck was screened by light works, effective against small arms fire, and offering at least an illusion of general protection. At the forward end of the deck, however, looking across the waist towards the forecastle, was only an open rail, and it was here, or on the gangways which prolonged the deck forward on either side (and in some ships on the centre-line), that a captain stood to command his ship, or an admiral his squadron, with the master at his side to con the ship. The position was natural for either purpose; roughly amidships, with a clear view over the whole ship, and good visibility in every direction except aft. It was also prominent and exposed, particularly to fire from before the beam.

Moreover it was often the admiral and commander, alone of all on board, who had leisure to think – that, indeed, was part of their job. A captain might have a great deal to occupy his mind (in chase, for example, striving to get the best out of his ship), and a flag officer had his squadron to manoeuvre, but in either case hours usually elapsed (except in darkness or thick weather) between sighting and identifying the enemy and opening fire, and once action was firmly joined there was often little admiral or captain could do but encourage his men by word and example. The officers on the quarter deck ran greater risks, and had more time both before and during action to contemplate them, than anyone else on board, and it is not surprising that sometimes their nerve failed them. It was not unusual in action for casualties to be virtually confined to the quarter deck, or much the heaviest there. Many commanders in successful single-ship actions did not survive to enjoy their triumphs. The *Despatch*, a twelve-gun sloop, beat off the much larger privateer *Prince de Soubise*, but Captain Holburne was mortally wounded. The *Milford* took the *Gloire* privateer of Bordeaux in the Bay of Biscay with the loss of both captain and first lieutenant in succession.[3] The *Isis* took the *Oriflamme* with the loss of only four killed, of whom Captain Wheeler, a midshipman and a quartermaster were all on the quarter deck. On board the *Intrepid* at the Battle of Minorca, only the captain out of five officers on the quarter deck escaped.[4] Twenty-nine commanders were killed in action or drowned during the war.[5]

It was therefore perfectly rational for commanders to be afraid, but it was none the less disastrous for the Navy, for if ships were not carried into action the valour of everyone else on board was useless. It was bad enough if a captain built

> a most enormous large and high barricadoe of junk etc., much too high for small arms to be fired over, from the main mast to the taffrail round her stern, and athwart the fore part of the quarter deck,[6]

which not only damaged the ship's sailing qualities, but clearly proclaimed his fears and demoralized the ship's company. It was much worse when ships steered clear of the fighting altogether. A flagrant example occurred during the attack on Havana in 1762. Augustus Hervey proposed and commanded a characteristically dashing and hazardous close attack on the Morro Castle, and the *Stirling Castle* which was supposed to lead the line in, instead hauled off out of range and watched the other ships get badly damaged, and Captain Goostrey of the *Cambridge* killed. For this Captain Campbell was dismissed the Service, and was probably lucky not to have been shot, considering the strength of naval opinion.[7] Captain Carpenter of the *Coventry*, meeting a larger French frigate, proposed to run the ship ashore to escape,

> but this was prevented by the violent behaviour and remonstrance of Mr Dalrymple our second lieutenant, who was exceedingly severe in his language, and almost mutinous, to save the King's ship from being run on shore and to prevent our own infamy and disgrace.[8]

It turned out to be a British frigate after all. Cases as obvious as this did not often occur, but flag officers were always conscious of the possibility, and ready to assume the worst if ships did not come into close action. It was thus that Pocock, after an indecisive action fought in light airs in the Indian Ocean, caused three of his captains to be court-martialled for failing to support him. It seems likely that in two of these cases the charge was unfair, and Pocock himself came to think the sentences over-severe,[9] but his reaction illustrates the extent to which senior officers bore the possibility of cowardice constantly in mind, and in view of the events of the previous war, and in particular of the Battle of Toulon, in which the larger part of the British fleet refused to come into action in support of the commander-in-chief, it is easy to understand why.[10]

This background helps to explain the fury with which the news of Byng's conduct in 1756 was received in the Service. The Admiral was sent with a squadron to relieve the British colony of Minorca, where a French force had landed and besieged the principal fortress. Byng met the French squadron with roughly equal forces, made a half-hearted attempt to engage, and withdrew to Gibraltar leaving the island to its fate. Most officers who heard of it at once assumed that it was a straightforward case of cowardice. Byng was specifically acquitted of physical cowardice by his court martial, perhaps fairly, but the officers were at bottom correct, for his was a clear case of moral cowardice, of preferring the certainties of failure to the risks of success. 'What a scandal to the Navy', Boscawen wrote when he heard the news, 'that they should be premeditated cowards that have been so long bred to arms.'[11] Captain Samuel Faulknor thought the same:

> No doubt but Mr Byng's behaviour on the late occasion off Mahon must anger and surprise you and every thinking man in the kingdom. Sad indeed; he's brought more disgrace on the British flag than ever his father the great Lord Torrington did honour to it.[12]

In his own squadron

> All the fleet are open-mouthed against Byng, his own division more than ours, as well as all the land officers that were on board to be landed at Minorca.[13]

This brings us to the delicate question of honour, a matter highly subjective at the time, and perilous for the historian to interpret. It is clear enough that courage was one quality that officers expected of one another, and of themselves, and that they were quick to resent any implication that it might be lacking. No doubt this was in part because it sometimes was lacking – the insinuation would have been less wounding if it had been less plausible. If ships for one reason or another failed to come into action in support of their friends, it was necessary to produce a good explanation. Lieutenant Philip Durrell, acting commander of the *Senegal* sloop under particular Admiralty orders for a scouting cruise which forbade him to engage any enemy he might meet, was allowed to reveal as much 'for your private and personal satisfaction'.[14] Captain Suckling of the *Dreadnought*, reporting how nearly he had caught the French *Palmier* while the *Assistance* lay becalmed within sight, was careful to guard Captain Edwardes's reputation by emphasizing how hard he had tried to come up.[15] Officers in Edwardes's position might demand a court martial to clear their names, as Captain Marlow of the *Dolphin* did after an action in which the *Solebay* had engaged a French privateer which escaped, and Captain Cornewall of Byng's squadron did after the Minorca battle.[16] Some took it more hardly than that. Arthur Gardiner, Byng's flag-captain and one of his few followers to stick by him in his disgrace, knew of Anson's opinion that Byng's squadron had brought disgrace upon the nation and dishonour upon its officers. In February 1758 he was commanding the *Monmouth* 64, one of the smallest ships of the line in the Navy and also one of the fastest, when chance threw him in the way of the *Foudroyant* 80, which had been flagship of the French squadron at the Battle of Minorca. He chased her all evening and into the night, and brought her to a running action. Gardiner was killed late in the evening, but the first lieutenant continued the fight, and about one in the morning the *Foudroyant* struck to her opponent. It was an extraordinary action in every way, for the disparity in broadside was two and a half to one, and among the factors which overcame these odds, Gardiner's drive to redeem his honour, if necessary with his life, must have been one.[17]

Other officers defended their honour in other ways. In 1750 Vice-Admiral Griffin, lately commanding the East Indies squadron, was cashiered by court martial for conduct in avoiding action in circumstances somewhat like Byng's. The charge was brought by Captain Lord Harry Powlett, or as Griffin put it, 'by the inveterate malice of a capricious turbulent young man', whom in turn he had court-martialled for cowardice, in spite of Powlett's attempts to avoid it by going on half-pay. This charge failed for want of evidence, and there ensued an unseemly pamphlet war, which led to a duel on Blackheath in 1756.[18] This undignified affair might be termed the dishonourable face of the affair of honour, but it was not typical, for both officers had more political friends than professional merits. An abler man whose career survived an embarrassing incident was Mostyn, who in 1745, commanding the *Hampton Court*, avoided engaging a French line-of-battle ship in conditions in which he could not open his lower-deck gun ports and the Frenchman could. It was perhaps prudent, and the court martial which he demanded cleared his name, but it did not stop him being hooted through the dockyard at Portsmouth by a mob of seamen and artificers calling after him, 'All's well! There's no Frenchmen in the way!'[19]

Of seamen themselves there were no complaints of cowardice. Sometimes they were unhappy; we hear of times when the 'the regret of being pressed hangs heavy on many', and of 'the peevishness and despondency which foul and contrary winds, and a lingering voyage, never fail to create',[20] but those who encountered seamen in action were always struck by their enthusiasm. 'People in high spirits in expectation that the chase will bring to and engage us', an officer of the *Dunkirk* noted in May 1758;[21] the *Dunkirk* was a sixty-gun fourth rate, and the 'chase' the *Formidable* of eighty-four guns, or about three times the weight of broadside. The seamen, who were practised judges of such things, were certainly in no doubt of the odds against them, and their eagerness was not for an easy victory. In quite different circumstances, ashore at the attack on Fort Royal, Martinique, an infantry officer witnessed the enthusiasm of seamen well led:

> You may fancy you know the spirit of these fellows, but to see them in action exceeds any idea that can be formed of them. A hundred or two of them, with ropes and pullies, will do more than all your dray-horses in London. Let but their tackle hold and they will draw you a cannon or mortar on its proper carriage up to any height, though the weight be never so great. It is droll enough to see them tugging along with a good 24 pounder at their heels; on they go, huzzaing and hullooing, sometimes up hill sometimes down hill; now sticking fast in the brakes, presently floundering in the mud and mire; swearing, blasting, damning, sinking and as careless of everything but the matter committed to their charge as if death or danger had nothing to do with them. We had a thousand of these brave fellows sent to our assistance by the Admiral, and the service they did us, both on shore and on the water, is incredible.[22]

Implicit in accounts like these, and frequently explicit in others, was one powerful reason for eagerness: 'You can't think how keen our men are, the hopes of prize money makes them happy, a signal for a sail brings them all on deck.' For a stranger to be aboard a ship in chase 'was amazing, as it exhibited a sample of the spirit and eagerness of the whole ship's company'.[23] It was common ground among officers and men that courage deserved, indeed required, its reward, whether in money or in honour. 'Officers must be brought to lose the idea of danger in that of glory,' as Augustus Hervey advised Lord Sandwich.[24] It was also evident to intelligent observers that leadership and training were the keys to success in action, and in particular that thorough preparation, practical and psychological, was the way to overcome fear: 'ridiculous to suppose courage dependent upon climate. The men who are best disciplined of whatever country they are, will always fight the best.'[25] If it is possible to make generalizations about such intimately human and therefore individual qualities as courage or cowardice, we may say that they are at all times affected by the prevailing moral climate, by the expectations men hold of each other, and of themselves, and by the degree to which their training has prepared them for the dangers they may have to face. Morale in the Navy, and bravery in the face of danger, were certainly strengthened among officers by the ideals of honour, and among everyone by the hope of gain, but there seems little doubt that it was chiefly the high level of professional skill and training which carried most people, most of the time, through the ordeal of battle.

CHAPTER VII

Officers

A A CAREER AT SEA

It is a fact worthy of more notice than it has received that the Navy never experienced any difficulty in finding enough officers. The same Service which had such trouble in wartime in recruiting ratings, had no lack of volunteers eager to become officers. Yet the Navy was for officers, at least as much as for ratings, an arduous, dangerous and ill-paid profession. In some respects its disadvantages were both absolutely and relatively greater for officers. The discomforts of life afloat must have seemed the worse for those from comfortable homes. Officers' pay was not good, and like the men's it was usually long in arrears. The captain of a first rate received twenty shillings a day in sea pay, the lieutenant of a third rate or smaller four shillings.[1] The endless complications of a captain's accounts could take years to pass, and his pay might be four years or more in arrears. From 1747, when sea officers were allowed to receive their pay annually in arrears, this became less likely, but twelve months was still the least time an officer could wait.[2] There was little here to tempt a gentleman into an arduous and perilous profession.

In order to understand why young men of good family did go to sea in large numbers we need to look at the alternatives open to them. For the sons of the nobility and gentry in the eighteenth century, the number of possible careers was not very large. The eldest sons of any families of property had a career automatically, managing the family estates and interests, perhaps sitting in Parliament, almost certainly engaging in local politics. It was the younger sons who had to earn a living, for it was very unusual for

252

estates to be divided. Most of the honest and respectable ways of making a living had obvious disadvantages. Politics and the court offered limitless prospects to those with the right connections, but it was useless to attempt them without. The regular army was highly honourable, but it called for capital to buy a commission, and in a fashionable regiment a substantial income as well. It was effectively only a part-time job, for commissioned officers were seldom with their regiments in peacetime, and by no means always in war. Beauclerk's Regiment, the 19th Foot, sailed for the attack on Belle Isle in 1762 missing fifteen officers, including the major and five captains.[3] The army neither required professional ability nor provided professional training. For those with money and influence it provided an attractive and not overly demanding career, but the purchase of a commission was as much an investment as the introduction to an active life, and the purchase system discouraged the officer from risking his investment in action. Moreover a captaincy involved financial commitments, and risks, analagous to those of a purser in the Navy.[4] The Church was another respectable profession in which an initial investment was required. It called for some hint of academic ability, or at least inclination, enough money to see a man through university, and some prospect of securing a church living. Without influence, a vocation from God was little help on the road to clerical advancement. As for the law, it was 'the hard way to social preferment: it required abilities, constant application, and a measure of good luck'. It also required money to study at one of the Inns of Court – £200 a year at the Middle Temple in 1718.[5] It was the natural field of the well-educated and ambitious – which often meant Scotsmen. Beyond these professions, there was not a great range of choice. Medicine and trade were not generally respectable, and those parts which were tended to be expensive; the commander of an East Indiaman, for example, could expect to pay a premium of upwards of £5000 for his berth. The artillery and engineers, which were not part of the regular army but came under the Ordnance Board, did not permit the purchase of commissions and provided a thorough professional education, but they were unfashionable, and not a likely prospect for a gentleman's son.[6]

The Navy was the only profession for a gentleman which did

not require – indeed, did not admit – the application of money or influence. It took its future officers young and provided them with a rigorous, and free, professional training with which they might rise to fame and fortune. The younger son of an impoverished family, like George, third son of Lord Elphinstone, could join the Sea Service 'to acquire his education and business together and without expense'.[7] For the harassed father anxious to launch his sons into the world as quickly as possible, the Navy offered a tempting prospect; put at its simplest, the boys left home young and cost little or nothing. It is true that Lord Cornwallis considered that his son as a lieutenant would hardly be able to live without an allowance of £100 a year, but he was rich and unfamiliar with the Service.[8] The majority of young officers managed on their pay. The Navy's attraction for future officers, or their parents, was straightforward; it offered excellent prospects and required negligible capital, financial or political. These advantages were sufficient to counterbalance many dangers and discomforts.

Moreover the Navy appealed not only to prudent fathers calculating how their sons might get on in the world, it attracted the boys themselves, at an age when perhaps thoughts of adventure were nearer their hearts than rational estimates of their prospects. Most young men destined for a naval career were at sea by the time they were fourteen at the latest. A few, like Vernon, left it till later, and it is even said (not very plausibly) that Thomas Grenville remained at Eton until he was nineteen before joining the Navy.[9] Many more went afloat well before fourteen. Matthew Michell went to sea at eight, James Burney and Samuel Barrington at ten, William Cornwallis and Hugh Palliser at eleven.[10] The future Admiral Duckworth had fought in two major fleet actions before his twelfth birthday. When John Cormack sailed to the East Indies as first lieutenant of the Tiger he took with him his nephews George and John Fielding, aged nine and seven. After his death they were looked after by other officers of the Tiger, and then taken on by Captain Colvill of the Sunderland (this was James Colvill, Lord Colvill's brother). With him they were drowned when the ship was lost in the great storm of New Year's Day 1761.[11]

The reason why boys left home so young was not only the requirements of a profession which had to be learnt young, but their own enthusiasm for it. No doubt there were many who were pushed into it by their parents, and there were certainly some who gave up after a few voyages,[12] but the keenness of boys to go to sea, often in the face of parental opposition, was mentioned by contemporaries too often for it to have been imaginary. Fathers proposing to send their sons to sea often did so explicitly at their desire: 'I intend him for the sea, as it's his inclination.'[13] There are stories of boys, 'seized, like many other boys, with a strong passion for the sea',[14] running away to sea. The stories are not easy to verify in individual cases, but appear too often to be altogether implausible.[15] It was not only a passion for the sea as such which animated them; one of the attractions of the Navy was the prospect of escaping from parental control. There was a great deal a young man of spirit might get up to in the Navy which could not be achieved in the nursery or the schoolroom. In the course of a few years in the Mediterranean (in peacetime, if that is the right word), the young Captain Augustus Hervey managed to seduce some hundreds of women in every class. His conquests included princesses, marchesas, countesses, a Portuguese royal duchess, the wife of the Doge of Genoa, and several nuns.[16] This was the kind of grand tour it was difficult to have with a tutor at one's heels. Such opportunities ranked among the Navy's attractions, though no doubt they were far from the mind of the five-year-old enthusiast who wrote this letter to Hawke after his victory at Quiberon Bay, in a careful round hand, ink over pencil:

> Sir Edward Hawke,
> I hear you have beat the French fleet when they were coming to kill us and that one of your captains twirled a French ship round till it sunk. I wish you was come home, for I intend to go to sea if you will take me with you.
>
> I am Lord Granby [sic] second son
> Charles Manners[17]

Enthusiasm like this was certainly one reason, and not the least important, why the Navy, for all its risks, never lacked noblemen's younger sons ready to join.

It is difficult to estimate exactly how great were the risks officers ran. It has been suggested that the loss of life in the Service as a whole was less than might be imagined,[18] but there certainly were real dangers not presented by other professions. Of the 443 captains made post between 1720 and 1750, more than one-third had by the end of the Seven Years' War ended their careers either in death or disgrace. The actual figures are as follows:

17 killed in action
15 drowned
38 dismissed or disgraced by court martial
4 suicides
82 died in service of natural causes
6 other causes of death (duels, executions, etc.)[19]

Less than 4 per cent of these captains died either by shipwreck or by enemy action, but nearly a fifth succumbed to illness, and it was probably this, rather than the more dramatic risks, which really thinned the ranks of the Navy. For the young officer toasting his hopes of promotion, a bloody war was less promising than a sickly season.

The young man contemplating a career at sea, however, had more attractive prospects than promotion for its own sake, and first among them all was prize money. It was considered entirely proper in the eighteenth century that patriotism should have its reward, and no class of persons were so highly rewarded for serving the Crown as sea officers. The entire value of any prize lawfully condemned in an Admiralty court was awarded to the captors, and the largest part went to the officers. Between 1756 and 1763 a total of 1855 merchantmen were taken from the enemy, plus a considerable number of warships.[20] Many were of no great value, but even small sums will mount up, and there was always the hope of some very large sum just over the horizon. Many an officer, like Admiral Medley, dreamt of a landed estate gained in an afternoon: 'such a lucky hit as Anson's last would do the business, and I most heartily wish it'.[21] 'I flatter myself', Admiral Boscawen wrote of his new house, 'to make the French pay for this building this summer. I have got at least one-fifth of it already, and another trip to the southward will bring three or four sugar ships more in our way.'[22]

The less prudent officers ran heavily into debt, 'trusting to the chance of war and success of prizes to be able to repay it all'.[23] Boscawen again, writing to his wife in the summer of 1756, urged her not to worry at his staying so long at sea: 'to be sure I lose the fruits of the earth, but then I am gathering the flowers of the sea'.[24]

The flowers of the sea included some very attractive blooms. Anson's 'lucky hit', the first battle of Finisterre in 1747, gained prizes worth £300,000. His second in command, Rear-Admiral Warren, made over £48,000 in that year, and £125,000 in that war.[25] At the fall of Havana in 1762, the naval and military commanders-in-chief, Admiral Pocock and Lord Albemarle, received £122,697 each. Albemarle's younger brother, Commodore Keppel, the naval second-in-command, received £24,539, and every one of forty-two captains gained £1600.[26] In 1746 Captain Saunders took a single ship which netted him nearly £40,000, and in 1762 the *Active* and *Favourite* shared the capture of the Spanish register ship *Hermione*, worth £519,705 clear of expenses, of which each captain received over £65,000.[27] Augustus Hervey, a favourite of his commander-in-chief and sent on all the best cruises, made £9000 in the course of 1748.[28] These were exceptional cases, but everyone had heard of them, and hoped that he might be the next lucky man. In any case, even the small gains of commanders who enjoyed no remarkable luck or favoured cruises would mount up to a very desirable addition to their pay. The young Captain Alexander Hood, serving under Hawke between 1757 and 1759, made over £1054. Only £295 of this was for the battle of Quiberon Bay, an unproductive action, since most of the French losses were sunk or wrecked.[29] Captain Tiddeman of the *Eltham* calculated in 1748 that he had about £2000 owing in prize money.[30] Captain Elliot of the *Hussar*, reporting taking a French privateer of no great value in January 1758, admitted that 'I have no reason to complain for if I share with the *Unicorn* I shall go near to get two thousand pounds by the *Hussar* within these three months'. Two years later he calculated that in three years he had made four or five thousand pounds, sharing in the capture of five men-of-war (plus two sunk), two privateers, six merchantmen (plus two retaken) and a large island.[31] All these officers were commanders or admirals, and the chances of making a fortune increased sharply with a command, but we hear even of a chaplain who left £10,000 earned at sea.[32] For anyone with a prospect of becoming a sea officer, there was a real hope of making at least a modest fortune, and there were many who at the close of their careers could write, as Lord Colvill did, that he had 'acquired all I am possessed of in the service of my King and country in the last two wars'.[33]

Prize money, moreover, was not the only additional reward an officer might hope for. Merchants expressed their gratitude to the protectors of trade in tangible forms. The famous Captain Lockhart of the *Tartar*, who took seven privateers in a year, received plate worth two hundred guineas from the London underwriters, and more from Bristol and Plymouth.[34] The Levant Company gave Captain Evans of the *Preston* a chest of plate for his care in escorting their ships, and in the West Indies another captain was voted a gold-hilted sword by the merchants of Barbados.[35] This sort of reward was distributed very unfairly, to those who had made their names in action against privateers, not to the convoy escorts who did most of the real work of protecting trade, but it was another aspect of the Navy's character as a profession in which money and honour came hand in hand – its laurels 'handsomely tipped with gold', as Admiral Vernon put it.[36]

In peacetime, when prize money was naturally unobtainable, there was for commanders always a chance of freighting specie. The eighteenth-century system of international trade required a considerable flow of gold, and it was very much safer to send it in a man-of-war than a merchantman. The Articles of War specifically excepted bullion from the general prohibition on private trade, and as London was taking over from Amsterdam as the principal bullion market, there were excellent chances for captains homeward-bound to carry a few tens of thousands of pounds in gold, at 1 or 2 per cent commission.[37]

The advantages to a younger son of a profession which offered opportunities like these were obvious. Equally obvious were the risks to a family of property in sending the eldest son into such a dangerous career. Moreover the Navy was much more a full-time profession than the army, and offered little leisure to cultivate the interests and occupations incumbent on an eldest son. Eldest sons in the Navy were therefore confined to those of families without property, or those whose fortunes were so badly damaged that they were prepared to run risks in the hope of recouping them. The point can be simply illustrated by the case of noble families, a category whose eldest sons are easy to distinguish. Peers in the Navy fell into three groups; those like Anson who had earned their peerages by their service, those like Howe who had succeeded unexpectedly on the deaths of elder brothers, and those like Colvill whose estates were so enfeebled that they were obliged to go to sea. What was true of the nobility was true of every family possessed of an estate or business of even modest extent. The Hills, for example, were a family of shipwrights in Sandwich, who owned a small shipyard. Over several generations each eldest son succeeded to the running of the yard, and the younger sons went into the Navy.[38] It may be taken as axiomatic that a first-born son in the Navy must have come from an impoverished family.

This was true of a naval family as much as any other. A successful officer who established a landed estate expected to hand it on to his heir, and would certainly not risk him unnecessarily. Younger sons or nephews might follow him into the Navy, but only an officer who had failed to make his fortune would send his heir to sea. Captain Sir William Hewitt died in 1749 leaving his son the baronetcy and one guinea. Young Sir William, then a lieutenant, carried all the family's hopes to sea with him, and with him, and his brother, they perished when his ship the *Duc d'Aquitaine* foundered in the Indian Ocean in 1761.[39] Captain Samuel Faulknor commanded Sir John Balchen's flagship the *Victory* in 1744 when she was wrecked on the Casquets with the loss of all on board. He left £50 to the three eldest of his ten sons, 'and as they are all lieutenants they can't expect more'. The eldest, Samuel, died captain of the *Windsor* in 1759. He was the son, grandson and great-grandson of captains in the Navy.[40] The Faulknors were perhaps unlucky, and certainly prolific, for succession from father to eldest son through four generations, each reaching post rank and none making a fortune, was unusual.

The quality which above all determined an officer's fortunes in the Navy, and marked it out from other professions, was his practical ability as a seaman. The capacity, not merely to command and to navigate, but to hand, reef and steer, was the basic requirement for an officer. Young gentlemen were expected to go aloft with the topmen, and to learn all that an experienced 'sea-daddy' could teach them.[41] Other attainments were highly desirable, but this alone was indispensable. 'Your young gentleman', Captain Gordon wrote to John Elliot's father,

> for his years is one of the prettiest seamen of all the youth I have, and though miserably neglected of late as to his education, has acquired the principal thing in our way, I mean, the knowledge of that business he is to follow through life.[42]

Eleven years later Elliot, now a captain himself, was remarking of one of his young gentlemen that 'he's not seaman enough for this ship', and must gain further experience before he could be recommended for a commission.[43] Officers themselves were well aware how necessary it was to perfect their seamanship. Lieutenant Charles Medows was offered by Boscawen a place in his flagship, with the virtual certainty of promotion to follow, but he declined, being conscious of a lack of seamanship, and preferring to stay with Keppel to acquire it. 'I don't think him in the wrong,' Boscawen wrote, 'there is no better seaman than Keppel, few so good, and not a better officer.'[44]

It was generally felt that a flagship was a bad place for a young gentleman to begin his professional training, for it was in smaller ships that he would acquire the all-important seamanship.[45] An accomplished seaman, however, could profit by service in a flagship to acquire that education and polish which were easily neglected at sea. By the time of the Seven Years' War thinking officers had been saying for some time that seamanship by itself was not enough. In 1744 an ill-educated captain inspired the cry 'For God's sake let all boys have a proper school till twelve years old at least. 'Tis terrible to think when they are captains that it will be a shame for them to write to the Admiralty.'[46] When Anson joined the Admiralty Board in 1745 his friend Captain Barnet wrote to him:

> I am stupid enough to think that we are worse officers though better seamen than our neighbours; our young men get wrong notions early, and are led to imagine

that he is the greatest officer who has the least blocks in his rigging.[47]

The same view is expressed in a pamphlet, probably by Admiral Vernon, published in 1747:

It is certainly necessary that a sea officer should have good natural courage: but it is equally just that he should have a good share of sense, be perfect master of his business, and have some taste for honour; which last is usually the result of *a happy education, moderate reading, and good company, rarely found in men raised on the mere credit of being seamen* ... The general notion about sea officers is that they should have the courage of brutes without any regard to the fine qualities of men, which is an error themselves too often fall into. This levels the officer with the common seaman, gives us a stark wrong idea of the nature design and end of the employment, and makes no distinction between the judgement skill and address of a Blake and a mere fighting blockhead without ten grains of common sense.[48]

Vernon is overstating his case, and he was himself a most unusual officer, who had studied first at Westminster and then at Oxford until he was nearly seventeen before going to sea. By then he had mastered Latin and Greek, traversed mathematics, navigation, geometry, fortification and gunnery, and made some progress in Hebrew. Thus equipped, he was inclined to look down on his less well-educated fellows, but he was certainly not the only officer of polish or learning. His contemporary Admiral Martin spoke French, Italian, Spanish and German with ease: 'we scarcely know which most to admire, the finished gentleman, the elegant scholar, or the brave commander'.[49]

Moreover observers were agreed that the standards of education and politeness in the Navy were rising considerably in the years before and during the Seven Years' War. 'My young lads', Keppel wrote in 1753, '... are such as I confess I never saw at sea before, well-bred, genteel, good and diligent to a degree. When I say I never saw before, I mean such numbers together.'[50] It is still possible to find complaints from gentlemen ashore of ill-bred 'sea-monsters',[51] but with decreasing justification. We find officers collecting portraits and sculptures, sketching the ruins of Herculaneum, and playing the harpsichord.[52] There were some fine draughtsmen among them.[53] Many of them knew French well enough to read letters or converse with French officers, even if, like Boscawen, not well enough to read Montaigne with pleasure.[54] Latin, Italian and other languages were not unusual – Latin and French were on the curriculum of the Royal Navy Academy at Portsmouth.[55] Near illiteracy was regarded as a bar to a commission, or even a warrant. [56] It was still possible for John Elliot to reach flag rank without learning to spell the simplest English words ('I'm non of the best of clarcks'), but Henry Medley was probably the last admiral unable to write a legible hand, and a buffoon like Thomas Pye was most untypical of senior officers by the time he received his flag in 1758. Even among junior officers the least educated seem often to have been also the least successful.[57] Officers in correspondence used what were for the day advanced scientific concepts, like Commodore Boys's discussion of the effect on a ship's centre of gravity of remounting her guns. It should be said that Boys had been educated for the nonconformist ministry, an unusual start to a naval career, but there were officers of high scientific achievements in the Service.[58] Men like John Campbell, one of the inventors of the sextant, and his namesake Alexander Campbell, both of them prominent in experiments with mathematical and other instruments, were among the leading practical scientists of their day.[59] It is interesting to note that both Campbells were of fairly humble birth, John the son of a Scots country minister, and Alexander the son of a purser, which suggests that a good education may have been among the qualities which raised them, respectively, to vice-admiral and commander.[60]

With rising politeness went a decline in boorishness. Drunkenness was the vice of the age, but there were degrees of drunkenness which were socially unacceptable in the wardroom, as well as professionally unacceptable in the Service.[61] For officers to drink or fight with their ratings was thought disreputable,[62] and the suspicion of theft would result in an officer being ostracized by his fellows.[63] Public quarrels between officers were increasingly thought of as disgraceful as well as damaging to the Service.⁶⁴ All these are indicators of a trend which the historian cannot measure, but which thoughtful contemporaries believed they could discern, and which is undoubtedly indicated by the evidence which has come down to us.

All officers in the eighteenth century had begun their careers as ratings. It is therefore impossible to speak in the modern fashion of officers 'promoted from the lower deck', implying officers promoted from a lower social class than the usual, officers who were not, or had once not been, gentlemen. In the eighteenth century such distinctions were meaningless, for there was no neat correspondence between the official system of ranks and ratings and the social realities of class. The regulations required a candidate for a commission to pass an oral examination in seamanship, to have served six years at sea, and two of those in the Navy in the ratings of midshipman or master's mate. The qualifications for warrant rank were less exactly specified, but long sea service was indispensable. In both cases the necessary experience had to have been gained as a rating. Gentleman or no, every officer had begun his career on the lower deck. Nevertheless not all careers followed the same pattern, and it is possible to identify three routes by one of which the great majority of sea officers gained their commissions or warrants. The first was to go to sea in boyhood as an officer's servant, usually a captain's servant, and under his patronage, or that of other friends or connections, to gain experience and serve the qualifying time. This was the usual method for young men of respectable families who hoped to become commissioned officers. They generally began as servants, and at some time served as midshipmen or mates for the qualifying two years, but otherwise they occupied any ratings which happened to be available in the ship's authorized complement. Young gentlemen in this position were often rated as able or ordinary seamen or landmen, and these ratings followed one another in an order dictated only by chance or convenience. It was of no consequence if a young gentleman moved from servant to midshipman to able seaman and back to servant, for none of these titles had much to do with his actual duties. In practice he was growing in years and knowledge, taking on more responsibilities and behaving more and more like the lieutenant he hoped one day to be. His progress was dictated by ability and experience, and quite unaffected by the rating in which he happened to be borne on the ship's books.

The second route to the quarter deck was to join the Navy in boyhood, with no more expectations than to grow up as a fore-mastman, but instead to rise by merit to a petty officer's rating, and thence to a warrant or commission. This was the typical pat-tern for a warrant officer, but many commissioned officers came up this way. Any petty officer who had been a midshipman or mas-ter's mate for two years was eligible to be examined for lieutenant, and many of them passed and received their commissions. These were men who had not, on entering the Service, had any clear pros-pect of reaching the quarter deck, and their opportunities often opened late in life. Almost always lieutenants promoted in this way were older than those who had been reckoned as 'young gentlemen' from the start. In the records they may often be dis-tinguished by their ages, as well as by having occupied the ratings of working petty officers and others not likely to have been avail-able for the accommodation of young gentlemen.

Lastly we must define a category of officers, probably smaller than the others but including several prominent men, who had be-gun their seagoing careers in the merchant service. The word 'be-gun' must be emphasized to distinguish these men from those sea officers, already committed to a naval career, who improved their experience or eked out their half-pay by serving in merchant ships in peacetime. It was of course possible to go to sea in merchant-men, generally in boyhood, and to rise by ability to the status of mate or even master, but as a rule mate was the highest a man could hope to go without capital, for masters of merchant ships usually owned shares in their ships.[65] Even masters, though gener-ally well rewarded, were professionally and socially insecure. With luck a master might become a successful merchant, but he was not likely to be reckoned a gentleman. By comparison the Navy offered the chance of honour, gentility and wealth, and some offi-cers of merchantmen were sufficiently attracted to abandon their careers in the hope of bettering themselves in the Navy. A mate was reckoned equivalent in standing to a petty officer in the Navy, so the accepted course was to enter the Navy in that rating, or with the prospect of being rated petty officer almost at once, and to aim for a warrant or commission thereafter.[66] Simply to reach warrant rank was, socially and financially, to 'break even' by the change, for low pay in the Navy was counterbalanced by prize money, half-pay and widow's pensions. To reach commissioned rank was to open new worlds of honour and profit.

To these three methods of rising to officer's rank should be added a fourth, numerically almost insignificant. In 1730 the old scheme of volunteers per order or 'King's letter boys' established in the previous century by Pepys, was modified by the foundation of the Royal Naval Academy at Portsmouth, to which the young gentlemen under Admiralty patronage were sent for an education of three years or so before going to sea. In principle this was a praiseworthy attempt to improve the education of future officers, but in practice it had fatal disadvantages. The Academy was expensive, and 'some progress in the Latin tongue' was required for admission, which effectively confined it to the sons of the wealthy.[67] Worse, the scholars at the Academy, for all their theoretical studies, were not learning seamanship, and the two years' sea time credited to them on graduation was no substitute for real experience when it came to an examination. Nor were the boys at Portsmouth making those vital personal contacts with future flag officers on which their promotion was likely to depend, and beside which the patronage of the Admiralty was a very insubstantial asset. Add to all this the fact that the 'academites' had a reputation for indiscipline and vice, and it is easy to see why those who knew the Navy did not send their sons there.[68] The Academy's theoretical capacity was forty, which would have been insufficient for more than a small proportion of the Navy's needs even if it had been full, which it seldom was.[69] In practice few successful officers came from it, and not many of any kind.

It is a matter of some interest to assess what proportion of officers used each of the methods of promotion, but apart from the Academy, there is little hard evidence. The certificates given to young men passing for lieutenants, which show their previous service, are the best indication, but it is necessary to use the pattern of ratings in which they had served as a guide. In its nature this is a matter of interpretation, and it seems likely that the number showing strong evidence of having begun as foremastmen, and risen as working petty officers understates the real proportion in that situation, many of whom must have passed through successive ratings indistinguishable, on paper, from those of young gentlemen. Moreover not all the lieutenants' passing certificates survive, and those which do may not be representative. For what it is worth, it can be said that of 815 who passed for lieutenant between 1745 and 1757, about 70 (9 per cent), including several future post-captains, show clear indications that they had bettered their social as well as their professional condition in reaching the quarter deck.[70]

It is most unlikely that any man of respectable family would willingly see his son go to sea with no better expectations than to become a common seaman, but beyond this it is difficult to attach social implications to the three main methods of officer entry. One can be fairly sure that the 9 per cent of lieutenants were not gentlemen by birth, and that most young gentlemen began their careers as captain's servants, but beyond this it is not safe to go, except to say that the level of education required of the future commissioned or warrant officer effectively excluded those who had not had some schooling. There were schoolmasters in the larger ships of the Navy for instructing the young, but they were not universal, nor universally good, and the possession of education, together with such elementary social graces as a man needed to pass in respectable company, must in almost all cases have derived from an upbringing in a class not below what might nowadays be called the lower middle class. The obstacles against the really poor reaching the quarter deck, though not insuperable, were very high.

Those who came from the lower middle class, the artisans, shopkeepers, small tradesmen and the like, had opportunities to send their sons into the Navy by any of the three routes. They appear chiefly to have come from seaports, and especially from dockyard towns, where they had many opportunities to make the acquaintance of captains or other officers who might take their sons to sea. For the captain with many servants' berths to fill,[71] it was a small favour to grant, for the only risk he ran was in getting a troublesome or useless boy who would have to be sent back to his parents. It happened sometimes, but this was the price one had to pay in the search for talent.[72] Many fathers might be in a position to ask such a favour. It is said that tradesmen in the dockyard towns were sometimes prepared to forget awkward bills in return for having an awkward son taken off their hands, and there is nothing unlikely in the suggestion. The officers of the dockyards were in a particularly good position, for then as now captains were anxious to be on good terms with those on whom depended the speed with which their ships were refitted, to say nothing of all those invaluable little comforts and refinements not sanctioned by the Navy Board's standing orders, which a word from the Master Shipwright might arrange. In just these circumstances Captain Middleton of the *Ardent* took on board in 1776 a son of the Assistant Master Shipwright at Chatham:

> Another young man, son to one of the Builder's assistants, walks the quarter deck, but is rated landman. He is a modest boy, and his father has been very civil and attentive in fitting the ship.[73]

Attentions of this sort advanced many sons of yard officers, among them Commodore Tiddeman, son of the Master Attendant of Plymouth, and Admiral Sir Peircy Brett, son of the Master Attendant of Chatham.[74]

Warrant officers in the Navy were another group who were in an excellent position to get their sons set on the road to a commission by starting as captains's servants, if not as servants to their own fathers. So too were Customs officers (like the fathers of Charles Middleton, Phillip Patton and William Bligh), shipbuilders, and anyone whose trade brought them into contact with commissioned officers in circumstances of mutual advantage.[75] Artificers as well as officers of yards found opportunities to advance their sons. John Pasco, Nelson's signal lieutenant at Trafalgar, who died a rear-admiral, was the son of a caulker who entered Plymouth Yard in 1760.[76] Moreover it was quite possible to rise directly from a warrant to a commission. Thomas Regon, for example, was an able seaman in the *Liverpool* in 1760. By 1776 he was carpenter of the *Ariel*, during the American War he distinguished himself, and when he died in 1782 he was first lieutenant of the flagship and poised to receive the next vacant command.[77] William Smith, gunner of the *Alcide*, was in 1758 pro-

moted directly to second lieutenant of the *Shannon*.[78] Justinian
Nutt sailed with Anson on the *Centurion*'s famous voyage round
the world in 1740 as a lieutenant's servant, and as he was then
about thirty-six he was certainly not a young gentleman in the
usual acceptance of the phrase. By the end of the voyage he had
risen first to master, then to acting third lieutenant, and he died a
post-captain.[79] Masters, being the best-educated warrant officers,
were in a particularly good position to reach commissioned rank,
though few left it as late as Richard Hinde, master of the *Dreadnought*, who received his commission in January 1743/4 the day
after he had passed his examination, being then upwards of sixty-
one years old.[80]

There are not many people who can be said with certainty to
have risen from foremastmen to senior officers, probably because
there were not that many in fact, but also because they were not
necessarily keen to advertise their origins. Admiral Cornish, for
example, is always stated to have been born in the humblest circumstances, and to have risen from a foremastman. It is not unlikely, but his father's real calling seems not to be recorded.[81] A
clearer case is James Alms, the son of a domestic servant of the
Duke of Richmond, who became a post-captain, and whose son
died a vice-admiral.[82]

Of the officers of merchantmen who joined the Navy in hopes
of preferment by far the best known is James Cook, the son of the
farm-hand who rose to post rank, and would probably have gone
further had he lived.[83] Arthur Forrest, a former petty officer, was
master of a merchantman in the Jamaica trade when Vernon persuaded him to sail with him as a pilot on the Porto Bello expedition. Seeing his opportunity, he declined payment of £50 for his
services in favour of a promise of preferment in the Navy if he
could pass the lieutenants' examination. This he soon did, was
appointed to command the *Pilot* sloop and employed to teach the
masters of the squadron the pilotage of Port Royal harbour. This
was the start of a career which made him a post-captain and a
wealthy planter.[84] Another who reached post rank from the merchant service was John McLaurin.[85] James Kempthorne, who
entered the Navy as an able seaman at the age of twenty, and died
a rear-admiral, was apparently a recruit from the merchant ser-

vice, though whether an officer or no does not appear.[86] Doubtless there were many who attempted the change with less success, and we hear of some of them.[87] There were certainly a good many who achieved modest good fortune in the Navy, reaching warrant or commissioned rank without ever making a mark in history. Thomas Porter was master of the *Roebuck* when he passed for lieutenant in 1755, most of his stated experience having been in merchantmen. He was then fifty, but still managed to reach master and commander's rank.[88] Lieutenant John Mathison, who passed in 1745, was another who entered the Navy as a petty officer.[89] William Traill was master of his father's ship in 1739 when he left her to join the Navy 'in hopes of preferment', and his hopes were not misplaced, for though his career eventually ended in drunkenness and disgrace, he at least reached acting commander.[90] Patrick Renney, son of a baillie of Falkirk, went to sea as a surgeon in whalers and slavers before entering the Navy in 1756, and leaving for posterity a entertaining memoir of his service. [91]

This sort of transition was the easier because of the frequent traffic in the other direction. In times of peace before the Seven Years' War the strength of the Navy was only ten thousand men, and only sixteen thousand before the American War.[92] This was far too few to provide employment for every officer who wished to serve and needed to earn a living, or every young gentleman who needed to get in his sea-time. Consequently they went to sea in merchantmen in large numbers. The Admiralty regarded it as demeaning for a post-captain to command a merchantman, or for a lieutenant to serve as mate of anything smaller than an Indiaman, but otherwise it imposed no restrictions, and it was easy for officers on half-pay to get leave to join merchant ships. From the peace in February 1763 to the end of 1764 a total of 120 lieutenants had done so, plus others who commanded customs vessels and packets, became harbour-masters and consuls, or served in the navies of foreign powers.[93] One in this situation was William Phillips, who wrote in 1752: 'By the assistance of my friends I have raised a subscription and purchased a snow of 160 tons ... I am chartered to sail next week to Dublin, and shall go from thence to Barbados.'[94] Similarly, Lieutenant Archibald Dorrock was in the Antigua trade, James Bremer traded to Portugal, and Michael Pascal to the West Indies.[95]

Young gentlemen who had not yet passed for lieutenant did the same in order to gain seatime and experience, for there were far too few berths available in the Navy. 'I have a very uphill work from the great number who I wish to serve,' Keppel wrote in 1753, 'but such are the times and such is the nature of the Sea Service that I see no encouragement for introducing into it such as are deserving. Lord Anson feels it as much as we all do, and yet has not power to amend it.'[96] George Elphinstone was one of many young men who turned to the East India Company to sustain his career. Having served in the Navy from 1761 to 1766, he became third mate of the *Triton* East Indiaman (commanded by his brother) until in 1769 he was able to return to the Navy as an acting lieutenant and resume the progress which took him eventually to be a full admiral and a peer.[97] John Elliot, despairing of getting on in the Navy in peacetime, reckoned an Indiaman or Customs vessel his best prospect, failing which he would ship in a London or Glasgow merchantman and work up to be master.[98] George Johnstone was another young Scot who served in merchantmen as a boy. He was the son of a baronet, Elliot of a law lord, Elphinstone and John Ruthven of peers, Thomas Geary of an admiral.[99] All of them sailed in merchantmen as young men, and it is not credible to suggest that no son of good family would ever darken the deck of a merchant ship. It is necessary to emphasize this, because Sir John Laughton, who stamped his views on naval history by writing all the naval entries in the *Dictionary of National Biography*, was convinced that the claims of age and length of service in lieutenants' passing certificates were frequently falsified, and was apt to dismiss purported merchant service as obviously false. There are cases in which it can be shown that officers had falsified these details, and there is a reference to a young man 'who scorned to plead the merchants' service, where he had not been', but there is reason to think that Laughton's ideas were far too sweeping.[100] Of those 815 who passed for lieutenant between 1745 and 1757, the number showing service in merchantmen before or after joining the Navy was 172, or 21 per cent.[101] The object of falsehood is to deceive, and it is hardly credible that over one-fifth of young men passing for lieutenant would have claimed merchant service if such service had in fact been rare and the claim implausible. There is really nothing unlikely in the suggestion that the young Richard Howe went to sea in a merchantman.[102]

The different opportunities of two methods of becoming an officer, by joining as a petty officer from the merchant service, and by entering as an officer's servant, can be illustrated from the diverse careers of two men, both born at Deal in Kent within a few years of one another, both of very similar social background. John Bentley entered the Navy about 1720 as a lieutenant's servant. He passed for lieutenant in 1726, but did not receive his first commission until eight years later, and then served ten years as a lieutenant. The turning point in his career came at the Battle of Toulon in 1744, when his gallantry, in an action discreditable to many who were present, earned him a command and the notice of Lord Anson. He was Anson's flag-captain at the first Battle of Finisterre in 1747, was present at the second victory of that name later in the year and again distinguished himself in the Battles of Lagos and Quiberon Bay. It was said of him that he had fought with distinction in every action of consequence which took place in over fifty years in the Service. Bentley died in 1772 a vice-admiral and a knight, but his most senior employment was as an an Extra Commissioner at the Navy Board from 1761 to 1764. His parentage I do not know, but he had kinsmen in such trades as shipwright, pastry-cook, boatbuilder, engraver and mariner, which seems to give a good idea of the social milieu from which he came.[103]

His contemporary William Boys was the son of a nonconformist woollen draper, and distantly related to a Kentish gentry family. He was baptized in the Independent Chapel at Deal on 26 June 1700, and was originally destined for the ministry. Instead he went to sea in a merchantman commanded by a friend of his father's. After a spell as a midshipman in the Navy, he sailed as mate of the slaver *Luxborough Galley*, which was burnt at sea on passage home from the West Indies. Boys was one of only seven who survived, by eating the bodies of their dead shipmates. This experience confirmed his austere piety; for the rest of his life he fasted and prayed for a fortnight beginning on the anniversary of his rescue. He was twenty-eight when he entered the Navy for good, and thirty-five before he received his first commission. He was made post in 1743, and for much of the Seven Years' War he served as commodore and commander-in-chief at the Nore, one of the most onerous administrative positions in the Navy. Because he had reached post-rank comparatively late in life, he had little hope of ever hoisting his flag, but his diligence, compassion and integrity earned him as responsible a position as Bentley achieved, in spite of his higher rank and more distinguished record at sea. He died in 1772 (the same year as Bentley) as Lieutenant-Governor of Greenwich Hospital.[104] In the end both men reached near the top of their profession by different routes. Some, though not all, of higher birth rose faster than they, but their careers are good illustrations of the varied opportunities the Navy opened to a young man of fair education, whatever his background.

But undoubtedly the most striking example of the Navy as a profession open to merit wherever it appeared is the life of John Perkins. Nothing certain is known of him before 1775, when he entered the flagship of the Jamaica Squadron as a pilot extra, but he must already have been an experienced local master or mate. Within a few years he was commanding the *Punch* schooner tender with brilliant success, and in 1782 he was commissioned as lieutenant in command of the *Endeavour* brig by Sir Peter Parker. Two years later, in a characteristically irregular manoeuvre, Rodney gave him a commission as master and commander of the same vessel, but it was not confirmed, and he had to wait until 1797 to advance to commander's rank. In 1800 he was made post, commanding the *Arab* and *Tartar* frigates. In 1805 he retired because of ill health, and in 1812 he died in Kingston. Apart from the unusual, if not unique fact that his career was spent entirely on a single station, and he appears never once to have visited England, Perkins's rise was not more remarkable than that of other men who entered from the merchant service and displayed outstanding merit. What marks him out is that he was a mulatto, and may well have been born a slave.[105] No more striking example could be found of the Navy's character as a career open to talent.

B PATRONAGE AND PROMOTION

We have seen that there was in the Navy a substantial minority of officers who had risen from relatively humble origins, showing that the Service was not only a highly honourable profession attractive to the nobility and gentry, but also to a large degree a career open to talent wherever it might be found. It remains to explain how talent was identified and promoted. In doing so it is necessary for the modern reader to jettison one of the basic assumptions with which he is likely to approach the subject. It is the custom in modern states for merit to be judged in public service by the medium of examinations or other methods of assessment intended as far as possible to eliminate the subjective prejudices of the examiners, and the effects of personal or political influence. The ideal cannot always be attained, but it is an ingrained assumption nowadays that some such methods are more or less synonymous with the advancement of merit. Conversely, the old régime's acceptance of a system openly based on personal influence, 'interest', as the eighteenth century called it, has been judged by generations of readers, and historians, as a corrupt method which sacrificed public interest for private gain.[1]

A glance at the senior officers of the Navy during the Seven Years' War appears to give unquestionable evidence of the effects of interest. There at the Admiralty we find Lord Anson, son-in-law of the Lord Chancellor; Admiral Boscawen, brother of Lord Falmouth the principal man in Cornish politics; Admiral Forbes, son of the Earl of Granard; and Admiral West, cousin of Pitt and the Grenvilles. Among the commanders at sea were Hawke, nephew of a Commissioner of Trade; Knowles, the bastard son of the Earl of Banbury; Smith, the half-brother of Lord Lyttelton and consequently another near kinsman of Pitt and the Grenvilles; Pocock, the nephew of Lord Torrington, First Lord of the Admiralty for six years, and Osborn, Torrington's son-in-law's brother; Watson, nephew of Torrington's successor Sir Charles Wager; Townshend, half-brother of a viscount; Holburne, a protégé of the Duke of Argyll; Frankland, nephew of a former Lord of the Admiralty; Hardy, the grandson of Josiah Burchett, Secretary of the Admiralty for forty-eight years; Northesk and Colvill, peers in their own right. Among the rising younger officers who first hoisted their flags during that war we find Holmes, son of the Governor of the Isle of Wight; Rodney, kinsman of the Duke of Chandos; Keppel, son of the Earl of Albemarle; Douglas, follower of the Earl of Morton; and Howe, an Irish viscount.

Unfortunately for those who disapproved of interest, this list includes those responsible for virtually every significant British victory for thirty years, and it would hardly be possible to find one of them – except Admiral Byng, son of Lord Torrington – who did not deserve his promotion. The paradox is clear: how could good men have been selected by a system which, according to the usual modern approach, seems bound to have shown deplorable results?

This approach is characteristically Victorian in its equation of means and ends. The means used in the eighteenth century to advance men in the public service were self-evidently wrong, runs the argument, and the results must consequently have been bad. Morality and efficiency walked hand in hand, and when public opinion tolerated advancement by interest, it was to be expected that the public service would suffer. This was the counterpart to many of the mid-Victorian reforms of government, concerned to establish, for example, the employment of public money and the recruitment of civil servants on a strictly regular basis, exactly as sanctioned by Parliament, in the confidence that from this efficiency and economy would naturally flow.[2] How far the Victorians were justified in this idea is not for this book to say, but it is clear that its application in reverse, as it were, to the eighteenth century, has landed many historians in difficulties. Short of extraordinary luck, or the ineffable superiority of the English character, no explanation seemed able to reconcile the history of the Service with its system of promotion. So bad a system could not possibly produce such good results.

The flaw in the logic, it may be suggested, lies in the two assumptions that personal influence deployed in the public service was morally wrong, and that in consequence it must lead to failure. As to the first, the historian has little useful to say; the application of interest was accepted in the eighteenth century as a normal and inevitable aspect of civil society, a means of exchange, like money, to be rightly or wrongly used according to each man's lights. We may disagree, but there is nothing to be gained by trying to shout across the abyss of two centuries to persuade our ancestors of their fault. What can be said is that we are mistaken if we suppose that a system based on personal influence must necessarily have chosen unworthy men. This would have been so if those with the power of choice had placed other qualities above professional ability – for example, if they had insisted on choosing officers only from those of noble blood, as the French navy normally did.[3] But if, from inclination or necessity, they used a system of patronage to identify and advance men of ability, that system might be at least as efficient as any examination or annual report in bringing skilful officers to the head of their profession.

There is no doubt that the system of personal followings was as fundamental to social relations among officers as it was between officers and ratings. There was no real distinction between a senior officer's followers among junior officers, and those among ratings; they were part of the same following, obeying the same imperatives, and even the barriers of rank between them were easily and often crossed. If there was a difference, it was that the officers were socially and professionally closer to one another than to ratings, and so the personal ties of the patronage system were stronger. The officer corps has been likened to a club,[4] which perhaps implies a body smaller, more homogeneous and more exclusive than it was, but it was just like a club in that the natural ways in which its members dealt with one another were personal rather than institutional or bureaucratic. In that it mirrored British society in general. The vertical links of mutual dependence and obligation which we call patronage were still the natural cement of society in the middle years of the eighteenth century. Class interests were discernible in embryo, but for most practical purposes, they were still unimportant.[5] In the Navy people found, and expected to find, much the same sort of social relations as they were accustomed to ashore.

This meant that every senior officer had his following of junior officers and would-be officers. For both him and them the system was a social and professional necessity. The captain commissioning a ship had an urgent need of reliable officers, and in wartime when they were scarce, it would have been rash simply to wait for whomever the Admiralty and Navy Board happened to send him. Commanders of energy applied for the officers they wanted. What the captain needed were good followers, men of whose qualities he had personal knowledge, who were willing to serve with him. The more and better his followers, the better chance he had of collecting a good set of officers, and that in turn was a major step in the direction of an efficient ship's company. In the Navy everything depended on teamwork; without a reliable ship's company the most brilliant officer was helpless, and the most ambitious frustrated. Often it meant the difference between death and survival at sea, between victory and defeat, and between wealth and penury. A captain like Richard Tiddeman, about to sail for the East Indies in 1758 with his first and another lieutenant ill, the two other very junior and inexperienced, and his boatswain 'eternally drunk', was in a dangerous position: 'I have certainly the worst quarter deck that ever man had.'[6] Tiddeman was a good officer, and no doubt unlucky, but it was the sort of ill luck which was much less likely to befall the officer with a healthy following. In the Navy professional success, if not survival, required that an officer have able subordinates eager to follow him.[7]

A following was built up by looking out for young men who hoped to become officers, and advancing them. The first and most obvious source of them was young gentlemen. There were many servants' berths to be filled, and commanders acquired the sons of their friends and relations, their neighbours and brother officers.[8] Often they took their own sons, though some felt that 'brothers and sons to officers often made mischief in ships', and John Elliot declined to take his young brother for this reason.[9] Sometimes a chance acquaintance forged the link. Captain Thomas Smith, as he then was, travelling through Somerset, had an accident near the village of Butleigh. He stayed with the vicar while his coach was repaired, and the upshot was that the vicar's youngest son, aged thirteen, went to sea with him, soon followed by his fifteen-year-old brother. This was the beginning of the careers of Alexander and Samuel Hood, subsequently Viscounts Bridport and Hood respectively.[10]

The captain or admiral who hoped to acquire, and keep, young men as his followers had to demonstrate his power to advance them. To do that he had to convince his seniors, and especially the Admiralty, that he was a man of judgement and discretion whose recommendations could be relied on. Then he would be in a position to reward merit, and young men would be eager to serve one who could advance their careers. Patrons therefore needed to be careful how they gave recommendations, lest their credit suffer by an injudicious choice – hence the care with which Boscawen distinguished between followers of his own whom he could vouch for, and one whom he had advanced at the request of a brother officer:

> I never saw him in my life. Mr Grierson and Mr Pollard I did recommend; the former was recommended by the late General Wolfe for some very gallant action in the landing at Louisbourg, but had not then served his time in the Royal Navy, the latter has served his time, has passed, and is well qualified.[11]

Even for Anson, at the head of his profession, it was not unimportant that his protégés should do well, and be seen to do well, which explains the pleasure with which he noted, writing to Hawke to congratulate him on his great victory at Quiberon Bay, that so many of his own 'friends' had distinguished themselves in the battle.[12] The follower to support was one who 'will always do honour to those that prefer him', as Keppel put it.[13] The one to avoid was a man like John Miller, a follower of Rodney's for twelve years who at his request was made a boatswain, only to prove drunken and useless.[14] This sort of débâcle did an officer's reputation for sound judgement no good at all, and the senior officer with a poor reputation, and consequently a poor chance of advancing his followers, would be avoided by all good men. Rear-Admiral Norris, for example, was personally unpopular, and known to be held in no high regard at the Admiralty, so the young John Elliot declined an offer to serve as his sixth lieutenant:

> I am extremely happy where I am. I thought it a pity to give up this to be the youngest lieutenant of the youngest admiral, who has no chance to have a separate

277

command, and consequently not in his power to be of
any use to me if he should take a fancy to me.[15]

For the young follower it was of great importance to his career
to become known to officers who were able to give expression to
their approval, now or in the future. 'I have but one piece of advice
to give you at present,' Lord Cornwallis wrote to his son in the
Navy,

> which is to endeavour to keep company with the cap-
> tains of ships and of your superior officers as much as
> you can. It will certainly be advantageous to you.

'In all professions,' he added later, 'the character superior officers
give of young men is all in all.'[16] Cornwallis was no expert on the
Navy, but in this he was quite right. In promoting officers, one
captain explained, 'regard has been paid not only to solicitation
but even to the character given to gentlemen by their commanders,
of any tolerable repute'.[17]

This 'even' is curious, for a young officer's 'character', his
reputation, was really the determining factor in his career. Without a good reputation for professional ability even the well-connected fared badly.[18] Lieutenant the Hon. James Wemyss, heir to a
great estate, resigned his commission in disgust in 1759 having
waited fourteen years in the vain hope of promotion.[19] Captain
Thomas Grenville was brother of Lord Temple and of George
Grenville, a member of the Board of Admiralty, both of whom
made persistent efforts on his behalf which hindered rather than
helped his naval career.[20] Lieutenant the Hon. Philip Tufton Perceval was 'a son of Lord Egmont's, but with a very indifferent character from [Admiral] Saunders of him', as Augustus Hervey noted
when he arrived on board. Perceval did reach post-captain, but he
was never trusted with responsibility, and spent thirty years 'commanding' yachts in harbour – not an impressive career for a man
whose father was for some time First Lord of the Admiralty.[21]

It was possible under the patronage system for officers of
undoubted competence and interest to rise surprisingly slowly.
Admiral Hawke was noted above as a man with interest, and he
certainly did derive some benefit from his uncle's influence, but the

striking thing about his career is how a man of his abilities, the follower of Warren and Sir Chaloner Ogle and a post-captain at twenty-nine, was nearly passed over for a flag in 1747. One may suggest that Hawke's own character could have contributed to this. He was a great sea commander, in moments of crisis calm and resolute, always a gentleman of the strictest integrity, but he was naïf and unwordly in political affairs, a fine judge of professional merit but capable of being deceived by men less honourable than himself, sometimes irritable in face of the petty vexations of daily life, and touchy when he felt his honour was impugned. In some respects he was a prickly and difficult man, and in a system which worked entirely by personal contacts, one can see that he was perhaps at a disadvantage compared with others, not necessarily less honest than he, but more urbane and worldly-wise.[22]

As a patron himself, Hawke was especially the friend of men who had no other friends, like Lieutenant James Hobbs who wrote to ask his help after his great victory in 1747, and later became his flag-captain. Hawke's letter asking for Hobbs's promotion to commander in 1755 is a model of a characteristic diffidence not at all justified by his rank and reputation: 'it is the first favour of the kind that I have ever asked, and shall be very much obliged to their Lordships . . .'[23] It was typical of him, too, to concern himself not only with the advancement but also the personal well-being of his followers. 'It is impossible to deny the asking of small favours for officers that have served with one and behaved well,' he wrote in 1762, asking for two carpenters to be allowed to exchange ships so that they could remain at the ports where their families lived.[24]

Throughout the Service, flag officers were asking for small favours or large for their followers, and especially naming those they wished to have as officers or young gentlemen in their flag-ships, and those they wished to promote.[25] When they shifted or hauled down their flags they listed the followers they wished to take with them. Admiral Saunders, for example, shifting his flag in 1757, took his flag-captain Alexander Hood, all six lieutenants (among them Alexander Holburne) and his chaplain.[26] The presence of Hood, a follower of Admiral Smith, and Holburne, nephew of Vice-Admiral Francis Holburne, illustrates a common practice among patrons, to swap recommendations. It was a natural response to a practical need; not every senior officer was always in a position to help his followers, and even a man with a large following might be in want of a particular officer. The admiral or captain who needed to fill a position would ask among his fellow officers for a candidate. The commander who recommended, say, a petty officer for a warrant, lost a good man and thereby weakened his ship's company, but it was very much in his interest to do so, for by demonstrating his power to reward merit he drew other and better men to follow him. It was almost a cliché that 'many a good man is lost to the world by being overlooked',[27] but senior officers had a constant need to identify these good men and attract them as followers. No doubt they could never promote all those who sought advancement, but neither could they ever have too many able followers.

The qualifications for promotion were understood by all officers, and often stated explicitly by patrons anxious to underline the suitability of their candidates. They needed to show that their protégés were men of experience and ability, preferably known to the patron for some time, ideally 'a gentleman of my own bringing up', as Sir John Bentley put it.[28] Thus Lord Colvill, reporting that he had promoted Lieutenant James Ferguson to a command, wrote:

> I beg leave to recommend this gentleman to their Lordships for confirmation. He has sailed with me more than fourteen years, in the stations of midshipman, mate and lieutenant. I know him well to be an excellent and alert seaman, a brave and good officer, and a very modest and honest man. His own merit has been his only recommendation.[29]

Although patrons freely swapped recommendations, and individuals passed easily from one following to another, a following as a whole was entirely dependent on its patron. His death or disgrace destroyed at a stroke the expectations of all his followers. When Boscawen died in 1761 his 'little Navy of your own making' as his wife called it, was dispersed.[30] Acting Lieutenant Thomas Breton, for example, was described in the following year as 'a very deserving young man, and who lost in Admiral Boscawen his only patron'.[31] Another of his followers, Lewis Gellie, was even more unlucky. He had first come to Boscawen's notice at the taking of Louisbourg, where his gallantry got him made sixth lieutenant of the flagship. He had risen to be first, poised for the next vacancy, when his patron died. He applied to Anson for help, who recommended him to Pocock, and he sailed on the Havana expedition as sixth lieutenant of his flagship. Again he rose to first, and in that position he returned with Pocock to England, only to find that his second patron, Anson, had also died. From this blow his career never recovered.[32] When Rear-Admiral Durrell died four days after arriving at Halifax to take command of the North American station in 1766, twenty-four young gentlemen applied for leave to return home at once, their prospects shattered.[33] When Vice-Admiral Watson died in India in 1757 Rear-Admiral Pocock actually offered to take on such of his followers as chose to remain with him, but this was an extraordinary mark of esteem for the dead admiral.[34] Normally no officer would injure his followers by favouring outsiders over them. If an officer was disgraced, like Byng, his following would disperse as swiftly as if he had died, or more swiftly, for it was worse to be associated with a living coward than a dead hero. Of all Byng's numerous followers, only three stood by him in his disgrace: Arthur Gardiner his flag-captain, John Amherst and Augustus Hervey, all old lieutenants whom he had made commanders. A large proportion of the senior officers of the Mediterranean squadron chose to return home when Hawke came out to relieve Byng, rather than remain on the scene of their patron's downfall.[35]

These three captains, and Byng's other followers who can be identified, did not share his weakness, and few officers in the Service equalled Hervey for audacious gallantry. It is curious nevertheless to observe that bad patrons often had bad followers. It does not seem to have been simply a matter of good officers looking elsewhere and leaving the doubtful patron with the ullage; there is a strong suspicion that bad officers actually bred up bad followers. Augustus Hervey's uncle William, for example (under whom he began his career), saw most of the officers of his ship court-martialled in the two years before he himself was dismissed the Service for cruelty. Several of them were his followers for many years, and

281

his first lieutenant, John Sbirrel ('a very troublesome man, and one that I believe nobody would like to have for a lieutenant') had been with him from boyhood.[36] Exactly the same pattern occurred in the case of Penhallow Cuming, dismissed the Service in 1758 by the same court martial which dealt likewise with his follower and first lieutenant Samuel Gribble.[37]

The twin poles of the naval patronage system were the Admiralty, or to be exact the naval members of the Board, and the commanders-in-chief of squadrons overseas. Because of slow communications it was necessary that admirals commanding abroad should supply vacancies among their officers without first referring to the Admiralty. Only a minority of the ships and men of the Navy were serving abroad at any time, but for various reasons the turnover of officers was much higher than at home. Mortality was greater in the fever zones, and many who did not die had to be invalided home. Personal or professional reasons often compelled officers to come home, though the Admiralty had for long been campaigning against those who returned, or declined to sail, because they disliked serving in dangerous waters, and under Anson it was necessary to produce convincing excuses for resigning abroad.[38] In some circumstances prizes or purchases might be commissioned as King's ships, and there were usually a few officers left behind when a squadron sailed whose places would have to be supplied. For all these reasons the overseas commanders-in-chief disposed of patronage out of proportion to the size of their squadrons. This and the good chances of prize money made their situation the most enviable, as well as the most arduous and dangerous available for a flag officer, and the power to appoint to overseas commands was the Admiralty's most valuable piece of patronage. Naturally it went only to those of whom their Lordships thought well, and specifically to those who could be trusted with the power of patronage. The orders of commanders-in-chief overseas always circumscribed their power to grant commissions and warrants, to a degree which varied according as the officer himself was trusted, but in every case they were subject to confirmation by the Admiralty. This appeared to leave the ultimate dependence beyond dispute, but in practice the Admiralty needed the commanders-in-chief at least as much as they needed it, for even Anson and Boscawen at the Board could satisfy all their deserving claimants for promotion only by private arrangement with the admirals who disposed of so much of the available patronage. It was often the case that Anson could most effectually help a follower by sending him overseas with a friendly admiral ('he designed to send you with the first commanding officer that went abroad, which was intending everything in his power to promote you early').[39]

This traffic was regulated by private correspondence, carried on in parallel with the official orders and despatches. At the same time as the admiral wrote formally to John Clevland, the Secretary of the Admiralty, for their Lordships' information, he would write privately to Anson, or to his secretary Philip Stephens, who was installed as Second Secretary of the Admiralty in 1759, and succeeded Clevland in 1763. Sometimes the official and private letters were virtually identical, apart from the address.[40] The replies invariably came from Stephens, for Anson hated the labour of correspondence. In these private letters commanders-in-chief solicited the confirmation of their commissions and warrants, and reported how far they had been able to serve 'the young gentlemen you did me the honour to recommend for preferment'.[41] It was a process of mutual accommodation in which favours were granted and returned on each side. It would have been unnecessary and indelicate to spell the matter out, but it was obvious to all involved that the process was essentially a matter of exchange. The unspoken idea was that the patron (and this applied equally to admirals or civilians at home) had an invisible balance, in credit or debit, of favour with the Admiralty, and specifically with Lord Anson. An officer who had asked little and done much had a good credit balance, and could decently ask for the advance of a follower. Lord Sandwich, in 1756, had exhausted his credit, and could only recommend a friend to go out to Hawke in the Mediterranean:

> I have been so often troublesome to Lord Anson that I don't choose upon this occasion to apply through his channel, though I know it would be the most expeditious method.[42]

In this system, each party needed the other, but in order for the arrangement to work, they needed to trust one another. If that trust were broken, or never established, the position of an overseas commander-in-chief was untenable.

The system can be seen at work in a letter from Keppel in 1763, justifying the unusual promotion of a lieutenant directly to post-captain:

> ... there being at that time no master and commander upon the station ... their Lordships confirming Mr Gregory in the *Syren* will be doing what I shall think myself under obligation to them for, and which I flatter myself they will not look upon me as unreasonable in hoping, as Mr Gregory is the only lieutenant I have appointed to a command since my being commander-in-chief in these seas, and when I acquaint their Lordships that he was my first lieutenant during the siege of the Havana, and employed by Lord Albemarle most constantly in essential services.[43]

The obligation that Keppel spoke of was not a mere figure of speech, for he was really in a position to do the naval members of the Admiralty Board essential service in advancing their followers. Admiral Cornish made the relationship between Board and commander-in-chief very clear in a private letter to Anson written in 1761:

> I hope your Lordship will be good enough to look in a favourable light upon my appointment of Captain Tiddeman to a broad pendant and a captain [under] him; I assure your Lordship that I was in great want of [an] assistant of rank in this country to carry on the public service with me, and to send on detached services. Captain Isaac Ourry I have appointed his captain, and my nephew Captain Pitchford into the *South Sea Castle* in his room, a young man who I flatter myself bears a very good character, and as I have no children of my own I look upon him in the light of a son. Lieutenant Mathison, your Lordship's recommendation, I shall put into the *Tyger* hulk ...[44]

This was neatly contrived; unless Anson confirmed the rather dubious promotions of Tiddeman and Pitchford, his own protégé would lose his advancement to commander. All other commanders-in-chief, with more or less finesse, operated the same system.[45] So also did other First Lords. Rodney's relations with George Grenville while he was at the head of the Board were particularly close.[46] In December 1762, for instance, Grenville wrote explaining that Admiral Cotes had applied for his son-in-law Charles Kendall to be made lieutenant, but the Board having made it a rule to grant no more commissions now the preliminaries of peace were signed, he could only recommend the young man to Rodney in the West Indies. Less than two months later Kendall received his promotion.[47]

This must have been at the expense of young gentlemen who had gone out with Rodney and still awaited their commissions: an example of Rodney's unhappy ability to alienate his natural supporters, and a breach of the conventions governing promotion overseas. As a rule the flagship of a commander-in-chief going overseas was officered with his followers, who had the first claim on promotion. The same free market in talent which made the flagship the best manned of the squadron, gave her also the best, or at least the best-placed, officers and young gentlemen. If a command became vacant, the first lieutenant of the flagship had a natural claim on it, and the other lieutenants would move up accordingly. The first lieutenant of a private ship hoped to be advanced to sixth lieutenant of the flagship, because that in effect meant sixth in line of succession for the next vacant command. James Patterson, for example, was first lieutenant of the *Dreadnought* in the action off Cape François on 21 October 1757, 'and his good behaviour in that action', wrote Admiral Cotes, 'induced me to take him for one of my officers the first opportunity'.[48] In the same way Boscawen in 1756 asked for the first lieutenant of the *Harwich* to be promoted sixth of his flagship.[49] Joining the admiral's flagship was more or less the same as joining his following, and it was the high road to promotion.

The same system operated with other officers. When warrant officers' places fell vacant, the officers of smaller ships were promoted to larger, and the mates of the flagship received their first warrants. When the first lieutenant of the flagship received his command, the eventual vacancy at the end of a chain of consequential removals would go to a young gentleman from the flagship. An admiral was not bound to confine his promotions to his own followers or his own flagship, but it was always to them that he looked first. Between 24 February and 2 November 1758, for example, Boscawen, commanding on the Louisbourg expedition, advanced ten commanders, forty-nine lieutenants, seven masters, twelve boatswains, ten gunners, five carpenters, four pursers, five chaplains, nine surgeons, eleven surgeon's mates, four masters-at-arms, four cooks, two sailmakers, a schoolmaster and four yard officers. Many of these were consequential moves, but nearly all of those actually promoted in rank came from the flagship. The three new commanders were the first three lieutenants of the flagship, fifteen of the nineteen newly-commissioned lieutenants and both the new masters had been midshipmen or mates in her, all seven of the new boatswains had been Boscawen's boatswain's mates, and all four of the new gunners had been gunner's mates with him. Two new carpenters had been carpenter's mates in the flagship, and one carpenter's crew. Three new pursers had been clerks in the flagship, two new masters-at-arms her corporals, and both the sailmakers, sailmaker's crew.[50]

This was a typical pattern of promotions, repeated with minor variations by all flag officers overseas. Between March and October 1757 Commodore Steevens in the East Indies made three new lieutenants, two out of his ship, and one master promoted to a commission in his own ship. Of nine new warrant officers, four were promoted in their own ships, and five came from the flagship.[51] Between May and November 1757 Francis Holburne made two new commanders (the first two lieutenants of his flagship), nine lieutenants (six of them former young gentlemen in her), five boatswains, two gunners and two carpenters (all of them from his flagship).[52]

For the warrant officers of the flagship herself there was a chance of becoming senior officer of an overseas yard, for the commander-in-chief would have to fill any vacancies in the local yard, subject to the Navy Board's confirmation. Thus in 1761 Commodore Douglas installed the master of his flagship to replace the suspended Master Attendant of English Harbour, the dockyard at Antigua.[53] In 1759 Boscawen was able to do a service to two followers simultaneously, when he supported a request for superannuation from Robert Haswell, the Master Attendant of Gibraltar since 1739, and recommended in his place David Patterson, the master of his flagship.[54] The same principle applied if a yard were captured, as both Havana and Manila were during the Seven Years' War. In the event, both were handed back at the peace, but not before the victorious admirals had appointed a complete set of yard officers. Pocock's purser, master and carpenter became respectively Storekeeper, Master Attendant and Master Shipwright of Havana.[55] They all lost their places at the peace, but they had acquired a good claim to some compensating position, and to a pension.

As a rule the only direct interference with the patronage of an overseas commander-in-chief which was possible for the Admiralty was to order home an officer whom they intended to provide for, leaving the admiral to supply his place, which of course he would be happy to do.[56] The Mediterranean, however, was near enough for the Admiralty to retain some of the patronage in its own hands, which was a source of intermittent complaint from flag officers there.[57] They felt this interference implied a lack of that trust which was so essential to them, for without it they could not serve their own followers and maintain their position in the Service. It was an understood thing that regular commissions granted abroad carried an entitlement to confirmation, and even an unconfirmed promotion in plausible circumstances gave a young man some claim to consideration.[58] But what was justified and what was not always remained, however carefully an admiral's orders were worded, a matter of interpretation, and the spirit in which the Board interpreted these questions was crucial to a commander-in-chief overseas. The Admiralty was perforce delegating a great deal of valuable patronage together with the power to abuse it. The temptation to make more vacancies than was strictly necessary was very great for even the most scrupulous senior officer, and the scope for interpretation of what was necessary was very wide. Every senior officer needed his commissions and warrants to be scrutinized by an accommodating and trustful

Board which would support his credit and gain him more followers to add to those he had been able to advance, but some
allowed themselves to be seduced by the chances of irregular
vacancies into undermining their own reputations with the Board.

The simplest and commonest means of creating a vacancy was
to permit resignation on grounds of ill health.[59] Medical certificates were required, but in the then state of medicine there were
many conditions for which the only hope of relief appeared to be
return to a cool climate, and it was impossible for the Admiralty to
know which certificates were justified. Another fruitful source of
patronage was the commissioning of new men-of-war, particularly
in the West Indies, where there was an urgent operational need for
sloops of a type which could only be purchased locally. Commanders-in-chief in the Leeward Islands were sometimes authorized to buy and officer such vessels, but there remained many
delicate circumstances. Commodore Douglas felt sufficiently sure
of himself to report that he had recommissioned and officered a
former King's sloop recaptured from the French, but when the assembly of Barbados offered to replace the sloop which they had
formerly purchased for the Navy, but was now quite worn out and
unserviceable, he accepted clandestinely and did not reveal to the
Admiralty that he had substituted one *Barbadoes* sloop for
another.[60] Even though no additional patronage was involved in
this case, commissioning a new ship was extremely sensitive.
Admiral Holmes was severely reprimanded for commissioning
prizes at Jamaica in 1761:

> Let him know that as he is expressly forbid by their
> Lordships' additional instructions to him to purchase
> any ships for his Majesty without their Lordships' pre-
> vious order, he could have no authority or even preten-
> sion to put those ships into commission, and that he has
> therefore no right to expect that the commissions and
> warrants he gave in consequence of so irregular a pro-
> ceeding should be confirmed.[61]

An irregular commission like this might do its recipient more
harm than good. The young Lieutenant William Cornwallis went
abroad in 1763 under Sir William Burnaby, an officer with stronger

political contacts than professional merits, and susceptible to the lobbying of Lady Cornwallis on her son's behalf. Her approaches, more enthusiastic than discreet, would have damaged his chances by themselves if made to a more professional flag officer, and in the event Burnaby's support damaged him just as effectively. He gave Cornwallis a commission in transparently irregular circumstances, 'which prevented the inclinations of some in power from helping you', as Keppel informed him privately.[62] Keppel himself, whose relations with Anson were so close that he even felt able to admit in private correspondence that he was bearing unmustered supernumeraries to bolster his ship's company without his commander-in-chief's knowledge, went to great lengths to justify his promotions. No one knew better than he how easy it was to create a vacancy ('a commander-in-chief can always find reasons for such occasion'), and how easy it was for the Admiralty to suspect.[63]

There is no doubt that especially in peacetime officers on overseas stations did arrange resignations to create vacancies. The officer who resigned had his rank already, and might think it well worth losing full pay to gain the favour of powerful men.[64] Thomas Grenville became lieutenant in 1740 thanks to a contrived resignation of his kinsman Thomas Smith.[65] Anson knew of such an arrangement proposed in the Mediterranean in 1751 by an acting lieutenant seeking confirmation by persuading another to resign in return for the pay he would forfeit, 'or any other little thing he shall ask'.[66] In 1765 Hawke was privy to a scheme to make a follower of his post in this way ('had we been at Bombay, Captain Jackson should have quitted for him').[67] At about the same time Admiral Pocock was asked by a follower

> If by the help of my friends or the *proper* application of a little money I could get appointed to a command whilst on the station, whether I might hope for his countenance and concurrence with regard to the confirmation of my commission. He answered that in a case of that sort, if not too open and glaring an impropriety, I might rely upon him.[68]

This raises the question of how money might be applied, properly or otherwise. This was of great consequence for the efficiency of the Navy, for if officers could be bribed to quit with the connivance of the admiral, their commissions were in effect being purchased, with all that that implied. It is surprisingly difficult to be sure if this ever happened. Lord Cornwallis, for example, wrote to his brother reporting some advice which he had received from Keppel about the chances of an exchange:

> I cannot thoroughly understand him, but if anything of that sort can be done, I believe Lord Egmont [First Lord] will be inclined to serve you. If any sum of money should be necessary for it, for I have heard there are sometimes bargains of that sort, I will answer any draft that you may find it necessary to draw a month after sight; perhaps I am talking very ignorantly, but I am so very anxious to have you made post.[69]

Was Cornwallis talking very ignorantly? Men who knew more of the Navy than he did, agreed. Soon after taking office as First Lord in 1771 Lord Sandwich wrote of his determination to put a stop to 'the abuses which have crept into the Service, by allowing the sale of commissions (coloured by quitting for want of health) in foreign countries'.[70] This seems strong evidence, and the related practice of captains offering money to swap ships certainly occurred. Augustus Hervey offered the commander of a cruiser £400 to exchange, though the offer was refused.[71]

Unfortunately what ought to be the clearest case of a commission purchased by bribery is also the most perplexing. In May 1765 the Hon. Edward Michael Pakenham was second lieutenant of the *Romney*, flagship of Lord Colvill on the North American station, when the *Crown* naval store ship arrived at Halifax. Pakenham kept a private journal, and in it he wrote on 28th:

> Captain Feattus of the *Crown* having given me to understand that he was willing to quit his ship upon a consideration being paid him, I obtained leave from the admiral to make an agreement with him, Mr Denne the first lieutenant having declined. I accordingly made an agreement to give Captain Feattus twelve hundred pounds to quit his ship, which he did this day, and I was

appointed master and commander of her by the admiral.[72]

Official records confirm that Feattus did resign 'for the benefit of his health', Pakenham took command and brought the *Crown* to England, where the first thing he learnt on his arrival was that 'I was promoted by the Lords of the Admiralty to the command of his Majesty's sloop the *Bonetta* on 20th June last, so that the money I gave Captain Feattus was absolutely thrown away'.[73]

The account is highly circumstantial and comes from an unquestionably authentic source, and yet almost everything about it is very difficult to believe. Pakenham must have known, if he had learnt anything at all about the Navy during his service, that a commission granted in such circumstances had virtually no chance of confirmation. That no doubt was why the first lieutenant declined it, and wisely, for their Lordships did indeed refuse to confirm Pakenham's commission: 'as the vacancy was not regular, it is inconsistent with the rules of this office to comply with his request'.[74] If Pakenham had any acquaintance with the political world, he surely should have known that his friends were working on the Board of Admiralty to get him a command. Again, what could persuade Lord Colvill to imperil his reputation with the Admiralty, upon which his entire career and fortune were founded? Not only were the circumstances extremely suspicious, but the *Crown* was under Admiralty orders and not even part of his squadron. He apparently had nothing to gain by the transaction, and a great deal to lose. Lastly, there is question of the money itself. Pakenham was the eldest son of the first Baron Longford, an Irish peer in modest circumstances, who had no doubt sent his heir to sea in the hope of improving his fortunes, not completing their ruin. Lord Longford had difficulty managing on a gross income of about £2000 a year, and it seems improbable that the family could have found the enormous sum of £1200. In the circumstances it looks imprudent of Feattus to accept a note of hand which was far from certain to be honoured.[75] (I assume that even a wealthy man could hardly have found cash or bills to that amount at a few days' notice in one of the remoter parts of North America.)

So for many reasons this apparently clear evidence of a commission purchased turns out to be far from clear. What is certain, however, is that the system was of its nature open to this and other abuses, and that only a strong mutual trust between commanders-in-chief abroad and the Admiralty would permit it to work efficiently. Officers like Rodney who needed to take much space in their despatches to assure their Lordships with what rigorous propriety they had administered promotions were already in danger, even if their protestations did not themselves arouse disquiet.[76] It was much better to be above suspicion than to try to dispel it.

There was however one apparent abuse of the patronage system, chiefly though not entirely practised by admirals overseas, which was officially tolerated. The sons or near kinsmen of senior officers were accepted as a special case to whom the normal requirements of competence and experience need not be stringently applied. Lord Sandwich, always an accurate barometer of naval convention, explained it thus in 1764:

> As to Sir William Burnaby's making his son a captain, it was very natural for him to do it; if he is under age, it rests with the Admiralty Board to confirm him or not as they think proper, but I am satisfied in my opinion that no one has a right to complain that he has given his son the preference over every recommendation.[77]

'A brother officer who has a son a lieutenant in the Navy has a very just title to ask and to expect the favour you ask from any admiral,' Sir James Douglas wrote, and fifty years later Nelson considered 'the near relations of brother officers as legacies to the Service'.[78] Nelson himself, nephew of the Controller of the Navy, was one such legacy, and there were a considerable number of able senior officers who owed their rise, or at least the speed of their rise, to the same circumstance. Admiral Forbes's father and Pocock's uncle had been flag officers before they became peers, Watson and Frankland were nephews of admirals who reached the Admiralty Board, Hardy the son of another. There was a presumption that the merits of senior officers' sons deserved, at least, sympathetic consideration. Thus Commodore Moore appointed Lieutenant St Lo to command a sloop, 'a very deserving man and son to a very old officer in our service', and Keppel recommended a young man for preferment in the marines because his father, as adjutant during the attack on Belle Isle, 'has exerted himself in a particular manner during the whole service, and the young lad himself has shewn good spirit'.[79] It was with obvious pleasure that their Lordships informed old Admiral Harrison, the port admiral at Plymouth in 1757, that after a recent victory they had appointed his son a post-captain, 'not only on account of his being the son of so worthy a father, but for his late gallant behaviour and good conduct which hath given the Lords great satisfaction'.[80] In all these cases the young men had real professional merits regardless of their parentage, but it was not always so, and the custom of favouring the sons of senior officers was undoubtedly a weakness. It is necessary to look no further than the career of John Byng, favoured son of the great Lord Torrington, to see why.

What St Lo and Harrison had, and Byng had not, was success in action, a claim to advancement which operated throughout the Service, but especially in home waters where the Admiralty controlled promotions and followings made their impact less directly. Certainly those favoured by Anson or Boscawen were in a strong position, and so were those who followed their followers. Admiral Saunders was a member of the inner core of Anson's following, those who had survived his voyage round the world, and he could be sure that Anson would attend to his recommendations. Leaving the Mediterranean,

> Sir Charles Saunders going home would carry his people with him and leave his ship for Mr Broderick, as he would have no doubt of getting them provided for with him in England whilst Lord Anson presided, an indulgence which Mr Osborn perhaps could not have obtained.[81]

This comment was made in envy and overstates Anson's partiality, but it rests on truth, for the essence of the patronage system was trust, and Anson could trust his old friend and follower in a way he never could trust Osborn, whom he did not know well, and who was Byng's brother-in-law. Nevertheless it was not possible for the naval lords to make all promotions from their own followings and those of their friends, for they constituted too small a proportion of those eligible. It was necessary to have a criterion which did not depend on personal knowledge, and in the absence of any system of confidential reports, Anson, and to a large degree all flag officers, based their choice on success in action. This was what gave Harrison and St Lo their real claim to advancement, and with them very many others. 'My constant method,' Anson wrote,

> since I have had the honour of serving the King in the station I am in, has been to promote the lieutenants to command whose ships have been successfully engaged upon equal terms with the enemy, without having any friend or recommendation, and in preference to all others, and this I would recommend to my successors if they would have a fleet to depend on.[82]

'Nothing is so difficult', John Elliot wrote, 'as to establish as [sic] a character at sea.'[83] The way to do it was, as he had, to take a French privateer in single action. Simply to have served aboard a ship in a successful action was useful to a young officer. To be first aboard the enemy was, in the slang phrase, 'to gain the commission' ('which is not only a point of honour, but also a matter of interest'). Charles Middleton, trying to 'gain the commission', hoisted a boat out to board a French privateer without taking the way off his ship, filled the boat, and nearly drowned the boat's crew.[84] Good seamanship also could gain the commission, even without the presence of the enemy. Acting-lieutenant Hammond commanded the *Albany* sloop in 1757 when she was sent out to Hawke's squadron with an urgently needed shipment of spars:

> He behaved remarkably well in the gale of wind by preserving the topmasts for the squadron at the utmost risk, and notwithstanding the remonstrances of the whole company for cutting them away.[85]

Lord Howe, Hawke went on, had a vacancy for a lieutenant and would be glad of so resolute a seaman to fill it. Thus the career of a future Controller of the Navy (and baronet) profited from his courage and skill.

Nevertheless, for a young officer who hoped for command, or for post rank, nothing was more swiftly effective than to take an enemy ship of equal or greater force. When the *Isis* took the *Oriflamme* in 1761, Captain Wheeler was killed early in the action and the first lieutenant, James Cunningham, was appointed to command the prize.[86] In similar circumstances Michael Clements took two privateers in succession, and was raised from lieutenant to post-captain at a stroke.[87] Ezekiel Nash, second lieutenant of the *Milford* when she took the *Gloire* privateer of Bordeaux after both the captain and first lieutenant had been killed, was not promoted. He may been thought too junior (he had been a lieutenant less than two years), but it is also possible that the Board disapproved of his having spent much of the war commanding a privateer himself.[88] It was not necessary for the captain to be killed for the first lieutenant to profit from a creditable action. When John Elliot took the *Vengeur* he secured his first lieutenant's promotion to commander.[89] Thomas Baillie was first lieutenant of the *Tartar*, which under Captain Lockhart took seven privateers in a year, but when Lockhart was ill early in 1757 Baillie took her to sea himself, and immediately captured the *Victoire* privateer of Le Havre. For this he was made post to command her.[90] William Newson, commanding the *South Sea Castle* store ship in the Indian Ocean, led the boats of the squadron in a daring expedition to cut out two French ships from under the guns of Pondicherry. He was made post and given command of one of them.[91] Captain Bray of the *Adventure* armed ship, one of the smallest and weakest commander's commands in the Navy, took the fourteen-gun privateer *Machault*, and learnt by return of post that 'the Lords are extremely pleased with Captain Bray's gallant behaviour, and ... they will very soon give him a post ship as a reward for his services'.[92] In the same way Captain Burnett of the *Happy* sloop and Captain Hotham of the *Fortune* sloop reached post rank after successful actions.[93] It was not even necessary to succeed provided the action were sufficiently creditable. Lieutenant James Orrock commanded a three-gun press-tender when he was attacked by a 12-gun privateer. He fought for two hours, and when all his powder was exhausted they threw shot and handspikes at the enemy before finally striking. For this gallant defence he was promoted commander.[94]

For post-captains who distinguished themselves in action there were several possible rewards. In a few cases, officers were knighted for gallantry.[95] Those who were at the top of the captains' list, like Boscawen after the first battle of Finisterre in 1747, could be given a flag. Those too junior for flag rank, like John Bentley at the same battle, might be rewarded by being given the chance of a lucrative cruise.[96] In such circumstances it was promotion to move from a larger to a smaller ship; the largest ships were mostly flagships, but flag-captains were usually junior and inexperienced protégés of the admiral, learning their trade under his eye, and it was insulting for an experienced captain to be offered a flagship.[97] For Bentley, the move to a small cruising ship meant more freedom, more responsibility, and potentially more money. This was true to an extent even of junior officers, which is why Commodore Boys was flattered and surprised that a follower of his chose to leave a cruising ship to serve under him at the Nore.[98]

Warrant as well as commissioned officers could advance their careers by distinguishing themselves in action. Patrick Lukey was master of the *Tartar* 28 under Captain Lockhart when she took the *Melampe* 36 in the Channel. For this Lockhart was given a fourth rate, his first lieutenant made commander, and the Admiralty offered to promote any of his lieutenants he desired to be first. He replied that none had sufficient experience, and instead asked for Lukey, who was duly commissioned.[99] John Elliot wanted to have his master promoted in the same way after he took the *Vengeur* in 1758, 'as he's both a good officer and a gentleman', but was unable to do so as the master had not served his time in the Navy.[100] John Thane was commissioned by Sir Peter Warren at the seige of Louisbourg in 1745 having served both as a master and a gunner.[101]

Even such unwarlike figures as pursers, who were not expected to expose themselves in action, could win promotion by gallantry. When the *Badger* sloop, 12, took the *Escorte* privateer of St Malo, of 18 guns, it was Andrew Rutherford the purser who took charge of the small-arms men, the sloop being too small to carry any marines. Captain Taylor was made post, and Rutherford was promoted into a frigate.[102] In 1760 Samuel Hood asked Anson for a commission in the marines for his young cousin and follower Thomas Hoskins, who

> has been my clerk four years, and my view for him was a purser's warrant, but he has shown himself so very spirited and clever in the service I have had against the enemy, that I think it a pity to place him in a cockpit.[103]

When John Bray took the *Machault* the three men who lashed the privateer's bowsprit to the rigging (thus preventing her using her broadside) were the captain himself, the pilot, and the midshipman commanding a cutter which was operating with the *Adventure*. The midshipman was made lieutenant, the Admiralty having to get a royal dispensation to do so as he had not served his time.[104] The same thing was necessary in the case of John Vesey, who was made a lieutenant for his services as a pilot on the Quebec expedition.[105]

The principle of promoting officers who had distinguished themselves in action was unquestionably healthy for the Service. It encouraged men to run risks in the hope of advancement, and it was one of the ways in which flag officers were able to identify candidates to adopt as followers. Its only weakness was that it could occasionally benefit 'a mere fighting blockhead without ten grains of common sense'.[106] The famous action between the *Foudroyant* and the *Monmouth* advanced Robert Carkett overnight from first lieutenant of one of the smallest line-of-battle ships in the Navy, to captain of the largest. He was certainly a gallant officer and a good seaman, but not the most intelligent of post-captains. Twenty-two years later his failure to observe signals and follow the admiral's orders ruined Rodney's plans off Martinique and lost him a potential victory.[107]

Besides the recommendations of friends and the credit of success in action, there was one further principle which operated on the promotion of officers, which was seniority. It applied to young gentlemen to the extent that they had to show six years' service at sea, including two in the Navy as midshipmen or mates, and had to be twenty years old to receive a commission (though it was possible to pass the examination younger). It is often said that these re-

quirements, or at least the minimum age, were easily circum-
vented, but how easily is a matter of doubt.[108] In 1780 John Ibbetson, a senior clerk in the Admiralty, was attempting to arrange
some false time as midshipman for his nephew:

> As the want of a little rated time may be of the utmost
> consequence to him hereafter, may I request that he may
> be rated (if it can be done without impropriety) as far
> back as the ship's books will admit of it, in the room of
> anyone to whom such time is not of equal consequence;
> the person giving up his rank to be no lower in point of
> pay or prize money – I am told it often is done.[109]

Ibbetson was presumably well informed, and practices of this sort
certainly occurred,[110] but the evidence, at least at the end of the
century, suggests that it was very unusual for lieutenants to evade
the requirement of six years' experience, that the examination in
seamanship was a real test, formidable to the unprepared, and that
only limited breaches in the requirement of age were made, quite
intentionally, in order to provide accelerated promotion for the
best young officers at times when lieutenants were in short supply.[111] There were undoubtedly far more deviations in the opposite
direction, of men passing for lieutenant when long past their first
youth at sea, though few left it so late as Richard Hinde, or the
celebrated Billy Culmer, who was a midshipman with Lord Hood
in 1757, and still at sea in that rating in 1790.[112]

Within the list of lieutenants seniority mattered to the extent
that it regulated the order in which the lieutenants of a ship took
rank, but it had only an indirect influence on promotion, in that
the first, and consequently most senior, lieutenant was in the strongest position, and the most junior, and consequently most inexperienced, in the weakest. 'The stations betwixt third and first are
quite different,' as one lieutenant put it. When John Rogers, formerly first lieutenant of the *Sapphire*, was appointed third of the
Penzance, being senior to the first and second, his objection was
upheld by the Admiralty, which was anxious to support the claims
of seniority.[113] On the other hand neither the Board nor any flag
officer paid much regard to seniority when it came to promotion.
Any officer was eligible so long as he was neither too inexperienced

nor too elderly, and there was no question of taking the most senior first. It was thought improper to make a lieutenant post in preference to a master and commander save in exceptional circumstances, and in the same way commanders-in-chief at home were discouraged from putting in midshipmen to act for missing lieutenants, when there were always lieutenants available to fill the places temporarily,[114] but beyond that seniority was not very important. Among warrant officers, who qualified for successively larger rates of ship, seniority was of less consequence than the rate for which an officer had passed. 'The Lords do not approve removing warrant officers from sloops into 74-gun ships, as there must be good men in the intermediate rates.'[115] This, however, had little to do with length of service in the rank as such.

Where length of service counted a great deal was in promotion from captain to admiral. It was an inviolable convention that flag officers could be chosen only from the top of the captains' list, and moreover that those who reached that enviable position had a virtual right to their promotion.[116] These criteria applied in no other case, and it is not difficult to see how damaging they would have been to the efficiency of the Service had they been applied unmodified. There were, however, two modifications of crucial importance. The first was the rank of 'rear-admiral without distinction of squadron', commonly known as 'yellow admiral', instituted by Anson's board in 1747. In effect this was a compulsory retirement scheme for captains, who received the title and half-pay of a rear-admiral on the distinct understanding that their sea careers were at an end. It was then possible for the Admiralty to reach as far down the captains' list as it desired, selecting the able for active command and retiring the rest as yellow admirals. This still confined the choice of flag officers to those at the head of the captains' list, for it was impracticable to retire half the captains in the Navy just to make a commader-in-chief of someone half-way down the list. The temporary rank of commodore solved this problem, allowing any captain to be appointed to command a squadron without affecting his permanent seniority. In 1761 Augustus Keppel, at the age of thirty-six, was commanding a squadron of sixty-three sail, with two junior commodores under him. There was no doubt that he had the experience to do so; when he first hoisted his flag the following year he was a post-captain of eighteen years' seniority, and had been a commander-in-chief, off and on, since 1749.[117]

There was a further safeguard which acted to preserve the Navy from promotions justified more by seniority or influence than merit, for to make an officer an admiral did not oblige the Admiralty to employ him. George Clinton, for example, whose brother was the Duke of Newcastle's brother-in-law, and who stood as near to the fount of civil patronage as any man, was made an admiral at the Duke's request, but it was an empty honour since he was never allowed to go to sea again.[118] Much the same considerations applied to the promotion of Captain Lord Harry Powlett in 1756. His professional reputation was dubious, the King had misgivings, but Anson, who fiercely protected the Navy from Newcastle's interference in any essential matter, was quite content to leave it to the Duke to decide, 'if any civil consideration make it necessary to include him'.[119] He could afford his equanimity, for if the Board did not choose to employ Powlett, there was no real difference between promoting him on the active list and retiring him as a yellow admiral. He did in fact serve a few months as relief commander-in-chief in the Downs.

The real problem with admirals was that there were not enough of them, and even Anson, with his unrivalled knowledge of the Navy, did not feel he knew the senior captains well enough to make the best choice. In the summer of 1756 he was thinking of the names of new rear-admirals: 'I know few of them, and yet several must be recommended.'[120] This was a natural uncertainty at the outbreak of war, before a younger generation had had the chance to distinguish itself, but as late as 1758 there was great difficulty in choosing a junior flag officer to serve under Hawke in the Western Squadron:

> I believe the list consists of Knowles, Holburne (who sent a letter to the Board but little short of the other affair just at the same time), Smith, Harrison and another, I think hors de combat from age and infirmities, with Norris and Lord H. Powlett.[121]

Knowles was able, but a difficult character who had made so many

enemies that it was almost impossible to employ him. On another
occasion Anson explained his feelings to Hawke:

> Knowles' imprudence always hurts him, and he has
> enemies enough to seize every occasion that offers. I
> have always wished him well with all his indiscretions;
> his busy spirit constantly draws him into difficulties.[122]

Holburne, as Lady Anson indicates, had written to the Board in
very insubordinate terms, and was out of favour for failing to take
Louisbourg the previous year. Smith was too gouty and Harrison
too elderly for active sea command. Powlett, as we have seen, was
a political admiral, and Norris (the son of the late admiral of the
fleet) in little better odour. It is easy to see why it was during this
summer that the first substantial commands in home waters were
entrusted to commodores.

Promotion to flag officer was to an extent an exception to the
general principle which operated throughout the Navy, that patronage was the spring which drove the machinery of promotion.
Because the relation of patron and client was by its nature a personal one, it could not avoid being affected by personal considerations. However great was senior officers' need of good followers,
they would have been less than human if they had not found some
men more congenial than others. No sensible man would choose to
share the stress and confinement of shipboard life for many
months or years with someone he found it impossible to get along
with. Friendships and enmities, likes and dislikes, were inevitably
woven into the fabric of the patronage system. But in order for it to
work effectively they had to be kept in their place, and in this the
attitude of the First Lord was crucial. A man who carried private
animosities into his public duties could have done much to pervert
the system and undermine the efficiency of the Service. One of the
strengths of the Navy before and during the Seven Years' War was
the austere impartiality with which Anson administered it. Of
course he favoured his followers, as he was bound to do by obligation and prudence, but he did not penalize the others, even
under considerable provocation. Augustus Hervey, for example,
was prominent in the opposition to the 1749 Navy Bill, a measure

promoted by Anson's Board, and led the defence of his patron, Byng. In both cases he went well beyond the limits of prudence or propriety, and he ostentatiously associated himself with the Prince of Wales's opposition circle.[123] Unlike some of his relatives, Augustus Hervey was sane, but he wholly lacked one of the leading characteristics of sanity, which is moderation. In everything he did, he gravitated naturally to extremes. His private life was marked by extravagant infidelities, his professional career by daring brilliance, his personal and political opinions by unbridled passion. Having done all he could to attack Anson, he attributed to him just that resentment which a lesser man would undoubtedly have felt. Anson, who knew his abilities as an officer, steadily favoured him with command, protected him from his own imprudence, and ignored his personal attacks.[124] Hervey's mother begged him to respond, but in vain:

> I know that both he [Admiral Forbes] and Lord A——
> have spoke very handsomely about you to different
> people. Why therefore perpetuate enmity and be perpe-
> tually blowing those embers that are near ext-
> inguished?[125]

So long as Anson was at the head of his profession, the professional skills of even so reckless a partisan as Hervey were recognized. It was, however, in the nature of the system that in hands which were, or simply which seemed to be, less impartial, it could swiftly divide the Service with envy and suspicion. It may be suggested that something of this lies behind the disastrous unpopularity of that able and diligent First Lord, Lord Sandwich, during the American War. So the patronage system was not perfect; to work at its best it needed patrons of the right temperament, and it needed a strong lead in the right direction. But it is difficult to see what other system was possible in the eighteenth century, and far from clear that any method since devised has identified and promoted merit any more efficiently.

C AUTHORITY

We have seen that it was of the greatest professional importance to officers that they should be effective patrons, seen to be able to reward merit. Only thus could they assemble the following of able men which was the essential foundation of a successful career. But beyond this there was a still more compelling reason for senior officers, and for the Admiralty, to depend on patronage. Their powers to coerce the reluctant or punish the recalcitrant were quite insufficient to enforce obedience from either officers or men. What really supported their authority was that they had things to give which their subordinates badly wanted. For officers, their ambitions for command, for honour, and above all for wealth could only be satisfied if their seniors bestowed promotion and opportunity on them, and they could not be expected to do that except to loyal and trustworthy men. Patronage not only facilitated an officer's career, it was the real strength of his authority. The Admiralty controlled the Navy not by formal bonds of discipline and obedience, but by its control of patronage.

This was the real reason why the delegation of patronage to overseas commanders-in-chief was so delicate, for this patronage was power. They had to have power to support their authority and command their squadrons, but every piece of patronage granted to them was so much removed from the Admiralty's control, and so much lessening of its own powers of command. The situation was analogous to the classic one of a central government obliged to sustain over-mighty subjects to defend its frontiers, but perpetually in fear of their disloyalty. The Admiralty's ultimate control of the Navy was never in doubt only because its powers to appoint and, still more important, to remove officers were not disputed. Lacking most of the apparatus of modern centralized government, the Admiralty kept control of the Service, in so far as it did, almost entirely by the control of patronage.[1]

Senior officers who, for whatever reason, found themselves unable to advance their followers were therefore in serious trouble, for with the power to promote they lost the only real reason why men should obey them. 'I am convinced', Hawke complained to

Anson, 'that it is the intentions of many of the captains to dispute everything with the commanding officer, as this will always be the case with a person like myself, who has it not in his power to do them favours.'[2] Complaints like this came most often from the Mediterranean, where the boundary between Admiralty and local patronage was ill defined. Soon after taking command there in 1757 Saunders had occasion to complain of the 'slight' put on him by the Admiralty putting in officers in place of those he had appointed to a purchased xebec.[3] A few months later his successor Osborn was expressing 'concern' at a similar incident, and in 1759 he felt himself 'much hurt' when some of his commissions were not confirmed; 'their Lordships' approbation ...', he pointed out, 'must always give credit to those who command'.[4] The same point was made in 1767 by Captain Tinker, thanking Hawke, then First Lord, for confirming a promotion, which 'does me credit also in my corps, and sets me in a light among our people, showing that I am honoured with your friendship and regard'.[5] Command and credit were mutually dependent. This is what lies behind Rodney's remark that 'the carrying on his Majesty's Service with success so much depends upon the commander-in-chief having those officers about him whom he most approves';[6] not simply the benefit of working with congenial spirits, but successful patronage as a crucial element in the senior officer's authority. It was not entirely hypocritical of Barrington to write in 1777 that he

> had not a wish beyond the serving of those who had
> been brought up under me ... Was I promoted to a flag
> and honoured with a command to have it in my power
> to serve them, it would make me truly happy and sur-
> pass every other consideration;[7]

for flag rank without the power of patronage would have been an enpty honour.

This meant that the Admiralty had to support the power of its commanders-in-chief by confirming their commissions and warrants, and leaving them the scope to grant them. It was, for obvious reasons, a matter of delicate judgement; too much power given away undermined the Board's own authority and weakened its control of the Navy, but too little would prevent the commander-in-chief from effectively doing his job. How much power to delegate was a matter to be decided afresh in each case, having regard to the admiral's responsibilities, and to his character. The East Indies were so remote that it was usually necessary to allow the commander-in-chief to commission prizes or purchases, but this was allowed in the West Indies only to favoured officers like Commodore Frankland, whose commissions into a brigantine bought by public subscription in 1757 were confirmed.[8] It was a matter of nice judgement whether to trust a commander-in-chief with private orders to supplement and explain his public instructions. This implied that he was trusted to interpret their Lordships' wishes, a latitude only to be allowed to those of reliable judgement. In 1749 Lord Sandwich felt able to give private guidance to the senior officer in Nova Scotia, Captain Rodney:

> It is judged improper as yet to send any public order upon a business of so delicate a nature, which is the reason of my writing to you in this manner, and I am satisfied that your prudence is such as will not suffer you to make any injudicious use of the information you now receive. There are some people that cannot be trusted with any but public orders, but I have too good an opinion of you to rank you among them, and shall think this important affair entirely safe under your management and secrecy.[9]

Having appointed an officer it trusted, it behoved the Admiralty not to interfere with his powers more than absolutely necessary. At the same time the Board had to protect, not only its own authority, but the interests of all its officers, which might be threatened by an unscrupulous, or simply injudicious, commander-in-chief. Frankland, for example, found himself obliged to court martial one of his captains whose insubordination had extended to challenging the admiral to a duel,

> and as it is by subordination alone that the few rule the many, I flatter myself that their Lordships will take into consideration whether such a person ought to be retained in the Service, which I apprehend can never be

carried on if an inferior is permitted either to dispute the
orders or to insult the person of a commanding officer,
upon putting the laws of his country against him, and
by which he had been found culpable.[10]

Frankland's problem was not unique, for other aggrieved officers
sought their revenge against authority. Lieutenant Ross of the *Seaford*, court-martialled by his captain, attacked him ashore, and in
1761 Lieutenant Montagu, first of the *Maidstone*, dangerously
wounded his captain in a duel at Deal.[11] It was relatively straightforward to condemn this sort of assault on authority, but in more
difficult cases the Admiralty might easily find itself obliged to judge
between its commander-in-chief and his officers. In 1762 in the
Leeward Islands Rodney's unhappy talent for alienating his officers raised such complaints as this:

> He has in contriving these disappointments told me a
> thousand *lies*, made me a thousand promises which he
> never can perform, yet thinks me fool enough to believe
> ... I don't think any captain secure *now*, without the
> limits of the jurisdiction of the Admiralty, unless their
> Lordships immediately put a stop to such arbitrary pro-
> ceedings. *They* never injure one captain or officer to
> serve another, and therefore I take the liberty to say, all
> commanding officers should make the maxims of that
> Board the rule of their actions.[12]

Rodney ejected Captain Robert Duff from his ship in order to take
her as his flagship, which in Duff's view,

> must, I am convinced, injure his Majesty's service by
> putting a stop to the emulation there is amongst the cap-
> tains to get their ships well manned and disciplined, and
> by creating a reluctance in officers to go from under the
> eye or immediate power of the Admiralty into distant
> services, when they find themselves thus liable to be
> turned from an eligible ship, which at a considerable
> expense to themselves and at great pains and troubles
> they have got well manned and disciplined, into such

ships as the commanding officer abroad may think proper to order them.[13]

Whether these complaints were justified or not, they illustrate the destructive possibilities of patronage unwisely handled. The damage to the efficiency of a squadron thus divided was obvious, and the mischief was done by the time the Board could hear of it. The only effective remedy was to appoint commanders-in-chief of approved judgement, and remove them as soon as the Board ceased to have confidence in them, for once they were appointed, interference was likely to make matters worse.

No commander-in-chief could afford to see his patronage, and therefore his authority, attacked, for it was his most sensitive and vulnerable point. Least of all did he expect to see it threatened by the Admiralty Board, which was supposed to be supporting him. In November 1756 Pitt's brief triumph drove Lord Anson from office with the rest of the Newcastle connection, and put in his place Lord Temple, who knew nothing of the Navy and was not prepared to learn. Temple sent Frankland public orders which included recommended promotions. To have made a private request in a private letter as Anson did would have been acceptable, though it was always doubtful if a civilian First Lord could properly manipulate the naval patronage system to the same extent as an admiral at the head of the Board. What was beyond doubt was that Temple's approach directly threatened Frankland's patronage, and therefore his authority. This explains the fury of his response, surely one of the most remarkable ever to have been addressed by an officer to the First Lord of the Admiralty:

> You will please to inform Lord Temple that I have friends of my own to provide for as pursers in larger ships when vacancies happen. Such a public manner of recommending people savours so much of an order that I beg you will inform his lordship that one great inducement for our going abroad is to provide for our friends, and [it] is a privilege I never have or can give up.[14]

Frankland was a man who spoke his mind, but he had reason to do so, for Temple's interference threatened the basis of authority in the Navy.

Compared with the delicacies of patronage, warlike operations were in many respects a simpler and less divisive field for the exercise of authority. Frankland, for example, detained a ship passing through his station (the Leeward Islands) under orders for Jamaica, in response to a crisis unknown to the Admiralty. Later receiving reinforcements, he sent an extra ship to Jamaica to replace that he had taken. This intelligent initiative was subsequently approved by the Admiralty, and a year later a complaint of the commander-in-chief at Jamaica of a similar 'encroachment and insult upon his command' received a magisterial rebuke:

> it being a sort of language they [their Lordships] have not been used to from any, more especially from those under their command, who they will take care shall be properly supported in their authority, and at the same time expect to be treated with the respect and decency due to the office the King has honoured them with, wherefore they admonish him to be more circumspect in his style of writing in the future.[15]

This was a mild example of a problem which repeatedly plagued the Admiralty: the combination of officers touchy over their honour and independence, and the many situations in which rank or seniority were not unambiguously established. Even in matters which were supposed to be settled, there were dissentient voices. Frankland, for example, was unhappy at always promoting masters and commanders in preference to lieutenants, 'as I should be most exceedingly chagrined at being the instrument of promotion to anyone whose only merit was being a commander, and even that far above their deserts'.[16] When it came to the position of commodores, in which there was much that was unclear, problems multiplied. Sometimes commanders-in-chief like Cornish appointed commodores when they had no orders to do so,[17] and at least one officer made himself a commodore, complete with a flag-captain. This was Captain Forrest, who was left senior officer at Jamaica by the death of Admiral Holmes, and but for the tact of Sir James Douglas, the first senior officer to reach the island, the incident might have had worse consequences.[18] Other captains felt themselves threatened by the position of commodores; Captain Rodney, on his way to North America in March 1756 when Commodore Keppel, who was junior to him on the captains' list, commanded there, felt that if they met either the commodore must strike his broad pendant, or Rodney himself resign.[19] This was absurd, because the Admiralty's right to appoint whomever it chose to command in chief was undeniable, but Rodney's feelings, and the feelings of others in similar circumstances, were real, and posed a real problem for authority. Much the same problem occurred in Boscawen's squadron when the news came in 1759 of Rodney's own promotion to rear-admiral, over the head of Captain Smith Callis, who promptly applied to resign his commission:

> As you was pleased to inform me that Mr Rodney was made rear-admiral of the blue, by which promotion I am superseded and deprived of my rank, therefore beg you will give me leave to quit his Majesty's ship *Culloden* under my command, as I cannot serve with honour under him.[20]

Callis, whose reputation was blemished, had no real expectations of active flag rank, but the convention was strong that the most senior captains had a right to promotion, and in fact he soon after was retired as a yellow admiral.

A similar issue of rank arose at Plymouth in 1759. For some time after the death of Admiral Harrison, there was no port admiral appointed, and Captain Thomas Hanway was ordered to hoist a broad pendant and act as commander-in-chief. In November he found himself in dispute with Captain Roddam to whom he had given orders concerning the mooring of his ship. Hanway was senior to Roddam on the captains' list as well as being a commodore, yet still he had trouble enforcing his authority.[21]

This was a trifling incident of no lasting importance, but a much more serious, indeed potentially disastrous, problem arose in 1758. In the previous year Hawke had commanded the naval side of an attack on Rochefort which had failed miserably. The

fault was not primarily his, but he was blamed by Anson for allowing himself to be entangled in councils of war, always a recipe for
indecision: 'why Hawke put his name to any council of war, when
I warned him so strongly against it, astonishes and hurts me.'[22]
Evidently Anson formed the conclusion that in a future landing it
would be better to divide the command, leaving Hawke to cover
the operation with the main fleet to seaward, while a more junior
officer, better at co-operating with the military, commanded the
actual landing force. In May 1758 a scheme for an attack on St
Malo was set in motion, and Commodore Howe was ordered to
command the landing squadron. Hawke was in port at the time,
and found himself bidden to assist Howe in what he took to be
another attack on Rochefort. Hawke was touchy about his honour
and authority, and assuming that he was in effect superseded as a
failure by an officer twelve years his junior, he hauled down his
flag without orders and set off for London, preceded by a highly
insubordinate letter of resignation. By the time he reached the
Admiralty to be interviewed by the Board forty-eight hours' later
he had discovered his mistake about the destination of the expedition, and realized the extent of his own folly. His explanation to
the Board was lame:

> [he] acknowledges that he has done an irregular thing,
> but he did not do it with any view of disregard to disres-
> pect to the Board, but merely from thinking it would ap-
> pear a slur upon him to the world ... and he thought he
> had better not serve at all, if he could not serve with
> honour.[23]

For Anson and the Board the affair was extremely embarrassing. If officers were to abandon their responsibilities in the midst of
war at every fancied slight there would be no hope of commanding
the Service. 'This step of Sir E. Hawke has spread a very improper
spirit of discontent in the fleet at Spithead.'[24] An example had to be
made, and yet it was out of the question to dispense with Hawke's
services, for he was one of the very few senior officers with the experience and capacity to command the country's principal fleet.
The only solution was for Lord Anson himself, at the age of sixty-
one, to leave the Cabinet and the Board and take command of the

Western Squadron for the summer, with Hawke as his subordinate. In fact Hawke soon fell ill, 'a good deal occasioned by the uneasiness of his mind from his own late conduct',[25] leaving Anson alone in command. In his absence (and Boscawen's) the naval business of the Board was paralysed, and the Cabinet bereft of one of its Service heads for the whole summer. The consequences could easily have been more serious than they were.

Hawke was not the first senior officer to clash with the Board in this way. In the previous war Admiral Vernon had finally ended his stormy career afloat by hauling down his flag when the Board refused to allow him to warrant a gunner on his own authority in home waters.[26] Unlike Hawke, he was not indispensable, and the principle was well established that only overseas commanders-in-chief were entitled to make officers. In practice the Board frequently asked its home commanders-in-chief to fill up blank commissions or (more often) warrants,[27] when the circumstances and the admiral made it useful and safe to do so, but there was no question of any general dissipation of the power of patronage, least of all towards so ungovernable an officer as Vernon.

More resignations of admirals occurred at the time of Admiral Byng's trial and condemnation. Admiral Forbes resigned his seat at the Board,[28] and Temple West, who had been Byng's second in command, refused an active command. This was not because he supported Byng's conduct, of which he was privately very critical, but because

> I can only be answerable for my loyalty and fidelity to my King, and resolution of doing what appears to me best for his service, which it seems an officer may not want and yet be capitally convicted for his misconduct or inability of judging right, and I am not so presumptuous as to imagine that my actions can always be so rightly governed, nor am I altogether certain that the judgement of others is infallible, and as in either case the consequences may be fatal . . .[29]

Forbes was soon back at the Board, however, and West with him, so their gestures did not harm their careers.

Resignations on grounds of honour mark out one of the weaknesses of a system of authority which depended so heavily on self-interest. Officers who cared sufficiently about something to sacrifice their careers were in a position to embarrass the Admiralty considerably. Nevertheless the strength of bonds of mutual interest was great, and they worked both ways, for in some circumstances junior officers had patronage to offer their seniors. This was notably the case with the matter of prize agency in large squadrons. There were strong practical reasons for the captains of the squadron to choose a joint (though not usually sole) prize agent for all the ships. It was more efficient, and it greatly lessened the risk of divisive quarrels. For the latter reason, it was permissible for the flag officer to hint at the desirability of making a joint appointment, but anything like interference in the sacred rights of property was considered most unwarranted. Saunders ('it has always been my intention to recommend my secretary ... in as advantageous a manner as I could') went at least as far as decency allowed.[30] What made the matter more delicate was that the agency was extremely valuable, and the appointment therefore put much money in the pocket of a friend or follower of the admiral's, often his secretary. The captains had lucrative patronage to bestow, not on the admiral himself, but (what was nearly as direct a compliment) on his follower. It was a good example of a distinction which occurred elsewhere in the Service, between those things which a senior officer had a right to expect, and if necessary demand, from his juniors, and those things which they could quite properly withhold, but might find it very wise to offer. Captains in squadrons did not necessarily appoint a joint agent, nor if they did was he always the admiral's protégé,[31] so that if they did proffer this gift, they had a right to expect gratitude in return – and the gratitude of flag officers was valuable. Thus in 1747 Anson wrote to one of his captains that he

> was extremely flattered by the remembrance of the Western Squadron in appointing my secretary agent for their prizes. I should be glad of any opportunity of shewing them how much I think myself obliged by it, as it was done unasked.[32]

Anson was already a member of the Board, and in a very good position to repay an obligation.

Like other aspects of the patronage system, however, this had the weaknesses of its strengths. If the flag officer and his captains failed to come to mutually satisfactory arrangements, there was a real risk of divisions between and among them. Admiral Cotes at Jamaica allowed himself to become embroiled in a quarrel over prizes with several of his captains, and in the middle of it had the officer who was managing their legal case arrested and court-martialled for insubordination, alleging a 'Scotch faction' got up to undermine his authority.[33] The appearance of partiality was glaring, and the cohesion of his squadron could not but suffer from it.

Admiral Hawke aroused great resentment, not by malpractices of his own – he was the last officer of whom such things might be suspected – but by employing a secretary who was an unprincipled schemer and abused the admiral's trust. Hawke alone failed to perceive his character; Anson was well aware of the damage done by that 'very bad man his secretary',[34] and many other officers remarked that

> this secretary had too much influence with the old admiral ... and this occasioned much discontent and murmuring in the fleet or Western Squadron, as much partiality was shown in the appointment of cruising ships.[35]

By 1762 one of Hawke's captains wrote that

> he's lost a great deal of his popularity in the fleet by the means of his secretary, who for the sake of putting money in his own pocket has led the a[dmira]l to do things about agency that hurt him not a little.[36]

This is but one more illustration of the importance of judgement of character to the patronage system, and consequently to the functioning of the Navy. Trust was the essence of the system, and if trust were ill bestowed the whole structure of authority was threatened. It is an indication of Hawke's greatness as a sea commander that his career survived two disastrous misjudgements, either of which would have ruined a lesser man. The Navy as a whole could not afford such blunders. When so much depended on personal connections, men had to feel able to rely on one another, for only then could authority function effectively.

D DUTY

There was so much scope for abuse of the opportunities of naval life, and so little intrinsic strength in Admiralty authority to restrain it, that it was doubly important that officers should be men of integrity. But because Admiralty authority rested largely on its power to reward, it found itself in the position of trying to restrain the abuse of opportunity by dispensing it, of putting within reach of temptation those officers who it hoped would be least likely to succumb. It does not appear a very promising means of keeping officers to their duty when there were so many chances of making money or avoiding trouble and danger by neglecting it. It is therefore surprising and noteworthy how infrequently the Service in fact suffered from serious dereliction of duty by officers. There were many petty deviations from the letter of the regulations by which officers or ratings might profit without affecting the efficiency of the Navy much, or at all, and these were widespread and tolerated, but in serious matters, duty generally won over self-interest.

The most prominent of naval temptations was prize money. It was not often that a commander openly flouted his orders and left his station in pursuit of prizes, the crime for which Captain Bentinck of the *Niger* was superseded in 1762,[1] but there were many less obtrusive ways in which the lure of prizes might distort naval operations. It was very well to suggest sending out cruisers, as Keppel did to Pocock off Havana in 1762, as 'success would make it a very essential service to the public as well as to individuals';[2] the problem was the damage it might do to the public in the process. Officers might easily find themselves having to choose between private profit and public duty; the very terms with which they congratulated themselves in their reports ('I thought it my duty to prefer the public good to my own private advantage')[3] testify to the suspicion they needed to dispel. Moreover a commander-in-chief's patronage in the disposal of cruising stations, sending a favoured commander on a lucrative cruise while others languished with the main squadron, was a divisive force within the squadron. A captain like Augustus Hervey, who made £9000 in a year under the indulgent command of John Byng,[4] was undoubtedly not endearing either himself or the admiral to his fellow officers.

A particularly interesting test case concerning the choice of a cruising ship from a squadron occurred in 1747. Captain Thomas Grenville commanded the *Defiance* in the Western Squadron under Anson, and his brother George, an ambitious young politician, was a member of the Admiralty Board. George wanted to get his brother a lucrative cruise, and had secured some sort of undertaking from his fellow commissioners. It must be emphasized that this was a perfectly proper transaction by the standards of the day. The decencies of eighteenth-century politics permitted, indeed required, that the kinsmen of senior politicians should be looked after. There is no reason to doubt that whatever assurances George Grenville had been given were sincere, and that his brother would at a suitable opportunity have been given his cruise. What the rest of the Board – guided, undoubtedly, by Anson himself, who was its leading naval member – did not mean to do was to give Thomas his cruise until the strategic situation permitted. In the spring of that year, George grew impatient and demanded the fulfilment of the promise, but there was at that time reason to expect that the French fleet would soon put to sea, and there was no question of weakening Anson's squadron at so critical a time. George therefore met what he interpreted as a straightforward breach of faith. He was extremely angry and refused to sign the order:

> the Board are so much afraid, or so little anxious about keeping their word so solemnly given, that they have signed the order and gratified Mr Anson in his request.[5]

315

Soon after the French did indeed come out, and in the ensuing battle Tom Grenville was killed.

This episode has been variously interpreted,[6] but from the naval point of view it appears as the clash of two cultures. Grenville represented the normal standards of the political world, while the rest of the Board, led by Anson, stood for the professional standards of the Navy. The gap between them was not wide, and Anson did all he could to mollify Grenville without conceding the point of principle; he promised to release the *Defiance* as soon as possible, and mentioned that he had been able to get Temple West (Grenville's cousin) made a commander, 'Mr Warren having consented to take him upon my recommendation'.[7] But though the gap was narrow, it was very significant, for it turned on the primacy of operational requirements. The principle was here successfully asserted, that the needs of the Navy took precedence over other claims, however well founded. It was a principle of crucial importance for the efficiency of the Service.

There was in fact a good means of avoiding many such conflicts of interest by arranging prize-sharing agreements. Sometimes a group of commanders would agree among themselves to go shares in any prizes they might take, whether or not they were present at the capture,[8] but better from the Service's point of view were the agreements which embraced an entire squadron. It then did not matter which ships were detached to cruise or sent in to refit, for all would profit equally by the opportunities gained by any. This was a practice encouraged by many prudent flag officers, even though it cost them a piece of patronage.[9]

When temptation was put in their way, captains frequently rejected it. In May 1758 Captains Digby and Proby, detached from Keppel's squadron in the Western Approaches, encountered a large French man-of-war escorting eight store ships. The escort fled leaving the rich prizes defenceless, but the two captains, though they passed within gunshot, ignored them and chased the warship for five days and nights. Digby (who was the senior officer) 'gained much credit, as we had chased ... and had left a French convoy of merchant ships every one of which we might have taken'. In this case Anson was privately regretful that the prizes had been missed: 'he certainly did right as an officer, and yet it would have distressed the enemy much to have cost them ships'.[10] In general, however, it was very much for the good of the Service that captains should 'do right as officers', and gain credit by doing so, and incidents like this are indicative of the public standards of officers under Anson.

If prizes were taken and disagreements arose over prize money, as they easily could, it was not necessary or even usual for them to take the dangerous turn that Admiral Cotes's did. There certainly was a violent dispute between Sir Charles Knowles and Captain Thomas Graves, but Admiral Knowles was a quarrelsome and litigious character.[11] Many people found means to compose their differences – arbitration by some respected senior officer was often resorted to[12] – and did not allow those which remained to sour their official relations. In 1742 Admiral Vernon at Jamaica was in dispute with his second Sir Chaloner Ogle, but remained on good terms with him throughout.[13]

Prizes more often entangled commanders in dubious practices which did not much affect the efficiency of the Service. Ransoming was one such: the common method of privateers to save themselves the trouble and danger of actually manning and bringing in prizes by releasing them for money, keeping the master or mate as security for its eventual payment. This reduced cruising to a system of kidnapping, and many people thought it at best unbecoming a King's ship, but from the strictly military point of view it was much less of a distraction from warfare than keeping the prizes.[14] Much the same was true of collusive captures, like that which Augustus Hervey arranged with the Maltese master with a French cargo whom he met in Sardinia, and who agreed to be taken for 10 per cent of the proceeds.[15] It was dishonest, but only the enemy suffered.

Sea officers themselves suffered greatly from the dishonesty of colonial vice-admiralty courts, whose chief interest was in their fees, if it was not in screening the local merchants who were trading with the enemy. This last was common in the West Indies, where Holmes at Jamaica had occasion to complain about the judge's

outrageous acts of injustice ... [he] expresses the most

317

determined intention of defrauding the officers and seamen of his Majesty's squadron, as well as encouraging
and protecting the trade carried on with the enemy.[16]

Holmes was scarcely a disinterested witness, but outrageous is not
too strong a word to describe the actions of some colonial authorities. In December 1759 the *Amazon* took some prizes to windward
of Barbados, and brought them to anchor there, but because of the
notoriously exorbitant charges of the colony's vice-admiralty
court it was decided to take them down to Antigua to get a better
price. In order to keep the profits in the island, the governor laid an
embargo on private vessels, and when the *Amazon* and her prizes
sailed, he ordered the batteries to open fire on her, shooting away
her topgallantmast head.[17] The standards of eighteenth-century
colonial government, remote from the supervision of London,
were in many ways lax, but it was not acceptable for a royal governor to fire on a King's ship, even to line his friends' pockets.

Another method for commanders to make money was freighting specie. This happened both in peace and war, but it seems to
have been more in peacetime that it seriously affected ships' movements. It was almost a matter of course for ships coming home
from the Mediterranean to touch at Lisbon in hopes of a freight;
Augustus Hervey found four other ships there when he arrived in
the Tagus at the peace of 1749.[18] Even in wartime there were considerable temptations. Early in 1761, when the Spaniards were still
neutral, the agent of Captain Arthur Forrest at Jamaica was urging
him to find means to visit Havana where there were opportunities
of carrying Spanish silver to Europe.[19] The transaction would have
been disapproved of by the Spanish authorities almost as much as
by the Admiralty, and Forrest either could not, or did not chose to,
do anything about it.

Freights, like prizes, were productive of disputes. Captain
Darby of the *Devonshire* was ordered by Sir Jeffery Amherst, the
commander-in-chief of land forces in North America, to carry
£57,000 down to the West Indies to pay some of his troops operating there, but the Captain (backed by Lord Colvill, who was entitled to one-third as commander-in-chief) declined to take it
without the customary 1 per cent for an overseas voyage, and

Amherst professed himself unable to pay more than half that rate.[20] This dispute was referred to the Treasury. There were other disagreements over freights, between captains, or between captains and their commander-in-chief, but though they undoubtedly preoccupied those involved, they seem to have been able to avoid much general animosity or disruption of operations.[21]

Further temptations and problems were offered by the related matters of prize goods and private trade. The carrying of any private cargo except specie in the King's ships was strictly forbidden, but there was nothing in the regulations to prohibit officers from having commercial interests elsewhere, and there were many temptations in doing so. Commodore Douglas, an officer who drew the line between duty and profit with some strictness, declined to invest in a sugar cargo taken by one of his captains, in case the manning of his squadron (in the Leeward Islands) suffer indirectly:

> you would have asked me for some invalids to have carried her home, which I will never consent to, lest they should get able seamen instead of invalids.[22]

Captain Forrest, by contrast, invested extensively in prize cargoes of indigo and other colonial produce, and was in consequence much interested in the protection of homeward-bound convoys – though as a substantial planter in Jamaica he would have been anyway.[23] Other officers were involved in trade as part of their financial involvement with their brother officers. Sir Peter Warren, who lent money extensively to officers and ratings, provided his nephew Captain Richard Tyrell with over £3800 in 1751–52 to go into the Antigua sugar trade.[24]

Another method by which captains in the West Indies might profit was by chartering to the Crown the small sloops which many of them had bought as private tenders to their ships. Despatches or orders had often to be carried, and these fast little vessels, with their reliable naval crews, were much better than the alternatives. The operational reasons for employing them were strong, and if officers profited from the advancing of the King's service, that seemed to them only proper.[25]

Some of these transactions involved at least potential conflicts of interest, but they do not seem to have had any real effect on naval operations – unlike the situation in the French navy, where the carrying of *pacotilles* (private consignments of goods) was widespread, and even the Minister of Marine was concerned in it.[26] Compared to these, such dealings as those of Captain Tiddeman, who sailed for the East Indies in 1746 with various parcels of cloth, hats, cutlery and trinkets for sale, were fairly harmless. He was carrying a cargo for trade, but in practice most of the goods were bartered to victual the ship or replenish the captain's stores in ports where money or bills were not acceptable, and if he made a profit (which is not clear) it was arguably incidental to a proper concern for the welfare of his ship.[27] Straightforward corruption, like selling the King's stores or freighting cargoes for profit, for which Lieutenant Bourgeois was dismissed in 1764, or Lieutenant Dugdale of the *Magdalen* schooner in the same year, was rare among commissioned officers.[28]

There were various other species of fraud or dishonesty by which officers might enrich themselves. Theft was probably the simplest, usually in the form of pillaging prizes. This was a normal accompaniment of privateering, and still to an extent permitted in the French navy, but regarded in the British service as dishonourable. Officers accused of this crime were ostracized by their fellows, and suspended by admirals as a 'scandal to the Service'. There are hints in several cases that those concerned were promotees from the lower deck or the merchant service.[29]

Another sort of fraud was false mustering. This was common, but not usually with the prime object of making money. Young gentlemen were rated able seamen, or domestics concealed under other ratings, as a matter of course, and so long as people were actually on board in the numbers, if not in the characters, listed in the muster, the Admiralty was not unduly perturbed. Mustering persons who were not actually in the Navy, however, was not well regarded. Lord Harry Powlett was detected mustering under false names his coachman, footman and thirteen-year-old son, together with the eight-year-old son of the first lieutenant, none of whom were on board. This was passed off as the work of his clerk, as was a very similar case involving Sir William Burnaby.[30] Neither officer bore a good character, and there do not seem to have been similar cases among the generality of sea officers, except that it was not unusual for captains to bear their sons as servants in infancy. This is usually interpreted as a means of advancing their future careers with false seatime, but it is not clear that the practice either could or did have that effect, and it seems more likely that it was just an unofficial addition (of £12 a year) to the captain's wages. This generally happened only in peacetime, when ships on a standard complement were over- rather than under-manned (there were plenty of applicants to fill servants' berths in wartime), and it had no effect on the efficiency of the Service apart from costing it money.

This is an important distinction which applies to most aspects of corruption or dishonesty in the Navy. Things which directly affected the efficiency of the Service or the interests of its personnel were by their nature easily detectable, and always intolerable to naval opinion, but things which simply put more money into men's pockets than they were supposed to receive for doing their duty were much easier to accept and much more difficult to expose. One of the great strengths of the British Navy in the eighteenth century, arguably its decisive advantage over its rivals, was that in wartime money was never really lacking. Ministers like the Duke of Newcastle quailed at the debts the Navy accumulated, but in practice the money was always there. Some proportion of that money certainly went in directions not sanctioned by the law or the regulations, and a part (by no means all) of that would have been regarded by authority as improperly diverted, but in practice the Navy could afford it. This marks the difference between the authors of some of the frauds mentioned above, and officers like the surgeon who extorted extra money for venereal cures, those who took their full allowance of beef when their men were on only two-thirds, or 'picked' for the largest pieces from the cask before the other messes had their turn.[31] All these were disgraceful because they directly affected the men's well-being, and were therefore an abuse of trust.

A more difficult matter to regulate, because it had nothing to do with money, was the zeal with which officers faced the exertions and perils of their profession. It was a common observation that 'their Lordships should make great allowance between peace and war in the officers' hurrying to sea',[32] but even in wartime people were tempted to linger. The Board carefully scrutinized the 'daily states' of their commands sent up by the port admirals, and were quick to remark if they detected unwarrantable delays. The same applied to diversions, such as ships lingering in the Tagus (doubtless in search of freights) on their way home.[33] Captain Penny of the *Firebrand* 'prevailed upon the good nature' of his commander-in-chief to allow him to call at Weymouth where his wife and family lived, and whence he was sharply recalled when Boscawen heard of it. Penny was unlucky in that he was supposed to be escorting a convoy of ships laden with tin ore from Falmouth to South Wales, where they would pick up coal for the return voyage to fuel the steam pumps which drained the mines. Delay threatened the safety of the mines, and nothing was nearer to Boscawen's heart than the welfare of Cornish industry. Penny would have been wiser to neglect some interest with a less powerful and alert patron.[34]

Another temptation was for captains at sea to return to port on less than convincing pretexts. By the time of the Seven Years' War, with Anson ten years at the Board, this was not a prudent move. Lord Harry Powlett, 'Captain Sternpost' as he was afterwards known, returned to port with an alleged defect in that timber in 1755. He managed to escape conviction at the subsequent court martial, but never commanded a ship again.[35] Captain Gambier, a discontented member of Hawke's fleet in 1760, might well have suffered the same fate had the admiral not refused to send home his list of fictitious defects.[36] Equally little patience was shown to officers who went sick in suspicious circumstances, especially to avoid sailing to unpopular stations.[37]

It was much more common, however, for officers to show eagerness to get to sea in wartime. Quite apart from their sense of duty and honour, there were rewards to be had from their profession which were not to be had ashore. Standing officers in Ordinary, if not too aged, always exchanged for duty in wartime in order to get to sea. Commissioned officers also volunteered for sea duty, like the lieutenant of a fire-ship who volunteered to replace a dead officer in a cutter in 1760, even though that was an arduous and obscure service.[38] Captain Baird of the *Defiance* insisted in putting to sea though very ill (he had been delirious only two days before).[39] Probably Augustus Hervey's attitude was indicative of the general spirit of officers of the time:

> I cared very little about anything but my pleasures in these days, till I got to sea, and then my profession was all my pleasure.[40]

It is always tempting to generalize from the case of Hervey, because we know so much about him, but it must be done with caution, for he was in many respects quite untypical. The same applies to an even greater extent to George Rodney, and it is necessary to digress to say something about that singular character, because so many generalizations have been unwisely founded on his career. It cannot be emphasized too strongly that Rodney was unique; qualities were combined in him which in other men were never associated. He was an officer of brilliant professional gifts which secured him early promotion, but he never displayed that reliability and trustworthiness upon which, as we have seen, a senior officer's position in his service largely depended. Unlike every other admiral, he found that his abilities had carried him to high rank without securing him real power. Almost alone among senior officers, he found his promotions repeatedly blocked, his followers disadvantaged, and the loyalty of his officers in doubt. His career presents a succession of professional triumphs continually undermined by his disastrous relations with those he had to work with. In spite of the sort of achievements which raised other admirals to wealth and power, Rodney suffered repeated disappointment and ruin.

These troubles befell him because of defects of character whose origins it is not easy to explain. Those who incline to a psychological interpretation of history may see in his behaviour the symptoms of insecurity typical of the *parvenu*. Rodney in fact came of respectable parents, but so poor that he was brought up as a charity boy in the household of distant relatives. In adult life he was a compulsive and ostentatious spender, he approached his seniors with obsequiousness (only Pitt had a more unctuous style in letters), treated his equals with hauteur,[41] and was only truly at ease, and truly popular, with his social and professional subordinates. His friends begged him to deal frankly and honestly with them,

323

and to restrain that 'indifference and contempt that you have always held them in', but in vain. 'If you will be open and candid with your friends many will stir to save you – but you must be faithful to them, or they cannot be so to you.'[42] He attributed to others just those qualities of avarice and malice which independent observers thought characteristic of him.[43] Rodney's pompous and snobbish manner tended to infuriate men, and amuse intelligent women like Fanny Boscawen, who wrote to her husband in February 1758 to tell him that Rodney's ship the *Dublin* was ordered to join his squadron in place of the wrecked *Invincible*:

> How great Mr Rodney will be in America, and how much more he'll always know of his admiral's plans and designs than anyone else ever pretended to. If he had to do with any other commander I can figure to myself that he would always know *better* than the admiral, 'for George Grenville and he would have consulted that point together the last time they met at Pitt's'. You will say that I am very hard upon poor Rodney, but indeed he is *très fanfaron*. According to his company, when he knows he cannot be found out he talks with those whom he never saw, and is consulted about affairs which he never hears of. However, the *Dublin*'s a good ship.[44]

It is easy enough to see why such a man was disliked, but dislike alone is not sufficient to explain his troubles. Rodney's most extraordinary characteristic was that he repeatedly broke the rules of the Service, not as other men did, in ways which were socially acceptable or in circumstances in which they were unlikely to be detected, but when he was certain to be discovered, and could not rationally have expected to gain anything but opprobrium.

Rodney repeatedly injured his brother officers by interfering with their followers. We have observed his trying to steal good men by alleging links with them; he also harboured deserters from other ships, and attempted to dispose of his sickly and useless men by exchange.[45] He did much the same with officers. Captain Keith of the *Amazon* had occasion to complain that John Cowling his first lieutenant had been taken away and replaced with a worthless man 'who has been bandied from ship to ship', not to promote Cowling, but just to gratify a mediocre captain who was the son of an earl.[46] He tried to curry favour with the Admiralty by telling tales on his brother captains, and he carried himself to his immediate subordinates in a high style of haughty dignity, resenting mild remonstrance or tactful suggestion.[47]

His dealings with the Admiralty were equally unhappy. Almost alone among senior officers, he allowed his operations to be severely distorted by the search for prizes,[48] and his handling of prize goods was not above suspicion. In 1755, before the declaration of war, when French merchantmen were being taken but their cargoes impounded until the Prize Commissioners should determine their fate, a ship called the Astrée was taken aboard which was a valuable horse, private property and not liable in any circumstances to be condemned as lawful prize. The animal was missed, and discovered in Rodney's possession.[49] He consistently treated his captains' prize agency as a matter for him to dispose of.[50] In his first independent command, off Le Havre, he was applying pressure on his subordinates to place their prize agency with the commodore's nominee. This in itself was disgraceful, but what was more, Rodney's agent was Mr Cooley, the Collector of Customs at Portsmouth. Customs officers were not natural allies of sea officers, and it is certain that Cooley must have been giving something in return for this business. What it was does not appear, but it is not difficult to guess the opportunities opened by operating on the coast of France with a complaisant custom house officer at home.[51] Rodney's reputation for untrustworthiness in financial matters was a direct cause of his bankruptcy. In 1775 he desperately needed to pass his contingent accounts as commander-in-chief in the Leeward Islands in 1761–62, which were held up for want of vouchers to £1500 allegedly spent on intelligence. This sort of expenditure was very difficult to support with orthodox vouchers, and other commanders-in-chief had little difficulty getting them dispensed with, but Stephens, the Secretary of the Admiralty, remarked on Rodney's case 'that he believed not one of these sums had been paid'.[52] Fair or not, it was the nemesis of the reputation Rodney had earned for himself.

The same fatality attended his promotions as commander-in-chief overseas. Soon after he was first appointed, instances of irregular or suspicious advancement began to come to their Lordships' attention.[53] By the end of the Seven Years' War, his reputation was so well established, for all his undoubted professional merits, that Lord Sandwich was taking a considerable risk in giving him a command in 1771. He sailed with private instructions imploring him not to imperil the First Lord's position by abusing this trust. He did so immediately:

> which is directly contrary to your instructions and to the assurances you gave me before you left England and since by letter, that you would not draw me into any difficulties by making officers upon irregular vacancies. Can you imagine that after I have refused confirmation to officers in North America and the Leeward Islands under similar circumstances, I would make a distinction at Jamaica . . . ?[54]

Worse was to come. It has been remarked that admirals' sons were an accepted special category, but there were decencies to be observed in exploiting this. In 1774 Sandwich refused to confirm the advancement of Rodney's son James, then twenty years old, from lieutenant to post-captain directly. 'I do assure you,' he wrote,

> that if he was my own son I would not confirm his commission. No service can go on if fixed rules are not adhered to, and I must beg you to tell me how I could withstand the same thing on other stations, if a precedent was established in your case.[55]

Other men would have profited by the warning. Rodney, when he was next in command in 1780, advanced his younger son John, who was fifteen years old and had been at sea for less than a year, from midshipman to post-captain in a few weeks.[56]

Rodney was an intelligent man who knew the Navy as well as any officer; whatever drove him repeatedly to damage himself was not miscalculation but some inner compulsion whose nature the historian can hardly guess. No other officer displayed his extraordinary talent for self-destruction. In every other case sea commanders of his ability were also reliable judges of professional merit and reasonably trustworthy in their handling of money. Those who lacked these qualities also lacked professional merits. Rodney alone showed abilities which raised him to high rank combined with weaknesses which destroyed the basis of trust upon which alone an officer could effectively command. It was an extraordinary combination, and unique, for in the Navy as a whole it was only bad officers who seriously neglected their duty.

327

CHAPTER VIII

❦

Politics

A   THE NAVY IN POLITICS

Politics in the eighteenth century was not an activity confined to small class of semi-professionals, but an aspect of the affairs of everyone who was involved in public life at any level of society, and by no means the entire occupation of even the greatest. Cabinet ministers were far from being full-time politicians, or even full-time ministers, and the Seven Years' War was effectively fought on a four-day week.[1] At the other end of the scale no one who held an office under the Crown, however lowly, was unconnected with the process of maintaining local influence, and ultimately of supporting a ministry in power. Every employment in the gift of the Customs, the Post Office or any other branch of government was needed to conciliate local interests and aid in electing Members of Parliament who would support the ministry of the day. Ministers bestowed the jobs and titles, contracts and favours in their gift on those who they expected would return these attentions with gratitude and support. In an age of weak ideology and almost no party structure beyond personal followings and connections, there was no other way of sustaining Parliamentary government.

The Admiralty and the Navy inevitably took their place in this system. In October 1761 Lord Hardwicke, the Lord Chancellor, calculated that his son-in-law Lord Anson controlled the largest 'faction' in the new House of Commons, fifteen members.[2] This group consisted largely of sea officers sitting for seats which they owed to government nomination. Some of these seats were actually in the Admiralty's control, others that of other branches of government, and others again belonged to private interests which had offered them to the ministry to dispose of. These officers, nearly all of them admirals, were on the same footing as other Crown servants in Parliament, that is to say that they were expected to support the ministry with their votes on all matters of importance. This was a function of the circumstances in which they had been returned to Parliament, and not of their profession, for other officers who owed their seats to private or family interest voted as they pleased. There was some sense that in strictly naval measures the First Lord of the Admiralty was entitled to hope for their favour, but it fell a long way short of an obligation. Thus Henry Pelham wrote to the Duke of Bedford, the First Lord in 1747, of Admiral Steuart, who sat in his family's interest, 'Besides, to whom does he belong? Not to your Grace, otherwise than as his profession obliges him.'[3] Shortly afterwards the proposals of the 1749 Navy Bill set a large part of the naval MPs against the policy of Anson and his Board.

This was one reason why the naval influence in Parliament was less than it might have been, for though there were twenty or more naval MPs, their profession did not unite them in any politically significant way.[4] It also kept them away from the House for long periods, especially in wartime, and gave them an alternative focus for their careers and ambitions which discouraged many of them from taking an active part in debates. A seat in Parliament was a recognized reward for success and eminence, in the Navy as in other walks of life, but it did not usually lead to an active Parliamentary career. Naval men could get leave from their ships to attend the House,[5] but Parliamentary duties do not seem to have sat very heavily on their shoulders. It was quite possible for an officer like Captain Edmund Affleck, chosen for Colchester in 1782, to enter Parliament without even being aware he was a candidate, and in 1747 Commodore Edward Legge achieved the still more unusual distinction of being elected posthumously.[6]

The Navy's direct influence on national politics was largely confined to the boroughs which it controlled, or partly controlled. These were six: Dartmouth, Plymouth, Portsmouth, Rochester, Saltash and Sandwich, plus Queenborough shared with the Ordnance Board. They yielded ten seats in all.[7] These represented half the boroughs at the disposal of the Crown, but still only a tiny proportion of the number of votes an administration needed in order to survive. The Admiralty's control was based on its patronage in the dockyards which lay in or near each of these boroughs. The commissioners and officers of the yards had political duties to perform to sustain the naval interest,[8] which might extend at least to threatening dismissal for the recalcitrant. In 1767 Commissioner Hanway at Chatham was trying to eject Alderman Sparks, a violent opponent to the Admiralty's interest in Rochester, from his place as surgeon to the Chatham Chest.[9] In 1733 the Clerk of the Cheque at Woolwich was ordered to drop heavy hints to those of the yard artificers who were electors at Shoreham that they would be dismissed if they did not vote correctly.[10] The trouble with threats like this was that they were largely bluff, for the artificers were skilled men well aware of their scarcity. Moreover in boroughs with a popular franchise, electors were in a strong position, and knew it.[11]

The real control of these boroughs, as of others, rested not on threats but on patronage. The Admiralty could rely on the electors' votes as long as it attended to their interests. 'As I am circumscribed with regard to this corporation,' Hawke remarked in his letter covering a petition from Portsmouth, for which he sat, 'I could not avoid giving attention to a case where their interest seems to be so much concerned.'[12] Sea officers like Hawke or Admiralty officials like Clevland and Stephens were in a good position to steer naval contracts their constituents' way,[13] and, even more important, to act as their patrons in the Service. It was said of Boscawen, MP for Truro, that he took the sons of the electors to sea with him, and Keppel was suggested as a candidate for Chichester no only because he was a cousin of the local magnate the Duke of Richmond, but 'because of the Commodore's merits as a good officer, and a rising man in the Navy, where he would be able, and if chosen, willing, to serve the sons of his friends who should go into the sea service.'[14] Of Dartmouth in 1757 the Duke of Devonshire reported that 'the corporation have desired a seaman, so I proposed Captain Howe'.[15] The sort of transaction they had in mind is illustrated by a letter from Captain Lord Edgcumbe to Newcastle in 1761:

One of the electors [of Fowey] has a son on board my

ship who has passed his examination, and if he could be
made a lieutenant the father's vote would be secured; I
have asked this favour of Lord Anson, and if your Grace
would back my solicitation he certainly would do it.[16]

The fact was, as Lord Egremont put it in a letter to Rodney, 'to an
important man in a corporation almost nothing can be refused', or
as Admiral Moore complained of the ill behaviour of a cutter's
master, 'I suppose such a great man as a voter for Queenborough
may do anything with impunity'.[17]

For the ministry of the day it was essential that the wishes of
such important people should be gratified, but if the efficiency of
the Navy were not to suffer, there were many requests, of just the
sort which they were likely to make, which could not be granted.
This dilemma occurred in other walks of public life in which ability, experience or diligence were required, but in the eighteenth
century they were few and relatively insignificant. There was no
service in the least like the Navy in its requirement for professional
competence from all its officers and men, and the nature of a political system which measured merit by quite different criteria, evidently presented the Navy with grave threats to its efficiency. How
it dealt with them will be discussed in the next section.

B POLITICS IN THE NAVY

In their continual struggle to create and maintain a Parliamentary
majority, ministers needed all the patronage they could get. When
the Duke of Newcastle threatened to resign unless his nominee was
chosen as Dean of Gloucester,[1] he was not just being petulant, for
control of appointments was an essential support of any government, and the principal preoccupation of Newcastle's political
career. In effect he held office as the ministry's political manager,
and he was entitled to demand of his colleagues the wherewithal to
sustain them all in office. It was calculated in 1759 that the 'civil

service' of the Crown employed about 16,000 people.[2] In the same year the Sea Service had nearly 85,000 officers and men. Even allowing that a rating's place was not usually of much political consequence, this leaves several thousand sea officers whose commissions and warrants represented valuable patronage in the gift of the Crown. If the King's government were to be carried on, it was highly necessary that every piece of patronage should be available to support it, not only to sustain a Parliamentary majority, but to encourage obedience. In civil government as in the Navy, authority rested chiefly on its power to reward, for its other means of enforcing obedience were frail, and diminished in proportion to distance from London. For all these reasons, politicians needed the Navy.

For the Navy, however, there were obvious risks in this embrace. The qualities by which sea officers were judged always began with skill and experience, which were criteria not in common use ashore. As late as 1797, when the old system was running into severe criticism, a Commissioner of Stamps was appointed because he was the nephew of a duke, and because 'a natural, constitutional indolence governed him with irresistible sway', disabling him from other employment.[3] It is easy to see how dangerous this charitable spirit was to senior officers, whose whole careers depended on detecting and cherishing professional ability. Even in the Navy the 'merit' of birth was sometimes advanced, especially by officers like Lord Harry Powlett whose naval claims to advancement were in doubt: 'as setting aside my service, I hope my birth is some reason for desiring to be promoted to a more honourable post'.[4] Similarly Captain Lord Aylmer complained that he had been passed over for a flag although he was related to a former Lord Commissioner, to Admiral Sir Peter Warren, and to the late Admiral of the Fleet, Sir John Norris.[5] But for senior officers to concede any general force to this sort of claim was to undermine not only the efficiency of the Service, but the real basis of their own authority in it. Their control depended on their exercise of patronage; if noble birth, or indolence, or any other civilian criterion of advancement were admitted to have force in the Navy, it must to an extent undermine their own freedom of choice, and consequently their power.

It was for this reason that Anson and all sea officers so strenuously resisted the nominations of Newcastle and other politicians. It was not, as we shall see, because they disapproved of political influence as such, and it was not even because politicians' choices were necessarily bad ones. Newcastle's record in this respect was not entirely discreditable. He made his choices on explicitly political grounds, but they were often able men none the less. John Ommanney owed his position as Agent Victualler at Plymouth to Newcastle's patronage, but under the test of war he proved diligent and efficient.[6] Jonas Hanway, a man of conspicuous honesty and independence, was appointed to the Victualling Board in 1762 after applications to Newcastle by the Archbishop of Canterbury.[7] Even in the choice of generals to command expeditions he was not always inferior to Pitt.[8] The danger for senior officers was not only, or even chiefly, that Newcastle and other politicians would choose the wrong men; it was that they were the wrong men to make the choice.

It is not true to say, as Sir Lewis Namier did, that Anson had to struggle against political nominations made by his brother officers.[9] Anson himself was concerned in political nominations, and like almost all senior officers he was himself a Member of Parliament (in the Lords, of course) with the customary political obligations to discharge. The degree of involvement in and enthusiasm for politics varied from officer to officer, but it would have been unreasonable, indeed impossible, for any flag officer to withdraw altogether from the political world to which rank, if not birth, had automatically introduced him. The crucial question for Anson and his colleagues was not the nature of the proposition, but the quarter from which it came. Political patronage in their own hands was relatively safe, not only because they understood the importance of professional merit, but because it then supported rather than undermined their own authority. Recommendations from politicians were therefore acceptable only if they were adopted and sponsored by an admiral. For a junior officer the favour of an admiral was far more valuable than that of a politician. Young Lieutenant Rodney was advised in 1740 by his kinsman the Duke of Chandos to apply to Admiral Wager the First Lord rather than to Walpole the chief minister, and he was quite right.[10] The fate of pleas from Newcastle to Anson shows how unwise officers were to approach the politician rather than the officer. Anson's abrupt, not to say savage dismissal of what were, by conventional political standards, perfectly reasonable requests, leave one with some sympathy for Newcastle.[11] The only sea officer with whom Newcastle seems to have had success was Powlett, and this, as we have seen, was a meaningless concession. Even in the dockyards and victualling establishments, which had until recently been a clear field for government patronage, Newcastle found himself rebuffed by Anson[12] – and not only by Anson. In the summer of 1758, with both Anson and Boscawen at sea and Forbes the sole sea officer left at the Board, the wretched Duke found himself worse off than ever, dependent on the Secretary of the Admiralty for news of naval affairs: 'Admiral Forbes is the great man here, and though I see him frequently at court, he takes no more notice of me than if I was not in the Kings's service.'[13]

It was not only Newcastle who suffered in such circumstances. Anson was undoubtedly the strongest naval First Lord of the period, personally and politically, but other officers in his position rebuffed other senior ministers likewise. A civilian First Lord also could find himself snubbed, especially if like Temple he was ignorant and unpopular, and when Hawke was First Lord the Duke of Cumberland discovered that even the royal family could not expect to interfere in naval promotions. He wrote to Hawke about various protégés:

> I do not mean that you should prefer them to any of your own who have served well and deserve every attention from you, but should hope after you have provided for them, that you will think of mine.

Of course the Duke did expect that his clients would have preference, and when Hawke took him at his word, he was very angry. Hawke was a weak First Lord politically, but the Duke was quite unable to touch him, and he was obliged to swallow his anger and conciliate the admiral as best he could.[14] The slow rise of officers with powerful patrons – powerful, that is, in the political world – is noteworthy. The Duke of Grafton employed his influence to get Lieutenants William Affleck and Arthur Phillip made commanders; they had to wait eleven and eighteen years respectively. William Lockhart, a protégé of the Duke of Roxburgh, had to wait seventeen years.[15] If it came to a contest between an officer and a politician, for instance between Admiral Holmes's and the Earl of Buckingham's candidates for a chaplaincy in 1760,[16] the officer was likely to win. The decencies of the day required peers to be treated with due deference (there is a note by Clevland to one of his clerks to write a reply to a request of Lord North's 'on quarto paper, very complaisantly'),[17] but the reality was that civilian politicians were carefully excluded from real influence on naval promotions.

One apparent exception to this is the undoubted influence of Clevland himself and his successor Stephens, both of whom were MPs, and in a sense civilian politicians. Clevland's son Archibald was made a commander by Boscawen in 1755, and reached post rank the following year at about eighteen. Clevland claimed that Anson had done this unasked, which is very probable, for it was the sort of favour which Clevland could not decently request, but Anson could very properly offer.[18] The fact was that Clevland was in a pivotal position of great trust and importance, depended upon not only by Anson but by senior officers who all knew how influential he was.[19] He was treated not as an outsider but as a civilian within the naval system, and his son enjoyed the advantages an admiral's son would have had. It is also worth pointing out that his brother-in-law Captain Towry seems to have enjoyed no special favour or remarkable rise.[20]

The only effective method for the great men of the civilian world to influence naval promotions was indirectly, by persuading an admiral to adopt and forward their applications. This surmounted the real obstacle by restoring the patronage to naval hands. Thus at the very time that Newcastle was being rebuffed by Anson, his wife, wiser than he, was getting Boscawen to make two 'loyal young burgesses of the borough of Leicester' lieutenants in the marines.[21] In the same way in the previous war Pulteney had advanced his clients by persuading Admiral Vernon to favour them.[22]

This was possible because senior officers often had their own political reasons for advancing followers. Most of them were

Members of Parliament, virtually all of them were of that standing in the civilian world which automatically carried some political obligations. Their political followings merged naturally and imperceptibly into their naval followings. Probably those who had political claims were a minority in an admiral's following, and certainly it was as true for them as for the others that the admiral's credit depended on the choice of men of ability, but some political claims did no harm to an officer of professional merit and might well make the difference between him and another, equally able but less well-connected. Anson did not object to the process, which was natural and inevitable, so long as the political clients were also the followers of officers, who understood the paramount importance, both to the Service and to themselves, of professional competence. Anson himself often accepted and sometimes originated political promotions.[23] He made David Shuckforth a lieutenant in 1753 at his father-in-law's request,

> which would not have done but by your Lordship's recommendation, for we must be very sparing in making officers in time of peace, as we have already so many on our lists that cannot be employed.[24]

Other senior officers with more political connections and obligations than Anson sponsored more numerous political promotions. Boscawen was particularly active in this,[25] and when he 'wrote to Lord Anson to make the bearer of this a lieutenant, he is very well recommended to me by Cornish friends', Anson can have been in no doubt what sort of friendship was implied.[26] Boscawen made Henry I'Anson a lieutenant to please the Duke of Dorset, and later Hawke made him commander at the request of the Secretary of the Treasury.[27] In the same way Hawke made Hood a commodore at Lord Chatham's request.[28]

In all these and many similar transactions there is an implicit understanding that the candidates' political claims were additional to, and not a substitute for, professional abilities. Often the patrons made this clear in their recommendations: 'he is related to Lady Warren, an old [i.e. senior] lieutenant and a very worthy officer'; 'Mr Douglas my fifth lieutenant, who is a good clever sensible man ... Lord Morton knows him very well.'[29] It is in fact remark-

ably difficult to find cases of officers advanced on political recommendations whose professional claims to promotion were not
sound. In 1761, for example, two followers of Sir George Pocock
sought his favour in getting them promoted commanders. William
Owen was disappointed, as the admiral explained that he had
exhausted his credit with Anson and could not for the moment ask
him any further favours. James Hawker, on the other hand,
received Pocock's support and his promotion. Sir George was able
to make this approach not as an officer, but as MP for Plymouth,
Hawker having married an alderman's daughter. It is a clear case
of political advantage, but upon examination not as simple as it
might seem. Hawker was brother-in-law and follower of that excellent officer Captain Lucius O'Bryen, and a lieutenant of nearly
six years' seniority. He had been at sea throughout the war, and as
far as one can tell had the experience necessary for a command.
Owen on the other hand had been a lieutenant only three years,
much of which time he had spent on shore recovering from losing
his arm in action. His wound gave him a claim to consideration,
but he was clearly less well qualified than Hawker. So a promotion
made on explicitly political grounds turns out to have been equally
justifiable by professional standards.[30]

A similar case is presented by a request made in 1758 by Sir
Peircy Brett, MP for Queenborough, in a private letter to Stephens:

> I must beg the favour you will give me leave to trouble
> you with some requests from my friends at Queenbor-
> ough. I am desired by the Recorder to beg the favour of
> Lord Anson to remove Mr David Weller, carpenter of
> the *Cornwall*, into the *Bellona*, a new third rate ordered
> to be set up at Chatham. This man is a near relation to
> the Recorder, whom I shall be glad to oblige, and must
> desire you will pay my respects to his Lordship.[31]

It seems to be an unmistakable case of a 'borough recommendation' such as Anson deplored,[32] and at first sight surprising that he
ordered Brett's request complied with at once. In fact, the transaction had nothing to do with the efficiency of the sea-going Navy,
for both Weller and his ship were long past service. He had been a

carpenter twenty-eight years, and the *Cornwall* had not been in commission since 1749. Standing officers were borne in old ships like her, as well as in new ships entered on the Navy list but not yet built, in effect to secure a pension to deserving officers who could not be accommodated on the limited superannuation lists. There was talk of the *Cornwall* being broken up (which happened in 1761) and Weller was anxious to secure the continuance of his pension. By custom and equity he had a strong claim, and it was much in the Navy's interest that officers should be able to look forward to support in old age as a reward for long service. Almost certainly he would have had his request granted by whatever channel he had happened to make it.

These transactions, like everything else to do with patronage, depended on mutual trust. It was essential that the patron be an officer who could be relied on not to place political merit above professional skill. As with the normal naval patronage, there were temptations to be resisted, but in the long run it was in senior officers' own interest to resist them, and most of them did. As with the normal naval patronage, however, there was one conspicuous exception to that rule, George Rodney. He alone was found by experience to advance men whose chief or only merit was their relevance to Rodney's political ambitions. As a result his candidates were rejected in circumstances when most other officers of his seniority and ability would have had no difficulties. Namier describes at length Rodney's efforts to promote Lieutenant Joseph Hunt, against Anson's implacable opposition, as part of his campaign to be elected to Parliament for Okehampton.[33] Hunt, who was the son of the Assistant Master Shipwright of Plymouth Yard, appears to have been a good officer who was unlucky in becoming attached to so dangerous a patron as Rodney. He did in the end get his promotion, which was more than some of Rodney's political recommendations managed. In 1761 the admiral was trying to get elected for Penryn, and wanted Captain Peard of the *Savage* sloop, a freeman of the borough, made post. He asked indeed to have him as his own flag-captain, a choice never denied any other flag officer, but all in vain. Peard died a master and commander.[34]

Rodney's case was exceptional, probably unique (which makes it unfortunate that Namier founds generalizations about the Navy on it), but it was true that all flag officers needed political friends to support their position. The actual appointments of officers to commands at sea were at least susceptible to political influence, especially in peacetime when there was some sense that the Navy could afford political choices. Rodney's election for Penryn is supposed by his biographer to have improved his chances of an overseas command, and Boscawen's political consequence certainly did no harm to his desire for sea commands.[35] In either case the admirals' professional claims were strong, and politics may have had nothing to do with the choice of them, but there is room for much more suspicion in the case of Commodore Pye's command in the Leeward Islands before the Seven Years' War, or Sir William Burnaby's afterwards. Indeed these two are rare cases of political interest advancing officers of less than outstanding ability. Pye's professional character has been mentioned, and he seems to have owed his rise to his connections with the Bathursts and Montagues.[36] As for Burnaby, whom Vernon called a dancing-master, he has been described as 'one of the unluckiest admirals on the Navy list' from his repeated failure to get a command during the American War, but it seems rather his reputation than his luck which should be blamed.[37]

There were perfectly respectable reasons for good officers to cultivate political connections, for an admiral's position could be an exposed and vulnerable one, especially overseas.[38] Few would be able to apply pressure on the First Lord himself, as Admiral Matthews in the Mediterranean was able to do in 1742–44,[39] and few, at the other extreme, would find themselves in so much need of friends as Admiral Byng, but in between there were risks and pressures which might be warded off. Officers might be attacked by mercantile interests complaining that their trade was not well protected; the Russia Company had Captain William Brett court-martialled on such a charge in 1759,[40] while in 1762 Governor Dalrymple of Guadaloupe was sending Rodney thinly veiled threats:

> for having unlimited credit in the Treasury, I will not sit
> with my arms across and suffer every insult that the
> most paltry of all privateers can offer this government,
> nor would I make use of any uncommon means, out of

regard to you and respect to your Service, till I can receive your answer.[41]

Protection in such situations as these did not come amiss, and it is easy to understand the motives of Captain Duff in writing to Lord Bute in 1762 that 'it was by your Lordship's benevolence I got my first preferment in the Navy'.[42] It is most unlikely to be true, for Duff was a lieutenant of 1739, when Bute was a young man without any influential position, but it did no harm for a fellow Scot to establish links with the new chief minister.

This leads naturally to the question of how far political and professional obligations could be exchanged. It is clear that officers with political advantages could in some circumstances apply them to help their naval careers, but there remains the expression of naval obligations in a political context. This was a tricky point, and few encountered it in the form of so sharp a dilemma as Lieutenant Nigel Gresley, a follower of Admiral Smith's, at whose request Anson had given him his first commission. Gresley came of a Staffordshire land-owning family, and had a vote in the borough of Lichfield. In the by-election of 1753, he thought himself obliged to choose between two candidates: his own brother, and Lord Anson's. In this perplexing situation he wrote to Smith for advice, and his reply is worth quoting at length:

> It behoves you greatly, both in honour and interest, to vote in such a manner as will be most agreeable to Lord Anson. I say in honour, because you were not made a lieutenant by him in stipulation for your vote, but as a young gentleman recommended by me to him and his brother, who had voted for him and for whose behaviour I would be answerable as an officer and a gentleman ... He, as first commissioner of the Admiralty, has it more in his power to hurt or to help you than any man in England, and I who know how small your fortune is at present, and how precarious any great addition to it is from any other source but your profession, must as a friend insist that as a man, a father, and a hus-

> band, you ought to continue to follow that, and use all
> means consistent with honour to advance yourself in
> it.[43]

Smith is drawing another version of that distinction which we have noticed before, between the obligations a junior owed his seniors, which he could not decently evade and they could properly demand, and those things which he might withhold, but which, if offered, entitled him to expect some gratitude. Gresley's promotion was a strictly professional affair, in which Smith as patron engaged himself for his follower's character. No political connection was implied – but should Gresley choose to establish one, he might reasonably hope to profit by it.

As Smith's advice implies, Anson was himself involved in political promotions as other officers were, but it is true that he was by temperament and circumstances much less a political officer than, say, Boscawen. By nature austere and withdrawn, disinclined to correspondence or even to conversation, he did not invite applications, and was notoriously difficult to speak to.[44] His personal political connections, with Lord Hardwicke by marriage, and in Lichfield by purchase, had come late in life and encumbered with relatively few obligations. This made it easier for him to take a stiff line with recommendations of which he did not approve, especially those from civilian politicians, or in the case of Rodney, naval politicians. His personal qualities helped him to keep undue political influence out of the Service. Twenty years later Lord Sandwich found his situation much more exposed. By nature gregarious, with a wide circle of correspondents including many officers, a leading politician by, and almost from, his birth, Sandwich inherited and sustained a great number of contacts and connections which naturally laid him open to pressure:

> What I go through with regard to solicitations for preferment is not to be conceived by anyone but the person who feels it; it really makes me tired of my situation. More is wanted than there is a possibility of giving, and there is scarce a friend I have in the world, or a person in authority in government, who is not ready to quarrel

with me for not making the lieutenant he patronizes a captain. Was I to give commissions for ships not in service merely to give rank it would only multiply claims and make it still more intolerable. I declare to you that I have the strongest applications for above half the first lieutenants in your fleet, exclusive of those in other parts of the world. Admiral Keppel pesters me without relaxation for two of his lieutenants, and to keep him in good humour, which at this time is a matter of consequence, I have promised him that they shall be promoted as opportunities offer. In this situation, my dear Lord, what can I do, and have I not a little reason to complain that my friends, instead of feeling for my distresses, will help to multiply them? You well know that everything that comes from you makes its due impression upon me, and that I never neglect any point that I know you have at heart, but I own I am so sore upon this subject of giving promotion that I can scarcely trust a pen in my hand for fear of disobliging those I write to.[45]

Sandwich's situation in 1778 also points a weakness in the naval patronage system. It depended heavily on mutual trust, and nowhere more so than where political recommendations were concerned. If the Navy became divided on political, or indeed on personal lines, the links of trust might be severed and the mutual authority of First Lord and senior officers alike imperilled. To what extent this really happened during the American War it is not for this study to determine, but it is clear enough that contemporaries perceived divisions of a new and dangerous type.[46] In Anson's day no real differences of ideology troubled the political world,[47] or at least the Navy. Both earlier and later in the century there were real reasons for officers to distrust one another, and to the extent to which they did, the naval patronage system and its control of political influence was endangered. Under Anson the principle was preserved that the naval system, though it closely resembled the methods by which a Parliamentary majority was maintained, and could on occasion be used for that purpose, was

342

divided from the political world ashore by a barrier permeable by officers alone. Only in the hands of reliable sea officers was the corrosive influence of political interest permitted in the Navy. Almost alone among the responsibilities of Georgian government, war at sea was too serious a business to be left to the politicians.

Conclusion

It has always been difficult to believe that the eighteenth-century Navy was really as harsh and divided a world as it has been presented. Historians are nowadays inclined to emphasize the essential order and cohesion of British society in that era, the extent to which 'oligarchical government ... stood four-square on its foundations in the tacit consent of the people'.[1] It was a society which, in spite of great disparities of wealth, power and opportunity, displayed no great gulfs between classes, but rather an infinite number of little gradations, collectively wide but individually easy to surmount. It was a society in which men could rise as far as their abilities would carry them, not untrammelled by social prejudice, but with a freedom from legal and customary restraints unknown in any other major European state of the day. In this society, the vertical bonds of patronage and protection were still far stronger and more important than the nascent interests of class. As individuals, great men stood close to, and especially in electoral politics depended on, a multitude of lesser folk: 'there was no substitute for the establishment of harmonious personal relationships'.[2] The social world was far more united by shared interests and a common understanding than it was divided by mutual fear and incomprehension.

A view of the social life of the Navy which presented it as a sort of floating concentration camp could only be reconciled with all this if officers and men had been drawn from groups completely isolated from the currents of national life, unrepresentative of the mass of their fellow countrymen, thinking and acting in ways wholly unlike those of their age and rank. It is true that seafaring was of its nature an isolated profession, a silent service whose voice was heard less clearly than others, but it has always been next to impossible to believe that seamen and sea officers were really so different from the rest of the world.

344

Approaching the matter from another point of view, no one who has ever commanded ships or men imagines that cruelty and oppression are the way to mould an efficient fighting force. It is true that eighteenth-century infantry fighting demanded of the foot soldier the obedience to command of an automaton, but even in the army it was never true that harsh discipline alone made good troops, and the nature of the seaman's profession, which required the constant exercise of trained initiative in circumstances in which the officers could not possibly have taken control, ruled out any such rigid system. Yet it is an undoubted fact that British ships, collectively and individually, were during the Seven Years' War conspicuously better handled and better fought than their enemies'. It offends against every canon of experience and common sense to suppose that men who proved under the supreme test of battle to be brave, disciplined, skilful and daring, were in their everyday lives the degraded subjects of an arbitrary tyranny.

The reality was that for all its undoubted peculiarities, the Navy resembled the society from which it was recruited in many more ways than it differed from it. It has been said that 'British society in the late eighteenth century displayed a sort of disordered cohesion ... which owed little to the bonds of authority'.[3] That 'disordered cohesion' exactly describes the Navy. It was by modern military standards an ill-disciplined, even chaotic force, in which the obedience of officers and men was at best qualified by temperament, convenience and self-interest. Officers could not give orders to their men, nor the Admiralty give orders to them, backed by an omnipotent State; they had to persuade and to reward if they were to hope for co-operation. This made for a loose and disorderly system, but it also linked officers and men together by the bonds of mutual need. Officers were not in a position to get what they wanted by the simple exercise of force or authority, and those who might have been inclined by nature to do so were restrained by the knowledge that the attempt would be counterproductive. The men for their part were the possessors of a scarce and valuable skill, and they knew it. If their interests seemed to diverge from their superiors', they well knew how to make use of their position. But in fundamental matters they seldom did feel that their interests diverged.

This emphasizes the extent to which the Navy, like society as a whole, changed continually, for it is clear that the Service which suffered the mutinies of 1797 must have been very different from that of forty years before. How and why it changed are questions which this study cannot answer, and perhaps it did not change as much as might appear. Except in being collective movements in which ships co-operated, these mutinies followed more or less the 'unwritten rules' which had long governed such affairs. Like popular riots throughout the century, they were essentially conservative,[4] aimed to restore the just system which had formerly obtained, to rescue the Navy from the deformations recently introduced into it. To men, both on the lower deck and the quarter deck, who had seen the excesses of the French Revolution, the mutinies of 1797 seemed very dangerous. Certainly they displayed evidence of class and political sentiments which would have been unthinkable a generation earlier, but it is not clear with hindsight that they were really as novel or as revolutionary as they then seemed. In forty years material conditions in the Navy had worsened. Inflation had ground away the value of the naval wage, and the coppering of ships had removed the chance of frequent leave. The Service had expanded not only absolutely but relative to the population as a whole, to recruit many more men (and officers) unacquainted with the traditional accommodations of seafaring. When all these things have been considered, however, we should still beware of exaggerating the changes of forty years.

At all events, it seems certain that in the middle years of the century the Navy, considered as a society in miniature, was very much a microcosm of British society in general. It was peculiar in almost all its superficial aspects; it had its own customs and traditions, its dress and language, and in the important matter of Parliamentary politics it operated a private system insulated from conventional politics ashore. But in its fundamentals, in the ways in which people dealt with one another and thought of one another, it closely resembled British society ashore. In the last analysis, the wooden world was built of the same materials as the wider world.

APPENDICES

APPENDIX I

COMPLEMENT

This table gives the authorized complement of officers, ratings and marines of each rate and size of ship, and from that calculates the percentage which seamen formed of each ship's company, and the ratio of tons to men, and tons to seamen. It will be understood that 'seamen'

| Rate | Guns | Complement | Tonnage | Commissioned Officers | | Warrant Sea Officers | | | | | |
				Capt	Lieut	Mr	Bts	Gnr	Ctr	Sgn	Prs
1st	100	880	1800–2090	1	6	1	1	1	1	1	1
1st	90	780	1800	1	6	1	1	1	1	1	1
2nd	90	750–780	1570–1870	1	6	1	1	1	1	1	1
2nd	84	750	1920	1	6	1	1	1	1	1	1
3rd	80	600–700	1350–1980	1	4	1	1	1	1	1	1
3rd	74	600–700	1550–1830	1	4	1	1	1	1	1	1
3rd	70	480–550	1400–1440	1	4	1	1	1	1	1	1
3rd	66	520	1470–1480	1	4	1	1	1	1	1	1
3rd	64	480–520	1220–1400	1	4	1	1	1	1	1	1
4th	60	400–435	1060–1300	1	3	1	1	1	1	1	1
4th	50	300–350	850–1050	1	3	1	1	1	1	1	1
4th	44	250–280	690–850	1	3	1	1	1	1	1	1
5th	38	250	940	1	3	1	1	1	1	1	1
5th	36	240	720–750	1	3	1	1	1	1	1	1
5th	32	220	650–720	1	3	1	1	1	1	1	1
6th	28	200	580–610	1	1	1	1	1	1	1	1
6th	24	160	430–520	1	1	1	1	1	1	1	1
6th	22	160	430–470	1	1	1	1	1	1	1	1
6th	20	160	400–450	1	1	1	1	1	1	1	1
sloop	18	120–130	320–380	1	1	1	1	1	1	1	1
sloop	16	125	310	1	1	1	1	1	1	1	1
sloop	14	110–125	150–190	1	1	1	1	1	1	1	1
sloop	12	80–110	100–220	1	1	1	1	1	1	1	1
sloop	10	100–110	210–230	1	1	1	1	1	1	1	1
sloop	8	80	140	1	—	—	1	1	1	1	—
bomb	8	60	230–310	1	—	—	1	1	1	1	—
fireship	8	45	250–400	1	1	—	1	1	1	1	—
yacht	10	70	230	1	—	—	1	1	1	1	—
yacht	8	40	160–170	1	—	—	1	1	1	1	—

Capt = Captain or Commander; Lieut = Lieutenant; Mr = Master; Bts = Boatswain; Gnr = Gunner; Ctr = Carpenter; Sgn = Surgeon; Prs = Purser.

included landmen if necessary, and that certain miscellaneous ratings such as barber and midshipman extra were, if borne, subtracted from the total of seamen. The tonnages given are approximate. A few ships, chiefly prizes, did not conform to any of these establishments.

	Inferior Warrant Officers						Petty Officers						
Ch	Ck	SM	SMk	Ar	SMt	MA	MM	Md	CCk	QM	QMM	BM	YS
1	1	—	1	1	5	1	6	24	1	8	6	4	4
1	1	—	1	1	5	1	6	24	1	8	6	4	4
1	1	—	1	1	4	1	4	24	1	8	6	4	4
1	1	—	1	1	4	1	4	24	1	8	6	4	4
1	1	1	1	1	3	1	3	16	1	6	4	2	4
1	1	1	1	1	3	1	3	16	1	6	4	2	4
1	1	1	1	1	3	1	3	16	1	6	4	2	4
1	1	1	1	1	3	1	3	16	1	6	4	2	4
1	1	1	1	1	3	1	3	16	1	6	4	2	4
1	1	1	1	1	2	1	2	10	1	4	4	2	2
1	1	1	1	1	2	1	2	10	1	4	4	2	2
1	1	1	1	1	2	1	2	10	1	4	4	2	2
1	1	1	1	1	2	1	2	6	1	3	3	1	2
1	1	1	1	1	2	1	2	6	1	3	3	1	2
1	1	1	1	1	2	1	2	6	1	3	3	1	2
1	1	—	1	1	1	1	2	4	1	2	2	1	1
1	1	—	1	1	1	1	2	4	1	2	2	1	1
1	1	—	1	1	1	1	2	4	1	2	2	1	1
1	1	—	1	1	1	1	2	4	1	2	2	1	1
—	1	—	1	—	1	—	1	2	1	2	1	1	—
—	1	—	1	—	1	—	1	2	1	2	1	1	—
—	1	—	1	—	1	—	1	2	1	2	1	1	—
—	1	—	1	—	1	—	1	2	1	2	1	1	—
—	1	—	1	—	1	—	1	2	1	2	1	1	—
—	—	—	—	—	—	—	1	1	1	1	—	1	—
—	—	—	—	—	—	—	1	1	1	1	—	1	—
—	—	—	—	1	—	—	1	2	1	2	1	1	—
—	—	—	—	—	—	—	1	1	1	1	1	1	—
—	—	—	—	—	—	—	1	1	1	1	—	1	—

Ch = Chaplain; Ck = Cook; SM = Schoolmaster; SMk = Sailmaker; Ar = Armourer; SMt = Surgeon's Mate; MA = Master at Arms; MM = Master's Mate; Md = Midshipman; CCk = Captain's Clerk; QM = Quartermaster; QMM = Quartermaster's Mate; BM = Boatswain's Mate; YS = Yeoman of the Sheets.

		Petty Officers									Idlers		
Rate	Guns	Cx	SMM	GM	YPR	QG	CM	St	Cp	Tp	SC	CC	StM
1st	100	1	1	4	2	25	2	1	2	1	2	12	1
1st	90	1	1	4	2	22	2	1	2	1	2	12	1
2nd	90	1	1	4	2	22	2	1	2	1	2	10	1
2nd	84	1	1	4	2	21	2	1	2	1	2	10	1
3rd	80	1	1	2	2	20	1	1	2	1	2	8	1
3rd	74	1	1	2	2	18	1	1	2	1	2	8	1
3rd	70	1	1	2	2	17	1	1	2	1	2	8	1
3rd	66	1	1	2	2	16	1	1	2	1	2	8	1
3rd	64	1	1	2	2	16	1	1	2	1	2	8	1
4th	60	1	1	1	1	15	1	1	2	1	2	6	1
4th	50	1	1	1	1	12	1	1	2	1	2	6	1
4th	44	1	1	1	1	11	1	1	2	1	2	6	1
5th	38	1	1	1	1	9	1	1	2	1	1	5	—
5th	36	1	1	1	1	9	1	1	2	1	1	5	—
5th	32	1	1	1	1	8	1	1	2	1	1	5	—
6th	28	1	1	1	1	7	1	1	1	1	1	4	—
6th	24	1	1	1	1	6	1	1	1	1	1	4	—
6th	22	1	1	1	1	5	1	1	1	1	1	4	—
6th	20	1	1	1	1	5	1	1	1	1	1	4	—
sloop	18	1	—	1	1	1	1	1	1	—	1	2	—
sloop	16	1	—	1	1	1	1	1	1	—	1	2	—
sloop	14	1	—	1	1	1	1	1	1	—	1	2	—
sloop	12	1	—	1	1	1	1	1	1	—	1	2	—
sloop	10	1	—	1	1	1	1	1	1	—	1	2	—
sloop	8	—	—	1	—	—	1	1	—	—	—	1	—
bomb	8	—	—	1	—	—	1	1	—	—	—	1	—
fireship	8	1	—	1	1	—	1	1	1	—	1	1	—
yacht	10	—	—	1	1	1	1	1	—	—	—	—	—
yacht	8	—	—	1	—	—	1	1	—	—	—	—	—

Cx = Coxswain; SMM = Sailmaker's Mate; GM = Gunner's Mate; YPR = Yeoman of the Powder Room; QG = Quarter Gunner; CM = Carpenter's Mate; St = Steward; Cp = Corporal; Tp = Trumpeter; SC = Sailmaker' Crew; CC = Carpenter's Crew; StM = Steward's Mate.

Servants	Widows' Men	Seamen	Tons per Man	Tons per Seaman	Marines						
					Ct	1L	2L	Sg	Cp	Dm	Pte
52	18	569 (65%)	2.0–2.4	3.2–3.7	1	1	1	3	3	2	100
48	16	478 (62%)	2.3	3.8	1	1	1	3	3	2	100
47–48	15–16	455–483 (61–62%)	2.1–2.4	3.4–3.9	1	1	1	3	3	2	100
47	15	466 (62%)	2.6	4.1	1	1	1	3	3	2	90
39–43	12–14	352–446 (59–64%)	2.2–2.8	3.8–4.4	1	1	1	3	2	1	90
39–43	12–14	354–448 (59–64%)	2.6	4.1–4.4	1	1	1	3	2	1	90
34–36	10–11	264–321 (55–59%)	2.7–2.9	4.5–5.3	1	—	1	2	2	1	70
35	10	304 (58%)	2.8	4.8–4.9	1	—	1	2	2	1	70
34–35	10	264–304 (55–58%)	2.5–2.7	4.6	1	—	1	2	2	1	70
30–31	8–9	219–252 (55–58%)	2.6–3.0	4.8–5.2	1	—	1	2	2	1	60
26–28	6–7	137–184 (46–53%)	2.8–3.0	5.7–6.2	—	1	1	2	2	1	50
24–25	5–6	104–132 (42–47%)	2.8–3.0	6.4–6.6	—	1	—	1	2	1	40
24	5	117 (47%)	3.8	8.0	—	1	—	1	2	—	40
23	5	108 (45%)	3.0–3.1	6.7–6.9	—	1	—	1	2	—	40
22	4	91 (41%)	2.9–3.3	7.1–7.9	—	1	—	1	2	—	40
20	4	91 (45%)	2.9–3.0	6.4–6.7	—	1	—	1	1	—	35
18	3	55 (34%)	2.7–3.2	7.8–9.4	—	1	—	1	1	—	35
18	3	56 (35%)	2.7–2.9	7.7–8.4	—	1	—	1	1	—	35
18	3	56 (35%)	2.5–2.8	7.1–8.0	—	1	—	1	1	—	35
14–15	2–3	47–55 (39–42%)	2.7–2.9	6.8–6.9	—	—	1	1	1	—	25
15	3	50 (40%)	2.5	6.2	—	—	1	1	1	—	25
14–15	2–3	37–50 (34–40%)	1.4–2.3	3.8–4.1	—	—	1	1	1	—	25
13–14	2	36–65 (45–59%)	1.2–2.0	2.7–3.4	—	—	—	—	—	—	—
14	2	55–65 (55–59%)	2.1	3.6–3.8	—	—	—	—	—	—	—
7	2	57 (71%)	1.7	2.5	—	—	—	—	—	—	—
6	1	39 (65%)	3.8–5.2	5.9–7.9	—	—	—	—	—	—	—
7	1	14 (31%)	5.5–8.8	17.9–28.6	—	—	—	—	—	—	—
6	1	48 (69%)	3.3	4.8	—	—	—	—	—	—	—
5	1	22 (55%)	4.0–4.2	7.3–7.7	—	—	—	—	—	—	—

Ct = Captain; 1L = 1st Lieutenant; 2L = 2nd Lieutenant; Sg = Sergeant; Cp = Corporal; Dm = Drummer; Pte = Private

Sources: *Regulations and Instructions*, pp. 146–149; ADM 180/20, p. 219; ADM 2/1152, p. 454.

APPENDIX II

SEA TIME

These tables are compiled from abstracts of captains' logs received in the Admiralty from 1758 to 1762, and covering periods in commission from 1757. The sample includes logs from three 1st rates, twelve 2nd rates, sixty-two 3rd rates; fifty-two 4th rates; forty-five 5th rates; seventy 6th rates; sixty-two sloops and forty-five others (bombs, fireships, armed vessels, etc.). They distinguish time at sea from time in port, meaning either in harbour or (more often) at anchor in a secure road. In the first table the different rates are distinguished, expressed in actual 'ship-days' and as percentages of the total. In the second table the distinction is between different stations, omitting the few ships on the coast of West Africa. 'Home Waters' in this context includes the Channel, North Sea, Western Approaches, and the Atlantic coasts of France, Spain and Portugal. Commissions spent on more than one station have been roughly divided.

| | Ship-Days | | |
	In Port	At Sea	Totals
1st & 2nd	11,976 (77%)	3,499 (23%)	15,475 (5%)
3rd & 4th	70,068 (59%)	48,696 (41%)	118,764 (35%)
5th & 6th	58,118 (50%)	58,623 (50%)	116,741 (34%)
Sloops	29,201 (51%)	27,776 (49%)	56,977 (17%)
Others	23,950 (71%)	9,793 (29%)	33,743 (10%)
Totals	193,313 (57%)	148,387 (43%)	341,700
Home Waters	110,951 (61%)	70,871 (39%)	181,822 (54%)
Mediterranean	14,818 (43%)	19,453 (57%)	34,271 (10%)
West Indies	27,049 (48%)	29,668 (52%)	56,717 (17%)
North America	31,218 (65%)	16,736 (35%)	47,954 (14%)
East Indies	7,420 (56%)	5,751 (44%)	13,171 (4%)

Source: ADM 7/573.

352

APPENDIX III
ORIGINS OF SHIPS' COMPANIES

In this table some ships' companies are shown broken down into their origins. The figures are for complement only, including marines but excluding all supernumeraries. The totals include some men otherwise classified or unclassifiable, but are slightly less than the total numbers borne as given in the musters because they exclude widows' men and re-entries.

Ship	Pressed	Volunteers	Turned Over	Total
Achilles	45 (6.5%)	365 (52.6%)	281 (40.5%)	694
Ambuscade	36 (4.1%)	526 (60.1%)	304 (34.7%)	875
Arundel	25 (6.3%)	127 (32.1%)	131 (33.0%)	396
Elizabeth	258 (36.4%)	431 (60.9%)	19 (2.7%)	708
Hampton Court	246 (17.7%)	809 (58.3%)	315 (22.7%)	1,387
Totals	610 (15.0%)	2,258 (55.6%)	1,050 (25.9%)	4,060

Ship	Period	Sources
Achilles	Jan 1757–Apr 1758	ADM 33/541
Ambuscade	Feb 1755–May 1761	ADM 33/544
Arundel	May 1758–Jan 1761	ADM 33/542
Elizabeth	Feb 1755–Dec 1755	ADM 33/537
Hampton Court	Apr 1755–Mar 1759	ADM 32/94

DESERTION & LENGTH OF SERVICE

In these graphs the horizontal axis represents the period of each man's service in his ship, in months, and the vertical axis represents the proportion of the total number of deserters who ran in each month. The 'deserters' are all those run on their ship's books from her complement, excluding supernumeraries. The graphs are compiled from the books of the following ships, which, though not claimed as statistically random, provide a fair coverage of different types of ship in different circumstances. I know of no reason to suppose that any other sample would give very different results. Because of insufficient rigour in distinguishing men run between one and two months after joining their ships, it is probable that the figures for those run in the first month in these graphs are too high, and those for the second month correspondingly too low.

Ship	Rate	Period (months)	Sources	Ship	Rate	Period (months)	Sources
			ADM 36/				ADM 36/
Weymouth	4th	92	6833–6838	Jason	5th	39	5888–5893
Torbay	2nd	94	6839–6842	Hornet	sloop	93	5788–5793
Monmouth	3rd	82	6094–6104	Temple	3rd	26	6882–6887
Northumberland	3rd	120	6186–6197	Dragon	3rd	22	5454–5456
Colchester	4th	59	5232–5237	Blandford	6th	46	5125–5126
Invincible	3rd	11	5853–5855	Laurel	sloop	28	6034–6035
Valiant	3rd	41	6982–6988	Basilisk	bomb	22	5127–5128

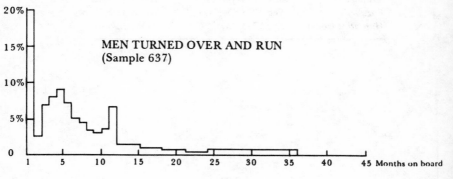

MEN TURNED OVER AND RUN
(Sample 637)

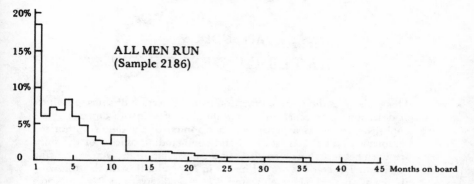

ALL MEN RUN
(Sample 2186)

Months on board

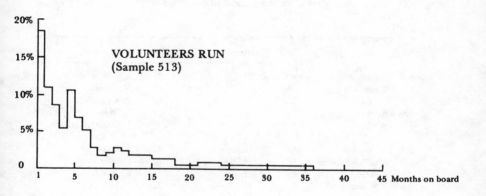

VOLUNTEERS RUN
(Sample 513)

Months on board

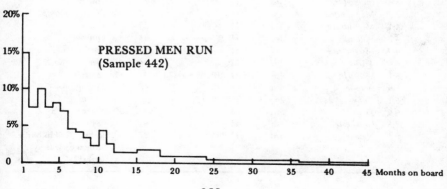

PRESSED MEN RUN
(Sample 442)

Months on board

355

RATES OF DESERTION

This table gives the rates of desertion from a selection of ships. The 'rate of desertion' is here defined as the number of men run on each ship's books, expressed as a percentage per annum of the ship's authorized complement. The rates, stations and commanding officers of the ships are given because these were three of the most important factors affecting desertion. The stations are defined as in Appendix II, with the following abbreviations: H = Home waters, M = Mediterranean, NA = North America, EI = East Indies, WI = West Indies, WA = West Africa. The 'Time' column represents the period in calendar months covered by that entry.

%	Ship	Rate	Station	Time	Captains
0.7	Weymouth	4th	EI	31	J. S. Somerset
1.2	Weymouth	4th	EI	18	N. Vincent[1]
1.9	Torbay[2]	2nd	H	48	A. Keppel
2.0	Burford	3rd	WI	9	J. Gambier
2.3	Barfleur	2nd	H	30	J. Bentley, S. Colby, S. Graves
2.7	Monmouth	3rd	H, M	12	A. Gardiner
2.9	Northumberland	3rd	H, NA	120	Colvill[3]
2.9	Colchester	4th	H	18	R. Roddam
3.0	Weymouth	4th	H	22	T. Hanway
3.3	Ambuscade	5th	H, M	75	R. Gwynn, C. Bassett
3.4	Weymouth	4th	EI	21	R. Collins
3.4	Invincible	3rd	H	11	J. Bentley
3.7	Magnanime	3rd	H	62	W. Taylor, Howe
4.1	Monmouth	3rd	H	24	A. Hervey
4.2	Valiant	3rd	H, WI	41	A. Duncan[4]
4.9	Monmouth	3rd	H	31	J. Storr
5.0	Torbay[5]	2nd	H	34	W. Brett
5.2	Lichfield	4th	H, NA, WA, WI	47	M. Barton
5.9	Achilles	4th	H	40	S. Barrington
6.1	Duke[6]	2nd	H	13	S. Graves
6.6	Jason	5th	H	39	T. Warrick
7.5	Colchester	4th	H	41	L. O'Bryen
8.1	Newark	3rd	H, NA, M	97	J. Barker, W. Holburne,[7] J. Montagu, J. Bray, C. Inglis[8]

%	Ship	Rate	Station	Time	Captains
8.2	*Hornet*	sloop	WI	20	C. Napier
8.4	*Monmouth*	3rd	H	15	H. Harrison
9.2	*Temple*	3rd	WI	12	L. O'Bryen
9.6	*Temple*	3rd	H	14	W. Shirley
11.3	*Dragon*	3rd	H, WI	22	A. Hervey
11.4	*Torbay*	2nd	H	12	C. Colby[9]
12.8	*Elizabeth*	3rd	H	11	J. Montagu
12.9	*Jamaica*	sloop	WI	55	T. Riggs, S. Hood, S. Thompson
17.0	*Lynn*	5th	H, NA, WI, M	92	J. Kirke, W. Stirling, A. Millar
17.1	*Hornet*	sloop	H	32	G. Johnstone
17.5	*Blandford*	6th	H, WI	25	R. Watkins
18.0	*Dolphin*[10]	sloop	H	8	B. Marlow
18.8	*Blandford*	6th	NA, WI	21	P. Cuming[11]
21.7	*Hornet*	sloop	NA, WI	52	S. Salt[12]
22.4	*Fame*	3rd	H	8	J. Byron
22.5	*Laurel*	sloop	H	8	P. Cosby
22.7	*Arundel*	6th	WI	32	C. Middleton, J. Innes
24.0	*Advice*	4th	WI	42	T. Pye[13]
24.8	*Deal Castle*	6th	H	26	G. Tindall
27.7	*Hornet*	sloop	H	9	J. Clapcott
30.0	*Laurel*[14]	sloop	H	20	J. Milligen
34.4	*Basilisk*	bomb	H	22	J. Clerke

Notes:
1. Dismissed his ship for misconduct in action.
2. Ship's company and officers turned over complete from *Swiftsure*.
3. Part of the time as captain, part as commodore with a captain under him.
4. Flag-captain to Commodore Keppel.
5. Ship's company turned over complete from *Valiant*.
6. Guardship in the Hamoaze.
7. Flag-captain to his brother, Vice-Admiral Francis Holburne.
8. Flag-captain to Rear-Admiral Brett.
9. Flag-captain to Vice-Admiral Boscawen.
10. Said to have a bad and mutinous crew.
11. Dismissed his ship for brutality.
12. Relieved on account of senility.
13. Commodore commanding in the Leeward Islands, 1752–1756 (a peacetime commission).
14. Ship paid off unseaworthy on the crew's petition.

Sources

Achilles	ADM 33/541 & 544
Advice	ADM 36/4798
Ambuscade	ADM 33/544

Arundel	ADM 33/542
Barfleur	ADM 33/547
Basilisk	ADM 36/5127–5128
Blandford	ADM 36/5125–5126
Burford	ADM 33/548
Colchester	ADM 36/5232–5237
Deal Castle	ADM 33/553 & 555
Dolphin	ADM 36/5382
Dragon	ADM 36/5454–5456
Duke	ADM 33/553
Elizabeth	ADM 33/534
Fame	ADM 33/558
Hampton Court	ADM 32/94, ADM 33/564
Hornet	ADM 36/5788–5793
Invincible	ADM 36/5853–5855
Jamaica	ADM 33/539
Jason	ADM 36/5888–5893
Laurel	ADM 36/6034–6035
Lichfield	ADM 33/568
Lynn	ADM 32/106 & 201, ADM 33/569
Magnanime	ADM 32/117–120
Monmouth	ADM 36/6094–6104
Newark	ADM 32/132–133, ADM 33/574–575 & 664
Northumberland	ADM 36/6186–6197
Temple	ADM 36/6882–6887
Torbay	ADM 36/6839–6842
Valiant	ADM 36/6982–6988
Weymouth	ADM 36/6833–6838

APPENDIX VI

RATES OF TURN-OVER

In this table the rate of turn-over is expressed as the annual percentage increase of the total number borne (excluding supernumeraries) over the authorized complement. This therefore covers all discharges, including desertions and deaths, and makes no deduction for re-entries. These are of course men discharged from individual ships, many of them into another ship and not out of the Service. A figure of 50 per cent would indicate that one man in two at the beginning of any twelve-month period would have left by the end of it, or that on average the ship's company changed completely every two years. The mean of the twenty-two ships below is in fact 52.9 per cent. The *Advice*'s figure comes from the same peacetime commission as in Appendix V; the others are all wartime commissions.

%	Ship	Rate	Sources
16.9	Lichfield	4th	ADM 33/568
21.3	Weymouth	4th	ADM 36/7029–7035
26.4	Valiant	3rd	ADM 36/6982–6988
29.7	Burford	3rd	ADM 33/548
40.8	Monmouth	3rd	ADM 36/6094–6104
45.1	Temple	3rd	ADM 36/6882–6887
48.1	Achilles	4th	ADM 33/541
50.0	Ambuscade	5th	ADM 33/544
52.3	Hampton Court	3rd	ADM 32/94
55.2	Jason	5th	ADM 36/5888–5893
55.5	Invincible	3rd	ADM 36/5853–5855
55.8	Arundel	6th	ADM 33/542
57.1	Hampton Court	3rd	ADM 33/564
58.8	Blandford	6th	ADM 36/5125–5126
59.5	Northumberland	3rd	ADM 36/6186–6197
61.4	Elizabeth	3rd	ADM 33/534
61.8	Advice	4th	ADM 36/4798
62.0	Colchester	4th	ADM 36/5232–5237
67.3	Barfleur	2nd	ADM 33/547
70.1	Torbay	2nd	ADM 36/6832
83.2	Hornet	sloop	ADM 36/5788–5793
85.0	Laurel	sloop	ADM 36/6034–6035

AGE OF SHIPS' COMPANIES

An Admiralty order of 1764 required the age and place of birth of every person to be entered in the muster books, though it was some years before the practice became general. The earliest evidence of the age structure of ships' companies therefore comes from the years before and during the American War. These diagrams combine the ages of ships' companies at various dates between 1764 and 1782. There appear to be no great differences in this sample between ships' companies in peace and war, except that the category of ordinary seamen and landmen is almost completely lacking in peacetime. The ages of sea officers and marines were hardly ever recorded, and those of servants only occasionally, so the view of a ship's company is not complete.

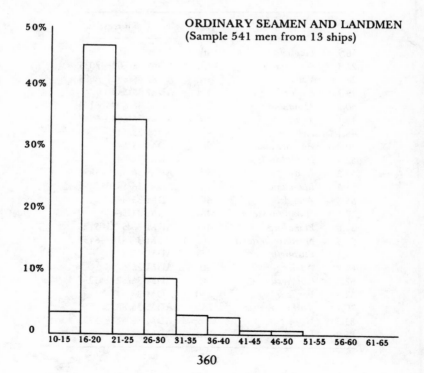

ORDINARY SEAMEN AND LANDMEN
(Sample 541 men from 13 ships)

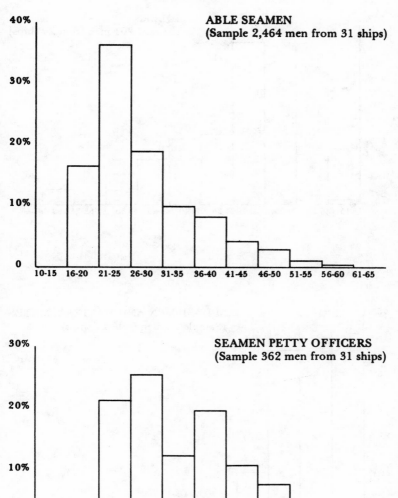

ABLE SEAMEN
(Sample 2,464 men from 31 ships)

SEAMEN PETTY OFFICERS
(Sample 362 men from 31 ships)

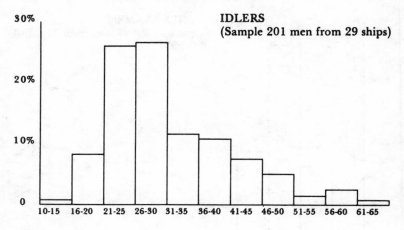

IDLERS
(Sample 201 men from 29 ships)

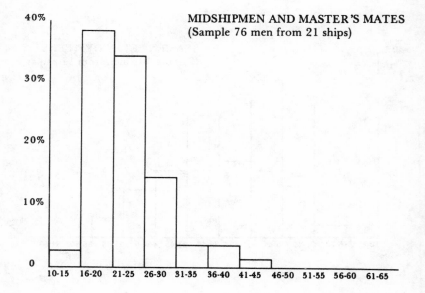

MIDSHIPMEN AND MASTER'S MATES
(Sample 76 men from 21 ships)

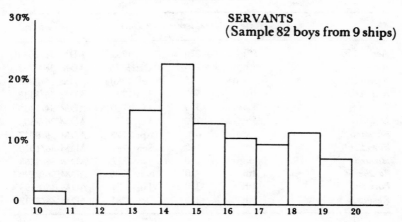

SERVANTS
(Sample 82 boys from 9 ships)

The evidence is drawn from the following ships' musters. Those in the first list are from peacetime, and many of the ships had reduced complements.

Ship	Rate	Complement	Date	Source
Achilles	4th	160	Sep 1764	ADM 36/7287
Achilles	4th	400	Jan 1773	ADM 36/7293
Active	6th	180	Aug 1771	ADM 36/7544
Aquilon	6th	160	May 1765	ADM 36/7546
Augusta	yacht	40	Jan 1765	ADM 36/7109
Beaver	sloop	180	Jul 1765	ADM 36/7328
Belle Isle	3rd	180	Jun 1765	ADM 36/7319
Boreas	6th	160	Jan 1765	ADM 36/7323
Boston	5th	180	Jan 1770	ADM 36/7563
Burford	3rd	180	Jan 1765	ADM 36/7316
Dragon	3rd	180	May 1765	ADM 36/7575
Edgar	4th	420	Jan 1765	ADM 36/7353
Edgar	4th	420	Mar 1771	ADM 36/7356
Fame	3rd	180	Jan 1765	ADM 36/7363
Favourite	sloop	100	Aug 1765	ADM 36/7370
Greyhound	cutter	28	Jan 1765	ADM 36/7204
Sir Edward Hawke	schooner	30	Jan 1770	ADM 33/685
Solebay	6th	160	Jan 1768	ADM 33/685
Southampton	5th	160	Sep 1772	ADM 33/685

Ship	Rate	Complement	Date	Source
Active	5th	220	Jan 1782	ADM 36/10441
Amazon	5th	220	Oct 1776	ADM 36/7743
Basilisk	fireship	55	Feb 1780	ADM 36/8062
Belle Isle	3rd	500	Jan 1777	ADM 36/8139
Bristol	4th	350	Jan 1780	ADM 34/116
Dolphin	5th	150	Aug 1775	ADM 36/7583
Elizabeth	3rd	600	Apr 1778	ADM 36/8017
Eurydice	6th	160	Sep 1781	ADM 36/10107
Hazard	sloop	60	Jan 1777	ADM 36/8268
Panther	4th	420	Nov 1780	ADM 36/8599
Portland	4th	350	Jan 1779	ADM 36/8595
Recovery	5th	220	Dec 1781	ADM 36/9732

APPENDIX VIII

WIVES

In this sample of pay books, 599 women are identified as wives, and a further 228 women are mentioned of unstated relationship who shared a surname with the person whose pay they drew, and might have been wives, mothers, sisters, cousins or aunts. Of this 827: 63 (7%) belonged to sea officers, 176 (21%) to petty officers, 441 (53%) to able seamen, 65 (7%) to ordinary seamen or landmen, and 82 (10%) to others.

In the same sample of pay books, 1407 men were discharged dead whose next of kin is stated, of whom 355 (25%) left widows.

In both cases there may be some degree of double counting, but there is no reason to doubt the ratios.

Ship	Source
Achilles	ADM 33/541 & 544
Ambuscade	ADM 33/544
Arundel	ADM 33/542
Burford	ADM 33/547–548 & 551
Deal Castle	ADM 33/553 & 555
Dorsetshire	ADM 33/555
Duke	ADM 33/553
Edgar	ADM 33/558
Elizabeth	ADM 33/557
Fame	ADM 33/558
Hampton Court	ADM 32/94, ADM 33/564
Invincible	ADM 33/539
Jamaica	ADM 33/539
Lichfield	ADM 32/105, ADM 33/568
Lynn	ADM 32/106 & 201, ADM 33/569
Magnanime	ADM 32/117–120
Monmouth	ADM 32/113
Newark	ADM 32/132–133, ADM 33/574–575 & 664

APPENDIX IX

REMITTANCES

This table examines the pay books of a sample of ships, showing the number of remittances, the number to wives or women of the same surname who might have been wives, the remittances as a proportion of the net pay, and the remitters as a percentage per annum of the authorized complement. It will be evident that only a small minority made remittances, and only just over half of them were to wives, or possible wives. It should be noted that three of the ships here listed began their commissions before the 1758 Navy Act came into force: the *Ambuscade* in February 1755, the *Hampton Court* (first entry) in June 1755, and the *Lichfield* in January 1757.

Ship	Period (months)	Remittances	'Wives'	% Net Pay	% Complement	Source
Achilles	15	12	10	1.5	2.3	ADM 33/541
Achilles	5	19	16	3.3	10.9	ADM 33/541
Achilles	5	4	3	0.7	2.3	ADM 33/541
Achilles	12	4	3	0.5	0.9	ADM 33/544
Ambuscade	75	71	27	18.5	4.5	ADM 33/544
Arundel	32	25	9	3.8	5.9	ADM 33/522
Burford	9	20	8	3.9	5.0	ADM 33/548
Burford	6	32	21	4.9	12.1	ADM 33/551
Deal Castle	5	1	0	1.3	1.5	ADM 33/555
Deal Castle	6	2	1	1.9	2.5	ADM 33/555
Deal Castle	6	2	1	1.6	2.5	ADM 33/553
Deal Castle	6	7	2	5.3	8.7	ADM 33/553
Dorsetshire	6	23	14	3.5	8.8	ADM 33/555
Duke	13	38	32	3.3	5.0	ADM 33/553
Edgar	9	23	14	4.0	7.3	ADM 33/558
Fame	8	14	7	1.8	3.2	ADM 33/558
Hampton Court	44	9	3	2.3	0.5	ADM 32/94
Hampton Court	6	3	3	0.6	1.2	ADM 33/514
Lichfield	45	29	7	4.3	2.2	ADM 33/568
Totals		**338**	**181**	**5.6**	**4.6**	

VENEREAL DISEASE

This table gives the incidence of venereal disease in various ships. The figures derive from the charge of 15s. for venereal cures noted in the pay books, ignoring the fact that some men were treated more than once, and expressing the result both as a number of cures, and as in other appendices, as a percentage per annum of the ship's authorized complement. Being charged for treatment must have discouraged men from reporting sick with this malady, so the figures may understate its true incidence; it is also possible that the figures may be inflated by fraudulent charges on the dead or deserted. The mean of these thirty-three commissions is 8.4 per cent per annum. In modern warships a low incidence of these illnesses is often taken as an indicator of a happy or well-run ship; if the same was true in the eighteenth century it does not appear to correlate well with more obvious indicators such as the rate of desertion.

Ship	Rate	Period (months)	No	% p.a.	Source
Duke	2nd	13	2	0.3	ADM 33/553
Lichfield	4th	45	12	0.9	ADM 33/568
Deal Castle	6th	6	1	1.2	ADM 33/555
Barfleur	2nd	31	30	1.7	ADM 33/547
Magnanime	3rd	13	25	3.2	ADM 32/117
Monmouth	3rd	10	13	3.2	ADM 32/113
Lynn	5th	6	5	3.6	ADM 32/106
Lynn	5th	28	24	4.1	ADM 32/106
Elizabeth	3rd	11	20	4.5	ADM 33/534
Achilles	4th	5	8	4.6	ADM 33/541
Hampton Court	3rd	44	93	5.1	ADM 32/94
Lynn	5th	7	10	6.1	ADM 33/569
Deal Castle	6th	6	5	6.2	ADM 33/555
Magnanime	3rd	13	55	7.0	ADM 32/117
Dorsetshire	3rd	6	19	7.3	ADM 33/555
Burford	3rd	9	30	7.5	ADM 33/548
Deal Castle	6th	5	5	7.5	ADM 33/555
Deal Castle	6th	6	6	7.5	ADM 33/553

Ship	Rate	Period (months)	No	% p.a.	Source
Burford	3rd	6	21	7.9	ADM 33/551
Invincible	3rd	12	59	8.2	ADM 33/539
Edgar	4th	9	29	9.2	ADM 33/558
Ambuscade	5th	75	161	10.3	ADM 33/544
Achilles	4th	15	56	10.6	ADM 33/541
Fame	3rd	8	48	11.1	ADM 33/558
Lynn	5th	13	30	11.1	ADM 32/106
Magnanime	3rd	6	41	11.4	ADM 32/118
Jamaica	sloop	54	61	13.5	ADM 33/539
Hampton Court	3rd	6	33	13.7	ADM 33/564
Arundel	6th	32	67	15.7	ADM 33/542
Achilles	4th	5	28	16.0	ADM 33/541
Lynn	5th	5	18	17.3	ADM 32/106
Lichfield	4th	12	54	18.0	ADM 32/105
Achilles	4th	12	88	20.9	ADM 33/544

APPENDIX XI

MANPOWER

These figures represent the mean numbers of men borne and mustered in the Navy as a whole, including marines, during the years stated. Those borne were on the ships' books either as part of complement or as supernumeraries; those mustered were actually on board. They are printed by Lloyd, *British Seaman*, pp. 287–288, from ADM 7/567.

Year	No. borne	No. mustered
1754	10,149	9,797
1755	33,612	29,268
1756	52,809	50,037
1757	63,259	60,548
1758	70,518	70,014
1759	84,464	77,265
1760	85,658	n.a.
1761	80,675	n.a.
1762	84,797	81,929
1763	75,988	n.a.
1764	17,424	17,415
1765	15,863	n.a.

SOURCES

ABBREVIATIONS AND CONVENTIONS

By some way the majority of the manuscript sources of this work come from the Public Record Office in London, and to save endless repetition in the notes I have adopted the convention that documents are in the P.R.O. unless otherwise stated. All P.R.O. references therefore begin simply with the letters of the record group, of which I have used the following:

ADM	'Admiralty', including Navy Board, Victualling Board, Sick and Hurt Board, etc.
C	Chancery
CO	'Colonial Office'; the eighteenth-century records are of course entirely from the Secretaries of State and the Board of Trade and Plantations.
PC	Privy Council
PRO 30	'Gifts and Deposits' of private records not originally in government custody
PROB	Probate records of the Prerogative Court of Canterbury
RG	Registrar-General of Births, Deaths and Marriages
T	Treasury
WO	'War Office', including Ordnance Board

Many of the documents I have used are letters, and of these a majority are official correspondence addressed by officers and others to the Secretary or Second Secretary of the Admiralty, for their Lordships' information. Since most of these letters come from unfoliated volumes or bundles it is necessary to cite the date and the correspondents in order to identify them, but to save ceaseless repetition of the names of Clevland and Stephens, the Secretaries

371

of this period, I have mentioned the addressee of each letter only when it was not directed to the Secretary. Where only the writer is named, the letter was written on official business to the Admiralty.

Repositories of documents other than the P.R.O. are identified by the following abbreviations:

B.M.	British Museum (now British Library) Department of MSS
E.S.R.O.	East Suffolk Record Office
H.L.	Henry E. Huntington Library, San Marino, California
M.C.	Mulgrave Castle Archives (in the possession of the Marquis of Normanby)
N.M.M.	National Maritime Museum, Greenwich
S.R.O.	Staffordshire Record Office, Stafford
W.S.L.	William Salt Library, Stafford

I have also used the following other abbreviations in the notes and the bibliography:

B.I.H.R.	*Bulletin of the Institute of Historical Research*
CM	Court Martial
D.N.B.	*Dictionary of National Biography*
E.H.R.	*English Historical Review*
H.M.C.	Historical Manuscripts Commission
M.M.	*The Mariner's Mirror*
N.R.S.	Navy Records Society

COLLECTIONS

It is not possible to describe all the record collections I have cited or consulted, but the following are the most important.

Public Record Office

ADM 1: This class contains the official in-letters of the Admiralty, of which I have read all those written during the Seven

Years' War by commanders-in-chief or flag officers, and a sample of those from captains and commanders. Both categories, especially the former, contain as enclosures much correspondence from subordinates and others. Much of the matter of these letters deals with naval operations rather than social conditions, but they contain a wealth of incidental information, not only in what they say but in the way they say it. An important and neglected aspect of these documents is the 'turn-over notes'. It was the custom of Clevland and Stephens, when they read the letters at the Admiralty Board, to turn over the bottom right-hand corner and scribble a note summarizing their Lordships' determination upon it. The letter was then removed from the Board Room and the clerks drafted their out-letters on the basis of the Secretary's notes. These out-letters are to be found in ADM 2, but their formal phraseology is a much more distant reflection of the Board's opinion than the Secretary's terse, pithy (and, it must be said, somewhat illegible) notes.

ADM 1/5294–5302:   These are the original minutes of evidence and verdicts in courts martial, as returned to the Admiralty by the judge-advocate in each case. They vary a good deal in the fullness and accuracy of the record, but taken as a whole they form an extremely important body of evidence for the inner life of the Navy, less for the actual crimes with which people were charged (important though they were) than for the incidental information about shipboard life and naval attitudes. See also ADM 12/22, an epitome or digest of courts martial, 1755–1806.

ADM 3:   The Admiralty Board minutes are solely a record of decisions taken, and reveal little of the discussion or argument which must have taken place. They are useful chiefly for verifying the facts and dates of particular decisions.

ADM 30/44:   This is a Victualling Office precedent book, of considerable value for the study of victualling and pursery.

ADM 32–36:   These are the musters and pay books of individual ships. The importance of these records for the social history of the Navy, and the use which I have made of them, will I hope be evident from the text. Much greater use could be made with the aid of a computer.

ADM 43: These Head Money Vouchers consist of papers submitted to the Navy Office in support of claims for the head money awarded to the captors of enemy men-of-war or privateers. Where the captors were privateers, the vouchers often include copies of the muster rolls and the articles of agreement of the ships' companies. This is a valuable and apparently unused source of information on the economics of privateering, which deserves to be much more thoroughly exploited than I have been able to do.

ADM 51 & 52: Logs of ships; primarily navigational documents with a minimum of other information, they can nevertheless be used as a check on the accuracy of other narratives.

ADM 107/3–5 and ADM 6/86: These are copies of certificates issued to candidates passing the professional examination for lieutenant. They include information about their age and previous sea experience from which it is possible to deduce something of the social and professional background of the commissioned officer corps.

PRO 30/8: An important collection, being the papers of William Pitt the elder. The relatively small amount of useful naval information reflects Pitt's distance from the practicalities of warfare.

PRO 30/20: These are the private papers of Admiral Rodney, a collection of capital importance for all eighteenth-century naval history. They must be used, though they often have not been, with the caution that Rodney was a most untypical officer.

PROB 11: These are copies of wills proved in the Prerogative Court of Canterbury, including those of many sea officers. They yield much evidence concerning their personal affairs, and in some cases, opinions.

British Library
Add.MSS 35359: This volume contains an important part of the scanty surviving correspondence of Lord Anson.

Huntington Library

Stowe and Grenville Papers: Unfortunately relatively little of this collection relates to George Grenville's time at the Admiralty.

Mulgrave Castle Archives

Box VI: This includes naval correspondence of Augustus Hervey, Lord Mulgrave and Lord Sandwich, chiefly of the period of the American War.

National Maritime Museum

ADM/B: These are Admiralty in-letters from the Navy Board, covering the whole range of their responsibilities. The Navy Board copy out-letters of the same correspondence are in the P.R.O., but are less valuable because they do not include the many enclosures.

CLE: Papers and accounts of Captain Michael Clements, including inventories of his private stores and wine.

COR: Correspondence of Admiral Cornwallis; the letters from his father and elder brother during his early service are interesting. Parts of this collection were printed by the H.M.C.

DOU: The letter books of Commodore Sir James Douglas give an unusually good view of the responsibilities of a commander-in-chief overseas; unlike so many such collections, they include private letters, often much more revealing than official correspondence.

DUF: The letter books and papers of Captain Robert Duff, which also include valuable private correspondence.

ELL: The correspondence of Captain (later Admiral) John Elliot. Most of this is private correspondence, particularly valuable for its vivid picture of the hopes and plans of an ambitious young officer.

HWK: Admiral Hawke's papers; with Rodney's this is for my purposes probably the most important collection of private papers (though strictly speaking both are largely a private collection of official and semi-official papers). There are in fact two distinct

Hawke collections in the N.M.M.; the first, which has been there some time, is catalogued under this reference, but the second consists of papers recently acquired from the Earl of Rosse, and not yet catalogued. I have referred to the latter as the Rosse Hawke MSS, using the existing bundle or volume references.

TID: This collection consists of the correspondence and papers of Captain Richard Tiddeman, including a valuable set of accounts.

UPC: This was formed as an autograph collection, but it includes a remarkable correspondence, chiefly between George Johnstone and Arthur Forrest, concerning a dispute with Admiral Cotes over prize money.

Staffordshire Record Office

Lichfield MSS D615: This collection includes most of the remainder of the surviving Anson correspondence.

William Salt Library

H.M. Drakeford MSS: Richard Drakeford was a purser who retired ashore as a Navy agent and man of business in the 1740s, keeping up extensive personal and business contacts with his friends at sea. This voluminous and disorderly collection of his accounts and papers would repay more study than I have been able to give it.

NOTES AND REFERENCES

INTRODUCTION

1. J. Ehrman, *The Navy in the War of William III, 1689–1697* (Cambridge, 1953); Baugh, *Naval Administration in the Age of Walpole; idem, Naval Administration 1715–1750.*
2. Lloyd, *British Seaman*; Kemp, *British Sailor*. Michael Lewis, *A Social History of the Navy 1793–1815* (London, 1960) is still valuable, but concentrates on officers and does not use documents. An important recent contribution for an entirely different period is Anthony Carew, *The Lower Deck of the Royal Navy 1900–1939* (Manchester, 1981).
3. See Rodger, 'Stragglers & Deserters', p.56.
4. Hutchinson, *Press-Gang*, is a notable example.
5. See bibliography.
6. John Harland, *Seamanship in the Age of Sail* (London, 1984).
7. Reprinted London, 1929, ed. G. Callender, Society for Nautical Research, Occasional Publication No.II.

CHAPTER IA

1. Diogenes Laertius I,104, cf. F.W.A. Mullach, *Fragmenta Philosophorum Graecorum* (Paris, 1860–81, 3 vols.) I,233.
2. ADM 1/922, enc. to H. Osborn, 13 Jun 1756.
3. Namier & Brooke, *House of Commons 1754–90*, III,7. Keppel, *Keppel*, I,328.
4. Erskine, *Hervey's Journal*, p.252.
5. Rodger, 'Douglas Papers', p.271.
6. *Advice to Officers*, p.50.

7. ADM 1/5298, CM of W. Pierpoint, 16 Aug 1759.
8. T.B. Macaulay, *The History of England* (Everyman ed., 1906, 4vv) I,228.
9. ADM 25/28, Sir J. Barclay & Sir J. Biers.
10. Renney, 'Journal', p.65.
11. ADM 1/90, f.18v. N.M.M: TID/14, R. Tiddeman to Navy Board, 27 Jan 1758.
12. ADM 1/5165, petition of S. Barclay, 28 Mar 1761.
13. Baugh, *Naval Administration 1715–50*, pp.192–3.
14. ADM 1/717, J. Boys, 26 Apr 1760.
15. ADM 1/307, J. Douglas, 27 Apr 1763.
16. Bulkeley & Cummins, *Voyage to the South Seas*, p.8.
17. ADM 33/673. ADM 1/936, enc. to F. Geary, 7 Dec 1761.
18. *Advice to Officers*, p.103.
19. ADM 1/5299, f.339, CM of R. Donington.
20. ADM 1/2245, L. O'Bryen, 24 Dec 1757.
21. Appendix VII.
22. Appendix I.
23. ADM 1/5300, CM of men of *Centurion*, 21 Jul 1761.
24. See note to Appendix VII.
25. Wallis, *Carteret's Voyage*, II,450.
26. ADM 73/404, No.993 (also Nos.939, 996, 1069); ADM 1/931, P. Durrell, 29 Apr 1760. See also T64/311, ff.7–9.
27. ADM 1/5299, CM of A. Richardson, 5 Nov 1760. Bellamy, *Ramblin' Jack*, p.39.
28. Kemp, *British Sailor*, p.129. Equiano, *Narrative*, p.109.
29. Appendix I.
30. Appendix VII.

31. N.M.M.: Rosse Hawke MSS, Bundle B16, Hawke to S. Barrington, 17 May 1780.

32. Houlding, *Fit for Service*, p. 382.

33. ADM 2/1152, pp.2–3.

CHAPTER IB

1. Middleton, 'Pitt, Anson & the Admiralty', p.192.

2. Rodger, *Admiralty*, p.58.

3. S.R.O.: Lichfield MSS, D615/P(S)/1/1, Lady Anson to Anson, [Jul 1750] & 19 Oct 1750. B.M.: Add.MSS 15956, f.32.

4. PRO 30/9/31, extracts from diary of Lord Berkeley of Stratton, p.1. Ilchester, *Letters to Lord Holland*, p.54. James, Earl Waldegrave, *Memoirs from 1754 to 1758* (London, 1821), p.85.

5. H.M.C.: *Various VI*, pp.38–39.

6. Middleton, 'Administration of Newcastle and Pitt', pp.56–61. N.M.M.: COO/1, p.5. B.M.: Add.MSS 35359, f.413.

7. G.F. James, 'The Admiralty Establishment, 1759', *B.I.H.R.* XVI (1938–9), p.24.

8. P. Coquelle, 'L'espionnage en Angleterre pendant la Guerre de Sept Ans', *Revue d'Histoire Diplomatique* XIV (1900), p.528.

9. Holmes, *Augustan England*, pp.246–248.

10. Wickwire, 'Admiralty Secretaries', p.235. David Syrett, *Shipping and the American War 1775–1783* (London, 1970), p.6.

11. ADM 1/578, F. Holburne, 6 May 1758.

12. Namier & Brooke, *House of Commons 1754–90*, II,221. Middleton, 'Administration of Newcastle and Pitt', p.63. Rodger, *Admiralty*, pp.65–66.

13. Middleton, 'Pitt, Anson and the Admiralty', pp.190–194. The minutes of one such Cabinet meeting are in ADM 1/5123/1.

14. ADM 1/925, C. Knowles, 14 Oct 1757.

15. ADM 1/89, f.129r. ADM 1/162, f.138. ADM 1/4120 *passim*. ADM 1/90, f.635.

16. Baugh, *Naval Administration in the Age of Walpole* and *Naval Administration 1715–50*, gives a most complete account, from which I have derived my summary.

17. J.M. Collinge, *Navy Board Officials 1660–1832* (Office-Holders in Modern Britain VII, London, 1978), p.5.

18. Kemp, 'Boscawen's Letters', p.230. H.L.: STG 23, No.42, T. West to G. Grenville, 11 Aug 1753.

19. ADM 1/90, f.526. ADM 1/236, f.15. ADM 1/715, W. Boys, 1 Dec 1758. ADM 1/93, G. B. Rodney, 18 Feb 1761.

20. A.W.H. Pearsall, 'Naval Aspects of the Landings on the French Coast, 1758', in Rodger, ed., *Naval Miscellany*, pp.218–219.

21. ADM 6/403. Surry & Thomas, *Book of Original Entries*, p.99. ADM 29/1.

22. ADM 1/161, f.77. ADM 1/162, ff.125–6. ADM 1/237, f.183.

23. ADM 1/93, Sir C. Hardy, 7 Nov 1762.

24. Baugh, *Naval Administration in the Age of Walpole*, Ch.9. Rodger, *Naval Records*, Ch.IV.

25. Baugh, *op.cit.supra*, Ch.8. Gradish, *Manning*, Ch.6.

26. Baugh, *op.cit.supra*, pp. 48–52. Gradish, *Manning*, Ch.7.

27. See H. C. Tomlinson, 'The Ordnance Office and the Navy, 1660–1714', *E.H.R.* XC, p.19. The organization had not much changed since 1714.

28. ADM 7/553.

29. This conclusion must be advanced with caution, for though the Admiralty during the Second World War felt the need for comparable statistics, it was not able to collect them. See, however,

ADM 219/32 & ADM 187/44.
30. Below, Ch.IIIA.

CHAPTER IIA

1. Bellamy, *Ramblin' Jack*, pp.40 & 43.
2. Appendix II.
3. Appendix I.
4. *Advice to Officers*, p.43.
5. Press, 'Seamen of Bristol', p.10. Davis, *English Shipping Industry*, pp.59–60.
6. Appendix I.
7. Spavens, *Narrative*, p.33. ADM 51/3788, 28 Oct 1758. Bellamy, *Ramblin' Jack*, p.89.
8. N.M.M.: OBK/9.
9. ADM 1/802, enc. in P. Durrell, 21 Aug 1761. Erskine, *Hervey's Journal*, p.251.
10. PRO 30/20/6, Admiralty order of 30 Aug 1758.
11. ADM 1/1488, S. Barrington, 9 May 1757. M.C.: VI 10/249, C. Middleton to Mulgrave, 11 Nov 1776.
12. Thompson, *Sailor's Letters*, p.119.
13. Gardner, *Above and Under Hatches*, p.22. ADM 36/8870, No.1081.
14. Wyndham, *Chronicles*, II.113.
15. Erskine, *Hervey's Journal*, p.264.
16. Kemp, 'Boscawen's Letters', p.181. B.M.: Add.MSS 35193, f.10.
17. ADM 1/801, S. Mostyn, 16 Mar 1755. ADM 7/744, order by C. Knowles, Feb 1747/8. N.M.M.: TID/14, order by G. Pocock, 26 Nov 1758. Erskine, *Hervey's Journal*, pp.249 & 303–304.
18. Vaughan, *Commodore Walker*, p.169.
19. Kemp, 'Boscawen's Letters', p.229. ADM 1/802, H. Harrison, 17 Mar 1758. ADM 1/926, F. Holburne, 14 Mar 1758.
20. B.M.: Add.MSS 35193, f.11. For the divisional system see Chapter VIB, p. 216.

21. ADM 1/801, H. Harrison, 6 Mar 1757.
22. N.M.M.: LBK/63, 3 Jan 1765.
23. ADM 1/928, F. Holburne, 10 Jan 1759.
24. Penry Lewis, ed., 'Portsmouth Dockyard in 1756', *Notes & Queries* 12th, III,224. For the identification of the writer as Slade, see ADM 95/17, p.239.
25. ADM 1/920, H. Osborn, 19 Dec 1755.
26. N.M.M.: DOU/6, p.11, J. Douglas to Governor of Santiago, 21 Jun 1762.
27. Equiano, *Narrative*, p.118.
28. Gardner, *Above and Under Hatches*, p.24.
29. Kemp, 'Boscawen's Letters', pp.178 & 182.
30. ADM 1/920, enc. to E. Hawke, 3 Jun 1755.
31. Erskine, *Hervey's Journal*, pp.68 & 131.
32. Vaughan, *Commodore Walker*, p.104.
33. Gardner, *Above and Under Hatches*, p.5. ADM 1/5301, CM of Lt. M. Abbot, 26 Aug 1762. *Advice to Officers*, p.72.
34. Kemp, 'Boscawen's Letters', p.181.
35. *Ibid.*, p.183. ADM 51/1001, 9 May 1755. N.M.M.: POC/1F, Navy Board to G. Pocock, 21 Aug. 1752. N.M.M.: PAK/1, *Romney*, p.318. [J. Byron], *A Voyage Round the World in His Majesty's Ship Dolphin* (London, 2nd. ed. 1767), p.59. ADM 49/146, p.4. B.W. Bathe, 'Fishing Tackle for the Royal Navy', *M.M.* 70 (1984), p. 118.
36. *Advice to Officers*, p.62.
37. ADM 1/384, P. Brett, 15 Mar 1763.
38. Williams, *Anson's Voyage*, p.375n. Newton, *Journal of a Slave Trader*, p.9. Powell, *Bristol Privateers*, p.222.
39. ADM 1/5299, f.630.
40. H.L.: STG 21, No.24, T. Brett to

G. Grenville, 20 Mar 1746. ADM 1/5297, CM of Capt. N. Vincent, 12 Jun 1758. ADM 43/16, No.602.
41. Wyndham, *Chronicles* II,120.

CHAPTER IIB

1. ADM 1/481, f.93.
2. ADM 1/90, f.148. ADM 33/585.
3. ADM 1/162, f.53.
4. ADM 1/803, P. Durrell, 12 Jan 1762.
5. ADM 1/308, enc. to R. Tyrell, 14 Nov 1763.
6. E.H. Jenkins, *A History of the French Navy* (London, 1973), p.127.
7. N.M.M.: TID/31. ADM 1/5297, CM of Mr A. Spratt, 7 Feb 1758.
8. H.L.: ST 15, p.6.
9. Davis, *English Shipping Industry*, p.126.
10. ADM 1/90, f.114.
11. N.M.M.: DOU/4, p.186. Bellamy, *Ramblin' Jack*, p.85.
12. ADM 1/384, enc. to T. Brodrick, 11 Jan 1758. N.M.M.: PAK/1, *Dunkirk*, p.27. A.J. Marsh, 'The Taking of Goree, 1758', *M.M.* 51 (1965), p.123, where 'miles' should read 'leagues'.
13. Newton, *Journal of a Slave Trader*, p.61. See also W.E. May, 'Navigational Accuracy in the Eighteenth Century', *Journal of the Institute of Navigation* VI (1953), p.71.
14. ADM 1/5297, CM of Mr A. Spratt, 7 Feb 1758.
15. ADM 1/657, J. Moore, 5 Feb 1762. ADM 1/90, ff.523–524. ADM 1/653, H. Powlett, 17 Jan 1757. ADM 1/655, W. Boys to J. Clevland (private), 8 Jul 1759. ADM 1/716, W. Boys, 6 Apr 1759.
16. ADM 1/1606, B. Clive, 14 Oct 1758. ADM 1/1442, J. Amherst, 4 May 1761.
17. ADM 1/932, P. Durrell, 22 Jul 1760.
18. ADM 1/5297, CM 6 Mar 1758.
19. ADM 1/936, F. Holburne, 2 & 3 Sep 1761.
20. *Ibid.*, enc. to F. Holburne, 23 Oct 1761. ADM 1/937, F. Holburne, 31 Jan 1762.
21. ADM 1/480, f.493B. ADM 1/5294, CM 11 May 1753. ADM 1/930, enc. to F. Holburne, 28 Oct 1759.
22. ADM 1/1486, J. Byron, 20 Jul 1755.
23. ADM 1/802, T. Hanway, 24 & 26 Oct 1760. ADM 1/5299, f.681. ADM 1/937, F. Geary, 11 Feb 1762.
24. ADM 1/2245, L. O'Bryen, 3 Jan 1752/3. ADM 1/655, enc. to W. Boys, 19 Jun 1759.
25. Mackay, *Hawke*, pp. 243–251. N.M.M.: Rosse Hawke A6, draft, Hawke to Anson, [Nov 1759]. Spavens, *Narrative*, p.46, cf. *Prometheus Vinctus*, l.88.
26. See the map in Syrett, *Havana*, p.356.
27. C. Fernandez Duro, *Armada Española desde la Unión de los Reinos de Castilla y de Aragón* (Madrid, 1895–1903, 9 vols.) VII,47.
28. Syrett, *Havana*, pp. xiii, 108–143, 206–207, 237.
29. Howse, *Greenwich Time*, pp.56, 61–64, 68.
30. N.M.M.: ELL/400, No.12.
31. Taylor, *Mathematical Practitioners*, pp.219 & 222.
32. ADM 1/2245, L. O'Bryen, 16 Jan 1757. Howse, *Greenwich Time*, pp.58–60.
33. ADM 1/1488, W. Boys, 13 Dec 1757.
34. ADM 1/481, f.308. N.M.M.: TID/31. ADM 1/306, T. Frankland, 18 Nov 1755.
35. ADM 1/306, T. Frankland, 18 Nov 1755.
36. ADM 14/179, No.756. ADM 1/1896, T. Hankerson, 24 Jan 1761.
37. Erskine, *Hervey's Journal*, p.136.
38. ADM 1/384, T. Broderick, 17, 22

& 26 Apr 1758. Erskine, *Hervey's Journal*, p.280.
39. Vaughan, *Commodore Walker*, p.152.
40. Bellamy, *Ramblin' Jack*, p.57.
41. ADM 1/384, enc. to T. Broderick, 11 Jan 1759.
42. Boys, *Luxborough Galley*.
43. Davis, *English Shipping Industry*, p.156.
44. ADM 1/384, enc. to T. Broderick, 16 Jan 1760. Lind, *Health of Seamen*, p.47.

CHAPTER IIC

1. Equiano, *Narrative*, p.148.
2. N.M.M.: PAK/1, *Neptune*, p.124.
3. Lavery. *Ship of the Line*, I,121–125.
4. Erskine, *Hervey's Journal*, p.272. ADM 1/307, enc. to J. Moore, 5 Apr 1760.
5. Ch.IIA above, n.19.
6. ADM 1/2245, L. O'Bryen [May 1756]. ADM 1/481, ff.180 & 184. Long, *Naval Yarns*, p.40.
7. ADM 1/802, enc. to P. Durrell, 9 Mar 1761.
8. Wyndham, *Chronicles* II,232.
9. Erskine, *Hervey's Journal*, p.272. ADM 1/384, H. Osborn, 30 Mar 1758. ADM 36/6098, slain list.
10. Schomberg, *Naval Chronology* I,356.
11. Bonner-Smith, *Barrington Papers* I,246.
12. ADM 1/653, T. Smith, 25 Feb 1757. ADM 51/77, 24 Feb 1757.
13. N.M.M.: PAK/1, *Dunkirk*, p.3.
14. Long, *Naval Yarns*, p.50.
15. ADM 1/236, f.78.
16. ADM 1/236, f.78.
17. ADM 1/236, f.167.
18. ADM 1/384, C. Saunders, 23 Apr 1757. ADM 51/4193, 3 Apr 1757.
19. Erskine, *Hervey's Journal*, p.272 n.1.
20. Russell, *Bedford Correspondence* I,214; cf. ADM 1/87, Anson, 11 May 1747.

21. Bentley, *Bentley*, p.37. Long, *Naval Yarns*, p.50.
22. Peter Padfield, *Guns at Sea* (London, 1973), p. 121.
23. Keppel, *Keppel*, I,357.
24. ADM 1/481, f.207; the French is as reported by an American.
25. Mackay, *Hawke*, p.249.
26. *Gentleman's Magazine* (1759), p.558.
27. Equiano, *Narrative*, p.146. Mackay, *Hawke*, p.248.
28. ADM 1/307, enc. to J. Moore, 13 Nov 1758. ADM 1/384, enc. to H. Osborn, 24 Aug 1757. Kemp, 'Boscawen's Letters', p.193.
29. Syrett, *Havana*, p.301.
30. ADM 1/3945, 24 Nov 1759.

CHAPTER IID

1. Spavens, *Narrative*, p.5. Robinson, *British Tar*, p.353.
2. For pensions, see Rodger, *Naval Records*, pp.34–35.
3. Lavery, *Ship of the Line* II, Ch.7.
4. For the Divisional System see below, Ch. VIB, p.216.
5. N.M.M.: LBK/63, 3 Jan 1765. N.M.M.: OBK/9. B.M.: Add.MSS 35193, f.9.
6. G.A. Ballard, *The Black Battlefleet* (Lymington, 1980), p.24. *Kilvert's Diary*, ed. W. Plomer (London, 1938–40, 3 vols.), I,189 (21 Jul 1870).
7. Lind, *Treatise of the Scurvy*, in Lloyd, *Health of Seamen*, p.14.
8. Kemp, 'Boscawen's Letters', p.188. ADM 1/384, f.595.
9. ADM 1/482, f.146, Colvill, 10 Apr 1761.
10. Mackay, *Hawke*, p.130.
11. Howard, *Sailing Ships of War*, p.219.
12. ADM 1/1488, T. Baillie, 4 Sep 1757.
13. ADM 1/656, P. Brett, 1 Sep 1761.
14. ADM 1/925, C. Knowles, 13 Oct 1757. ADM 1/653, H. Powlett, 27 Jan 1757. ADM 1/5297, CM of J. Mitchell

& W. Hardy, 4 Jan 1758. Other examples could be given.
15. ADM 1/656, P. Brett, 1 Sep 1761. ADM 1/927, F. Holburne, 2 Sep 1758.
16. Press, 'Seamen of Bristol', App.IX.
17. N.M.M.: OBK/9.
18. ADM 1/5301, CM of P. Clarke, 13 Apr 1762.
19. Jarrett, *Naval Dress*, pp.40–41. *Advice to Officers*, pp.79 & 109.
20. W. Falconer, *An Universal Dictionary of the Marine* (London, 4th ed. 1780, repr. Newton Abbot, 1970), p.300.
21. N.M.M.: COO/1 p.19.
22. ADM 1/651, T. Smith, 29 May 1756.
23. Jarrett, *Naval Dress*, pp.31–43. *Advice to Officers*, pp.40–41. See also ADM 7/298, No.101, concerning a person falsely claiming to be an officer; the fact that he wore no uniform aroused no suspicion in itself.
24. N.M.M.: TID/31, inventory of linen, 29 Mar 1750.
25. N.M.M.: ELL/400, No.15.
26. M.C.: VI, 1/122. This refers to the lieutenant's uniform.
27. On accommodation in general see Lavery, *Ship of the Line* II, Ch.7.
28. ADM 1/1487, J. Barker, 14 Jun 1756. ADM 95/17, pp.247–253. ADM 49/133, No.550.
29. N.M.M.: ADM/B/161, 29 Jan 1759.
30. Stone, *Family, Sex and Marriage*, p.255.
31. Taylor, *Sea Chaplains*, p.170.
32. Kemp, 'Boscawen's Letters', p.227.
33. N.M.M.: TID/31.
34. Renney, *Journal*, p.89.
35. N.M.M.: ELL/400, No.19.
36. Kemp, 'Boscawen's Letters', p.175.

CHAPTER IIE

1. Equiano, *Narrative*, p.112.
2. Bellamy, *Ramblin' Jack*, p.46.
3. *Ibid.*, pp.40–44 & 47.
4. Matcham, *Russell*, p.248.
5. ADM 1/651, T. Smith, 21 Mar 1756. PRO 30/20/8, p.358.
6. ADM 1/5296, f.494. ADM 1/5297, CM of J. Blake, 11 Aug 1758.
7. Kemp, 'Boscawen's Letters', p.170. Keith Thomas, *Man and the Natural World* (London, 1983), pp.111 & 227.
8. N.M.M.: UPC/2 No.114. Middleton, 'Administration of Newcastle and Pitt', pp.39–40.
9. Erskine, *Hervey's Journal*, p.172.
10. Baugh, *British Naval Administration in the Age of Walpole*, pp.422–430, describes it.
11. ADM 7/745, H. Palliser to E. Hughes, 13 Oct 1760. N.M.M.: TID/14, R. Tiddeman to H. Cowell, 1 Jan 1761. N.M.M.: HWK/14, E. Hawke to T. Hanway, 4 Nov 1759.
12. ADM 1/5297, CM of J. Blake, 11 Aug 1758.
13. Williams, *Anson's Voyage*, p.366. Lind, *Treatise of the Scurvy*, p.74. ADM 1/5300, CM of men of *Centurion*, 21 Jul 1761. (All references to men buying provisions for themselves.)
14. N.M.M.: TID/31.
15. N.M.M.: CLE/4/2, 9 Jun 1763.

CHAPTER IIF

1. *Advice to Officers*, p.86.
2. Drummond & Wilbraham, *Englishman's Food*, pp.197–198.
3. Bellamy, *Ramblin' Jack*, p.204.
4. Renney, 'Journal', p.63.
5. Spavens, *Narrative*, p.29.
6. N.M.M.: CLE/4/2.
7. N.M.M.: TID/31, 13 May 1749.
8. N.M.M.: TID/14, R. Tiddeman to T. Broderick, 20 Feb 1758. ADM 1/1788, J. Fortescue, 22 Jun 1762. ADM 1/5295, CM of R. Bainbridge, 31 Dec 1755. ADM 32/94 SB No.65.
9. ADM 1/5300, CM of W. Cuddy, 31 Oct 1761.
10. ADM 1/5294, CM of Capt. A. Campbell, 11 Sep 1751. ADM 1/5300,

CM of A. Vaughan, 5 Jan 1761. Lind, *Health of Seamen*, p.56.
11. N.M.M.: LBK/63, 3 Jan 1765. B.M.: Add.MSS 35193, f.11.
12. B.M.: Add.MSS 35193, f.11.
13. ADM 1/930, F. Holburne, 29 Oct 1759. N.M.M.: TID/14, R. Tiddeman to T. Broderick, 12 Feb 1758. ADM 1/5299, f.530.
14. Keppel, *Keppel* I,130.
15. ADM 1/90, f.175, E. Boscawen, 29 Feb 1760.

CHAPTER IIG

1. Wyndham, *Chronicles* II,102.
2. See, notably, Kemp, 'Boscawen's Letters'.
3. PROB 11/736, f.25.
4. N.M.M.: POC/1E, G. Pigot to G. Pocock, 8 Jul 1759.
5. ADM 1/306, T. Frankland, 28 Feb 1757. Spavens, *Narrative*, p.14. PC 1/9/47. PROB 11/957, f.123.
6. PROB 11/960, f.383. PROB 11/1059, f.98. PROB 11/1136, f.321. PROB 11/875, f.222. N.M.M.: COR/56, P.S. to A. Keppel to W. Cornwallis, 11 Jul 1764.
7. PROB 11/866, f.31.
8. PROB 11/1136, f.321.
9. Erskine, *Hervey's Journal*, p.xxxi.
10. Renney, 'Journal', pp.95–99.
11. Erskine, *Hervey's Journal*, p.131. N.M.M.: TID/8, E. Boscawen to R. Tiddeman, 4 Oct 1749.
12. ADM 1/5300, CM of G. Newton & T. Finlay, 2 Jul 1761. ADM 1/716, W. Boys, 14 Jan 1759. ADM 1/5295, CM of Capt. M. Arbuthnot, 13 Mar 1755.
13. Erskine, *Hervey's Journal*, p.147. ADM 1/482, f.466.
14. ADM 1/5294, CM of Capt. Vaughan & Lt. Pike, 13 Oct 1750.
15. ADM 1/933, F. Holburne, 29 Dec 1760. ADM 1/5297, CM of Capt. P. Cuming, 5–6 Dec 1758.
16. ADM 1/5302, f.129.

17. Dickinson, 'Naval Diary', p.241. ADM 51/3765. ADM 36/4825.
18. N.M.M.: COO/1, p.19.
19. E.g. Hutchinson, *Press Gang*, p.270.
20. Appendix VII. Stone, *Family, Sex and Marriage*, p.50. E.A. Wrigley & R.S. Schofield, *The Population History of England 1541–1871* (London, 1981), pp. 423–424.
21. Bromley, *Manning Pamphlets*, p.110.
22. Gradish, *Manning*, p.216. ADM 106/3107.
23. Appendix VIII.
24. ADM 1/718, enc. to W. Boys, 4 Mar & 29 Jun 1761. ADM 1/1441, E. Affleck, 17 Oct 1756, & H. Angel, 21 Feb 1756. ADM 1/1487, E. Barber, 15 Nov 1756.
25. Appendix IX.
26. J.S. Shaw, *The Management of Scottish Society 1707–1764* (Edinburgh, 1983), p.186. See also Cobbett, *Parliamentary History* XV,862.
27. Renney, 'Journal', p.63. In the ship's pay book, ADM 32/117, only seven wives can be certainly identified as receiving part of their husbands' pay.
28. ADM 6/332, pp.81, 83–84, 90, 125, 134, 136, 156, 162–163, 170, 176 & 182.
29. ADM 1/655, enc. to P. Brett, 30 Jan 1760.
30. Appendix X.
31. A.D. Harvey, 'Prosecutions for Sodomy in England at the beginning of the Nineteenth Century', *Historical Journal* XXI (1978), p.939.
32. ADM 12/26.
33. Stone, *Family, Sex and Marriage*, p.542. See also, for his evidence rather than his conclusions, Gilbert, 'Buggery and the British Navy', pp.72–98.
34. ADM 1/89, f.23. ADM 1/924, enc. to T. Broderick, 13 Jun 1757. ADM 1/653, T. Smith, 8 Jun 1757.
35. ADM 1/5301, CM of Capt. H.

Angel, 12 Jan 1762. ADM 1/307, G.B. Rodney, 10 Feb 1762. PRO 30/20/8, pp.56–57.

CHAPTER IIIA

1. J.R. Tanner, ed., *Samuel Pepys's Naval Minutes* (N.R.S. Vol.60, 1926), p.250.
2. Baugh, *Naval Administration in the Age of Walpole*, p.365.
3. Gradish, *Manning*, p.144.
4. Beveridge, *Prices and Wages*, p.529; cf. Baugh, *Naval Administration in the Age of Walpole*, p.407.
5. Gradish, *Manning*, p.144, where the figure of 822 gals. in the last line of the table reads 322 gals. in the original (B.M.: Stowe MSS 152, f.130).
6. ADM 1/90, f.333v.
7. ADM 30/44, p.262. N.M.M.: TID/14, report of survey, 2 May 1759.
8. Gradish, *Manning*, p.147. T.S. Ashton, *An Economic History of England: The Eighteenth Century* (London, 1972 ed.), p. 31. Beveridge, *Prices and Wages*, p.576. Rodger, 'Victualling', n.52. N.M.M.: HWK/11, J. Ommaney to E. Hawke, 7 Aug 1759.
9. PRO 30/20/6, D. Hailes to G.B. Rodney, 4 May 1758.
10. Gradish, *Manning*, p.140.
11. Lavery, *Ship of the Line* II,142–143. ADM 95/17, pp. 111 & 267.
12. T.S. Ashton, 'Changes in Standards of Comfort in Eighteenth Century England', *Proceedings of the British Academy* XLI (1955), p.177.
13. Watt, *Starving Sailors*, p.9.
14. Gradish, *Manning*, p. 197. ADM 1/922, H. Osborn, 24 May 1756. Beaglehole, *Cook*, pp.705–706. Lloyd & Coulter, *Medicine and the Navy* III,305. Wallis, *Carteret's Voyage* II,449.
15. ADM 1/5297, CM of H. Nelson, 27 Jan 1758.
16. N.M.M.: HWK/14, E. Hawke to P. Pett, 25 Sep 1759.

17. Thompson, *Sailor's Letters* II,25. Baugh, *Naval Administration 1715–50*, p.450.
18. Gradish, *Manning*, pp.159–160. ADM 1/2245, L. O'Bryen, 19 Apr 1757.
19. ADM 1/235, T. Cotes, 7 Aug 1757.
20. Rodger, 'Scorbut', argues this.
21. Rodger, 'Victualling'.
22. ADM 1/482, f.146.

CHAPTER IIIB

1. Matcham, *Russell*, p.191. ADM 1/922, enc. in H. Osborn, 30 Jul 1756.
2. N.M.M.: ELL/400, Nos.16–18.
3. Rodger, *Naval Records*, Ch.IV, describes musters and pay books in detail.
4. ADM 30/44, p.58.
5. ADM 1/715, W. Boys, 30 Jul 1758. ADM 1/718, W. Boys, 20 May 1761.
6. ADM 1/718, enc. to W. Boys, 18 Jan 1761. ADM 1/919, enc. to E. Hawke, 4 Apr 1755. ADM 1/654, T. Smith to J. Clevland (personal), 9 Aug 1757. ADM 1/922, H. Osborn, 10 May 1756.
7. ADM 30/44, pp.17 & 120. Admiralty *Regulations and Instructions*, p.117.
8. ADM 30/44, p.32.
9. *Ibid.*, p.19.
10. N.M.M.: TID/35. ADM 30/44, p.16.
11. Mountaine, *Seaman's Vade-Mecum*, p.233.
12. ADM 30/44, p.15.
13. *Ibid.*, p.170.
14. ADM 7/745, Admiralty order 17 Feb 1761.
15. ADM 30/44, p.18.
16. *Case of the Pursers*, p.1. ADM 30/44, p.190.
17. ADM 30/44, p.15.
18. Baugh, *Naval Administration in the Age of Walpole*, p.377. *Case of the Pursers*, p.2. ADM 1/925, enc. to C. Knowles, 15 Oct 1757. Renney, 'Journal', p.63.

19. *Case of the Pursers*, p.1—but this was written in 1711, when the Victualling Board's technical standards were lower, and of course it is not impartial.

20. ADM 1/656, P. Brett, 12 Apr 1761. N.M.M.: DOU/8, p.6.

21. N.M.M.: ROD/1, p.42. Bellamy, *Ramblin' Jack*, p.47.

22. ADM 30/44, pp.68 & 184. WO 34/56, f.17. N.M.M.: TID/14, R. Tiddeman to R. Grant, 10 Sep 1758.

23. ADM 30/44, pp.27–28, 37, 40, 47, 62, 69–70, 79, 167. Admiralty *Regulations and Instructions*, p.119. *Case of the Pursers*, p.3.

24. ADM 1/5297, CM of Capt. P. Cuming, 5–6 Dec 1758; CM of Mr H. Nelson, 27 Jan 1758.

25. Spavens, *Narrative*, p.73.

26. *Advice to Officers*, p.97.

27. N.M.M.: TID/35. ADM 1/5297, CM of H. Nelson, 27 Jan 1758; CM of Mr W. Parker, 23 Nov 1758. *Advice to Officers*, pp.90 & 97.

28. ADM 20/235.

29. PROB 31/598/489. ADM 68/322. ADM 43/16 No.602.

30. Baugh, *Naval Administration 1715–50*, pp.455–456. Bromley, *Manning Pamphlets*, p.113. *Case of the Pursers*, p.3 (but note that this was written in 1711, before bills in course bore interest). Beveridge, *Prices and Wages*, pp.519–525.

31. ADM 30/44, p.87. Baugh, *Naval Administration 1715–50*, p.458.

32. *Advice to Officers*, p.42. Gardner, *Above and Under Hatches*, p.2.

33. ADM 1/718, W. Boys, 10 Apr 1761.

34. W.S.L.: H.M. Drakeford MS 15A & 15B *passim*; H.M. Drakeford MS 9. B.M.: Add.MSS 35193, f.118.

35. Surry & Thomas, *Book of Original Entries*, p.101.

36. Namier & Brooke, *House of Commons 1754–90* I,228 & II,114.

CHAPTER IIIC

1. Aspinall-Oglander, *Admiral's Wife*, p.10. Marcus, *Heart of Oak*, p.128.

2. Kemp, *British Sailor*, p.109. Mackay, *Hawke*, p.18.

3. Syrett, *Havana*, p.304.

4. ADM 1/306, T. Frankland, 28 Apr 1757. Smith, *Grenville Papers* II,11.

5. Press, 'Seamen of Bristol', Ch.III, p.1. Crewe, 'Naval Administration', p.101.

6. ADM 1/235, T. Cotes, 18 Jan 1757 & 1 Aug 1759. On the rates of sickness in French ships, see the figures in Le Goff, 'Naval Recruitment', Appendix III.

7. Ranft, *Vernon Papers*, p.408. Kemp, 'Boscawen's Letters', p.230.

8. S.R.O.: D615/P(S) 1/10, G.B. Rodney to Anson, 10 Feb 1762. Spinney, *Rodney*, p.187.

9. Rodger, 'Scorbut'. Carpenter, *Scurvy*, pp. 53–63 & 69–74.

10. Admiralty *Regulations and Instructions*, p.203. Gradish, *Manning*, p.162. See also Baugh, *Naval Administration in the Age of Walpole*, pp.377–385, and *Naval Administration 1715–50*, pp.449–450.

11. Kemp, 'Boscawen's Letters', p.248.

12. Gradish, *Manning*, p.164.

13. Lind, *Health of Seamen*, p.121.

14. Drummond & Wilbraham, *Englishman's Food*, pp.182–184, 228 & 259. Peter Mathias, *The Transformation of England* (London, 1979), pp.268–269 & 278. ADM 1/1487, enc. to E. Boscawen, 4 Jul 1756. Leslie Clarkson, *Death, Disease and Famine in Pre-Industrial England* (London, 1975), p.28.

15. Kemp, 'Boscawen's Letters', p.185. ADM 1/935, F. Geary to Anson, 22 Jun 1761. ADM 1/1488, J. Bover, 7 Jun 1757.

16. B.M.: Add.MSS 35359, f.419.

17. ADM 30/51–52.

18. ADM 3/70, 1 Jul 1762.

19. Mackay, *Hawke*, p.126. ADM 1/90, f.479v.
20. ADM 1/235, T. Cotes, 26 May 1758. ADM 107/3, p.353. Rodger, 'Douglas Papers', p.254 & n.33.
21. Erskine, *Hervey's Journal*, p. 277; but the *D.N.B.* implies he may have been younger.
22. Mackay, *Hawke*, pp. 129 & 296.
23. ADM 1/235, T. Cotes, 3 Aug 1755. ADM 1/384, C. Saunders, 20 Dec 1760. ADM 1/481, f.594. Sedgwick, *House of Commons 1715–54* II,93–94.
24. Lind, *Treatise of the Scurvy* (1953 ed.), p.92. Kemp, 'Boscawen's Letters', p.180. ADM 1/925, C. Knowles, 9 Nov 1757. ADM 1/938, F. Holburne, 30 Sep 1762.
25. ADM 7/418 & 420.
26. ADM 1/924, enc. to T. Broderick, 3 Jun 1757.
27. ADM 102/374.
28. Gradish, *Manning*, pp. 201–2.
29. Gradish, *Manning*, p.212.
30. For total numbers, and the pitfalls of estimating them, see Ch.VA, p.148.
31. Houlding, *Fit for Service*, p.40.

CHAPTER IIID

1. G.E. Manwaring, *The Flower of England's Garland* (London, 1936), pp.53, 57, 66 & 72. Lloyd & Coulter, *Medicine and the Navy* III,133–134.
2. Erskine, *Hervey's Journal*, p.149. Etienne Taillemite, *Dictionnaire des Marins Français* (Paris, 1982), p.34.
3. Adrien Carré, 'Notes sur l'Histoire de la Médecine du Travail et de l'Ergonomie dans la Marine', *Revue d'Histoire Economique et Sociale* XLVII (1969), p.274. G. Lacour-Gayet, *La Marine Militaire de la France sous la règne de Louis XV* (Paris, 1902), p.360. Lloyd & Coulter, *Medicine and the Navy* III,72. Le Goff, 'Naval Recruitment', Appendix III, gives instances of rates of sickness in French ships.
4. Ives, *Voyage*, p.444.

5. ADM 1/927, enc. to C. Holmes, 10 Nov 1758.
6. N.M.M.: LBK/63, 3 Jan 1765. Lind, *Health of Seamen*, p.73. Lind, *Treatise of the Scurvy* (1953 ed.), pp.84–85; cf. Rodger, 'Scorbut'.
7. Lind, *Health of Seamen*, p.47. Kemp, *British Sailor*, pp.109–110. Kemp, 'Boscawen's Letters', p.199. Gradish, *Manning*, p.123. Lloyd & Coulter, *Medicine and the Navy* III,72–73. A.E. Clark-Kennedy, *Stephen Hales* (Cambridge, 1929), pp.153–168. ADM 106/2188, p.452. ADM 49/133, No.569. Admiralty *Regulations and Instructions*, p.215.
8. ADM 1/927, C. Holmes, 12 Nov 1758.
9. Vaughan, *Commodore Walker*, p.97.
10. ADM 1/925, C. Knowles, 24 Nov 1757.
11. B.M.: Add.MSS 35193, f.9.
12. Lloyd & Coulter, *Medicine and the Navy* III,128.
13. Gradish, *Manning*, p.174. Lind, *Health of Seamen*, pp.29–30.
14. Hutchins, *Hanway*, p.81.
15. ADM 1/654, T. Smith, 14 Aug 1757. Lind, *Health of Seamen*, p.114. ADM 1/719, W. Gordon 11 Aug 1762. ADM 3/70, 12 Aug 1762.
16. Lind, *Health of Seamen*, p.31.

NOTES TO CHAPTER IIIE

1. Lloyd & Coulter, *Medicine and the Navy* III,187–195.
2. H.L.: STG 18 No.7, pp.8–12.
3. ADM 1/306, T. Frankland to Dr J. Maxwell, 12 May 1756, & to J. Clevland, 22 Sep 1756.
4. Lloyd & Coulter, *Medicine and the Navy* III,210–212, 216 & 264–265. For the cost of a battleship, see Lavery, *Ship of the Line* I,96.
5. ADM 102/399 is an inventory of the drugs and medical equipment in Haslar in 1758.
6. H.L.: STG 18 No.7 p.7. Lloyd & Coulter, *Medicine and the Navy* III,216, 223–225. ADM 1/921, enc. to

H. Osborn, 2 Apr 1756. ADM 99/24, p.91.

7. Gradish, *Manning*, pp. 191–192.

8. N.M.M.: DUF/10, R. Duff to [E. Boscawen, Jun 1755]. ADM 1/481, f.7. ADM 1/803, Colvill, 15 Mar 1763.

CHAPTER IVA

1. Bromley, *Manning Pamphlets*, p.110. Press, 'Seamen of Bristol', Ch.III, p.12. Hutchinson, *Press-Gang*, p.40.

2. David Alexander, 'Literacy among Canadian and Foreign Seamen, 1863–1899', in Ommer & Panting, *Working Men*, p.3.

3. ADM 1/803, enc. to P. Durrell, 8 Jan '1761' [1762].

4. ADM 1/1486, W. Brett, 30 Jun 1755.

5. J. H. Plumb, *Georgian Delights* (London, 1980), pp. 8 & 18.

6. A. Smith, *The Wealth of Nations* (London, 1812 ed., 3 vols.) I,169.

7. ADM 1/5300, CM of G. Newton & T. Finlay, 2 Jul 1761.

8. Spavens, *Narrative*, p.1.

9. James Boswell, *Life of Dr Johnson*, ed. R. W. Chapman & J.D. Fleeman (London, 1970), p.927.

10. Davis, *English Shipping Industry*, pp.72–73. Appendix I.

11. Spavens, *Narrative*, p.33. ADM 51/3788, 28 Oct 1758.

12. ADM 1/716, enc. to W. Boys, 26 Feb 1759. ADM 1/5300, CM of Capt. C. Feilding, 10 Aug 1761.

13. Press, 'Seamen of Bristol', Ch. I, p.10. Baugh, *Naval Administration 1715–50*, pp.98–99. Blake, *Marine System*, pp.57 & 62.

14. Davis, *English Shipping Industry*, p.145.

15. Baugh, *Naval Administration 1715–50*, p.405. In 1748 the cost of provisions in the Navy was calculated as 21s. 4d. a lunar month, allowing 1 per cent of the cost of raw materials for

processing and packing costs – but this allowance must have been far too little. At 1752 prices the raw material cost was reckoned as 17s. 7$\frac{3}{4}$d. a man a month (ADM 30/44, pp.236–239). It would be remarkable if the elaborate industrial processes required to preserve victuals added less than a quarter to the market price of the raw foodstuffs.

16. Gradish, 'Wages & Manning', p.50.

17. N.M.M.: ROD/1, P. Pigou to R. Roddam, 9 Jun 1760, & W. Harold to R. Roddam, 10 Jun 1760. Newton, *Journal of a Slave Trader*, pp.69–71. Press, 'Seamen of Bristol', Concl., p.2.

18. Davis, *English Shipping Industry*, pp.154–5.

19. Press, 'Seamen of Bristol', Ch.V, pp.3–4. Powell, *Bristol Privateers*, p.188.

20. Rodger, *Naval Records*, pp.34–36.

21. ADM 1/482, f.495, Colvill, 12 Nov 1765.

22. Bromley, *Manning Pamphlets*, p.125; see also *ibid*., index references s.v. Seamen, Character, and Robinson, *British Tar*, pp.290 & 304.

23. Press, 'Seamen of Bristol', Ch.I, pp.3–4. Vaughan, *Commodore Walker*, pp.64–65.

CHAPTER IVB

1. ADM 1/481, f.346.

2. ADM 1/1478, E. Boscawen, 18 Aug 1742.

3. ADM 1/1787, A. Forrest, 23 Mar 1760.

4. ADM 1/5301, CM of Lt. Coates, 9 Mar 1762.

5. Erskine, *Hervey's Journal*, p.246. N.M.M.: ELL/400 No.24.

6. ADM 1/2245, L. O'Bryen, 23 Sep 1755.

7. Admiralty *Regulations and Instructions*, p.192.

8. ADM 1/90, ff.255–262. ADM 36/6102.

9. ADM 1/1606, B. Clive, 2 Oct 1758. For another example see ADM 1/929, F. Holburne, 9 May 1759.

10. ADM 1/88, F. Holburne, 10 Jan '1756' [1757].

11. ADM 1/384, C. Saunders, 9 May 1760. ADM 1/482, f.246.

12. N.M.M.: TID/14, G. Pocock to R. Tiddeman, 16 Feb 1759.

13. ADM 1/1486, P. Baird, 6 Jun 1755.

14. Keppel, *Keppel* I,119.

15. ADM 1/924, T. West, 26 Jan 1757. Spavens, *Narrative*, p.63.

16. ADM 1/1787, A. Forrest, 18 & 25 Nov 1760; cf. ADM 36/5226. ADM 1/928, F. Holburne, 13 Jan 1759. PRO 30/20/6, J. Worth to H. Harrison, 2 Jan 1759.

17. Spinney, *Rodney*, pp. 60, 64 & 70. PRO 30/20/6, S. Mostyn to G.B. Rodney, 31 May 1756. ADM 1/924, enc. to E. Boscawen, 6 Mar 1757.

18. ADM 1/652, T. Smith, 25 Dec 1756. ADM 1/715, W. Boys, 31 Dec 1758.

19. ADM 1/235, T. Cotes, 8 Mar 1757. N.M.M.: CLE/3/3, M. Clements to J. Bentsly, 14 Jan 1759.

20. ADM 1/88, F. Holburne, 25 Nov 1756. E.S.R.O.: HA 67/431/236, A. Keppel to Navy Board, 14 Dec 1761. ADM 1/482, f.294.

21. N.M.M.: UPC/3, No.8.

22. ADM 1/92, f.29. ADM 1/922, H. Osborn, 6 Jun 1756.

23. ADM 1/935, F. Geary, 28 May 1761.

24. ADM 1/482, f.262.

25. ADM 1/383, f.468.

26. ADM 1/93, G.B. Rodney, 14 Nov 1759, 30 Jun & 11 Oct 1760.

CHAPTER IVC

1. PRO 30/8/80, f.8.

2. Lloyd, *British Seaman*, p.249 gives the gross rates correctly, but understates the deductions. Michael Lewis, *The Navy of Britain* (London, 1948), p. 301, conflates the gross rate for ordinary seamen with the net rate for able seamen. Hutchins, *Hanway*, p.82, is completely adrift.

3. Rodger, *Naval Records*, pp.54–55.

4. Baugh, *Naval Administration in the Age of Walpole*, p.229 n.392. Barnes & Owen, *Sandwich Papers* III,247.

5. N.M.M.: CLE/4/1, narrative of George III's visit to Spithead. Namier & Brooke, *House of Commons 1754–90* I,145. ADM 1/926, F. Holburne, 16 Feb 1758.

6. ADM 1/306, T. Frankland, 8, 15 & n.d. [c.18] Oct 1755; 9 Dec 1757. ADM 1/5297, CM of Capt. T. Pye, 1–4 Mar 1758. *D.N.B.* s.v. Pye. S.R.O.: D615/P(S)/1/2, Lady Anson to Anson, 27 Jul [1758], 'by what I can learn about the affair of Commodore Pye, Admiral Forbes is the only person at the Board who had nothing to do with it.' Williams, 'Sandwich's Naval Administration', p.165.

7. Press, 'Seamen of Bristol', Ch.II, pp.2–6. Hutchins, *Hanway*, p.82.

8. ADM 1/5299, ff.229A & 482. ADM 1/654, T. Smith, 28 Jul 1757. PROB 31/474/259. Lloyd & Coulter, *Medicine & the Navy* III,229.

9. Davis, *English Shipping Industry*, p.137. Press, 'Seamen of Bristol, Ch.II, pp.2–4.

10. ADM 1/5299, f.587. Pares, 'Manning of the Navy', p.34. ADM 1/235, T. Cotes, 20 Apr 1759.

11. ADM 1/1487, J. Byron, 10 Oct 1756. Gradish, *Manning*, p.72.

12. ADM 1/1488, P. Brett, 21 Mar 1757. N.M.M.: DOU/6 p.11, J. Douglas to Gov. of St Iago, 21 Jun 1762.

13. Davis, *English Shipping Industry*, pp.140, 144 & 192. Press, 'Seamen of Bristol', Ch.II, pp.9–10. Conrad Dixon, 'Signing-On', *M.M.*70 (1984), p.311. Blake, *Marine System*, p.62.

14. ADM 1/5300, CM of Capt. C. Feilding, 10 Aug 1761. ADM 7/745, E. Hughes, 17 Apr 1760. Hutchinson,

Press-Gang, p.125. ADM 7/299 No.38. ADM 1/1442, P. Affleck, 26 Dec [1758].

15. Press, 'Seamen of Bristol', Ch.II, p.10. Bellamy, *Ramblin' Jack*, p.134.

16. W.E. Minchinton, ed., *The Trade of Bristol in the Eighteenth Century* (Bristol Record Soc. XX, 1957), p.153.

17. Gradish, *Manning*, p.75; cf. Pares, *Colonial Blockade and Neutral Rights*, pp.9 & 38–40; Vaughan, *Commodore Walker*, p.xvi.

18. PRO 30/20/8, p.114. ADM 43/16, No.1094.

19. Vaughan, *Commodore Walker*, p.94 – but this is my only example, and may not be typical.

20. These generalizations are founded on reading the many articles of agreement between privateer owners and their crews in ADM 43: e.g. ADM 43/14, Nos.1178, 1299, 1359, 1508, 1509; ADM 43/16, Nos.679, 680, 782, 715.

21. *London Gazette*, No.9542, 30 Dec 1755.

22. Brown, 'Privateering', pp.25 & 29; the mean size of privateers presumably increased after the 1759 Privateering Act forbade the issue of letters of marque to ships of less than 100 tons (*ibid.*, p.22).

23. As n.20 above.

24. See Ch. VD p. 185.

25. Press, 'Seamen of Bristol', App.IX.

26. As n.20 above.

27. For which process see Rodger, *Naval Records*, Ch.IV.

28. Appendix VI.

29. ADM 1/654, T. Smith, 20 Aug 1757. Surry & Thomas, *Book of Original Entries*, p.73. W.S.L.: H.M. Drakeford MS 2; *idem*, MS 22, E. Jasper to R. Drakeford, 11 May 1736. Baugh, *Naval Administration in the Age of Walpole*, p.227.

30. ADM 1/90, f.344. ADM 1/920, H. Osborn, 30 Oct 1755. Gradish, 'Wages and Manning', p.60.

31. Baugh, *Naval Administration 1715–50*, p.161.

32. ADM 30/44, p.54. This strengthened earlier legislation to the same effect.

33. ADM 1/925, enc. to C. Knowles, 29 Nov 1757.

34. ADM 49/80, p.69.

35. Kemp, 'Boscawen's Letters', pp.177 & 197.

36. ADM 33/539, pay book of *Jamaica* sloop with assignments of wages to Capt. S. Hood. Gwyn, *Enterprising Admiral*, pp.162 & 166.

37. Gradish, 'Wages and Manning', pp. 48–53. Gradish, *Manning*, pp. 89 & 95. For an insight into the administrative difficulties of paying ships more frequently see ADM 14/179, No.813.

38. ADM 1/654, T. Smith, 20 Aug 1757. PRO 30/20/7, G.B. Rodney to R. Hughes, 15 Jan 1760. ADM 1/1487, P. Brett, 19 Mar 1756.

39. ADM 1/939, F. Holburne, 13 Feb 1763. Pares, 'Manning of the Navy', p.37. Gradish, 'Wages and Manning', p.57.

40. Baugh, *Naval Administration 1715–50*, p.165. ADM 1/384, E. Boscawen, 10 Apr 1759. ADM 1/715, W. Boys, 22 Dec 1758.

41. ADM 1/235, T. Cotes, 5 Jul 1756. ADM 1/927, F. Holburne, 6 Sep 1758. ADM 1/930, F. Holburne, 12 Oct 1759.

42. ADM 1/2659, W.S. Willett, 31 Mar 1754.

43. ADM 1/930, F. Holburne, 29 Oct 1759.

44. Ch.VE p.198.

45. Barnes & Owen, *Sandwich Papers* III,246 n.1.

46. Gradish, *Manning*, pp.98–99. ADM 32/76.

47. ADM 174/291. Appendix IX.

48. ADM 33/547.

49. J.S. Bromley, 'Prize Office and Prize Agency at Portsmouth, 1689–1748', p.170, in J. Webb, N. Yates & S.

Peacock, eds., *Hampshire Studies* (Portsmouth, 1981). Corbett, *Seven Years' War*, p.321. Beatson, *Memoirs*, p.419.

50. Gardner, *Above and Under Hatches*, p.10.

51. Kemp, 'Boscawen's Letters', p.238.

52. ADM 1/162, f.191. ADM 1/383, f.507. Ranft, *Vernon Papers*, p.338.

53. Rodger, 'Douglas Papers', pp.268 & 270.

54. Mackay, *Hawke*, p.227. N.M.M.: HWK/14, E. Hawke to A. Hervey, 30 Sep 1759. *D.N.B.* sv. Hervey. Beatson, *Memoirs*, p.326.

55. Erskine, *Hervey's Journal*, p.250. ADM 1/5297, CM of Capt. P. Cuming, 5–6 Dec 1758. H.L.: STG 21 No.24, T. Brett to G. Grenville, 20 Mar 1746.

56. ADM 7/299, No.40.

CHAPTER IVD

1. Rodger, 'Stragglers and Deserters', p.58.

2. ADM 1/384, T. Broderick, 3 Apr 1760. Another example: ADM 1/927, F. Holburne, 6 Sep 1758.

3. ADM 1/90, f.595. ADM 1/714, H. Powlett, 15 Aug 1757. ADM 1/1895, Howe, 8 Jan 1760, & R. Harland, 27 Jan 1760.

4. ADM 1/719, W. Gordon, 23 Sep 1762. ADM 1/715, F. Geary, 6 Feb 1758. Baugh, *Naval Administration in the Age of Walpole*, p.209. Gradish, *Manning*, p.113.

5. ADM 1/925, C. Knowles, 9 Nov 1757. ADM 1/926, T. Broderick, 29 Jan 1758.

6. ADM 1/578, H. Osborn, 3 Aug 1758. ADM 1/922, H. Osborn, 6 Jul 1756.

7. ADM 1/929, F. Holburne, 31 Aug 1759.

8. Anderson, 'Prisoners of War', p.89. ADM 1/717, W. Boys, 1 Dec 1760. ADM 36/6554–6555, SLVO Nos.

18498–18572. ADM 36/5942. ADM 1/932, P. Durell, 22 Aug 1760.

9. Rodger, 'Stragglers & Deserters', n.37. ADM 1/90, f.440. ADM 1/716, L. Leslie, 27 Nov 1759. ADM 1/920, E. Hawke, 17 Jun 1755. ADM 1/923, H. Osborn, 23 Oct 1756.

10. ADM 1/2245, L. O'Bryen, [Nov. 1757].

11. Williams, 'Sandwich's Naval Administration', p.493.

12. ADM 1/650, T. Smith, 12 Sep 1755. ADM 1/654, T. Smith, 12 Oct 1757. ADM 1/924, E. Boscawen, 3 Mar 1757.

13. ADM 36/5454–5456, men turned over from *Revenge*. N.M.M.: LBK/35A, f.4. ADM 1/923, H. Osborn, 18 Sep 1756.

14. ADM 1/717, W. Boys, 20 Apr 1760. ADM 1/930, F. Holburne, 9 Oct 1759.

15. ADM 1/651, T. Smith, 31 May 1756. ADM 1/235, T. Cotes, 5 Jul 1756. ADM 1/935, F. Holburne, 17 Jun 1761. ADM 1/933, F. Holburne, 10 Nov 1760. ADM 1/1606, A. Campbell, 2 Dec 1757.

16. ADM 1/717, L. Leslie, 5 Jan 1760. ADM 36/6788, SLVO Nos. 385ff. ADM 1/924, E. Boscawen, 17 Mar 1757. ADM 1/938, F. Holburne, 4 Aug 1762.

17. ADM 1/933, P. Durell, 29 Sep 1760. Another example: ADM 1/717, W. Boys, 22 Oct 1760.

18. ADM 1/802, H. Harrison, 13 Oct 1758.

19. Rodger, 'Stragglers and Deserters', p.59.

20. ADM 1/5297, CM of R. Jenkins *et al.*, 11 Jan 1758, & of F. Green, 2 Mar 1758. ADM 7/744, E. Hughes, 18 Jan 1757.

21. ADM 1/933, enc. to F. Holburne, 29 Dec 1760. ADM 1/926, T. Broderick, 29 Jan 1758.

22. ADM 1/932, enc. to P. Durell, 10 Jul 1760.

23. ADM 1/5296, f.183. N.M.M.: TID/16, order of 12 Apr 1761. Erskine, *Hervey's Journal*, p.260.

24. ADM 1/5298, CM of W. Howson, 24 Jul 1759. ADM 1/650, T. Smith, 23 Aug 1755. ADM 1/928, enc. to F. Holburne, 26 Feb 1759.

25. ADM 36/5734. ADM 36/5790. ADM 1/653, T. Smith, 23 Feb 1757.

CHAPTER VA

1. Perrichet, 'Administration des Classes', p.99. Le Goff, 'Offre et productivité' & 'Naval Recruitment'.

2. Notably by Neale, 'Cost of Impressment' and 'Power and Profit'.

3. N.M.M.: ADM/B/161, 10 & 19 Jan 1759. *House of Commons Journal* (1803 printing) XXVIII, pp.281–282. ADM 106/2191, pp.24 & 49. N.M.M.: ELL/9, note by D. Devert, 11 Jan 1759.

4. E.g. Gradish, *Manning*, p.215.

5. Appendix XI. ADM 106/2190, pp.56 & 65–70.

6. Gradish, *Manning*, p.216. For Slain Lists see Rodger, *Naval Records*, p.43.

7. Appendix VI.

8. Appendix XI.

9. ADM 106/2190, p.141. Appendix XI. The figures presented by Gradish (*Manning*, p.116) in this connection are meaningless without reference to the total number of men borne in each category.

10. Bromley, *Manning Pamphlets*, p.xxx. Vaughan, *Commodore Walker*, p.94. Hutchinson, *Press-Gang*, p.20.

11. Bromley, *Manning Pamphlets*, *passim*.

12. Gradish, *Manning*, p.204.

13. B.M.: Add.MSS 38340, f.17. In the copy in the Mulgrave Castle MSS (VI, 1/401) the figure for 1762 differs slightly, probably from a copying error in one or other version.

14. Ralph Davis, 'Seamen's Sixpences: An Index of Commercial Activity, 1697–1828', *Economica* N.S.XXIII

(1956), p.328. Davis, *English Shipping Industry*, p.323. Brown, 'Privateering', p.30.

15. PC 1/6 No.38. ADM 1/1487, H. Barnsley, 1 Mar 1756. N.M.M.: ELL/9 & CLE/4/1, Instructions annexed to Press Warrants. Hutchinson, *Press-Gang*, p.77, maintains the contrary.

16. ADM 1/1441, T. Allison, 18 Mar 1756. ADM 7/298, No.99.

17. ADM 1/5299, f.641. N.M.M.: COO/1 p.21. Spavens, *Narrative*, p.36.

18. Baugh, *Naval Administration in the Age of Walpole*, pp.149, 159–161. Lloyd, *British Seaman*, pp.149–151. See also Bromley, 'British Navy and Its Seamen'.

19. Lloyd, *British Seaman*, p.182. Baugh, *Naval Administration in the Age of Walpole*, p.238.

20. ADM 1/925, T. Broderick, 4 Aug 1757. N.M.M.: CLE/3/3, M. Clements, Feb 1758.

21. M.C.: VI, 11/12, Sandwich to Mulgrave, 24 Dec 1776.

22. ADM 7/418 & 420.

23. ADM 1/930, F. Holburne, 19 Nov 1759.

24. ADM 1/933, F. Holburne, 9 Nov 1760. ADM 1/934, F. Holburne, 13 Jan 1761.

CHAPTER VB

1. Appendix III.

2. ADM 36/7158.

3. ADM 17/223.

4. ADM 1/235, T. Cotes, 3 Aug 1755. ADM 1/1892, J. Hales, 9 May 1757. ADM 1/1488, W. Bayne, 23 Dec 1757.

5. ADM 1/928, F. Holburne, 10 Jan 1759.

6. M.C.: VI, 10/249, C. Middleton to Mulgrave, 11 Nov 1776.

7. The point will be evident from any study of the musters of ships commissioning in peacetime.

8. ADM 1/714, T. West, 5 Mar 1755.

9. ADM 1/928, F. Holburne, 25 Apr 1759. ADM 1/1488, T. Baillie, 30 Apr

1757. N.M.M.: HWK/10, J. Clevland to E. Hawke, 27 May 1755.

10. Syrett, *Havana*, p.255.

11. Kemp, 'Boscawen's Letters', pp.173–174. ADM 36/5853–5855.

12. ADM 1/921, H. Osborn, 15 Apr 1756. ADM 1/939, F. Holburne, 12 Jun 1763. ADM 1/924, E. Boscawen, 21 Feb 1757.

13. ADM 33/685.

14. ADM 36/8017. Sir J. B. Paul, ed., *The Scots Peerage* (Edinburgh, 1904–14, 9 vols.) V, 316.

15. ADM 36/8139.

16. Bromley, 'British Navy and Its Seamen', pp.154–155. ADM 1/717, enc. to L. Leslie, 6 Feb 1760. Harriott, *Struggles through Life*, p.63. ADM 1/4120 *passim* for ambassadors' complaints. Ships' musters *passim*, e.g. ADM 36/8017 & 8139.

17. ADM 1/1442, E. Affleck, 6 Jul 1759. ADM 1/933, P. Durell, 11 Oct 1760. ADM 1/924, E. Boscawen, 27 Feb 1757. ADM 36/6546, SLVO Nos. 14150 & 14151.

18. ADM 36/5234, entries in July & August 1757. ADM 36/7083, entries at St Helena. N.M.M.: TID/8, H. Powlett to R. Tiddeman, 26 Mar 1749.

19. ADM 1/656, J. Moore, 18 Dec 1761. ADM 1/651, T. Smith, 24 Feb 1756. Beatson, *Memoirs*, p.449. ADM 1/658, J. Moore, 25 Aug 1762.

20. N.M.M.: HWK/3, 17 Apr 1755. ADM 1/715, W. Boys, 4 Aug 1758. B.M.: Add.MSS 32726, f.169.

21. ADM 1/654, enc. to T. Smith, 27 Aug 1757. ADM 1/924, T. Broderick, 30 Jun 1757. ADM 1/91, f.193. ADM 33/547, *Barfleur*, entries 8 & 27 May 1758. Anderson, 'Prisoners of War', p.87.

22. ADM 1/803, enc. to P. Durell, 8 Jan '1761' [1762]. ADM 1/936, F. Holburne, 6 Oct 1761. ADM 1/937, F. Holburne, 3 Jan 1762. ADM 1/657, enc. to J. Moore, 13 Jan 1762.

23. ADM 1/657, J. Moore, 28 May 1762.

24. ADM 1/1487, P. Baird, 2 Mar 1756. Bellamy, *Ramblin' Jack*, p.134. Blake, *Marine System*, p.57. PRO 30/8/78, f.63. ADM 49/3.

25. Syrett, *Havana*, p.49. PRO 30/20/6, S. Mostyn to G.B. Rodney, 28 May 1756.

26. *Pace* Hutchinson, *Press-Gang*, pp.200–201. Lloyd, *British Seaman*, p.136. Bromley, 'British Navy and Its Seamen', p.153. But see also ADM 1/4122, 31 Oct 1757 & 15 Jul 1758.

27. George, *London Life*, p.307. ADM 49/64. ADM 1/925, T. Broderick, 10 Jul 1757.

28. J. Boswell, *Life of Johnson* (ed. Chapman & Fleeman, Oxford, 1970), p.246.

29. In this I disagree with Pares, 'Manning of the Navy', p.32.

30. ADM 33/539, letter attached to *Jamaica*'s pay book. N.M.M.: LBK/63, W. Cornwallis to W. Burnaby, 4 Mar 1766.

31. ADM 1/5300, CM of G. Newton & T. Finlay.

32. ADM 1/236 f.60. CO 142/31 f.15. PROB 11/959 f.301.

33. Rodger, 'Douglas Papers', pp.264 & 275.

34. ADM 1/306, T. Frankland, 6 Jul 1757. Pares, 'Manning of the Navy', p.32. N.M.M.: ROD/1, R. Roddam to Gov. of Cap François, 11 Apr 1757.

35. ADM 33/542, Capt. Innes's followers Aberdeen, Tom Jupiter & Fortune.

36. N.M.M.: TID/31.

37. ADM 1/718, L. Leslie, 10 Oct 1761. ADM 1/482, f.244.

38. ADM 1/927, F. Holburne, 18 Dec 1758.

39. *Advice to Officers*, p.29. ADM 36/7083, entries at St Helena.

40. ADM 1/927, F. Holburne, 17, 22 & 27 Dec 1758.

41. ADM 1/307, J. Douglas, 25 Jul 1760 & 6 Feb 1761. Rodger, 'Douglas Papers', pp.245, 253–254, 257, 259, 261–2 & 267.

42. ADM 1/5299, f.110. ADM 1/1486, W. Boys, 7 Nov 1755.
43. ADM 1/920, enc. to H. Osborn, 15 Nov 1755.
44. Kemp, *British Sailor*, p.129. Bromley, *Manning Pamphlets*, p.98 n.2. Lloyd, *British Seaman*, pp.184–185. Hutchins, *Hanway*, pp.81–85.
45. P. McGrath, *The Merchant Venturers of Bristol* (Bristol, 1975), p.171. ADM 1/88, F. Holburne, 14 Nov 1756.
46. WO 34/42, f.8.
47. E. Gillett & K.A. MacMahon, *A History of Hull* (Hull, 1980), p.235. ADM 1/929, F. Holburne, 31 Jul 1759.
48. ADM 1/927, F. Holburne, 26 Oct 1758.
49. ADM 1/655, enc. to E. Wheeler to P. Brett, 29 Jan 1760.
50. N.M.M.: HWK/10, J. Clevland to E. Hawke, 11 Aug 1757. ADM 1/1486, P. Baird, 29 Apr 1755. Middleton, 'Administration of Newcastle and Pitt', p.74.
51. ADM 1/650, T. Smith, 8 Sep 1755.
52. ADM 1/801, enc. to H. Harrison, 6 Mar 1757. Appendix IV.

CHAPTER VC

1. Norman Baker, 'Changing Attitudes towards Government in Eighteenth-Century Britain', in *Statesmen, Scholars and Merchants*, ed. Anne Whiteman, J.S. Bromley & P.G.M. Dickson (Oxford, 1973), p.209.
2. Bromley, *Manning Pamphlets*, pp.xxx–xlii, gives the history of eighteenth-century attempts to establish some sort of registration or conscription of seamen.
3. *Pace* Bromley, *Manning Pamphlets*, p.124 n.2, it was in use during this war.
4. Lloyd, *British Seaman*, Ch.VII. Baugh, *Naval Administration in the Age of Walpole*, pp.149–153. Gradish, *Manning*, pp. 56–60. Hutchinson, *Press-Gang*, pp.57–65, on this as most other subjects, combines much useful research with the most extravagantly prejudiced opinions.
5. ADM 1/1487, H. Barnsley, 10 Mar 1756.
6. N.M.M.: COO/1, pp. 15–16. PRO 30/20/6, G.B. Rodney, 26 Sep 1756.
7. ADM 1/919, E. Hawke, 21 Feb 1755.
8. Gradish, *Manning*, p.215. Hutchins, *Hanway*, p.80. Hutchinson, *Press-Gang*, p.326.
9. N.M.M.: COO/1, pp.15 & 22.
10. *Ibid.*, p.15.
11. ADM 1/5166, 16 Mar 1763. ADM 1/803, P. Durell, 5 Jan 1762.
12. ADM 1/5167, 24 Jul 1767. PC 1/8/83. ADM 1/1486, P. Baird, 6 Jun 1755. ADM 1/1488, J. Bover, 7 Jun 1757.
13. Hutchinson, *Press-Gang*, p.57. ADM 1/653, T. Smith, 4 Feb 1757.
14. ADM 1/929, F. Holburne, 28 Jul 1759. ADM 1/933, F. Holburne, 11 Nov 1760.
15. ADM 1/922, H. Osborn, 4 Jul 1756. ADM 1/921, H. Osborn, 26 Apr 1755.
16. ADM 1/89, f.136.
17. ADM 1/480, f.581.
18. ADM 1/88, F. Holburne, 18 Mar 1756.
19. ADM 1/936, F. Holburne, 29 Oct 1761.
20. N.M.M.: COO/1 p.15.
21. ADM 1/1608, T. Cleland, 20 Nov 1762. ADM 1/1486, P. Baird *passim*.
22. ADM 7/298, No.102.
23. Baugh, *Naval Administration in the Age of Walpole*, p.149. Middleton, 'Administration of Newcastle and Pitt', p.82. George, *London Life*, pp.141–142. PC 1/6 No.71.
24. ADM 3/70, 23 Aug 1762. ADM 1/1787, J. Fortescue, 4 & 11 Aug, 6 & 10 Sep, 12 Dec 1761. ADM 1/1788, J. Fortescue, 19 Feb, 19 Mar, 5 Aug & 12 Sep 1762. ADM 1/1488, G. Blyke, 26 Nov 1757.
25. Bonner-Smith, *Barrington Papers*

I,150. ADM 1/1488, enc. to W. Boys, 4 Apr 1757.

26. ADM 1/578, S. Graves, 3 Apr 1765. ADM 1/801, H. Harrison, 12 & 14 Aug 1757. Namier & Brooke, *House of Commons 1754–90* I,284.

27. ADM 1/801, H. Harrison, 3 Aug 1757.

28. ADM 1/932, F. Holburne, 5 May 1760. ADM 49/64. ADM 1/307, J. Moore, 3 Oct 1759.

29. ADM 1/1787, W. Fortescue, 10 Jan 1760.

30. ADM 1/1486, W. Boys, 27 Nov 1755. ADM 1/1487, W. Boys, 6 May 1756. Hutchinson, *Press Gang*, pp.205–206.

31. ADM 7/298, No.99.

32. ADM 1/919, E. Hawke, 12 Feb & 29 May 1755. ADM 1/920, enc. to E. Hawke, 8 Jun 1755. ADM 1/1441, T. Allison, 18 Mar 1756.

33. ADM 2/1152 pp.451, 484–485, 489, 494 etc. ADM 1/5116/6.

34. Gradish, *Manning*, p.85. Bromley, 'British Navy and Its Seamen', p.153. Middleton, 'Administration of Newcastle and Pitt', p.86. ADM 36/7048, W. Scragg Ab. Lloyd, *British Seaman*, p.136, notes a possible case of a thief accepted by the Navy.

35. ADM 1/802, enc. to H. Harrison, 8 Oct 1758. ADM 1/927, enc. to F. Holburne, 10 Aug 1758. ADM 1/1487, W. Boys, 23 & 25 Mar & 8 Oct 1756. ADM 1/653, T. Smith, 21 Feb 1757.

36. ADM 1/1487, W. Boys, 21 Mar 1756. ADM 1/88, F. Holburne, 16 Mar 1756. Baugh, *Naval Administration in the Age of Walpole*, p.421.

37. Hutchinson, *Press-Gang*, p.313.

38. Thompson quoted by Geoffrey Marcus, *Quiberon Bay* (London, 1960), p.185, though I have not been able to trace the quotation. ADM 36/6731.

39. J.J. Tobias, *Crime and Police in England, 1700–1900* (London, 1979), p.10, quoting Fielding, *An Enquiry into the Causes of the Late Increase of Robbers* (London, 1751), p.76.

40. Basil Williams, *The Whig Supremacy, 1714–1760* (Oxford, 2nd ed. 1962), p.133.

41. Bellamy, *Ramblin' Jack*, p.101.

42. ADM 1/1488, S. Barrington, 25 Apr 1757. ADM 1/1787, W. Osborn to A. Forrest, 22 May 1760. ADM 1/1489, W. Burnaby, 6 Apr 1758. Bellamy, *Ramblin' Jack*, p.39.

43. ADM 1/1488, enc. to W. Boys, 4 Apr 1757.

44. ADM 1/650, T. Smith, 28 Dec 1755. Robinson, *British Tar*, p.358. ADM 1/919, enc. to E. Hawke, 26 May 1755. Hutchinson, *Press-Gang*, pp.188–189, 247–251, 260 & 271.

45. ADM 36/6554, SLVO No.18468. ADM 1/1487, E. Barber, 26 Jun 1756. George, *London Life*, p.230. ADM 106/2190, p.24.

46. Rodger, 'Stragglers and Deserters', p.64.

47. ADM 1/936, enc. to F. Holburne, 22 Oct 1761.

48. ADM 1/935, F. Holburne, 20 Aug 1761. N.M.M.: COO/1, p.18.

49. ADM 1/1478, E. Boscawen, 8 Aug 1742. ADM 1/5301, CM of J. Windover & J. Gibson, 15 Feb 1762. ADM 1/925, C. Knowles, 11 Nov 1757.

50. ADM 1/717, L. Leslie, 6 Feb 1760. ADM 1/803, P. Durell, 4 May 1762. The story related by Godfrey Anstruther, *The Seminary Priests* (Gt Wakering, Essex, 1966–77, 4 vols.) IV, 22 seems to have grown in the telling.

51. ADM 1/234, f.680. ADM 1/5116/10, Lord North, 14 Oct 1756.

52. ADM 1/306, T. Frankland, 13 Dec 1757.

53. ADM 1/650, T. Smith, 26 Aug 1755.

54. ADM 1/5299, f.606. ADM 1/5301, CM of S. Raycroft, 17 Aug 1762. ADM 1/5300, CM of R. Smith, 19 Feb 1761. ADM 1/482, f.443. ADM 1/5299, f.596. Powell, *Bristol Privateers*, p.206.

For background see Andrew Charlesworth, *An Atlas of Rural Protest in Britain, 1548–1900* (London, 1983), pp.48, 86 & 124.

55. ADM 1/1788, J. Fortescue, 27 Sep 1762.

56. *Ibid.*, 2 May & 27 Aug 1762. Williams, *Liverpool Privateers*, p.85.

57. Spavens, *Narrative*, pp.37–39. ADM 51/1029, 25 Jul 1759. Williams, *Liverpool Privateers*, pp.157–159, gives a characteristically lurid and inaccurate version of this incident.

58. Rodger, 'James & Thomas'. ADM 1/924, E. Boscawen, 21 Feb 1757. ADM 1/920, enc. to E. Hawke, 3 Jun 1755. N.M.M.: HWK/10, J. Clevland to E. Hawke, 30 May 1755.

59. ADM 1/718, W. Boys, 7 Jan 1761.

60. ADM 1/930, F. Holburne, 22 Oct 1759. ADM 1/931, F. Holburne, 8 Apr 1760.

61. Hutchinson, *Press-Gang*, pp.85–87. Bromley, 'British Navy and Its Seamen', p.157.

62. ADM 1/1788, J. Fortescue, 25 May 1762.

63. ADM 1/1486, P. Baird, 12 Apr 1755. ADM 1/1787, W. Osborn to A. Forrest, 22 May 1760.

64. ADM 1/650, W. Boys, 23 Aug 1755. ADM 1/931, enc. to F. Holburne, 29 Mar 1760.

65. Richmond, *Navy in War of 1739–48* I,268. Gradish, *Manning*, p.66.

66. PRO 30/20/6, Admiralty order of 21 Aug 1757.

67. N.M.M.: HWK/10, W. Hamock to E. Hawke, 11 Feb 1755.

68. ADM 1/919, E. Hawke, 18 Mar 1755.

69. N.M.M.: COO/1, p.17.

70. ADM 1/651, T. Smith, 6 Jan 1756. Middleton, 'Administration of Newcastle and Pitt', p.79. ADM 1/922, H. Osborn, 6 May 1756. ADM 1/919, E. Hawke, 29 Apr 1755. ADM 1/924, T. Broderick, 28 May 1757.

71. N.M.M.: COO/1, p.21.

72. ADM 1/4120, H. Fox to Admiralty, 5 Apr 1756. ADM 1/4121, 15 Sep 1756. ADM 36/6832, SLVO men pressed at Halifax. ADM 1/651, T. Smith, 7 Mar 1756. ADM 1/1489, F. Burslem, 5 Mar 1758. ADM 1/5116/10, J. Stevens, 27 Apr 1755.

73. ADM 1/1486, P. Baird, 27 Feb 1755. ADM 1/654, T. Smith, 20 Jul 1757.

74. ADM 1/651, T. Smith, 29 May 1756. ADM 1/926, T. Broderick, 9 Jan 1758. ADM 1/924, enc. to H. Osborn, 31 Mar 1757.

75. ADM 1/928, F. Holburne, 9 Apr 1759.

76. Pares, 'Manning of the Navy', pp.51–57. Baugh, *Naval Administration 1715–50*, pp.92–93. Gwyn, *Royal Navy and North America*, p.261. ADM 1/237, f.143.

77. Press, 'Seamen of Bristol', Ch.IV, p.8. Rodger, 'Douglas Papers', p.276. ADM 1/481, f.420.

78. PRO 30/20/6, H. Osborn to G.B. Rodney, 27 Jan 1756.

79. ADM 1/920, enc. to E. Hawke, 17 Jun 1755.

80. R. G. Marsden, ed., *Documents relating to the Law and Custom of the Sea* (N.R.S. XLIX & L, 1915–16, 2 vols) II,385–390. B.M.: Add.MSS 32726, f.169. ADM 1/651, T. Smith, 24 Feb 1756. ADM 1/658, J. Moore, 25 Aug 1762.

81. ADM 1/801, H. Harrison, 24 Dec 1756. ADM 1/1486, W. Brett, 1 Jun 1755.

82. ADM 1/88, F. Holburne, 11 Apr 1756. ADM 1/921, H. Osborn, 8 Mar 1756.

83. ADM 1/5116/10.

84. Charnock, *Biographia Navalis* VI,34–35. Thompson, *Sailor's Letters*, p.vii.

85. N.M.M.: HWK/10, G.B. Rodney to E. Hawke, 1 Jun 1755. PRO 30/20/6, G.B. Rodney to E. Hawke, 2

Jun 1755. ADM 1/5295, CM of Lt. R.Sax, 14 Nov 1755.

86. Baugh, *Naval Administration 1715–50*, p.127. ADM 1/1486, W. Brett, 30 Jun 1755. ADM 1/1441, E. Affleck, 10 Sep 1756.

87. Rodger, 'James and Thomas', p.297.

CHAPTER VD

1. ADM 1/718, W. Boys, 5 Jan 1761.

2. Bromley, *Manning Pamphlets*, p.109.

3. ADM 1/926, F. Holburne, 23 Mar 1758. Press, 'Seamen of Bristol', Ch.I, p.5. George, *London Life*, p.311. Blake *Marine System*, p.59. Hutchinson, *Press-Gang*, p.49.

4. ADM 1/925, E. Boscawen, 18 Dec 1757. ADM 7/299, Nos.6 & 21. ADM 1/923, H. Osborn, 23 Nov 1756.

5. ADM 1/1787, J. Fortescue, 29 Sep 1761.

6. Rodger, 'Stragglers and Deserters', p.64. ADM 1/928, F. Holburne, 4 Apr 1759. ADM 1/384, E. Boscawen, 11 Apr 1759. ADM 1/935, F. Holburne, 9 Jun 1761.

7. ADM 1/90, f.318. ADM 1/654, T. Smith, 11 Nov 1757.

8. Pares, *Colonial Blockade and Neutral Rights*, p.38.

9. ADM 7/89–90.

10. Press, 'Seamen of Bristol', Ch.I, p.3. See also W.E. Minchinton, *Politics and the Port of Bristol in the Eighteenth Century* (Bristol Records Soc., 1963), p.90.

11. Pares, 'Manning of the Navy', p.47. N.M.M.: DOU/6, p.18. ADM 1/1789, A. Forrest, 9 Feb 1764. Vaughan, *Commodore Walker*, pp.41–48. Rodger, 'Douglas Papers', p.280. Spavens, *Narrative*, p.49.

12. ADM 1/924, H. Osborn, 14 Apr 1757. ADM 1/926, F. Holburne, 19 Mar 1758. ADM 1/927, enc. to F. Holburne, 19 Oct 1758.

13. ADM 1/1606, A. Clevland, 5 Sep 1757.

14. Powell, *Bristol Privateers*, p.219. John Latimer, *The Annals of Bristol in the Eighteenth Century* (Bristol, 1893) II,321. Vaughan, *Commodore Walker*, pp.xiv, 74, 77, 83 & 134. Hutchinson, *Press-Gang*, p.133. ADM 1/926, F. Holburne, 21 Jun 1758. ADM 7/299, No.25.

15. Harriott, *Struggles through Life*, pp.64–73.

16. ADM 1/653, T. Smith, 21 Feb 1757. ADM 1/928, F. Holburne, 29 Mar & 22 Apr 1759.

17. ADM 1/306, T. Frankland, 6 Jul 1757.

18. ADM 1/384, C. Saunders, 9 Apr 1762.

19. ADM 1/90, ff.59 & 166. ADM 1/307, J. Douglas, 11 Apr 1761. ADM 1/384, T. Broderick, 30 Oct 1758. ADM 1/654, T. Smith, 20 Jul & 17 Aug 1757.

20. Powell, *Bristol Privateers*, p.186. H.S. Kent, *War and Trade in Northern Seas* (Cambridge, 1973), pp.144 & 148.

21. ADM 1/306, T. Frankland, 28 Apr 1757.

22. ADM 1/655, W. Boys, 27 May 1759. ADM 1/1488, G. Blyke, 1 Sep 1757. ADM 7/299 No.18.

23. Hutchinson, *Press-Gang*, p.133.

24. ADM 1/5297, CM of J. Owens, 11 Feb 1758. ADM 1/5301, CM of G. Houlder, 12 Jul 1762.

25. ADM 1/717, enc. to W. Boys, 24 Apr 1760.

26. Cobbett, *Parliamentary History* XV, pp.875ff. *Commons Journal* XXVIII, p.216. *Lords Journal* XXIX, pp.331, 337–341, 344–347, 352–353. Lilian Dickinson & Mary Stanton, eds., *An Eighteenth-Century Correspondence* (London, 1910), p.386.

27. ADM 1/927, F. Holburne, 24 Oct 1758.

28. *Ibid.*, 27 Oct 1758.

29. ADM 1/716, L. Leslie, 18 Nov 1759. ADM 1/928, F. Holburne, 11 Mar & 2 Apr 1759. ADM 1/930, F. Holburne, 21 Oct 1759.

CHAPTER VE

1. ADM 1/5299, f.614.
2. ADM 1/5297, CM of F. Green, 2 Mar 1758. ADM 1/652, T. Smith, 23 Aug 1756. ADM 1/930, F. Holburne, 1 Sep 1759. ADM 1/5298, CM of W. Howson, 24 Jul 1759. ADM 1/651, T. Smith, 22 Feb 1756.
3. ADM 1/1488, S. Barrington, 17 Apr 1757. ADM 1/801, T. West, 30 Jan 1756.
4. PC 1/6 No.39. These charges are a frequent entry in every pay book.
5. ADM 1/930, F. Holburne, 26 Dec 1759.
6. ADM 1/926, F. Holburne, 5 Apr 1758 & T. Broderick, 29 Jan 1758.
7. ADM 1/930, F. Holburne, 20 Nov 1759.
8. ADM 1/921, H. Osborn, 1 Apr 1756.
9. Spavens, Narrative, p.64.
10. N.M.M.: COO/1, p.21.
11. ADM 1/932, P. Durell, 10 Jul 1760.
12. PRO 30/20/6.
13. ADM 1/5297, CM of T. Wells, 27 Jul 1758.
14. ADM 1/2245, L. O'Bryen, 29 Nov 1757. ADM 1/5299, f.596. ADM 1/653, H. Powlett, 16 Jan 1757.
15. ADM 1/5296, f.273. ADM 1/5300, CM of H. Bell et al., 21 Apr 1761. ADM 1/5301, CM of J. Robinson, 15 Mar 1762; CM of J. Gissop et al., 12 Jul 1762. ADM 1/933, F. Holburne, 24 Dec 1760.
16. ADM 1/5297, CM of T. Ringspeare et al., 21 Jan 1758; see also ibid., CM of J. Wright, 6 Aug 1758.
17. Matcham, Russell, p.270.
18. ADM 1/519, enc. in W. Leaver to Anson, 10 Sep 1755.
19. ADM 1/651, T. Smith, 4 May

1756. ADM 1/653, H. Powlett, 27 Jan 1757.
20. Articles of War, Art.XVI. ADM 1/1985, G. Johnstone, 14 Mar 1760. PRO 30/20/6, H. Osborn to G.B. Rodney, 13 Sep 1756. ADM 1/932, P. Durell, 13 Jun 1760. ADM 1/1488, G. Balfour, 23 Aug 1757.
21. ADM 1/653, T. Smith, 23 Feb 1757. ADM 1/5300, CM of H. Bell et al., 21 Apr 1761.
22. ADM 12/22, p.12. ADM 1/801, S. Mostyn, 25 Feb 1756. ADM 1/1486, J. Byron, 30 May 1755.
23. ADM 3/70, 21 Mar 1763.
24. ADM 1/5301, f.148. ADM 1/939, F. Holburne, 25 Jul & 16 Aug 1763.
25. ADM 1/88, F. Holburne, 11 Feb 1756.
26. ADM 1/5299, f.667. ADM 1/1488, G. Balfour, 23 Aug 1757.
27. ADM 12/22, p.61. ADM 1/5300, CM of J. Grigg et al., 26 Oct 1761. ADM 36/5632. ADM 1/802, P. Durell, 27 Oct 1761.
28. Erskine, Hervey's Journal, p.294. ADM 1/235, T. Cotes, 5 Jul 1756.
29. ADM 1/717, W. Boys, 23 & 24 Dec 1760. ADM 1/718, W. Boys, 5 Feb 1761. ADM 36/7083. ADM 36/5934. ADM 1/1442, J. Amherst, 5 & 8 Feb, & 18 Apr 1761.
30. ADM 1/933, F. Holburne, 9 Nov 1760. ADM 1/1895, A. Hervey, 23 Nov 1760.
31. Appendix IV.
32. Appendix VI.
33. Advice to Officers, p.57. Rodger, 'Stragglers and Deserters', p.63.
34. ADM 1/718, W. Boys, 29 Jun 1761. ADM 1/936, F. Holburne, 7 Oct 1761. ADM 1/937, F. Holburne, 22 Jan 1762. ADM 1/924, T. Broderick, 17 May 1757.
35. ADM 1/925, T. Broderick, 18 Jul 1757.
36. ADM 1/803, P. Durell, 13 Aug 1762.
37. PRO 30/8/80, f.18. ADM 1/89,

f.185. ADM 1/5298, CM of J. Cowin, 23 Aug 1759.
38. Gradish, *Manning*, pp.89ff.
39. ADM 1/384, E. Boscawen, 10 Apr 1759. ADM 1/715, W. Boys, 22 Dec 1758. ADM 1/931, F. Holburne, 17 Mar 1760. ADM 1/934, F. Geary, 28 Mar 1761.
40. ADM 106/2190, p.139. I cannot account for the shortfall in the total borne, as compared with the figures given in Appendix XI.
41. Gradish, *Manning*, p.116.
42. Pares, 'Manning of the Navy', p.39; similar examples can be found in many pay books.
43. Spavens, *Narrative*, pp.63 & 76. N.M.M.: HWK/10, T. Hanway to E. Hawke, 6 Jun 1755.
44. Wallis, *Carteret's Voyage* I,110–111.
45. G.S. Graham, 'The Naval Defence of British North America, 1739–1763', *Transactions of the Royal Historical Society*, 4th Ser., XXX, p.100. Appendix V; see also any peacetime muster.
46. H.S. Kent, *War and Trade in Northern Seas* (Cambridge, 1973), p.26. Pares, 'Manning of the Navy', p.34. C.M. Andrews, *The Colonial Period of American History* (New Haven, 1938) IV,231. Conrad Gill, *Merchants and Mariners of the Eighteenth Century* (London, 1961), p.68. ADM 1/1487, T. Broderick, 15 Apr 1756.
47. Lewis R. Fischer, 'A Dereliction of Duty; The Problem of Desertion on Nineteenth Century Sailing Vessels', in Ommer & Panting, *Working Men*, p.55.
48. ADM 43/14, No.1509. Williams, *Liverpool Privateers*, p.134.
49. ADM 1/714, W. Boys, 30 Nov 1758. PRO 30/20/6, Art.VIII of Boscawen's orders of 28 May 1758. ADM 1/927, 15 Oct 1758.
50. Baugh, *Naval Administration in the Age of Walpole*, p.231.
51. Compare the numbers of volunteers and pressed men run in Appendix IV; but we really need to know the proportion of one to the other in the Service as a whole to state this with confidence.
52. ADM 7/745, E. Hughes to F. Holburne, 15 Apr 1760.
53. ADM 1/481, f.577. ADM 1/5297, CM of T. Hassey *et al.*, 7 Nov 1758. Erskine, *Hervey's Journal*, p.285.
54. ADM 1/717, L. Leslie, 23 Jan 1760. ADM 1/5299, f.110. Rodger, 'James & Thomas'.
55. ADM 12/22. Gradish, *Manning*, p.110, counts five men hanged from Admiralty Board minutes, but this takes no account of overseas commanders-in-chief, who could confirm sentences on their own authority. I know of at least six men hanged overseas during the war.
56. ADM 1/384, T. Broderick, 20 Aug 1759. N.M.M.: HWK/16, E. Hawke to Duke of York, 23 Jun 1762.
57. ADM 1/5297, CM of R. Jenkins, 11 Jan, & CM of W. Oakes, 8 Feb 1758. ADM 1/5299, f.17. ADM 1/5301, CM of D. Gannon, 8 Mar 1762 & CM of J. Bennet *et al.*, 17 Nov 1762.
58. ADM 1/5297, CM of R. Allen, 11 Jan 1758. ADM 1/5296, f.231.
59. ADM 36/6839, R 7 Jun 1760.
60. ADM 7/299, No.3. Hutchinson, *Press Gang*, p.301 n.2.
61. N.M.M.: ADM/B/161, 26 Mar 1759. ADM 1/924, T. Broderick, 3 Jun 1757. ADM 1/654, T. Smith, 25 Nov 1757.
62. ADM 3/70, 22 Mar 1763.
63. ADM 1/5297, CM of T. Ringspeare *et al.*, 21 Jan 1758.
64. Gradish, *Manning*, pp.111 & 212. Appendix XI.
65. Crewe, 'Naval Administration', pp.86, 92, 101, 107 & 112. Appendix V.
66. ADM 106/2190, p.141. Gradish, *Manning*, p.216.

67. ADM 1/653, T. Smith, 23 Feb 1757; the version printed by Gradish (*Manning*, p.113) is a paraphrase rather than a quotation.

CHAPTER VIA

1. Alan Davidson, *North Atlantic Seafood* (London, 1979), p.395.
2. Rodger, 'Douglas Papers', p.274.
3. PRO 30/20/20/11, p.17.
4. B.M.: Add.MSS 32902, f.390. Henry Fielding, *The Journal of a Voyage to Lisbon* (London, 1755), p.189.
5. N.M.M.: HWK/10, enc. to R. Hughes to E. Hawke, 22 Sep 1749. ADM 1/5297, CM of J. Ryan, 16 May 1758.
6. Harriott, *Struggles through Life*, p.99. Bulkeley & Cummins, *Voyage to the South Seas*, p.19. Bellamy, *Ramblin' Jack*, p.49.
7. ADM 1/384, T. Broderick, 17, 22 & 26 Apr 1758.
8. G.E. Mingay, *English Landed Society in the Eighteenth Century* (London, 1963), p.11.
9. ADM 1/801, C. Watson, 23 Nov 1753.
10. ADM 1/922, enc. to H. Osborn, 23 Jul 1756. ADM 1/930, F. Holburne, 30 Dec 1759.
11. ADM 1/935, F. Holburne, 16 Jun 1761.
12. Renney, 'Journal', p.107.
13. ADM 1/5298, CM of P. McMahon & W. Wilkinson, 20 Aug 1759.
14. ADM 49/64.
15. ADM 7/744, E. Hughes, 24 Jun 1757.
16. Art. XXXV.
17. ADM 7/299 No.3. ADM 1/1442, T. Allwright, 5 Oct 1759.
18. PRO 30/20/19.
19. Gilbert, 'Crime as Disorder' is a particularly ripe example.
20. Matcham, *Russell*, p.141. Baugh, *Naval Administration 1715–50*, p.71.

CHAPTER VIB

1. Daniel A. Baugh, 'Poverty, Protestantism and Political Economy: English Attitudes towards the Poor, 1660–1800', in S.B. Baxter, ed., *England's Rise to Greatness, 1660–1763* (Berkeley, 1983), p.75.
2. Rodger, 'Stragglers & Deserters', p.56.
3. Erskine, *Hervey's Journal*, p.176. ADM 1/5299, f.32.
4. ADM 1/5274, CM of Lt. E. Elwal *et al.*, 5 Jun 1741. ADM 1/5275, CM of Capt. W. Hervey, 19 Aug 1742.
5. ADM 1/235, T. Cotes, 22 Jan 1755. ADM 1/5299, f.424. ADM 1/5297, CM of Capt. P. Cuming *et al.*
6. ADM 1/921, enc. to H. Osborn, 16 Mar 1756. ADM 1/801, H. Harrison, 30 Dec 1757.
7. ADM 1/5294, CM of Capt. A. Campbell, 11 Sep 1751.
8. ADM 1/5298, CM of J. Halman & W. Teague, 8 Oct 1759.
9. ADM 1/803, P. Durell, 23 Feb 1762.
10. ADM 1/481, f.587. ADM 1/801, H. Harrison, 6 Mar 1757.
11. ADM 1/5300, CM of Lt J. Burr, 16 Jun 1761, & CM of W. Roach, 3 Nov 1761.
12. ADM 1/926, enc. to T. Broderick, 8 Jan 1758.
13. ADM 1/5299, f.160.
14. Spavens, *Narrative*, p.19.
15. Ranft, *Vernon Papers*, p.401.
16. ADM 1/5297, CM of Lt W. Nethersole, 6 May 1758. ADM 1/934, F. Holburne, 27 Apr 1761.
17. N.M.M.: HWK/10, J. Clevland to E. Hawke, 23 Feb 1755.
18. B.M.: Add.MSS 35193, ff.9–11. Wyndham, *Chronicles* II,54.
19. Gradish, *Manning*, p.177. N.M.M.: LBK/63, orders of 3 Jan 1765.
20. Lind, *Treatise of the Scurvy* (in Lloyd, *Health of Seamen*), p.13. ADM 1/2245, L. O'Bryen, 25 Oct 1758.

21. H.L.: HM 1000, G. Pocock, 25 Jul 1761. Rodger, 'Douglas Papers', pp.270–271. N.M.M.: HWK/15 E. Hawke to G. Cokburne, 20 Oct 1760. N.M.M.: Rosse Hawke MSS A6, E. Hawke to Anson, draft [Nov 1759]. ADM 1/938, F. Geary to J. Clevland (private), 20 Aug 1762.

CHAPTER VIC

1. ADM 1/934, enc. to F. Geary, 30 Apr 1761.
2. ADM 1/90, f.338.
3. ADM 1/650, T. Smith, 31 Oct 1755. ADM 1/651, T. Smith, 15 Feb 1756.
4. *Advice to Officers*, p.19. ADM 51/1001, 3–11 May 1755, cf. Kemp, 'Boscawen's Letters', pp.178 & 182. N.M.M.: PAK/1 *Neptune*, pp.203, 205 & 217 (cf. ADM 51/632, 21 Oct, 3 Nov & 21 Dec 1761); *Blenheim*, p.235 (cf. ADM 51/116, 7 Jul 1762); *Romney*, pp.262 & 277 (cf. ADM 51/793, 10 Sep 1763 & 5 Jan 1764). Kemp, *British Seaman*, p.245.
5. ADM 1/801, T. West, 30 Jan 1756.
6. ADM 1/5298, CM of F. Lally, 24 May 1759. ADM 1/5299, f.335.
7. ADM 1/934, enc. to F. Geary, 30 Apr 1761.
8. ADM 1/5297, CM of G. Liquorish, 18 Feb 1758. ADM 1/5298, CM of R. Wythe, 4 Jun 1759. ADM 1/5299 f.530. ADM 1/5300, CM of A. Vaughan, 5 Jan 1761.
9. ADM 7/298, No.98.
10. Erskine, *Hervey's Journal*, pp.78–84 & 311.
11. Art. XXXV.
12. Add. Art. 12. ADM 7/299 No.31.
13. ADM 1/923, H. Osborn, 21 Sep 1756. *Advice to Officers*, p.63.
14. ADM 1/5298, CM of R. Bird, 2 Jan 1759. ADM 1/939, F. Holburne, 4 Jan 1763 (in this case the court convicted, but the Admiralty cancelled the sentence as illegal). ADM 1/1488, J. Bentley, 28 Mar 1757.

15. ADM 1/938, F. Holburne, 15 Sep 1762. ADM 1/5301, 23 Sep 1762.
16. ADM 1/5298, 24 Jul 1759.
17. See Ch.VE, p.202.
18. ADM 1/5297, CM of W. Oakes, 8 Feb 1758. ADM 1/5298, 15 Jan 1759.
19. ADM 1/5299, f.17. ADM 1/1486, J. Byron, 30 May 1755.
20. ADM 1/5296, ff.82 & 133. ADM 1/5299, f.550. ADM 1/5301, CM of G. Jennings, 13 Sep 1762. ADM 1/929, F. Holburne, 22 Aug 1759.
21. ADM 1/91, f.352. ADM 1/5300, CM of W. Fairbrother, 15 Feb 1761.
22. ADM 1/5297, CM of T. Ringspeare *et al.*, 21 Jan 1758. ADM 1/5301, CM of J. Robinson.
23. ADM 1/5298, CM of J. Cowin, 23 Aug 1759. ADM 1/5300, CM of W. Scott, 1 Dec 1761. ADM 1/5297, CM of J. Ryan, 16 May 1758.
24. ADM 1/5297, 12 Jun 1758. ADM 1/161, f.275. H.L.: HM 1000, G. Pocock, 15 May 1761.
25. ADM 1/5297, CM of Lt W. Nethersole, 6 May 1758.
26. Douglas Hay, 'Property, Authority and the Criminal Law', in D. Hay *et al.*, *Albion's Fatal Tree* (London, 1975), pp.18 & 23.
27. Gilbert, 'Buggery and the British Navy', p.82.
28. Ch.VE n.55.
29. ADM 1/5299, f.320.
30. ADM 1/237, f.263. ADM 1/803, P. Durell, 13 Jul 1762.
31. ADM 1/927, F. Holburne, 19 Jul 1758. ADM 1/936, F. Holburne, 19 Oct 1761.
32. ADM 1/939, F. Holburne, 17 Jul 1763.
33. ADM 1/5301, CM of M. Billin, 13 May 1762.
34. ADM 1/5298, CM of W. Lewis *et al.*, 26 May 1759.
35. ADM 1/5296, ff.500 & 517. ADM 1/5299, ff.542, 556 & 730. ADM 1/5301, CM of P. Clarke, 13 Apr 1762.

Bulkeley & Cummins, *Voyage to the South Seas*, p.68.

36. ADM 1/5301, CM of J. Bryan *et al.*, 12 Oct 1762. Rodger, 'Douglas Papers', p.262.

37. ADM 1/932, enc. to P. Durell, 10 Jul 1760.

38. ADM 1/925, enc. to C. Knowles, 24 Nov 1757.

CHAPTER VID

1. See the *Gentleman's Magazine*, 1759, pp.566–568, for a letter of complaint purporting to be from a common seaman; its style and language are as far removed from that of a real seaman, and as close to that of an opposition politician, as could well be imagined, and the writer was evidently quite unfamiliar with naval life.

2. ADM 1/5297, CM of T. Wells, 27 Jul 1758.

3. ADM 1/939, F. Holburne, 15 May 1763.

4. ADM 1/5294, CM of Capt. A. Campbell, 11 Sep 1751.

5. ADM 1/924, E. Boscawen, 17 Mar 1757. ADM 1/939, F. Holburne, 25 Apr 1763.

6. PRO 30/20/7, G.B. Rodney to R. Hughes, 15 Jan 1760. ADM 1/1606, B. Clive, 2 Oct 1758.

7. N.M.M.: TID/14, R. Tiddeman, 28 Jan 1758.

8. ADM 1/655, P. Brett, 29 Feb 1760.

9. *Ibid.*, enc. to P. Brett, 30 Jan 1760.

10. ADM 1/480, f.655. Bonner-Smith, *Barrington Papers* I,145.

11. ADM 1/716, L. Leslie, 15 & 24 Sep 1759.

12. ADM 1/88, F. Holburne, 28 Mar 1756.

13. ADM 99/28, pp.327 & 340. ADM 99/29, pp.365, 381, 397, 407, 411–412.

14. ADM 1/802, 6 Nov 1759.

15. ADM 1/928, F. Holburne, 16 Mar 1759.

16. ADM 1/924, enc. to H. Osborn, 2 Apr 1757.

17. ADM 1/925, C. Knowles, 2 Dec 1757.

18. ADM 1/5297, 27 Jan 1758.

19. ADM 1/5295, CM of R. Bainbridge, 31 Dec 1755. ADM 1/650, T. Smith, 31 Oct 1755.

20. ADM 1/716, 28 Mar 1759. ADM 1/656, P. Brett, 1 Sep 1761. ADM 1/925, C. Knowles, 13 Oct 1757.

21. ADM 1/93, G.B. Rodney, 11 Feb 1761.

22. ADM 1/90, f.528. ADM 180/2, f.17.

23. Baugh, *Naval Administration 1715–50*, pp.142–143.

24. ADM 1/5294, CM of Capt. Vaughan, 13 Oct 1750. See also the case of Crane, Ch.VIB p.214.

25. ADM 1/89, f.156. ADM 1/5300, CM of W. Roach, 3 Nov 1761. ADM 1/801, H. Harrison, 6 Mar 1757. ADM 7/745, E. Hughes to F. Holburne, 15 Apr 1760. N.M.M.: LBK/35A, ff.19 & 23. ADM 1/1442, E. Affleck, 2 Aug 1759. ADM 1/1489, P. Brett, 7 May 1758.

26. ADM 1/929, F. Holburne, 20 May 1759. ADM 1/939, F. Holburne, 23 Aug 1763.

27. ADM 1/716, L. Leslie, 24 Sep 1759. H.M.C.: *Du Cane*, pp. 63–64.

28. ADM 1/715, W. Boys, 21 Sep 1758. ADM 1/5297, CM of H. Jackson, 21 Sep 1758. ADM 1/5294, 19 Dec 1751. ADM 1/5300, CM of men of *Centurion*, 21 Jul 1761.

29. ADM 1/5297, CM of Capt. P. Cuming, 5–6 Dec 1758.

30. ADM 1/922, enc. to H. Osborn, 8 Jun 1756.

31. ADM 1/925, enc. to C. Knowles, 15 Oct 1757.

32. Ch.IVC p.136.

33. ADM 1/5299, f.227.

34. ADM 1/5297, 30 Sep 1758.

35. *Ibid.*, 20 Jan 1758.

CHAPTER VIE

1. Baugh, *Naval Administration, 1715–50*, p.74.
2. ADM 1/519, C. Holmes, 1 Jul 1758.
3. ADM 1/934, F. Holburne, 9 Jan 1761. ADM 51/3782, 9 Jan 1761.
4. ADM 1/936, F. Holburne, 9 Oct 1761.
5. ADM 1/939, F. Holburne, 4 Apr 1763.
6. *Ibid.*, F. Holburne, 15 May 1763.
7. Baugh, *Naval Administration 1715–50*, pp.126 & 188.
8. ADM 1/930, F. Holburne, 30 Dec 1759. ADM 1/933, F. Holburne, 9 Nov 1760.
9. George Rudé, *The Crowd in History* (New York, 1964), p.254.
10. Bellamy, *Ramblin' Jack*, p.55.
11. Renney, 'Journal', pp.69 & 86.
12. ADM 1/939, F. Holburne, 2 Apr & 30 June 1763.
13. ADM 1/5301, 22 Mar 1762. ADM 1/803, P. Durell, 12 Mar '1761' [1762].
14. Laughton, *Barham Papers* I,xii.

CHAPTER VIF

1. For examples of masters' cowardice in action see: ADM 1/384, enc. to E. Boscawen, 9 Jun 1759; ADM 1/5296, f.299; ADM 1/5298, CM of E. Pomeroy, 6 Aug 1759.
2. Lavery, *Ship of the Line* II,145. Howard, *Sailing Ships of War*, p.185.
3. Schomberg, *Naval Chronology* I,270 & 366.
4. ADM 1/384, C. Saunders, 6 Jun 1761. Wyndham, *Chronicles* II,232.
5. Beatson, *Memoirs* III,430.
6. ADM 1/90, f.161.
7. ADM 1/237, f.65.
8. Renney, 'Journal', p.87.
9. ADM 1/161, ff.262–264 & 275. ADM 1/5297, CM of Capt. N. Vincent, 12 Jun 1758. H.L.: HM 1000, G. Pocock, 15 May 1761.
10. Richmond, *Navy in the War of 1739–48* II,1–57.

11. Kemp, 'Boscawen's Letters', p.228.
12. W.S.L.: HM Drakeford 22, S. Faulknor to R. Drakeford, 31 Aug 1756.
13. Wyndham, *Chronicles* II,233.
14. ADM 1/191, f.124.
15. ADM 1/235, M. Suckling to T. Cotes, 9 Sep 1758.
16. ADM 1/5298, 30–31 Mar 1759. ADM 1/383, ff.425 & 437.
17. J. Entick, *The General History of the Late War* (London, 1763–64, 5 vols.) III,58–59. Erskine, *Hervey's Journal*, pp.xxiv, 271–274. ADM 1/384, H. Osborn, 12 Mar 1758.
18. ADM 1/5294, 3–7 Dec 1750 & 1 Sep 1752. M.C.: VI,1/135, T. Corbett to H. Powlett, 8 Jun 1750. N.M.M.: GRI/24 & 25.
19. Charnock, *Biographia Navalis* IV,431.
20. Kemp, 'Boscawen's Letters', p.180. Williams, *Anson's Voyage*, p.31.
21. N.M.M.: PAK/1, *Dunkirk*, p.6.
22. Spinney, *Rodney*, p.187. See also S.R.O.: D 615/P(S)1/10, G.B. Rodney to Anson, 10 Feb 1762.
23. Kemp, 'Boscawen's Letters', p.238. B.M.: Add.MSS 32902, f.390.
24. M.C.: VI,1/441, A. Hervey to Sandwich, 13 Oct 1779.
25. Laughton, *Barham Papers* I,311.

CHAPTER VIIA

1. Baugh, *Naval Administration in the Age of Walpole*, p.110.
2. Bromley, *Manning Pamphlets*, p.112. N.M.M.: TID/31. ADM 7/678 No.10.
3. Keppel, *Keppel* I,301.
4. H.C.B. Rogers, *The British Army of the Eighteenth Century* (London, 1977), pp.53–57. Namier & Brooke, *House of Commons 1754–90* I,138. Houlding, *Fit for Service*, pp.100–107 & 272. J.H. Broomfield, 'Some Hundred Unreasonable Parliament Men', *Bulletin of the Society for Army*

Historical Research XXXIX (1961), p.91. Alan J. Guy, *Oeconomy and Discipline: Officership and Administration in the British Army, 1714-63* (Manchester, 1985), p.131.

5. Namier & Brooke, *House of Commons 1754-90* I,105 & 126. Edward Hughes, 'The Professions in the Eighteenth Century', *Durham University Journal* XLIV (1952), p.46.

6. L.S. Sutherland, *A London Merchant, 1695-1774* (Oxford, 1933), p.101. Hughes, *loc.cit.*, p.47. Namier & Brooke, *House of Commons 1754-90* I,142. Holmes, *Augustan England*, *passim*. L. & J.C.F. Stone, *An Open Elite? England 1540-1880* (Oxford, 1984), pp.229-230.

7. Namier & Brooke, *House of Commons 1754-90* II,400.

8. N.M.M.: COR/56, Lord Cornwallis to W. Cornwallis, 27 Jun 1761.

9. Wiggin, *Faction of Cousins*, p.65.

10. Sedgwick, *House of Commons 1715-54* II,255. G.E. Manwaring, *My Friend the Admiral* (London, 1931), p.4. *D.N.B.* s.vv. Barrington & Cornwallis. Namier & Brooke, *House of Commons 1754-90* III,245.

11. Bentley, *Bentley*, p.67. N.M.M.: COO/1 pp.8-9.

12. Sedgwick, *House of Commons 1715-54* II,206.

13. ADM 1/2245, L. O'Bryen, 8 Aug 1756.

14. E.H. Locker, *Memoirs of Celebrated Naval Commanders* (London, 1832) W. Locker, p.6.

15. Namier & Brooke, *House of Commons 1754-90* III,609. Marshall, *Biography* II,i,310.

16. Erskine, *Hervey's Journal*, p.xxx.

17. N.M.M.: Rosse Hawke H2, f.82.

18. Ch.IIC pp. 99 & 105.

19. ADM 6/424.

20. Davis, *English Shipping Industry*, p.68. ADM 7/352.

21. H.M.C.: *Du Cane*, p.188.

22. Kemp, 'Boscawen's Letters', p.219.

23. Erskine, *Hervey's Journal*, p.44.

24. Kemp, 'Boscawen's Letters', p.241.

25. Sedgwick, *House of Commons 1715-54* I,415. Gwyn, *Enterprising Admiral*, pp.19-20.

26. Syrett, *Havana*, pp. 298 & 305-313.

27. *D.N.B.* s.v. Saunders. Corbett, *Seven Years' War* II,321. Beatson, *Memoirs* III,419. ADM 43/14 No.1256.

28. Erskine, *Hervey's Journal*, p.xix.

29. B.M.: Add.MSS 35193, f.106.

30. N.M.M.: TID/31.

31. N.M.M.: ELL/400, Nos.23 & 31.

32. Philip Jenkins, *The Making of a Ruling Class: The Glamorgan Gentry, 1640-1790* (Cambridge, 1983), p.37. Taylor, *Sea Chaplains*, p.496.

33. PROB 11/960, f.383.

34. Beatson, *Memoirs* II,78.

35. Kate Hotblack, *Chatham's Colonial Policy* (London, 1917), p.119. Laughton, *Barham Papers* I,xvii.

36. PRO 30/20/20/4, p.55.

37. L.S. Sutherland, *A London Merchant* (Oxford, 1933), p.20.

38. Hills, 'Shipbuilding at Sandwich', pp.197-198.

39. ADM 1/5166, 14 Dec 1761. PROB 11/771, ff.307-308. PROB 11/873, f.54.

40. PROB 11/736, f.25. ADM 6/424. ADM 1/5167, 15 Sep 1769.

41. Gardner, *Above and Under Hatches*, pp.14 & 22. Wyndham, *Chronicles* II,113.

42. N.M.M.: ELL/400, No.4.

43. *Ibid.*, No.26.

44. Kemp, 'Boscawen's Letters', p.243.

45. N.M.M.: Rosse Hawke H2, ff.185 & B16, S. Barrington to Hawke, 22 May [1780].

46. E.F.D. Osborn, ed., *Political and Social Letters of a Lady of the Eighteenth Century* (London, 1898), p.31.

47. Richmond, *Navy in the War of 1739-48* I,xii.

48. *Ibid.* I,xii.
49. *Ibid.* I,39. Charnock, *Biographia Navalis* IV,78.
50. Wyndham, *Chronicles* II,110. Thompson, *Sailor's Letters*, p.144, is often quoted in this connection; he points in the right direction, but greatly exaggerates.
51. Robinson, *British Tar*, pp.81 & 274. Erskine, *Hervey's Journal*, p.80 n.4.
52. Erskine, *Hervey's Journal*, pp.89 & 141. PROB 11/1043, f.349.
53. Williams, *Anson's Voyage*, p.17. N.A.M. Rodger, 'The Galliot Hoy *Youfro Maria*', M.M. 68 (1982), p.210.
54. ADM 1/90, f.52. *D.N.B.* s.v. Charles Knowles. Erskine, *Hervey's Journal*, Ch.IV. Kemp, 'Boscawen's Letters', pp.185 & 190.
55. H.M.C.: *Du Cane*, p.81. Surry & Thomas, *Book of Original Entries*, p.xxii. *D.N.B.* s.v. John Blankett.
56. ADM 1/307, G.B. Rodney, 30 Sep 1763. ADM 1/481, f.578.
57. N.M.M.: ELL/400 No.16. C 108/361. Namier & Brooke, *House of Commons 1754–90* I,145. ADM 1/717, W. Boys, 1 Jun 1760. ADM 1/653, enc. to T. Smith, 8 Jun 1757.
58. ADM 1/715, W. Boys, 22 Sep 1758. Boys, *Luxborough Galley*, p.21.
59. Taylor, *Mathematical Practitioners*, pp.199 & 225. Howse, *Greenwich Time*, p.60.
60. *D.N.B.* s.v. J. Campbell. Matcham, *Russell*, p.175. Alexander was killed in action as a commander, or he would doubtless have risen further.
61. ADM 1/91, f.200. ADM 1/481, f.63. Bentley, *Bentley*, p.32.
62. ADM 1/5297, CM of W. Parker, 23 Nov, & of J. Cook, 11 Dec 1758. ADM 1/5298, CM of Lt R. Steel, 17 Feb 1759. ADM 1/5302, f.183.
63. ADM 1/88, F. Holburne, 1 Jul 1755. ADM 1/384, T. Broderick, 16 Jan & 31 Mar 1760. ADM 1/5297, CM

of Lt J. Richardson *et al.*, 25 Feb 1758. N.M.M.: TID/14, R. Tiddeman to C. Steevens, 14 May & 16 Jun 1760.
64. ADM 1/384, C. Saunders, 24 Oct 1761. Erskine, *Hervey's Journal*, p.278.
65. Davis, *English Shipping Industry*, p.159.
66. N.M.M.: TID/14, G. Pocock to R. Tiddeman, 21 Dec 1758. ADM 1/926, F. Holburne, 28 Feb 1758 (cf. ADM 36/6239) offers an example of an able seaman being offered command of a merchant ship.
67. Baugh, *Naval Administration in the Age of Walpole*, p.99, & *Naval Administration 1715–50*, p.38. PRO 30/20/19. Rodger, *Naval Records*, p.19. J.J. Cartwright, ed., *The Travels through England of Dr Richard Pococke* II (Camden Soc. N.S. XLIV), p.116.
68. Surry & Thomas, *Book of Original Entries*, p.xxii. ADM 1/928, F. Holburne & R. Hughes, 9 Apr 1759. ADM 6/427, pp.439–442. One experienced officer who did send his son to the Academy was Lucius O'Bryen; ADM 1/2245, O'Bryen, 8 Aug 1756.
69. ADM 1/5117/16.
70. ADM 107/4. Examples p.308 (N. Bateman), & ADM 107/3, p.372 (J. Clarke), p.501 (R. Carkett).
71. Appendix I.
72. ADM 1/926, enc. to T. Broderick, 23 Jan 1758. PROB 11/866, f.31.
73. M.C.: VI 10/249, C. Middleton to Mulgrave, 11 Nov 1776.
74. ADM 7/812, f.34. PROB 11/745, f.66. *D.N.B.* s.v. P. Brett.
75. Laughton, *Barham Papers* I,viii. *D.N.B.* s.v. Patton. George Mackaness, *The Life of Vice-Admiral William Bligh* (London, 2nd. ed., 1951), p.3. Hills, 'Shipbuilding at Sandwich', p.198.
76. ADM 1/2345, No.300. ADM 106/3006. ADM 11/1, p.284. ADM 106/2979, caulkers.
77. ADM 6/336.

78. ADM 6/18, pp.472 & 479.
79. ADM 6/86, 30 Aug 1744.
80. ADM 107/3, p.511.
81. Charnock, *Biographia Navalis* V,139; but there is nothing in his passing certificate (ADM 107/3, p.261) to substantiate it.
82. Charnock, op. cit., VI,546. *Naval Chronicle* II, p.549.
83. Beaglehole, *Cook*, p.3.
84. Ranft, *Vernon Papers*, pp.81, 100–101 & 147. PROB 11/959, f.301. CO 142/31, f.15.
85. Rodger, 'James & Thomas'.
86. ADM 107/5, p.380.
87. ADM 1/654, T. Smith, 28 Aug 1757. ADM 6/86, John Cleland, 1744/5.
88. ADM 107/4, p.299.
89. ADM 107/4, p.5.
90. ADM 1/717, W. Boys, 1 Jun 1760. ADM 1/5299, f.712.
91. Brian Tunstall, *The Anatomy of Neptune* (London, 1936), p.xv.
92. Appendix XI.
93. ADM 106/2972.
94. Wyndham, *Chronicles* II,52.
95. ADM 1/5297, CM of Capt. T. Pye, 1–4 Mar 1758. ADM 1/801, enc. to S. Mostyn, 8 Feb 1756. Equiano, *Narrative*, p.94.
96. Wyndham, *Chronicles* II,110.
97. Namier & Brooke, *House of Commons 1754–90* II,400.
98. N.M.M.: ELL/400, No.6.
99. Namier & Brooke, *House of Commons 1754–90* II,684. ADM 107/5, pp.282 & 197.
100. N.M.M.: Rosse Hawke A4, J.B. Kelly to Hawke, 26 Sep 1767. N.A.M. Rodger, 'The Royal Navy and Its Archives', *M.M.* (to be published), argues this.
101. ADM 107/4.
102. *D.N.B.* s.v. Howe. ADM 6/86, 24 May 1744.
103. Charnock, *Biographia Navalis* V,282. Bentley, *Bentley, passim*. PROB 11/974, f.322.

104. Boys, *Luxborough Galley*. RG 4/1003, f.15. ADM 1/5168, 20 Apr 1774. Kent Archives Office MS PRC/32/64/69.
105. Marcus, *Heart of Oak*, p.81. CO 140/75, pp. 30–31, 63 & 152. ADM 1/250, No.50. ADM 1/2322, No.176. ADM 36/7553. ADM 24/4, p.87. ADM 1/314, f.493. On the position of mulattos see Edward Braithwaite, *The Development of Creole Society in Jamaica, 1770–1820* (Oxford, 1971), pp.167 & 172–173.

CHAPTER VIIB

1. E.g. Michael Lewis, *The Navy of Britain* (London, 1948), pp.271 & 273.
2. Rodger, *Admiralty*, p.94, applies this to reform of naval administration.
3. Pritchard, 'French Navy 1748–62', p.149.
4. A.N. Ryan, ed., *The Saumarez Papers: The Baltic 1808–1812* (N.R.S. CX, 1968), p.xi.
5. I follow the argument of Harold Perkin, *The Origins of Modern English Society, 1780–1880* (London, 1969), Ch.II.
6. N.M.M.: TID/14, R. Tiddeman to T. Broderick, 20 Feb 1758.
7. Baugh, *Naval Administration in the Age of Walpole*, pp.124–126.
8. ADM 33/685, the pay book of the *Solebay*, commanded by Lucius O'Bryen in 1768, gives a good example. Among the young gentlemen of the ship can be identified several O'Bryens and Drurys of his family, some members of the intermarried Saumarez, Durell and Dobree naval families of Guernsey and Jersey (for which see Ryan, op. cit. n.4 above, pp.xi & 238), besides several others from his home county of Cork.
9. Wyndham, *Chronicles* II,120. N.M.M.: ELL/400, No.27.
10. Hood, *Hood*, p.11.
11. ADM 1/90, f.218.

12. N.M.M.: Rosse Hawke H2, ff.76–77.

13. ADM 1/91, f.372. See also PRO 30/20/8 p.303.

14. ADM 1/93, G.B. Rodney, 30 Jun & 11 Oct 1760.

15. Kemp, 'Boscawen's Letters', pp.239 & 253. N.M.M.: ELL/400 No.13.

16. H.M.C.: *Various VI*, p.299.

17. N.M.M.: ELL/400 No.5, W. Gordon to Minto, 4 Apr 1750.

18. Holmes, *Augustan England*, p.281.

19. Namier & Brooke, *House of Commons 1754–90* III,621.

20. Wiggin, *Faction of Cousins*, p.79.

21. Erskine, *Hervey's Journal*, p.252. Charnock, *Biographia Navalis* VI,403–404.

22. N.M.M.: Rosse Hawke H2, ff.1–7. Mackay, *Hawke*, p.51. E.H. Locker, *Memoirs of Celebrated Naval Commanders* (London, 1832) Hawke, p.15.

23. Mackay, *Hawke*, pp.91 & 124.

24. ADM 1/578, E. Hawke, 25 Dec 1762.

25. E.g. ADM 1/234, f.549; ADM 1/162, f.99; ADM 1/383, f.381; ADM 1/237, f.4; ADM 1/482, f.82; ADM 1/578, W. Rowley, 8 Aug 1756.

26. ADM 1/384, H. Osborn, 12 Jun 1757.

27. ADM 1/2245, L. O'Bryen, 5 Aug 1756.

28. ADM 1/1488, J. Bentley, 25 Dec 1757.

29. ADM 1/482, f.116. See also ADM 1/801, C. Watson, 25 Aug 1752.

30. Aspinall-Oglander, *Admiral's Wife*, p.218.

31. ADM 1/658, J. Moore, 4 Aug 1762. For a more junior member of the 'little Navy', a carpenter's mate, see ADM 1/934, enc. to F. Holburne, 2 Feb 1761.

32. ADM 1/5118/21, L. Gellie, 15 Nov 1790.

33. ADM 1/482, f. 530.

34. Schomberg, *Naval Chronology*, I,300. Ives, *Voyage*, p.180.

35. Erskine, *Hervey's Journal*, p.xxiv. N.M.M.: HWK/4, E. Hawke to T. Saumarez, 3 Jul 1756.

36. Baugh, *Naval Administration 1715–50*, p.71. ADM 1/5274, 25 Sep 1740. ADM 107/3 p.277.

37. ADM 1/5297, 5–6 Dec 1758.

38. Baugh, *Naval Administration 1715–50*, p.39.

39. Wyndham, *Chronicles* II,114.

40. ADM 1/384, C. Saunders, 30 Nov 1761.

41. ADM 1/235, T. Cotes to Anson, 29 Sep 1758.

42. PRO 30/20/20/5, p.1.

43. ADM 1/237, f.187.

44. ADM 1/162, f.139.

45. N.M.M.: UPC/2 No.110. S.R.O.: D 615/P(S)1/10, G.B. Rodney to Anson, 25 Mar 1762.

46. Smith, *Grenville Papers* II, 9ff.

47. *Ibid*. II,24. PRO 30/20/20/4, p.43.

48. ADM 1/235, T. Cotes, 26 Sep 1759.

49. ADM 1/90, f.52.

50. ADM 1/481, ff.82–86.

51. ADM 1/162, f.12.

52. ADM 1/481, ff.464–466.

53. ADM 1/307, J. Douglas, 30 May 1761. N.M.M.: DOU/6, p.20, J. Douglas, 16 Oct 1762.

54. ADM 1/384, E. Boscawen, 3 May 1759.

55. ADM 1/237, f.77.

56. ADM 1/384, C. Saunders, 17 Aug 1762. ADM 1/480, f.580.

57. Ch.VIIC p.304.

58. B.M.: Add.MSS 35359, f.376. Wyndham, *Chronicles* II,110.

59. Baugh, *Naval Administration in the Age of Walpole*, pp.117 & 122.

60. Rodger, 'Douglas Papers', p.263.

61. ADM 1/236, f.265.

62. N.M.M.: COR/56, A. Keppel to W. Cornwallis, 11 Jul 1764.

63. Keppel, *Keppel* I,131. H.M.C.: *Various VI*, pp. 307–308. Above, p.284.

64. Baugh, *Naval Administration 1715–50*, p.13.

65. H.L.: STG 22, No.14.

66. W.S.L.: HM Drakeford 22, J. Faulknor to R. Faulknor, 9 Jan 1751.

67. N.M.M.: Rosse Hawke H2, f.114.

68. N.M.M.: COO/1, p.43.

69. N.M.M.: COR/56, Cornwallis to W. Cornwallis, 14 Oct 1764.

70. PRO 30/20/20/5, p.1.

71. Erskine, *Hervey's Journal*, p.61.

72. N.M.M.: PAK/1, *Romney*, p.313. I am indebted to Mr A.W.H. Pearsall for drawing this reference to my attention.

73. ADM 50/4, 29 May 1765. N.M.M.: PAK/1, *Romney/Crown*, p.324.

74. ADM 3/73, 31 Jul 1765.

75. This was Pakenham's financial position when he inherited the title in 1766, and I assume that his father's must have been much the same a year earlier (though I do not know what portion the dowager Lady Longford retained, and the possibility must be admitted that he was impoverished in 1766 partly because he had been extravagant in 1765). I am indebted to Mr Thomas Pakenham for information about his ancestors' finances.

76. ADM 1/307, G.B. Rodney, 10 Feb, 31 May & 11 Dec 1762.

77. Namier, *Structure of Politics*, p.17 n.1.

78. N.M.M.: DOU/4, undated rough draft in Douglas's hand loose at p.123. Sir Nicholas Nicolas, *The Despatches and Letters of Vice-Admiral Nelson* (London, 1844–46, 7vols.) V,364.

79. ADM 1/307, J. Moore, 17 Jan 1760. ADM 1/91, f.279.

80. ADM 1/801, H. Harrison, 14 Jan 1757.

81. Erskine, *Hervey's Journal*, p.281.

82. Namier, *Structure of Politics*, p.34.

83. N.M.M.: ELL/400 No.26.

84. H.M.C.: *Various VI*, p.298. Spavens, *Narrative*, p.15.

85. ADM 1/92, f.25.

86. ADM 1/384, C. Saunders, 6 Apr 1761.

87. Beatson, *Memoirs* II,78.

88. Schomberg, *Naval Chronology* I,366. Powell, *Bristol Privateers*, pp.184, 193 & 217. I assume that the two persons of this distinctive name were the same, since they do not appear to have been at sea at the same time.

89. N.M.M.: ELL/400, Nos.22 & 24.

90. Beatson, *Memoirs* II,76. ADM 1/1488, T. Baillie [28 Mar 1757].

91. ADM 1/162, f.35.

92. ADM 1/655, T. Smith, 3 Jan 1758.

93. ADM 1/1488, T. Burnett, 20 Mar 1757. Beatson, *Memoirs* II,61.

94. ADM 1/5296, f.328. Beatson, *Memoirs* I,524. Schomberg, *Naval Chronology* I,271.

95. Namier & Brooke, *House of Commons 1754–90* III,44.

96. Russell, *Bedford Correspondence* I,214. Bentley, *Bentley*, p.29.

97. ADM 1/307, enc. to G.B. Rodney, 1 Jul 1762.

98. ADM 1/1486, W. Boys, 23 Oct 1755.

99. *D.N.B.* s.v. Ross, Sir J.L. ADM 36/6845.

100. N.M.M.: ELL/400, No.24.

101. ADM 1/653, T. Smith, 25 Feb 1757.

102. *Ibid.*, earlier letter of same day. Beatson, *Memoirs* II,82.

103. ADM 1/1895, S. Hood to Anson, 3 Jan 1760.

104. ADM 1/655, T. Smith, 3, 4 & 8 Jan 1758. ADM 3/18 p.543.

105. ADM 1/482, f.75. ADM 107/5, p.203. ADM 1/5165, 1 Feb 1759.

106. Ch.VIIA p.261.

107. ADM 1/384, H. Osborn, 12 Mar 1758. Erskine, *Hervey's Journal*, p.274. PRO 30/20/2011, p.17.

108. Baugh, *Naval Administration in the Age of Walpole*, pp.100–101.

109. M.C.: VI 10/109, J. Ibbetson to Mulgrave, 11 Nov 1776.
110. H.L.: STG 23, No.13, P.H. Ourry to G. Grenville, 23 Feb 1764.
111. Rodger, 'The Royal Navy and Its Archives', *M.M.*, (to be published).
112. Gardner, *Above and Under Hatches*, pp.75–89.
113. N.M.M.: UPC/3 No.10. ADM 1/715, W. Boys, 14 Dec 1758.
114. ADM 1/936, F. Geary, 15 Nov 1761.
115. ADM 1/927, F. Holburne, 17 Oct 1758.
116. Gwyn, *Royal Navy and N. America*, p.47.
117. Namier & Brooke, *House of Commons 1754–90* III,7. Keppel, *Keppel* I,328.
118. Baugh, *Naval Administration 1715–50*, p.42.
119. B.M.: Add.MSS 32865, f.251. Namier & Brooke, *House of Commons 1754–90* III,314. ADM 1/4121, 16 Jun 1756.
120. B.M.: Add.MSS 32865, f.222.
121. B.M.: Add.MSS 35359, f.407.
122. N.M.M.: Rosse Hawke H2, f.61.
123. Baugh, *Naval Administration in the Age of Walpole*, p.126. Erskine, *Hervey's Journal*, Ch.III.
124. Ilchester, *Letters to Lord Holland*, p.84. Smith, *Grenville Papers* I,232; Erskine (*Hervey's Journal*, p.79) takes this to refer to Anson, but Spinney (*Rodney*, p.141) is clearly right to read it as referring to Boscawen.
125. Erskine, *Hervey's Journal*, p.306.

CHAPTER VIIC

1. Baugh, *Naval Administration in the Age of Walpole*, pp.138–146 & 502.
2. Mackay, *Hawke*, p.188.
3. ADM 1/384, C. Saunders, 20 Mar 1757.
4. *Ibid.*, H. Osborn, 28 Oct 1757. ADM 1/578, H. Osborn, 31 Jan 1759.
5. N.M.M.: Rosse Hawke H2, f.120.
6. PRO 30/20/8, p.155.

7. Williams, 'Sandwich's Naval Administration', p.224.
8. ADM 1/306, T. Frankland, 19 Nov 1757.
9. G.B. Mundy, *The Life and Correspondence of the Late Admiral Lord Rodney* (London, 1830, 2vols.) I,47.
10. ADM 1/306, T. Frankland, 28 Feb 1757. Spavens, *Narrative*, p.14.
11. ADM 1/235, T. Cotes, 12 Jun 1758. ADM 1/656, P. Brett, 18 Jan 1761.
12. N.M.M.: DUF/9, J. Hollwall to R. Duff, 5 Jun 1762.
13. *Ibid.*, R. Duff, 2 Sep 1762.
14. ADM 1/306, T. Frankland, 12 May 1757.
15. *Ibid.*, T. Frankland, 11 Jun 1756 & 19 Feb 1757. ADM 1/236, f.40.
16. ADM 1/306, T. Frankland, 16 Jun 1757.
17. Ch.VIIB p.284. See also ADM 1/481, ff.216 & 224–225.
18. Rodger, 'Douglas Papers', pp.249 & 273–275. Syrett, *Havana*, pp.86–90.
19. Smith, *Grenville Papers* I,231.
20. ADM 1/384, S. Callis to E. Boscawen, 20 Aug 1759.
21. N.M.M.: ROD/1, p.55. ADM 6/19, p.87.
22. B.M.: Add.MSS 35359, f.401.
23. Mackay, *Hawke*, pp.194–197.
24. B.M.: Add.MSS 35359, ff.393–394.
25. *Ibid.*, f.410.
26. Richmond, *Navy in the War of 1739–48* II,182–183.
27. ADM 1/714, H. Powlett, 12 Sep 1757. ADM 1/716, W. Boys, 15 Feb 1759.
28. Wyndham, *Chronicles* II,245.
29. ADM 1/924, T. West, 27 Jan 1757.
30. Kemp, 'Boscawen's Letters', p.216. N.M.M.: DOU/4, p.115; CLE/3/2, C. Saunders to M. Clements, 1 Dec 1761.
31. Gwyn, *Royal Navy and North America*, pp.184 & 217.
32. PRO 30/20/20/4, p.2.
33. N.M.M.: UPC/3, Nos.12–19.

Cotes's handling of prizes taken before the outbreak of war also led to his being sued by the Treasury: see T 1/447, ff.1–105, T 1/453, ff.316–320, T 1/457, ff.243–244, T 1/458, ff.119–131 & 333–334.
34. B.M.: Add.MSS 35359, f.410.
35. Renney, 'Journal', p.83.
36. N.M.M.: ELL/400, No.37.

CHAPTER VIID

1. ADM 3/70, 24 Aug 1762.
2. Syrett, *Havana*, p.209.
3. ADM 1/235, F. Wyatt to G. Townshend, 20 May 1757.
4. Erskine, *Hervey's Journal*, p.xix.
5. Smith, *Grenville Papers* I,59.
6. Richard Pares, *King George III and the Politicians* (Oxford, 1953), p.19. Philip Lawson, *George Grenville, A Political Life* (Oxford, 1984), pp.48–50.
7. Smith, *Grenville Papers* I,60.
8. N.M.M.: CLE/4/1, 31 Jan 1760. Matcham, *Russell*, p.228. PROB 11/840, f.146. Gwyn, *Enterprising Admiral*, p.17.
9. B.M.: Add.MSS 35193, f.106. N.M.M.: DOU/4, p.233; ADL/X/13, 23 Aug 1755.
10. N.M.M.: PAK/1, *Dunkirk*, p.7. ADM 1/90, ff.538–539.
11. ADM 1/578, C. Knowles, 1 Mar 1759.
12. W.S.L.: HM Drakeford 22, T. Smith to R. Drakeford, 26 Apr 1755.
13. Ranft, *Vernon Papers*, p.262.
14. Pares, *Colonial Blockade and Neutral Rights*, pp.17–25. ADM 1/235, T. Cotes, 8 Oct 1757. PRO 30/20/7, G.B. Rodney to Spanish consul at Le Havre, 28 Jul 1760. Erskine, *Hervey's Journal*, pp.61, 186 & 189. Harriott, *Struggles through Life*, p.43.
15. Erskine, *Hervey's Journal*, p.260.
16. ADM 1/236, f.200.
17. Dickinson, 'Naval Diary', p.240. ADM 51/3765, 1 Jan 1760.
18. Baugh, *Naval Administration in*

the Age of Walpole, p.111. Erskine, *Hervey's Journal*, p.74.
19. N.M.M.: UPC/3 Nos.29–30 & 38.
20. ADM 1/482, f.179. WO 34/55, ff.25–26.
21. ADM 1/482, f.249. ADM 1/1443, E. Affleck, 1 Jan 1763. Erskine, *Hervey's Journal*, p.143.
22. N.M.M.: DOU/4, p.187.
23. N.M.M.: UPC/3, Nos.27–38.
24. Gwyn, *Enterprising Admiral*, p.166.
25. PRO 30/20/8, pp.75 & 82. Rodger, 'Douglas Papers', p.275.
26. J.F. Bosher, 'The French Government's Motives in the *Affaire du Canada* 1761–1763', *E.H.R.* XCVI, p.64.
27. N.M.M.: TID/31.
28. PC 1/8/26. ADM 1/482, f.431.
29. Pares, *Colonial Blockade and Neutral Rights*, p.17 n.2. N.M.M.: TID/14, R. Tiddeman to C. Steevens, 14 May 1760. ADM 1/88, F. Holburne, 1 Jul 1755. ADM 1/384, T. Broderick, 16 Jan & 31 Mar 1760. ADM 1/5297, CM of Lt J. Richardson, 25 Feb 1758.
30. N.M.M.: HWK/10, Navy Board to E. Hawke, 29 Dec 1755 & 7 Feb 1756; ADM/B/149, 8 Nov 1754.
31. N.M.M.: HWK/11, J. Lendrick to E. Hawke, 26 Oct 1759; TID/14, G. Pocock to R. Tiddeman, 28 Jan 1760. ADM 1/5298, CM of W. Thompson, 1 Jan 1759.
32. ADM 1/939, F. Holburne, 15 May 1763.
33. ADM 1/924, T. Broderick, 9 Jun 1757. ADM 1/937, F. Geary, 24 Feb 1762.
34. ADM 1/924, E. Boscawen, 13 Mar 1757.
35. Corbett, *Seven Years' War* I,71.
36. N.M.M.: HWK/15, E. Hawke to J. Gambier, 10 Dec 1760.
37. ADM 1/235, T. Cotes, 15 Nov 1755.
38. ADM 1/936, F. Geary, 5 Nov 1761.

39. ADM 1/932, F. Holburne, 26 May 1760.
40. Erskine, *Hervey's Journal*, p.294.
41. H.B. Wheatley, ed., *Historical and Posthumous Memoirs of Sir Nathaniel William Wraxall, 1772–1784* (London, 1884, 5 vols.) I,223.
42. PRO 30/20/20/6, pp.9 & 40.
43. Smith, *Grenville Papers* I,221 & 232.
44. Falmouth MSS, *ex inf.* Major H.G.R. Boscawen.
45. Ch.IVB p.122. PRO 30/20/6, H. Osborn to G.B. Rodney, 13 Sep 1756 & S. Mostyn to G.B. Rodney, 31 May 1756.
46. PRO 30/20/8, p.284.
47. ADM 1/93, G.B. Rodney, 6 Jun 1759. Rodger, 'Douglas Papers', p.271. PRO 30/20/8, p.289.
48. Corbett, *Seven Years' War* I,315 & II,243. Pares, *War and Trade*, pp.282–283.
49. ADM 1/4120, 26 Nov 1755. PRO 30/20/20/1, p.37.
50. PRO 30/20/8, p.85.
51. PRO 30/20/7, W. Stiles to G.B. Rodney, 14 Feb 1761.
52. PRO 30/20/20/6, p.27.
53. ADM 1/237, f.127. ADM 1/307, G.B. Rodney, 31 May 1762.
54. PRO 30/20/20/5, p.61.
55. *Ibid.*, p.69.
56. Spinney, *Rodney*, p.354.

CHAPTER VIIIA

1. Baxter, 'Conduct of the Seven Years' War', p.330.
2. L.B. Namier, *England in the Age of the American Revolution* (London, 1930), p.236.
3. Russell, *Bedford Correspondence* I,216.
4. Namier, *Structure of Politics*, p.31. Sedgwick, *House of Commons 1715–54* I,155.
5. ADM 1/90, f.435. PRO 30/20/20/4, p.23.

6. Namier & Brooke, *House of Commons 1754–90* II,13. Surry & Thomas, *Book of Original Entries*, p.104.
7. Namier, *Structure of Politics*, pp.141–142. Namier & Brooke, *House of Commons 1754–90* I,54.
8. Baugh, *Naval Administration in the Age of Walpole*, p.318.
9. N.M.M.: Rosse Hawke A4, T. Hanway to E. Hawke, 16 Sep 1767.
10. Matcham, *Russell*, p.44.
11. Namier, *Structure of Politics*, pp.115–116 & 124. Baugh, *Naval Administration in the Age of Walpole*, pp.9 & 315–318.
12. Surry & Thomas, *Book of Original Entries*, p.lvi.
13. *Ibid.*, pp.xxvi–xxx & 73.
14. Namier, *Structure of Politics*, p.127.
15. Namier & Brooke, *House of Commons 1754–90* I,252.
16. B.M.: Add.MSS 32924, ff.266 & 412. The young man was Thomas Rawe; see ADM 36/5838, SB No.758.
17. PRO 30/20/20/4, p.15. ADM 1/658, J. Moore, 22 Dec 1762, (private).

CHAPTER VIIIB

1. Baxter, 'Conduct of the Seven Years' War', p.331.
2. Holmes, *Augustan England*, p.255; cf. S.E. Finer, 'Patronage and the Public Service', *Public Administration* XXX (1952), p.346.
3. W.R. Ward, 'Some Eighteenth-Century Civil Servants: The English Revenue Commissioners, 1754–98', *E.H.R.* LXX, p.35.
4. Namier & Brooke, *House of Commons 1754–90* III,314.
5. ADM 1/1441, Aylmer, 6 Jul [1756].
6. Namier, *Structure of Politics*, pp.250–252. Baugh, *Naval Administration 1715–50*, pp.32–34. Rodger, 'Victualling'.

7. Hutchins, *Hanway*, p.7.

8. Baxter, 'Conduct of the Seven Years' War', p.337.

9. Namier, *Structure of Politics*, p.33.

10. Sedgwick, *House of Commons* II,390.

11. Namier, *Structure of Politics*, p.250. Gradish, *Manning*, p.13. B.M.: Add.MSS 32892, f.96.

12. B.M.: Add.MSS 32900, ff.280 & 351.

13. S.R.O.: D 615/P(S)1/9, Newcastle to Anson, 2 Aug 1758.

14. N.M.M.: Rosse Hawke H2, ff.148-152.

15. *Ibid.*, 'Letter Book II', list of lieutenants for promotion.

16. ADM 1/236, f.3v.

17. ADM 1/5116/10, North, 14 Oct 1756.

18. ADM 1/481, f.59. Mackay, *Hawke*, p.220. Aspinall-Oglander, *Admiral's Wife*, p.209.

19. Wickwire, 'Admiralty Secretaries', pp.249-250. Namier, *Structure of Politics*, pp.41-42. ADM 1/578, F. Holburne, 6 May 1758. PRO 30/20/20/4, p.23. Namier & Brooke, *House of Commons 1754-90* II,221. Middleton, 'Administration of Newcastle & Pitt', p.63.

20. PROB 11/829, f.85. He died in 1757 a captain of fifteen years' seniority.

21. ADM 1/578, enc. to E. Boscawen, 18 Dec 1755.

22. Ranft, *Vernon Papers*, pp.39, 79, 149, 240 & 247.

23. B.M.: Add.MSS 32924, f.412; Add.MSS 32920, f.84; Add.MSS 35359, f.397.

24. B.M.: Add.MSS 35359, f.376.

25. Kemp, 'Boscawen's Letters', pp.179-180. ADM 51/1001, 4 May 1755. ADM 1/384, E. Boscawen, 15 Sep 1759.

26. ADM 1/90, f.55.

27. Kemp, 'Boscawen's Letters', p.179,

where the name is mistranscribed 'Janson'. N.M.M.: Rosse Hawke A4, H. Bankes to E. Hawke, 17 Sep 1767.

28. N.M.M.: ELL/400, No.51.

29. ADM 1/308, R. Tyrell to G. Grenville, 11 Apr 1763. ADM 1/481, f.467. See also ADM 1/920, E. Hawke, 11 Jun 1755.

30. N.M.M.: COO/1, p.4. ADM 1/2245, L. O'Bryen, 27 Dec 1755.

31. ADM 1/1489, P. Brett, 2 Mar 1758. ADM 6/14, f.63.

32. B.M.: Add.MSS 32892, f.96.

33. Namier, *Structure of Politics*, pp.33-34. Spinney, *Rodney*, p.164. ADM 1/5165, 27 Feb 1761.

34. Namier, *Structure of Politics*, p.314. Spinney, *Rodney*, p.174.

35. Spinney, *Rodney*, p.174. Corbett, *Seven Years' War* I,44. N.M.M.: Rosse Hawke H2, f.61.

36. Williams, 'Sandwich's Naval Administration', p.165. *D.N.B.* s.v. Pye.

37. Charnock, *Biographia Navalis* V,131. Williams, 'Sandwich's Naval Administration', p.165.

38. Baugh, *Naval Administration in the Age of Walpole*, pp.142-143.

39. *Ibid.*, p.70.

40. ADM 1/5298, 19 Mar 1759.

41. PRO 30/20/8, p.232.

42. N.M.M.: DUF/9, R. Duff to Bute, 22 Oct 1762.

43. Wyndham, *Chronicles* II,64. Oddly enough, Gresley had misunderstood the electoral position. In the by-election of 1753 (the only one which his brother contested) the vacancy was caused by the death of Richard Leveson-Gower, and the rival candidates were Henry Vernon, representing Lord Gower's interest, and Sir Thomas Gresley. Thomas Anson sat for the other seat, which was not in contest. In essence, however, Gresley was right, for Gower and Anson had an electoral agreement, and Vernon was clearly the

ministerial candidate. See Sedgwick, *House of Commons 1715–54* I,319–320 & 415, II,499.

44. N.M.M.: COO/1, p.5.

45. M.C.: VI 11/40, Sandwich to Mulgrave, 13 Aug 1778.

46. Baugh, *Naval Administration in the Age of Walpole*, p.145. Namier, *Structure of Politics*, p.32.

47. L.B. Namier, *Crossroads of Power* (London, 1962), p.89.

CONCLUSION

1. Christie, *Stress and Stability*, p.35.

2. *Ibid.*, p.55.

3. *Ibid.*, p.54.

4. *Ibid.*, p.155.

SELECT BIBLIOGRAPHY

(This consists of the works most useful in writing this book, or most often cited in it, and makes no pretence to be a comprehensive list of books on naval history in the period.)

Articles of War. Those in force during the Seven Years' War were contained in the statute 22 Geo. II c.33, the 1749 Navy Act. They may be consulted in any copy of the Statutes, or in N.A.M. Rodger, ed., *Articles of War* (Havant, Hampshire, 1982).

Anon.: *The Case of the Pursers of Her Majesties [sic] Navy* [London, 1711]. An informative pamphlet, though not all that was true in 1711 was true fifty years later, nor indeed were all the pamphlet's claims true in 1711.

Anon.: *Advice to Officers of the British Navy* (London, 1785). A satirical pamphlet, advising officers how to convert their service from a tedious duty into a profitable racket. The author evidently knew what he was talking about.

Admiralty: *Regulations and Instructions Relating to His Majesty's Service at Sea*, 1st ed. 1731. From at least the 7th ed. of 1747 to the 10th of 1766, the text is unaltered, but from the 8th of 1756 Additional Articles were appended. I have quoted from a copy of 10th ed., but the 8th and 9th, current during this war, were identical.

Anderson, Olive: 'The Establishment of British Supremacy at Sea and the Exchange of Naval Prisoners of War, 1689–1783', *E.H.R.* LXXV, p.77.

Aspinall-Oglander, Cecil: *Admiral's Wife, The Life and Letters of Mrs Edward Boscawen, 1719–61* (London, 1940). A charming and valuable correspondence, indifferently edited.

Barnes, G.R. and Owen, J.H.: *The Private Papers of John, Earl of Sandwich* (N.R.S. Vols. 69, 71, 75 & 78, 1932–38).

Baugh, Daniel A.: *British Naval Administration in the Age of Walpole*, (Princeton, 1965).

Baugh, Daniel A.: *Naval Administration 1715–50* (N.R.S. Vol. 120, 1977). These works (much wider in scope than their titles suggest) have transformed our understanding of eighteenth-century naval history, and are the foundation of all subsequent work, including this book.

Baxter, Stephen B.: 'The Conduct of the Seven Years' War', in *England's*

Rise to Greatness, 1660–1763 (Berkeley, 1983). This relates to the higher direction, not the actual fighting of the war.

Beaglehole, J.C.: *The Life of Captain James Cook* (London, 1974). The standard life, though not always reliable in details.

Beatson, Robert: *Naval and Military Memoirs of Great Britain from 1727 to 1783* (London, 1804, 6 vols.). A good near-contemporary operational history.

Bellamy, R.R., ed.: *Ramblin' Jack, The Journal of Captain John Cremer, 1700–1774* (London, 1936). Vivid and eccentric reminiscences of a merchant seaman who began his career in the Navy.

[Bentley, Richard]: *John Bentley, Knight, Vice-Admiral of the White* (Guildford, 1921). Not very informative.

Beveridge, Sir William, *et al.*: *Prices and Wages in England from the Twelfth to the Nineteenth Century* (London, 1939). A massive compilation of statistical raw material; the later volumes which were intended to analyse it never appeared.

Blake, John: *A Plan for regulating the Marine System of Great Britain* (London, 1758). A well-informed government pamphleteer writing in support of Grenville's Bill.

Bonner-Smith, David, ed.: *The Barrington Papers* (N.R.S. Vols. 77 & 81, 1937–41).

[Bonner-Smith, D., *et al.*]: *The Commissioned Sea Officers of the Royal Navy, 1660–1815* (Greenwich, National Maritime Museum, 1954, privately circulated, 3 vols.). Gives names and dates of commissions of all known commissioned officers, though it is neither complete nor completely accurate. I have used the version annotated by the late Cdr Pitcairn-Jones, with details of appointments taken from the List Books (ADM 8). The original of this is in the National Maritime Museum, with a copy in the P.R.O.

Boys, William: *An Account of the Loss of the Luxborough Galley* (London, 1787). A brief memoir of the author's father Commodore Boys.

Bromley, J.S.: *The Manning of the Royal Navy: Selected Public Pamphlets, 1693–1873* (N.R.S. Vol. 119, 1974). The editor's Introduction is one of the most thorough and perceptive statements of the manning problem.

Bromley, J.S.: 'The British Navy and Its Seamen after 1688: Notes for an Unwritten History', in Sarah Palmer and Glyndwr Williams, eds., *Charted and Uncharted Waters* (London, 1981). Demonstrates Professor Bromley's sensitive talent for asking the questions other scholars prefer to ignore.

Brown, J.W.: 'British Privateering during the Seven Years' War, 1756–

1763' (Exeter M.A. thesis, 1978). Contains useful work, but its statistics are vitiated by elementary errors, such as failing to distinguish between ships commissioning and ships in commission in any given year.

Bulkeley, John and Cummin, John: *A Voyage to the South Seas in the Year 1740–41* (London, 1743). The loss of the *Wager*, by two of her warrant officers.

Carpenter, Kenneth J.: *The History of Scurvy and Vitamin C* (Cambridge, 1986). An important corrective to traditional views on the subject.

Charnock, John: *Biographia Navalis* (London, 1794–8, 6 vols.). A biographical dictionary of all post-captains and above from 1660; invaluable but unreliable, and especially apt to confuse different persons of the same surname.

Christie, Ian R.: *Stress and Stability in Late Eighteenth-Century Britain* (Oxford, 1984).

Cobbett, William, ed.: *Cobbett's Parliamentary History of England* (London, 1806–20, 36 vols.). Prints reports of Parliamentary debates.

Colledge, J.J.: *Ships of the Royal Navy: An Historical Index* (Newton Abbot, 1969, 2 vols.). This is my source for all statements about the number of guns, tonnage, dates of construction, etc. of H.M. ships.

Corbett, J.S.: *England in the Seven Years' War: A Study in Combined Strategy* (London, 1907, 2 vols.). Concerned with strategy, diplomacy and naval operations. It has nothing to say about social conditions.

Crewe, Duncan G.: 'British Naval Administration in the West Indies, 1739–48' (Liverpool Ph.D. thesis, 1978). An almost unique example of intelligent research based on the ships' musters.

Davis, Ralph: *The Rise of the English Shipping Industry* (Newton Abbot, 2nd. ed. 1972). A classic history of merchant shipping.

Dickinson, J.C.: 'A Naval Diary of the Seven Years' War from Flookburgh', *Transactions of the Cumberland and Westmorland Antiquarian and Archaeological Society* N.S. XXXVIII (1938), p.238. Fragmentary but interesting diary of a surgeon's mate, from a poor nineteenth-century transcript.

Drummond, J.C. and Wilbraham, Anne: *The Englishman's Food* (London, 2nd ed. 1957).

Equiano, O.: *The Interesting Narrative of the Life of Olaudah Equiano or Gustavus Vassa the African, by Himself* (London, 1789, 2 vols.). As a young slave he was for some time owned by a sea officer.

415

Erskine, David, ed.: *Augustus Hervey's Journal* (London, 2nd ed. 1954). A remarkable and vivid memoir of a singular man, here excellently edited.

Gardner, J.A.: *Above and Under Hatches*, ed. C.C. Lloyd (London, 1955). An amusing and illuminating memoir. It is also edited by Sir R.V. Hamilton and J.K. Laughton as *The Recollections of Commander James Anthony Gardner, 1775–1814* (N.R.S. Vol. 31, 1906).

George, M.D.: *London Life in the Eighteenth Century* (London, 1925).

Gilbert, A.N.: 'Crime as Disorder: Criminality and the Symbolic Universe of the 18th Century British Naval Officer', in R.W. Love, ed., *Changing Interpretations and New Sources in Naval History* (New York, 1980).

Gilbert, A.N.: 'Buggery and the British Navy, 1700–1861', *Journal of Social History* X, p.72. These papers show a curious combination of useful research and tenacious misconceptions; from the tenor of some of the footnotes it is possible to conclude that the author's treatment of the eighteenth-century Royal Navy is little more than a colour for his feelings about the U.S. army in Vietnam.

Gradish, Stephen: *The Manning of the British Navy during the Seven Years' War* (London, 1980). An important and valuable work, but published after the author's untimely death in a very imperfect condition, and marred by serious misunderstandings.

Gradish, Stephen: 'Wages and Manning: The Navy Act of 1758', *E.H.R.* XCIII, p.46.

Gray, Ernest, ed.: *Surgeon's Mate; The Diary of John Knyveton, Surgeon in the British Fleet during the Seven Years' War* (London, 1942). Since it appears in several standard bibliographies, I mention this work as a warning to others; it is a crude forgery.

Gwyn, Julian: *The Enterprising Admiral: The Personal Fortune of Admiral Sir Peter Warren* (Montreal, 1974).

Gwyn, Julian: *The Royal Navy and North America: The Warren Papers, 1736–1752* (N.R.S. Vol. 118, 1973). Respectively the biography and the papers of a successful admiral; particularly valuable for their coverage of his financial and business dealings.

Harriott, John: *Struggles through Life* (London, 3rd. ed. 1815, 3 vols.). Some experiences at sea.

Harland, John: *Seamanship in the Age of Sail* (London, 1984). 'An account of the shiphandling of the sailing man-of-war 1600–1860'.

Hills, B.F.: 'Shipbuilding for the Royal Navy at Sandwich in the Eighteenth Century', *Archaeologia Cantiana* XCIV (1978), p.195. Symbiotic relation of a shipbuilding family and their naval cousins.

H.M.C.: *Du Cane Manuscripts* (No.61, 1905). Prints correspondence of Admiral Medley.

H.M.C.: *Various Manuscripts VI* (No.55, 1909). Prints correspondence of Henry Fox and of the Cornwallis family; the originals of much of the latter are now in the N.M.M.

Holmes, Geoffrey: *Augustan England; Professions, State and Society 1680–1730* (London, 1982).

Hood, Dorothy: *The Admirals Hood* (London, 1941).

Houlding, J.A.: *Fit for Service: The Training of the British Army 1715–1795* (Oxford, 1981). Also deals with the marines.

Howard, Frank: *Sailing Ships of War 1400–1860* (Greenwich, 1979). A technical history; compared with Lavery [q.v.], it is more concerned with details of rig, fittings and appearance than with design. See also James Lees, *The Masting and Rigging of English Ships of War, 1625–1860* (Greenwich, 1979).

Howse, Derek: *Greenwich Time and the Discovery of the Longitude* (Oxford, 1980).

Hutchins, J.H.: *Jonas Hanway, 1712–1786* (London, 1940). Life of the founder of the Marine Society. J.S. Taylor, *Jonas Hanway, Founder of the Marine Society* (London & Berkeley, 1985), appeared too late to be used in this book.

Hutchinson, J.R.: *The Press-Gang Afloat and Ashore* (London, 1913). Upon a foundation of extensive and quite accurate research, the author erected an airy superstructure of extravagant prejudices almost completely unsupported by the material he presents.

Ilchester, [Giles Fox-Strangeways] Earl of: *Letters to Henry Fox, Lord Holland* (Roxburghe Club, London, 1915). Fox was Secretary of State during much of the Seven Years' War.

Ives, Edward: *A Voyage from England to India in the Year 1754* (London, 1773). Ives was Physician of the East Indies Squadron.

Jarrett, Dudley: *British Naval Dress* (London, 1960). A sketchy sartorial history.

Kemp, Peter: *The British Sailor, a Social History of the Lower Deck* (London, 1970). A good brief history, but does not entirely escape the weaknesses of its sources.

Kemp, Peter: 'Boscawen's Letters to his Wife', in *The Naval Miscellany* Vol. IV, ed. C.C. Lloyd (N.R.S. Vol. 92, 1952). Valuable and engaging personal correspondence.

Keppel, Thomas: *The Life of Augustus Viscount Keppel* (London, 1842, 2 vols.). Prints some useful correspondence.

Laughton, Sir J.K.: *Letters and Papers of Charles, Lord Barham, 1758–1813* (N.R.S. Vols. 32, 38 & 39, 1907–1911).

Lavery, Brian: *The Ship of the Line* (London, 1983–84, 2 vols.). A fine study of the development of warship design. For similar work on smaller ships, see Robert Gardiner, 'Frigate Design in the Eighteenth Century', *Warship* Nos. 9–12 (1979).

Le Goff, T.J.A.: 'Offre et productivité de la main d'oeuvre dans les armements français au xviiie siècle', *Histoire économie et société* II (1983), pp.457–474.

Le Goff, T.J.A.: 'Naval Recruitment and Labour Supply in the French War Effort, 1755–59' [paper delivered at a conference at Annapolis, Md., in September 1981; to be published. I am grateful to Professor Le Goff for allowing me to read it.] These papers are an important corrective to the starry-eyed view of the French system held by most British historians. See also his 'L'Impact des prises effectuées par les Anglais sur la capacité en hommes de la marine française pendant les guerres de 1744–1748, 1755–1763, 1778–1783', in M. Acerra, J. Merino and J. Meyer, eds., *Les marines de guerres européennes XVII–XVIIIe siècles* (Paris, 1985); and 'Les gens de mer devant la système des classes (1755–1763): résistance ou passivité?', in 'Les hommes et la mer dans l'Europe du Nord-Ouest de l'Antiquité à nos jours', ed. Alain Lottin, Jean-Claude Hocquet and Stéphane Lebecq, *Revue du Nord* extra number, 1986.

Lind, James: *An Essay on the most effectual Means of preserving the Health of Seamen* (London, 1757). My quotations come from the 3rd ed. of 1779 as printed in Lloyd, *Health of Seamen* [q.v.].

Lind, James: *A Treatise of the Scurvy* (Edinburgh, 1753). My quotations are from either the 1953 edition (Edinburgh, ed. C.P. Stewart and D. Guthrie) or the extensive extracts printed in Lloyd, *Health of Seamen*.

Lloyd, C.C.: *The Health of Seamen* (N.R.S. Vol. 107, 1965). Extracts from the writings of Lind, Trotter and Blane.

Lloyd, C.C.: *The British Seaman* (London, 1968). My quotations are from the U.S. edition of 1970. Particularly good on the manning problem.

Lloyd, C.C., Keevil, J. and Coulter, J.L.S.: *Medicine and the Navy, 1200–1900* (Edinburgh, 1957–63, 4 vols.; vols. 3–4 by Lloyd and Coulter). A monumental but uneven medical history of the Navy.

Long, W.H.: *Naval Yarns* (London, 1899). An odd anthology of historical accounts of unstated provenance, among then Renney's 'Journal' [q.v.].

Mackay, Ruddock F.: *Admiral Hawke* (Oxford, 1965). The standard life of the admiral.

Marcus, G.J.: *Heart of Oak* (London, 1975). An impressionistic and lightweight survey of the social life of the Navy in the eighteenth century.

Marshall, John: *Royal Naval Biography* (London, 1823–35, 4 vols. in 8 parts + 4 vols. of Supplement). Succeeds Charnock, but also covers commanders.

Matcham, M.E.: *A Forgotten John Russell* (London, 1905). The career of a purser and naval officer in the 1730s and 1740s, with extensive quotation from his papers.

Middleton, Richard: 'The Administration of Newcastle and Pitt: The Departments of State and the Conduct of the War, 1754–60, with Particular Reference to the Campaigns in North America' (Exeter Ph.D. thesis, 1968). A thorough and illuminating piece of research. His *The Bells of Victory: The Pitt-Newcastle Ministry and the Conduct of the Seven Years' War, 1757–1762* (Cambridge, 1985), appeared too late to be used in this book.

Middleton, Richard: 'Pitt, Anson and the Admiralty, 1756–1761', *History* N.S. LV, p.189.

Mountaine, William: *The Seaman's Vade-Mecum* (London, 1767). A handbook combining advice on seamanship, naval tactics, keeping a ship's accounts and other matters, with a nautical dictionary.

Namier, L.B.: *The Structure of Politics at the Accession of George III* (London, 2nd ed. 1957).

Namier, Sir Lewis, and Brooke, John: *The History of Parliament: The House of Commons 1754–90* (London, 1964, 3 vols.).

The Naval Chronicle (London, 1799–1840, 40 vols.).

Neale, Larry D.: 'The Cost of Impressment during the Seven Years' War', *M.M.* LXIV (1978), p.45.

Neale, Larry D.: 'Interpreting Power and Profit in Economic History: A Case Study of the Seven Years' War', *Journal of Economic History* XXXVII (1977), p.20. If the author had considered the limitations of his knowledge and his evidence, verified his references and restrained his enthusiasm, these might have been more useful contributions.

Newton, John: *The Journal of a Slave Trader*, ed. B. Martin and M. Spurrell (London, 1962). The celebrated evangelical preacher and hymnodist was for some time master of a slaver. See also *An authentic Narrative of some Remarkable and Interesting Particulars in the Life of [John Newton]* (London, 1764).

Ommer, R. and Pantin, G., eds.: *Working Men Who Got Wet* (St. John's Newfoundland, 1980). Papers on Canadian maritime history.

Pares, Richard: *Colonial Blockade and Neutral Rights, 1739–1763* (Oxford, 1938).

Pares, Richard: 'The Manning of the Navy in the West Indies, 1702–63', *Transactions of the Royal Historical Society* 4th Ser. XX, p.31.

Pares, Richard: *War and Trade in the West Indies, 1739–1763* (Oxford, 1936).

Perrichet, Marc: 'L'Administration des Classes de la Marine et ses Archives dans les Ports Bretons', *Revue d'Histoire Economique et Sociale* XXXVII (1959), p.89. Valuable study of French manning problems.

Powell, J.W.D.: *Bristol Privateers and Ships of War* (Bristol, 1930). An excellent and scholarly study.

Press, Jon: 'The Living and Working Conditions of the Merchant Seamen of Bristol' (Bristol Ph.D. thesis, 1973). An extremely useful piece of research; we need more like this for other ports. One irritating feature of it is that it is not continuously paginated.

Pritchard, James: 'The French Navy, 1748–62', in R.W. Love, ed., *Changing Interpretations and New Sources in Naval History* (New York, 1980).

Ranft, B.McL.: *The Vernon Papers* (N.R.S. Vol. 99, 1958).

[Renney, Patrick]: 'The Journal of a Naval Surgeon [1756–1763]', printed in Long, *Naval Yarns*, anonymously and with the wrong dates. The author can easily be identified on internal evidence. The present writer's copy of Long formerly belonged to W.C.B. Tunstall, who has annotated it with his descent from Renney, and it is possible that he was Long's unstated source for the narrative. Whatever its origin, it is an amusing and authentic account. On internal evidence, it appears to have been written in 1793 or 1794, but apart from a few slips with personal names, it seems remarkably accurate.

Richmond, H.W.: *The Navy in the War of 1739–48* (Cambridge, 1920, 3 vols.). An operational history, but with more attention to social and administrative factors than Corbett gives.

Robinson, C.N.: *The British Tar in Fact and Fiction* (London, 1911). Primarily a survey of the public image of the sailor in literature and art.

Rodger, N.A.M., ed.: *The Naval Miscellany* Vol. V (N.R.S. Vol. 125, 1985).

Rodger, N.A.M.: *The Admiralty* (Lavenham, Suffolk, 1979).

Rodger, N.A.M.: *Naval Records for Genealogists* (P.R.O., 1984).

Rodger, N.A.M.: 'Stragglers and Deserters from the Royal Navy during the Seven Years' War', *B.I.H.R.* LVII, p.56.

Rodger, N.A.M.: 'The Douglas Papers, 1760–62', in *The Naval Miscellany* Vol. V.

Rodger, N.A.M.: 'The Victualling of the British Navy during the Seven Years' War', *Bulletin du Centre d'Histoire des Espaces Atlantiques* (Bordeaux) 1985.

Rodger, N.A.M.: 'Le Scorbut dans la Royal Navy pendant la Guerre de Sept Ans', in 'Les hommes et la mer dans l'Europe du Nord-Ouest de l'Antiquité à nos jours', ed. Alain Lottin, Jean-Claude Hocquet and Stéphane Lebecq, *Revue du Nord* extra number, 1986.

Rodger, N.A.M.: 'The Mutiny in the *James & Thomas*', M.M. LXX, p.293.

Russell, Lord John, ed.: *Correspondence of John, Fourth Duke of Bedford* (London, 1842–46, 3 vols.). Bedford was First Lord 1744–48.

Schomberg, Isaac: *Naval Chronology* (London, 1812, 3 vols.). Detailed history of naval operations.

Sedgwick, Romney: *The History of Parliament: The House of Commons 1715–54* (London, 1970, 2 vols.).

Smith, W.J.: *The Grenville Papers* (London, 1852, 2 vols.). Includes much naval correspondence of George Grenville and others of the family.

Spavens, W.: *The Narrative of William Spavens, a Chatham Pensioner, by himself* (Louth, 1796). A rare lower-deck memoir, but a very useful one, by an intelligent man with an excellent memory and an interesting career.

Spinney, David: *Rodney* (London, 1969). The standard modern life of the admiral.

Stone, Lawrence: *The Family, Sex and Marriage in England, 1500–1800* (London, 1977).

Surry, N.W. and Thomas, J.H.: *Book of Original Entries, 1731–1751* (Portsmouth Record Series, Portsmouth, 1976). Not only a very useful record text, but an extensive essay in local history, with a great deal to do with the Navy. As an appendix is printed R. Wilkins's pamphlet, *The Borough, being a faithful, tho' humerous, Description* [of Portsmouth] (London, 1748).

Syrett, David: *The Siege and Capture of Havana, 1762* (N.R.S. Vol. 114, 1970). A particularly well edited and informative record collection.

Taylor, E.G.R.: *The Mathematical Practioners of Hanoverian England* (Cambridge, 1966). Navigation was at the leading edge of eighteenth-century mathematics.

Taylor, Gordon: *The Sea Chaplains* (Oxford, 1978).

Thompson, Edward: *A Sailor's Letters* (London, 2nd ed. 1767, 2 vols.). Studied literary productions, offering the public the view of naval life which the author thought they wanted to read. They should be treated with great caution as evidence of what things were really like.

Vaughan, H.S.: *The Voyages and Cruises of Commodore Walker* (London, 1928). An anonymous contemporary account of the fortunes of a privateer commander in the 1740s.

Wallis, Helen, ed.: *Carteret's Voyage round the World, 1766–1769* (Hakluyt Society, 2nd Ser., Vols. CXXIV & CXXV, 1965).

Watt, Sir J., Freeman, E.J., and Bynum, W.F., eds.: *Starving Sailors: The Influence of Nutrition upon Naval and Maritime History* (Greenwich, National Maritime Museum, 1981). Notwithstanding its title, a serious and important contribution.

Wickwire, F.B.: 'Admiralty Secretaries and the British Civil Service', *Huntington Library Quarterly* XXVIII (1965), p.235.

Wiggin, L.M.: *The Faction of Cousins* (New Haven, 1958). A political account of the Temple-Grenville-Pitt connection; its handling of naval affairs is unsure.

Williams, Glyndwr, ed.: *A Voyage around the World by George Anson* (London, 1974). See also his *Documents relating to Anson's Voyage round the World, 1740–44* (N.R.S. Vol. 109, 1967).

Williams, Gomer: *History of the Liverpool Privateers and Letters of Marque* (London, 1897). Heavily and uncritically dependent on unreliable sources, chiefly local newspapers.

Williams, M.J.: 'The Naval Administration of the Fourth Earl of Sandwich' (Oxford D.Phil. thesis, 1962). Presents much useful evidence, but its analysis is rather jejeune.

Wyndham, Maud: *Chronicles of the Eighteenth Century* (London, 1924, 2 vols.). Prints extensive selections from the Lyttelton MSS, including correspondence of Admiral Smith, the Hoods and other naval members and connections of the family.

GLOSSARY OF NAUTICAL TERMS

(In the senses current in the mid eighteenth century only)

afterguard *n*: a body of men working on the quarter deck and poop; one of the 'parts of ship'.

aloft *adv*: above decks, in the rigging.

amidships *adv*: in the central part of the ship (in relation to length or breadth).

athwart *adv*: across.

ballast *n*: weight (usually of stones, gravel or pig iron) carried in the bottom of a ship's hold to improve her stability.

batten down *v*: to close and secure hatchways or other openings in hull and deck to prevent the ingress of water or air.

bear a hand *v*: to assist.

beat *v*: to proceed obliquely to windward by sailing with the wind on one or other side, usually each in turn.

bilge *n*: the angle of the ship's hull between side and bottom. In the plural it usually refers to the bottom of the hold, where waste water collects.

binnacle *n:* A locker containing the steering compass, standing immediately before the wheel.

block *n*: a pulley.

boltsprit *n*: bowsprit, *q.v.*

bomb vessel (colloquially '**bomb**') *n*: a man-of-war designed to carry one or two heavy mortars for shore bombardment. [In practice bombs often landed their mortars and operated as sloops.]

bounty *n*: a sum of money paid as an inducement or reward, e.g. to seamen who had volunteered, or to seamen's widows in compensation for their loss.

bowsprit *n*: a spar projecting over the bow and supporting parts of the standing rigging.

brace *n*: one of a number of parts of the running rigging controlling the yards in their movement in a horizontal plane about the masts.

bream *v*: to burn off weed from the bottom of a ship in dock.

brigantine *n*: a two-masted square-rigged vessel, a brig.

broadside *n*: (1) the complete battery or batteries mounted on one side of a ship (2) The simultaneous fire of all the guns of the broadside. [The fighting strength of a warship could be roughly measured by totalling the weight of shot fired in a single broadside.]

bulkhead *n*: a vertical partition within a ship.

burgoo *n*: a sort of porridge.

buss *n*: A two-masted fishing vessel. [Several busses were chartered by the Navy and armed as warships.]

cable tier *n*: a part of the orlop deck where the anchor cables were stowed.

capstan *n*: A vertical cylinder mounted on a spindle and turned by men pushing on capstan bars inserted in holes in its circumference. Round it was taken a turn or two of any cable requiring great effort to haul it, especially the messenger by which the anchor cable was hove in.

captain *n*: (1) a post-captain; (2) a master and commander; (3) the form of address for the commander of a privateer or master of a merchantman.

careen *v*: to lighten a ship lying afloat and heel her over so that one side of her underwater hull was exposed to be cleaned or repaired. [This was the only way to work on a ship's bottom in the absence of a dock.]

cat *v*: To hoist an anchor out of the water to the level of the forecastle, using a tackle called the cat-fall from a projecting spar called the cathead. [This was necessary to avoid the flukes of the anchor striking the hull as it was hauled in, and to get it from main deck level (where the cables led in) to its stowage against the side of the forecastle.]

caulk *v*: to stop the gaps between seams of planking by forcing in threads of oakum and sealing with pitch.

chase *n*: (1) a pursuit of one ship by another; (2) the ship pursued.

claw off *v*: to beat off a lee shore.

clean *v*: to bream and scrape a ship's bottom, either in dock or by careening.

clear away *v*: to disengage, disentangle, unfasten, remove or prepare to remove.

close *v*: (of a ship) to approach another ship, or the land.

come home *v*: (of anchors) to drag.

commander *n*: (1) the commanding officer of a warship, privateer or merchantman, the captain; (2) an officer of the rank of master and commander; (3) the senior officer commanding a squadron of warships.

commanding officer *n*: (1) the flag officer commanding a squadron of men of war; (2) the officer commanding a ship in the absence of her commander, the first lieutenant. [The term was almost never used in its modern sense of captain.]

con *v*: to pilot a ship in confined waters.

cordage *n*: rope and materials made from it.

convoy *v*: to escort.

convoy *n*: (1) a warship employed in escorting merchantmen; (2) a body of merchantmen under escort [rare].

crimp *v*: to get seamen in one's power and sell them.

crimp *n*: a person engaged in this trade.

cruiser *n*: a man-of-war sent on detached operations, alone or in company with one or two others. [It was an employment not a type of ship, though the larger ships of the line seldom acted as cruisers.]

cutter *n*: a one-masted vessel rigged with a gaff mainsail, topsail, headsails and usually a square topsail.

deckhead *n*: the underside of the deck above.

disrate *v*: to reduce a man to a rate inferior to that he formerly held.

driver *n*: a gaff sail set on the mizzen mast of a ship, or the main mast of a brig.

find *v*: (of a ship) to equip or fit out; used chiefly in the phrases 'well found' and 'ill found'.

fireship *n*: a small warship fitted with 'fireworks' (combustibles) in order to destroy enemy ships by setting herself on fire and running alongside them. [In practice this method of warfare was obsolete, and fireships usually served as small cruisers.]

fish *v*: (1) to secure an anchor in its stowage, having first catted it, by making fast a tackle to the crown of the anchor and hauling it up until the shank is horizontal. The two ends of the anchor are then secured by the fish-tackle to the fish-davit, and by the cat-fall to the cathead. (2) to strengthen a damaged, or mend a broken, spar by lashing another spar (the fish) to it like a splint.

flag officer *n*: an admiral.

fleet *n*: a body of merchant ships, or of merchantmen and warships in company. [The term was seldom used of men-of-war by themselves.]

fore *adj*: relating to the forward part of the ship.

forecastle *n*: a short deck built over the fore part of the main deck.

forecastleman *n*: one of a group of men working on the forecastle, one of the 'parts of ship'.

foremastman *n*: a common seaman, one who (in a merchant ship) berths in the forecastle, before the [fore]mast.

forward *adj*: relating to or in the direction of the bows or fore part of the ship.

frigate *n*: (1) a ship-rigged sloop of 16–18 guns; (2) a fifth or sixth rate cruising warship with two internal decks, the lower unarmed and the upper mounting the main battery; (3) any small cruising warship.

gaff *n*: a spar supporting the head of certain sails.

gantline *n*: a line rove through a block secured below the top, and used by riggers to hoist up gear. When a ship was stripped for the Ordinary, the gantline (otherwise girtline) was the only running rigging left aloft, ready to begin the process of re-rigging.

go about *v*: to put a ship onto the other tack, either by tacking or wearing.

ground tackle *n*: anchors, cables and the gear to handle them.

halliard *n*: tackles used to hoist yards or sails.

hand *v*: to gather in square sails, the men hanging over the yards seizing the sail and hauling it in to reef or furl.

haul off *v*: (of a ship) to increase her distance from another ship or the land, especially to windward.

head reach *v*: to gain on, to overtake, to escape.

heads *n*: the crew's latrines.

headsails *n*: sails spread on stays between the foremast and the bowsprit.

heave down *v*: to careen.

keel *n*: a type of square-rigged sailing barge native to the Tyne.

landfall *n*: that point at which a navigator meets, or intends to meet, the coast. [It should ideally be easy to identify and safe to approach.]

lee shore *n*: a shore to leeward of a ship, towards which the wind blows her.

leeward *adj*: in the direction towards which the wind is blowing.

leeway *n*: the extent to which the wind blows a ship to leeward of her course.

let go *v*: to cast off, to free, to loose; particularly to drop anchor.

letter of marque *n*: (1) a licence from the High Court of Admiralty permitting a privateer to attack the ships of a named enemy [thus distinguishing her from a mere pirate]; (2) an armed merchantman, engaged in her trade, but furnished with a letter of marque and prepared to take advantage of any chance prize (to be distinguished from the privateer, cruising entirely for prizes and carrying no cargo.

libertyman *n*: a rating given leave.

line-of-battle ship *n*: a man-of-war large enough to lie in the line of battle; by convention 1st down to 4th rates were reckoned as line-of-battle ships [rarely 'battleships'].

linstock *n*: a length of slowmatch kept smouldering in a bucket by a gun, the traditional method of firing the gun.

loggerhead *n*: an iron tool used to apply hot pitch.

log line *n*: a line made fast to a large piece of wood and knotted at fixed intervals. The wood was thrown overboard and the line allowed to run out freely; the number of knots run in a given period gave the ship's speed through the water.

longboat *n*: the largest ship's boat.

mainyard *n*: the lowest yard on the mainmast, from which was spread the mainsail.

mast *n*: a vertical spar, supporting yards, gaffs and sails. A ship had three masts; fore, main and mizzen in order from fore to aft. A brig had fore and main masts only; a ketch main and mizzen only. [In all three cases the mainmast was the tallest.] Each mast was itself composed of three spars, the lower mast, topmast and topgallant mast, to which the word was applied (according to context) either individually or collectively.

mizzen *n*: the aftermost mast of a ship or ketch.

muster *n*: (1) a list of all persons actually on board a ship; (2) an assembly of the ship's company for the purpose of compiling such a list.

muster *v*: (1) to enter a person on the ship's muster; (2) to assemble the ship's company to muster them.

offing *n*: the open sea, viewed from the land. A ship is said to 'make an offing' by working to seaward; having done so, she is 'in the offing' of that coast.

Ordinary *n*: the dockyard reserve [in theory paid for by the Ordinary, as opposed to Extraordinary, Estimate of the Navy].

orlop *n*: the lowest deck, lying on or below the waterline.

packet *n*: a small vessel employed to carry mails.

part *v*: (of rope) to break.

part of ship *n*: one of a number of parties into which each watch of the company was divided for handling the ship.

pay *v*: to coat with pitch.

pay off *v*: (of a ship) to pay and discharge her company, to decommission her.

pendant *n*: a streamer flown from the mainmasthead, distinguishing a man-of-war from a merchant ship. Private ships flew an ordinary narrow pendant, commodores a broad pendant.

pinnace *n*: a type of ship's boat.

pipe *v*: to give an order, particularly one conveyed by a series of notes blown on the boatswain's call, or whistle.

pitch *v*: (of a ship) to plunge head and stern alternately into the waves.

point *v*: to direct a ship's head in a particular direction, relative to the wind. To point 'high' is to steer as near into the wind as possible; that ship which points highest and makes least leeway will work best to windward.

poop *n*: a short deck built over the after end of the quarter deck.

portable soup *n*: a form of preserved food made from beef bones and offal, reduced to a solid block which could be reconstituted with water to form a thick stock.

private man *n*: a rating or private marine.

private ship *n*: a man-of-war not carrying an admiral.

privateer *n*: an armed merchant ship, licensed by letter of marque to cruise against enemy ships to her owners' profit.

protection *n*: a certificate exempting from impressment either a named man, or a given number of men belonging to a named ship.

pull *v*: to row.

put about *v*: (otherwise cast about, go about) to put the ship onto the other tack by tacking or wearing.

quarter deck *n*: a deck above the main deck, running from the stern about half-way along the length of the ship.

quarter gunner *n*: a rating established (in the proportion of one to every four great guns) to assist the gunner in maintaining and handling them.

rate *n*: (1) one of six classes into which the larger men-of-war were divided, first rates with the greatest number of guns, sixth rates with the least; (2) a rating.

rate *v*: to assign a man to a particular rating.

rattan *n*: a cane.

reef *v*: to reduce the area of a sail by bundling part of it against a spar with short lines called reef-points, secured through the sail and made fast round the spar.

rating *n*: (1) a member of a ship's company holding no rank in the Navy, a 'private man'; (2) a rate of ship.

rowing port *n*: one of a number of small ports on the lower deck of certain sloops through which oars or sweeps could be worked to propel the ship in calm weather.

royal *n*: a square sail set above the topgallant.

run *v*: (1) to desert; (2) to make a man 'run', to mark an R against his name in the muster, formally declaring him to be liable to the penalties established for desertion.

run ashore *n*: a trip ashore, a day's leave.

scantling *n*: the materials of the ship's hull.

shoal *n*: a bank or reef, an area of shallow water dangerous to navigation.

sheet *n*: a rope led aft from the lower corner of a sail to control it.

ship *n*: a vessel square-rigged on three masts. [The word was not used of any other rig.]

ship of the line *n*: a line-of-battle ship, *q.v.*

shipwright *n*: a carpenter employed in shipbuilding.

sight *n*: a navigational observation of some heavenly body, most often the sun at noon.

sloop *n*: (1) a small man-of-war, below the sixth rate, rigged as ship, brig or ketch; (2) a large cutter, as used for war and trade in the West Indies; otherwise a 'one-mast' or 'West India' sloop.

snow *n*: a two-masted square-rigged vessel similar to a brig, but setting her driver on a separate spar stepped immediately abaft, and parallel to, the main lower mast.

spar *n*: a length of timber, used in masting and rigging to spread sails.

square-rigged *adj*: rigged predominantly with square sails, spread on yards.

start *v*: (1) to pierce a cask and pour out its (liquid) contents; (2) to strike a man at work with a rattan or rope's end; (3) to ease or cast off a sheet or other piece of running rigging under strain.

stern chase *n*: a chase in which the pursued flees directly away from the pursuer.

stern gallery *n*: an open gallery running the width of the stern outside the captain's or admiral's cabin.

stockfish *n*: dried cod.

stream *n*: (1) a current; (2) that part of a harbour in which tides or currents flow.

strike *v*: (1) (of a ship) to run aground; (2) to lower a sail, etc., particularly to lower one's colours in token of surrender.

supernumerary *n*: a person borne on the ship's books surplus to her established complement.

sweep *n*: a large oar.

tack *v*: (properly, to shift tacks, otherwise to stay) to put the ship about onto the other tack by passing her bows to windward.

taffrail *n*: the rail surmounting the stern, bounding the after end of the poop.

tartan *n*: a small Mediterranean trading vessel, usually lateen-rigged on one mast, with a topsail and headsails like a cutter.

tender *n*: a vessel employed to assist or serve another, an auxiliary.

thick *adj*: (of weather) foggy, with poor visibility.

top *n*: a platform built at the head of the lower mast, serving to spread the topmast rigging and provide a place for men working aloft.

tophamper *n*: the spars, rigging and gear aloft, considered as an encumbrance or cause of windage.

topgallant *adj*: referring to the topgallant mast, the topmost of the three spars making a complete mast, and to the yard, sail and rigging belonging to it.

topman *n*: a seaman who works aloft.

transport *n*: a cargo vessel engaged by the government to convey troops or stores. [Almost all transports were charted merchantmen, but the Navy owned and manned a small number, known as storeships.]

trice up *v*: to secure an article to something above it.

trip *v*: (of an anchor being weighed) to break free of the seabed.

turn *v*: to tack.

turn out *v*: to get up, to get out of a cot or hammock.

turn over *v*: (of men) to be discharged into another ship.

ullage *n*: liquid waste, especially the remaining contents of an opened cask.

waister *n*: a member of the 'part of ship' which worked in the waist, on the main deck amidships.

wardroom *n*: a compartment used as the commissioned officers' mess; its location varied in ships of different size and design.

watch *n*: (1) one of the seven divisions of the nautical day; (2) one of the two [rarely three] divisions of the seaman part of the ship's company.

way *n*: the motion of a ship through the water.

wear *v*: to put a ship about onto the other tack by passing her bows to leeward.

weather *v*: to sail to windward of something, usually a headland.

widows' men *n*: fictitious men borne in the proportion of two to every hundred of the ship's company, whose wages were assigned to the officers' widows' pension fund.

windage *n*: (1) the extent to which a ship is blown to leeward of her apparent course by the pressure of the wind, particularly when beating; (2) the gap between the bore of a gun and the diameter of the shot.

windward *adj*: in the direction from which the wind is blowing.

yard *n*: (1) a spar suspended from a mast athwartships and horizontal, from which a square sail is spread; (2) a dockyard.

yardarm *n*: the outer end of a yard.

xebec *n*: a lateen-rigged vessel used for war or trade in the Mediterranean.

INDEX

In this index ranks and titles are as in 1763 unless otherwise mentioned in the text, and all commanders are styled 'captain'. Men-of-war are distinguished by the number of their guns, and are British (prizes included) unless otherwise stated. The following contractions are used: Ab = Able Seaman, Adm = Admiral, Asst = Assistant, Bsn = Boatswain, Br = British, Capt = Captain, C-in-C = Commander-in-Chief, Clk = Clerk, Col = Colonel, Ctr = Carpenter, Fr = French, Gen = General, Gnr = Gunner, Ld = Lord, Lt = Lieutenant, Md = Midshipman, Mqs = Marquis, Mr = Master, Mt = Mate, OS = Ordinary Seaman, PH = Public House, PoW = Prisoner of War, Prs = Purser, RAdm = Rear-Admiral, RN = Royal Navy, Sec = Secretary, Sgn = Surgeon, Sp = Spanish, VAdm = Vice-Admiral, Visct = Viscount.

435